Legalizing Gay Marriage

In the series

AMERICA IN TRANSITION: RADICAL PERSPECTIVES
edited by Gary L. Francione

Michael Allen Fox, *Deep Vegetarianism*
Lawrence E. Mitchell, *Stacked Deck: A Story of Selfishness in America*
Martine Rothblatt, *Unzipped Genes: Taking Charge of Baby-Making
in the New Millennium*

Legalizing Gay Marriage

MICHAEL MELLO
FOREWORD BY DAVID L. CHAMBERS

TEMPLE UNIVERSITY PRESS
Philadelphia

Temple University Press
1601 North Broad Street
Philadelphia PA 19122
www.temple.edu/tempress

∞ The paper used in this publication meets the requirements of the
American National Standard for Information Sciences—Permanence
of Paper for Printed Library Materials, ANSI Z39.48-1992

Library of Congress Cataloging-in-Publication Data
Mello, Michael.
    Legalizing gay marriage / Michael Mello ; foreword by David L. Chambers.
      p. cm. — (America in transition : Radical perspectives)
    Includes bibliographical references and index.
    ISBN 1-59213-078-X (cloth : alk. paper) — ISBN 1-59213-079-8 (pbk. : alk. paper)
      1. Same-sex marriage—Vermont. 2. Same-sex marriage—Law and legislation—
Vermont. 3. Same-sex marriage—United States. 4. Same-sex marriage—Law and
legislation—United States. 5. Gay couples—Legal status, laws, etc.—Vermont.
6. Gay couples—Legal status, laws, etc.—United States. I. Title. II. America in
transition (series).

HQ1034.U5M45 2004
306.84'8—dc22   2003068703

2 4 6 8 9 7 5 3 1

For Mom

Michael Mello is Professor of Law at Vermont Law School and the author of five books on capital punishment, including *The Wrong Man: A True Story of Innocence on Death Row* and *Deathwork: Defending the Condemned*.

David L. Chambers is a Professor at the University of Michigan Law School.

Contents

Series Foreword

MICHAEL MELLO begins his book, *Legalizing Gay Marriage: Vermont and the National Debate*, with the astute observation that "like abortion and capital punishment, same-sex marriage sits on the cultural fault line of morality, religion, and law." Mello explores the topic of same-sex marriage through a fascinating discussion of *Baker v. State*, a 1999 decision of the Vermont Supreme Court, which, in recognition of "our common humanity," held that the Vermont constitution guarantees same-sex couples the same benefits and protections enjoyed by married heterosexual couples. In response to *Baker*, the Vermont legislature enacted a "civil unions" law that provided to gay couples more than 300 benefits enjoyed by married heterosexuals but stopped short of opening up the institution of civil marriage to include gay and lesbian couples.

Although others have written about the creation of civil unions in Vermont, Mello goes beyond the formal confines of the courtroom and the legislative chamber and, through a remarkable collection of primary sources, presents a fascinating description of the political and cultural environment that resulted in the creation of civil unions. Mello also takes issue with others who have unqualified praise for Vermont's approach. He acknowledges that Vermont's civil union represents a significant step forward in the struggle for gay rights, but insists that it ultimately fails because it stigmatizes same-sex unions through the same sort of "separate but equal" treatment that once characterized racial distinctions and that was ultimately rejected by the Supreme Court in *Brown v. Board of Education*. Mello's analysis makes clear that even in the most progressive quarters, our nation is in denial about the extent of our homophobia.

Legalizing Gay Marriage is a most timely and important discussion of an issue that is likely to dominate the social and legal agenda for years to come. Indeed, in 2003, several Canadian courts held that the prohibition on same-sex marriage violates Canada's Charter of Rights and

Freedoms, and Canada is expected to legalize same-sex marriage through statute sometime in 2004. On November 18, 2003, the Supreme Judicial Court of Massachusetts ruled that denying same-sex couples the right to civil marriage is a violation of the Massachusetts Constitution. The court stayed its judgment 180 days to allow the legislature to act on the decision. And in June 2003, the United States Supreme Court ruled in *Lawrence v. Texas* that the Texas "Homosexual Conduct Law," which criminalized certain sexual conduct between persons of the same sex, violated the right of privacy guaranteed by the Due Process Clause of the Fourteenth Amendment. Although the *Lawrence* majority made clear that its holding did not address whether the government must recognize relationships such as same-sex marriage, the dissent argued vehemently that the majority had taken sides in a "culture war" over whether discrimination against homosexuals is appropriate, and has "largely signed on to the so-called homosexual agenda" that will lead to the "judicial imposition of homosexual marriage."

Make no mistake about it: There is an imminent national battle over the issue of same-sex marriage. That battle will involve a profound and perhaps uncomfortable consideration of our most basic values, traditions—and prejudices. *Legalizing Gay Marriage* will serve as an important preview of the conflict ahead, as well as a framework for a sensible and just resolution.

Gary L. Francione

DAVID L. CHAMBERS

Foreword

THE SIGNIFICANCE and timeliness of Michael Mello's book was brought home to me recently when I participated in a conference on same-sex marriage at Brigham Young University Law School in Provo, Utah. Nearly everyone in the audience opposed permitting two men or two women to marry each other. Many favored an amendment to the United States Constitution to prevent any state from permitting same-sex couples to marry. Most regretted the decision of the United States Supreme Court in June 2004 holding sodomy laws unconstitutional. To them, the institution of marriage was under siege. The welfare of unborn children was at risk. Same-sex unions, one speaker believed, would offend "the dignity of children." Another speaker referred to the union of two men as "mere friendship, with the option of sodomy."

My task at the conference was to discuss the developments in Vermont. I drew on Professor Mello's manuscript and described the decision of the Vermont Supreme Court in the *Baker* case, the response of the Vermont legislature, and the responses of Vermont voters in the two elections that have followed. After I spoke, another member of the panel, a member of the Brigham Young faculty, delivered a short version of a 60-page law review article he had written appraising the *Baker* decision. He criticized the reasoning of the court and accused the justices of misusing their own precedents. He then went on at some length to point out that few appellate courts in other states had cited *Baker* in the nearly four years since it was decided. He never acknowledged that the absence of citations in other courts should be no surprise. After all, in the four years since *Baker*, no other appellate court in the United States has decided a case involving a claim for same-sex marriage. Moreover, the Vermont decision rests entirely on an unusual provision of the Vermont Constitution, the so-called Common Benefits Clause, that is found in only a few other state constitutions. What this speaker was trying to do was to make the *Baker* case go away.

But it won't.

The fact that a conference in Utah devoted an entire panel to *Baker* nearly four years after it was decided is a sure sign of its continuing importance. *Baker* was the first decision of a state supreme court requiring that the benefits and responsibilities of marriage be extended to gay male and lesbian couples. And Vermont's legislature was the first legislature to affirm those benefits for its gay and lesbian citizens. The decision and the action of the legislature in adopting the civil union legislation produced temporary political upheaval in Vermont. In the rest of the country, the decision was praised by liberal activists and used by many to push for expanded recognition of same-sex relationships in their own states. At the same time, the decision was condemned by conservative Catholics, Christian fundamentalists, and right-wing politicians.

Professor Mello's book preserves this historic set of events in Vermont, drawing on newspaper accounts, on letters to the editor, on the sometimes angry, sometimes joyous testimony of private citizens before the Vermont legislature, and on interviews with some of the principal actors in the drama. I believe you will find this a gripping story.

I am not an entirely impartial witness to these events. I am a Vermont resident now, after teaching law at the University of Michigan for 34 years. My partner, John Crane, and I are among the thousands of American couples who have joined in civil union. John and I both worked in support of the legislation while it was pending. On one occasion, John attended a public hearing in the chamber of the Vermont House. Over a thousand people were in the building. While he was waiting to learn whether his name would be pulled at random to be one of the witnesses in support of same-sex unions, he heard a different Crane called as a witness. It was his brother Les. Part of what Les said that night is quoted in Chapter 3 of this book as reported in the next day's *Rutland Herald*:[1]

> Leslie Crane of Williston read a letter from his 18-year old son, who was unable to attend the hearing.
>
> "I am shocked that we as a state and a nation are entertaining the idea of homosexual union." Crane said, reading from the letter. "I believe that if Vermont legalizes this unnatural behavior, I believe there will be a migration like none ever seen. Such an influx of homosexuals will be detrimental to the moral and family values that surround us in Vermont."

[1]Jack Hoffman, *Second Round of Hearings Held*, Rutland Herald, Feb. 3, 2000.

The eighteen-year-old was John's nephew, a young man who liked John a lot. John heard what Les said and was stunned. It was not Les's beliefs that caught him by surprise. John knew that Les is a fundamentalist Christian. His surprise was that, given his closeness to Les and his wife Suzanne and their four children, Les would say what he did in public.

John approached Les outside the House chamber after his testimony. Les seemed taken aback that John was there. He told John that he didn't mean to be referring to the two of us when he spoke. He had dissociated us, whom he loved, from an impersonal menace that he feared. John said little that evening, but wrote Les a long letter telling him how offended and hurt he was. Les, who cares as much about family as we do, wrote back saying he understood and offered to absent himself from a family gathering that he knew John would be attending soon. He closed by asking John if the two of us would join Suzanne and him for dinner sometime at a neutral restaurant to try to repair the damage. Many months later, when John felt less angry, he accepted their invitation. The four of us met at a restaurant and talked. Les and Suzanne discussed the place of religion in their lives. John and I talked about our own lives. None of us changed the others' beliefs, but the brothers did come away reaffirming the love they felt for each other. Six months later, when John and I celebrated our civil union, Les and Suzanne were there. So were John's parents and three other brothers.

Our story is not unique. John and I know many others whose civil unions have proved an opportunity to bring family members to a better understanding of loving gay and lesbian relationships.

I hope that thirty years from now the tale that Professor Mello tells here of the resistance to same-sex marriage will seem as peculiar to young people as the story of men's resistance to women's suffrage seems to me today. If it does, Professor Mello's book will probably have played a small but valuable role in making that shift of mind possible.

Acknowledgments

THIS PROJECT has left me with many debts, which I gratefully acknowledge. Judy Hilts and Laura Gillen word-processed the manuscript in all its incarnations. Ted Sweet and Pam Gatos provided invaluable research assistance. Pam Gatos and Brook Hopkins gave me permission to quote the entirety of their memo on the events leading up to the *Baker v. State* litigation. Ted Sweet gave me permission to reproduce his memo on his interview with the recipients of the first civil union in Vermont. Greg Johnson, Doug Samuels, and Jennifer Hammer read and commented helpfully on at least one incarnation of this manuscript. Nancy Levit, Christine Wiseman, and Gary Francione provided excellent reviews of the manuscript. All remaining errors of fact, law, nuance, or taste are solely my own. The views expressed in this book are my own. They do not reflect the policies or opinions of my employer, Vermont Law School, or any other member of the law school community.

I am deeply grateful to Emily LaPointe, my friend and former research assistant, for believing in this project and for encouraging me to write about subjects beyond my own areas of academic expertise.

I am grateful to Vermont Law School Dean Kinvin Wroth and Associate Dean Bruce Duthu for a generous summer research stipend to support this book project, to Temple University Press and Editor-in-Chief Janet Francendese, to Susan Yates and Alysia Cooley at Publication Services, Inc., and to Peirce Graphic Services, LLC for their superb work in making this book a reality.

Vermont's same-sex civil unions law has generated a number of outstanding books. I found three such books especially indispensable: *Equality Practice: Civil Unions and the Future of Gay Rights* by William Eskridge; *Marriage and Same-Sex Unions: A Debate*, edited by Lynn Wardle, Mark Strasser, William Duncan, and David Coolidge; and *On Same-Sex Marriage, Civil Unions, and the Rule of Law*, by Mark Strasser.

This book had its genesis in an article I wrote for a symposium issue of the *Vermont Law Review* published in Fall 2000. I learned a great deal from other symposium contributors David L. Chambers, David Coolidge, William Duncan, Barbara Cox, and Greg Johnson. Many thanks to *Law Review* editors Dave Ross, Julie Tower, Brian Maddox, and Sean Flynn for bringing the symposium to fruition.

My *Law Review* article, in turn, was a revised, updated, and expanded version of remarks I presented at a panel discussion on same-sex marriage. The panel was held on February 8, 2000, at Vermont Law School. The other panelists were Hal Goldman, Professor Greg Johnson, Professor Gil Kujovich, and Karen Kerin. I am grateful to Professor Greg Johnson, to the Vermont Law School Alliance of Gay, Lesbian, Bisexual, and Transgendered Persons and to the Alliance's president, Nicole Allard, for sponsoring the panel. The *Law Review* article also formed the basis of remarks I presented on March 5, 2000, at a Community Discussion panel held at Trinity Methodist Church in Montpelier and organized by the Washington County Freedom to Marry Task Force. The other panelists were all members of the Vermont Legislature: Senator Ann Cummings, Senator Bill Doyle, Representative Francis Brooks, and Representative Karen Kitzmiller. I want to thank Chuck Kletecka and the Washington County Freedom to Marry Task Force for organizing this panel. I want to express my thanks to the members of these two panels—as well as to the audience members who spoke and asked questions—whose thoughtful and heartfelt comments broadened and deepened my understanding of the matters discussed in this book.

Two heroic members of the Vermont legislature, Representative Michael Kainen and Representative Bill Mackinnon, shared with me their experiences during the same-sex unions firestorm that engulfed Vermont in the year 2000. The first couple to receive a civil union agreed to be interviewed by my student research assistant, Ted Sweet. The lead counsel for the plaintiffs in the landmark case *Baker v. State* were interviewed by my assistant Pam Gatos and her daughter, Brook Hopkins. Thank you all.

Finally, I want to thank my mother, Ida Mello, whose wisdom and courage inspires me.

1 Vermont

A Preview of America's War Over Same-Sex Civil Marriage

Spurred on by the Supreme Court's landmark ruling decriminalizing gay sexual conduct, both sides in the debate over gay rights are vowing an intense state-by-state fight over deeply polarizing questions, foremost among them whether gays should be allowed to marry.

—*New York Times*, July 6, 2003[1]

I KNEW something was wrong when the driver of the pickup truck behind me hit his high beams. It was night, and I was driving on a deserted two-lane road in Vermont. I was driving the speed limit. We were the only two vehicles on the road. The red Chevy, sporting a rifle rack, was occupied by two men, a driver and a front-seat passenger. I slowed to let the truck pass, but it rode my rear bumper, its high beams bathing my car in unwanted light for mile after mile. I was surprised. Most Vermont drivers aren't jerks.

Then I remembered the sticker I had scotch-taped to the rear window of my car. It was a sticker proclaiming my support for gay and lesbian marriage in Vermont. Somehow I knew that this was about my sticker. It was. Eventually, the truck, passed me and screeched off. As it did, the man in its passenger seat shouted to me, "You fucking faggot." This incident occurred at the height of the Vermont controversy over same-sex marriage.

Certain issues always have ignited—and for the foreseeable future will continue to ignite—strong passions in our nation. Same-sex marriage is one of these. Like abortion and capital punishment, same-sex marriage sits on the cultural faultline of morality, religion, and law.

The campaign to allow gay and lesbian couples to share in the legal benefits, legal obligations, and legal responsibilities of marriage has had many different battlefields; this same-sex marriage war, as a historian of the Civil War once said about that conflict, has been—and is being—fought in 10,000 places. The first battlefield in the twenty-first century was in Vermont.

To glimpse a preview of America's battles-to-come over same-sex marriage, study Vermont's recent experience with the issue: the halting steps forward, the backlash, and, finally, the crafting of a "third way"—civil unions—compromise. Make no mistake. This culture war is coming to a courtroom and a statehouse near you. A series of events in the summer of 2003 guaranteed it.

FREEDOM SUMMER, 2003

O, Canada

The summer of legalized love came early.[2] It began with The Kiss. On June 8, 2003, co-lyricists Marc Shaiman and Scott Whittman won a Tony Award for their work on the Broadway hit "Hairspray." The two men kissed on the lips, hard, on national TV.[3] Their liplock celebrated their Tony Award and their 25-year relationship. Shaiman explained to the nation, "We're not allowed to get married in this world. But I'd like to declare in front of all these people, I love you and I'd like to live with you for the rest of my life."[4]

Shaiman was right about not being able to marry when he spoke the words. Two days later, he was no longer right. On June 11, 2003, an Ontario appeals court declared Canada's prohibition against same-sex civil marriage a violation of the country's Charter of Rights and Freedoms,[5] Canada's counterpart to our Bill of Rights. The court ruled that "the restriction against same-sex marriage is an offense to the dignity of lesbians and gays, because it limits the range of relationship options open to them."[6] Hours after the court decision, an Ontario judge performed a civil marriage ceremony for Michael Leshner, 55, a Toronto lawyer, and Mike Stark, 45, a graphic designer.[7] Dozens followed, then hundreds, including several Americans who crossed the border.[8] An appeals court in British Columbia, Canada's westernmost province, joined Ontario in ruling that gay and lesbian couples have an immediate right to marry.[9] There was some talk of appealing the court decisions, but in the end the Canadian government decided to embrace it instead.[10] Prime Minister Jean Chrétien announced his cabinet would seek to codify the court decision. Legislation would be drafted, vetted by Canada's high court, and submitted to the federal parliament.[11] Polls suggested that roughly 55 to 60 percent agreed with the prime minister.[12] And so, "with a minimum of fuss, hardly any hysteria, and no rending of garments,"[13] Canada is on the verge of making it legal for people of the same sex to marry each other. By the time you read these words, gay marriage will almost certainly be the law of the land in all of Canada. That's how fast the world is changing with respect to gay marriage.

The Texas Privacy Case

Fifteen days after the Ontario appellate court ruled, the United States Supreme Court decided the Texas privacy case, *Lawrence v. Texas*.[14] In a class with the great civil rights landmark cases, *Brown v. Board of Education* and *Roe v. Wade*, *Lawrence v. Texas* should become the Magna Carta of gays and lesbians. If the Justices meant what they said, and if they apply their *Lawrence* ruling faithfully to the issue of same-sex marriage, *Lawrence* paves the way for gay marriage in the United States.

Lawrence itself did not involve marriage. Responding to a weapons disturbance complaint, Houston police officers entered the private home of John Lawrence, where they observed Lawrence and another man, Tyron Gardner, engaged in anal sex.[15] The men were charged with violating a Texas sodomy statute, the "Homosexual Conduct Law," that made it a crime for two persons of the same sex to engage in certain kinds of intimate sexual conduct,[16] including anal sex. Like a cleansing summer storm, the Supreme Court struck down the Texas sodomy law as a violation of the right to privacy guaranteed by the Due Process Clause of the Fourteenth Amendment. The Court overruled a 1986 decision that states could punish gays for what historically was defined as deviant sex. This much was not surprising. In 2003, only four states outlawed sodomy between gays, and nine others barred sodomy between any sexual partners.[17] These laws were rarely enforced. However, "even if sodomy laws are rarely enforced, they are frequently invoked in civil cases, particularly parental custody and discrimination ones, whether over equal employment opportunities or equal access to school facilities. Sodomy laws, in other words, actually matter a lot—and overturning them could mean toppling an entire edifice of antigay law."[18]

The surprise in *Lawrence* was the broad sweep of the Court's reasoning. Writing for the five-Justice majority, Justice Anthony Kennedy wrote that gays are "entitled to respect for their private lives."[19] This translated into a substantive due process right to privacy: "The state cannot demean their existence or control their destiny by making their private sexual conduct a crime,"[20] because "liberty presumes an autonomy of self that includes freedom of thought, expression, and a certain intimate conduct."[21] Many people call *Lawrence* a sodomy case. I call it a *privacy* case.

The *Lawrence* Court made clear that its holding was limited to invalidating sodomy laws. Justice Kennedy explained that the case "does not involve whether the government must give formal recognition to any relationship that homosexual persons seek to enter,"[22] such as same-sex marriage.

A WEDGE ISSUE IS BORN: GAY MARRIAGE AND 2004[23]

We [gays and lesbians] can win the freedom to marry. Possibly within five years.

—Evan Wolfson, 2003[24]

Justice Antonin Scalia, writing for himself, Justice Clarence Thomas, and Chief Justice William Rehnquist, in *Lawrence v. Texas*, was having none of this movement toward gay marriage. In a remarkably nasty dissenting opinion, the hang-hard bloc of the Court urged us to recognize that the majority opinion can lay the groundwork for legal recognition of same-sex civil marriage.[25] The Court has taken sides in the "culture war," and the next step would be "judicial imposition of homosexual marriage, as has recently occurred in Canada."[26] The Scalia/Thomas/Rehnquist dissent charged that the majority had "signed on to the so-called homosexual agenda."[27] The door was now wide open for same-sex marriage—and worse. "State laws against bigamy . . . adult incest, prostitution, masturbation, adultery, fornication, bestiality, and obscenity," as well as laws barring same-sex marriage, "are called into question by today's decision" in *Lawrence*.[28] The majority "effectively decrees the end of all morals legislation. If, as the Court asserts, the promotion of majoritarian sexual morality is not even a legitimate state interest, none of the above-mentioned laws can survive."[29]

Well, no. The only state interest asserted by Texas in support of its sodomy law was a general notion of promoting "morality." The Court majority held that "morality" was not a strong enough reason to make all gay sex a crime. In constitutional nomenclature, morality was not a sufficient "rational basis" to sustain sodomy statutes. By contrast, laws prohibiting incest, bestiality, and the rest are based on state interests beyond general morality. Justice Sandra Day O'Connor, concurring in *Lawrence*, explained that the Court's invalidation of the Texas sodomy law did "not mean that other laws distinguishing between heterosexuals and homosexuals would similarly fail under rational basis review. Texas cannot assert any legitimate state interest here, such as national security or preserving the traditional institution of marriage. Unlike the moral disapproval of same-sex relations—the asserted state interest in this case—other reasons exist to promote the institution of marriage beyond mere moral disapproval of an excluded group."[30]

Strictly speaking, O'Connor was correct. The brief by the State of Texas cited moral disapproval as the sole justification for the sodomy law. However, a collection of friend-of-the-court briefs asserted another justification: protection of the traditional, heterosexual family. For example, the brief of the Liberty Counsel argued that "states have the right to promote the institution of heterosexual marriage" and that "deregulating human sexual relations will erode the institution of marriage" and will lead to "the abolition of marriage as the union of one man and one woman."[31] The Family Research Council and Focus on the Family argued in their brief that "marriage is the union of a man and a woman" and that the Texas sodomy law "is a rational means by which to protect and promote marriage as the union of a man and a woman."[32] A brief filed by 69 members of the Texas legislature justified the sodomy statute as "rationally related to promoting [solely heterosexual] marriage and procreation," because "protecting marriage is important," and because the sodomy law "is part of a myriad of state laws promoting marriage and discouraging sexual activity outside of it."[33] There were many other such briefs, but you get the basic idea.

The Scalia/Thomas/Rehnquist dissenting opinion included this remarkable justification for banning gay love and, presumably, gay marriage as well: "Many Americans do not want persons who openly engage in homosexual conduct as partners in their businesses, as scoutmasters for their children, as teachers in their children's schools, or as boarders in their homes. They view this as protecting themselves and their families from a lifestyle that they believe to be immoral and destructive."[34] (One commentator invited us to "tweak that sentence to read 'persons who openly engage in Islam' and see how it reads as a high-court opinion in an allegedly free country."[35] The Scalia/Thomas/Rehnquist dissent did say they had "nothing against homosexuals."

The dissenting opinion by Justices Scalia, Thomas, and Rehnquist was important in its own right. However, the dissent's real importance might be its portents for the future. During the 2000 presidential campaign, George W. Bush was often asked what he would seek in a Supreme Court nominee. The first name Bush brought up as his ideal was Justice Scalia.[36] Further, one might recall that Anthony Kennedy, author of the *Lawrence* majority opinion, was not President Reagan's first choice for the Court. Reagan's first choice was Robert Bork, who didn't believe that the Constitution protected even a right to *marital* privacy. Had Bork, rather than Kennedy, been confirmed by the Senate, the outcome of *Lawrence* might have been quite different.

Lawrence was a great day for freedom in America. Marc Shaiman—of the Tony Awards kiss—enthused after *Lawrence* that he and his partner were "going to Canada to get married, then Texas for a honeymoon."[37]

Liberal publications, such as the *Boston Globe, New York Times,* and *Nation,* cheered *Lawrence,* along with libertarian conservatives like William Safire and Andrew Sullivan.[38] Perhaps taking the Scalia/Thomas/Rehnquist opinions prediction that *Lawrence* would lead to a "massive disruption of the social order"[39] as an invitation, some social conservatives took *Lawrence* as a call to arms. U.S. Senate Majority Leader Bill Frist called for a constitutional amendment to outlaw gay marriage.[40] The measure rapidly acquired 25 sponsors.[41] (As Congress considers this constitutional amendment, I hope they'll remember that many Representatives are alive only due to the courage of a gay man, Mark Bingham, a passenger on United Airlines Flight 93;[42] on September 11, 2001, Flight 93's target was the U.S. Capitol dome.[43]) President Bush declined to endorse the constitutional amendment drive.[44]

Some Republicans thought in gay marriage they had found a "wedge issue" for the 2004 presidential campaign.[45] Most of the nine Democratic contenders supported same-sex civil unions,[46] that is, extending the legal benefits of marriage but calling it something else—but not gay marriage—including Howard Dean, who, as Governor of Vermont, had signed Vermont's civil unions statute into law. As of November 2003,

Dean was looking like a front runner: He was leading the Democratic field in fundraising; he had won endorsements by labor unions and by Hollywood fundraising powerhouses such as Rob Reiner and Martin Sheen; he had won a "virtual" primary on the Internet; he was leading in polls in New Hampshire and Iowa; he was holding his own in the Democratic debates; and the media had anointed him as a contender.[47] On the campaign trail, Dean touted the passage of civil unions in Vermont.[48] But he wouldn't support gay marriage.[49]

Newsweek's cover-story on *Lawrence* was headlined *The War Over Gay Marriage*.[50] On its cover, *Newsweek* put a photo of two men, and asked the question, *Is Gay Marriage Next?* The editors had considered putting on the cover a Vermont couple who had been joined by civil union.

MASSACHUSETTS: MIRACLE OR MUDDLE?

Only time will tell whether Scalia, Thomas, and Rehnquist were correct that *Lawrence* will be a constitutional earthquake and whether *Lawrence* will lead to same-sex marriage in the United States. Before we can find out, some U.S. state must first recognize same-sex marriage. As of May 2004 no state definitively grants or recognizes gay marriage. The Supreme Judicial Court of Massachusetts could have done so; the court heard oral arguments in *Goodridge v. Department of Health* in March 2003.[51] The *Boston Globe* newspaper editorial page urged the court to recognize gay marriage, and a poll it conducted indicated that a slim majority of the Massachusetts public opinion favored allowing gays to marry.[52] As the Bay State waited for the court's decision, the four Catholic bishops of Massachusetts reaffirmed the Roman Catholic Church's opposition to same-sex marriage. Gay activists lashed back at the church[53]—an institution already mired in a sex abuse scandal in which male priests molested boys and young men.[54] The state legislature held hearings on a constitutional amendment to bar same-sex marriage.[55]

Decision day in *Goodridge v. Department of Public Health* came on November 18, 2003.[56] By a razor-thin margin, the Supreme Judicial Court of Massachusetts ruled that "the right to marry means little if it does not include the right to marry the person of one's choice."[57] The lead opinion in *Goodridge* explained that the "Massachusetts constitution affirms the dignity of all individuals" and "forbids the creation of second-class citizens."[58] The marriage ban "works a deep and scarring hardship" on same-sex families "for no rational reason."[59] The court stayed the entry of judgment for 180 days to permit the legislature to take such action as it may deem appropriate in light of this decision."[60] The *Goodridge* court did not rely upon the U.S. Supreme Court's previous ruling in the Texas privacy case, *Lawrence v. Texas*. However *Lawrence* provided the "background music that suffused"[61] the Massachusetts opinion. "The Massachusetts decision and the *Lawrence* rulings were linked in spirit even if not as formal doctrine."[62]

Media reports characterized *Goodridge* as a 4-3 decision. In fact, the court split 4-3 and 3-1-3, and there is no way to tell which portions of the lead opinion are majority and which are plurality. Chief Justice Margaret Marshall wrote the lead opinion, in which two other justices joined in full. Her opinion reformulated the common-law definition of civil marriage to mean "the voluntary union of two people as spouses, to the exclusion of all others." "Marriage is a vital social institution," wrote the chief justice.[63] "The exclusive commitment of two individuals to each other nurtures love and mutual support; it brings stability to our society."[64] For those people "who choose to marry, and for their children, marriage provides an abundance of legal, financial, and social benefits."[65] The court maintained that its decision "does not disturb the fundamental value of marriage in our society."[66] Limiting marriage to heterosexual couples prevents the children of same-sex unions "from enjoying the immeasurable advantages that flow from the assurance of a stable family structure in which children will be reared, educated, and socialized."[67] It cannot be "rational under our laws to penalize children by depriving them of state benefits because of their parents' sexual orientation."[68]

The lead *Goodridge* opinion discussed and rejected several rationales for prohibiting same-sex couples from marrying. The government asserted that the state's interest in regulating marriage is based on the notion that marriage's primary purpose is procreation. The court flatly responded: "This is not correct."[69] Marriage laws in Massachusetts "contain no requirement that applicants for a marriage license attest to their ability or intention to conceive children by coitus. Fertility is not a condition of marriage, nor is it grounds for divorce."[70] Heterosexual couples "who never consummated their marriage, and never plan to, may be and stay married."[71] Heterosexual "people who cannot stir from their deathbed may marry."[72] In short, "it is the exclusive and permanent commitment of the marriage partners to the marriage, not the begetting of children, that is the sine qua non of marriage."[73]

The state also argued that confining marriage to opposite-sex couples ensures the optimal setting for child rearing. However, the *Goodridge* court rebutted, the government "readily concedes that people in same-sex couples may be 'excellent' parents."[74] Gay and lesbian couples "have children for the same reason others do—to love them, to care for them, to nurture them. But the task of child rearing for same-sex couples is made infinitely harder by their status as outliers to the marriage laws."[75] The laws of Massachusetts provide a "cornucopia of substantial benefits to married parents and their children," but "we are confronted with an entire, sizable class of parents raising children who have absolutely no access to civil marriage and its protections because they are forbidden from procuring a marriage license."[76] The marriage ban is what harms the children of same-sex parents. Striking down the ban would help children.

The government further contended that broadening civil marriage to include gay couples would trivialize or destroy traditional marriage. The court countered that the couples in *Goodridge* "seek only to be married, not to undermine the institution of civil marriage. They do not want marriage abolished. They do not attack the binary nature of marriage, the consanguinity provisions, or any other gate-keeping provisions of the marriage licensing laws."[77] Allowing same-sex marriage "will not diminish the validity or dignity of opposite-sex marriage, any more than recognizing the right of an individual to marry a person of a different race devalues the marriage of a person who marries someone of her own race."[78] To the contrary, "extending civil marriage to same-sex couples reinforces the importance of marriage to individuals and communities. That same-sex couples are willing to embrace marriage's solemn obligations of exclusivity, mutual support, and commitment to one another is a testament to the enduring place of marriage in our laws and in the human spirit."[79]

At first blush, it appears that the *Goodridge* court was requiring gay marriage. But was it? Did the *Goodridge* court mandate gay marriage, or would a parallel system of benefits—civil unions, for example—pass muster under the state constitution? I honestly can't tell from the court's lead opinion. The commentary on *Goodridge* amounts to a Rorschach blot; it reveals more about the preconceived attitudes and biases of the commentators than it does the *Goodridge* opinion itself.

On the one hand, *Goodridge* emphasized the importance of the freedom of choice to marry and of the right to privacy in making intimate decisions. The court treated marriage as a civil right, and the ruling did not say whether civil unions might suffice. Harvard Law School professors Lawrence Tribe and Elizabeth Bartholet read *Goodridge* as requiring marriage.[80]

On the other hand, Governor Mitt Romney and State Attorney General Thomas Reilly read *Goodridge* to suggest that a civil unions statute would be enough.[81] The question before the court was "whether, consistent with the Massachusetts's constitution, the Commonwealth may deny the *protections, benefits, and obligations* conferred by civil marriage" to gay couples.[82] And the dispositional portion of the *Goodridge* opinion held that "barring an individual from the *protections, benefits, and obligations of civil marriage* solely because that person would marry a person of the same sex violates the Massachusetts Constitution."[83] Further, although the court said that the constitution "forbids the creation of second-class citizens,"[84] it is not clear that civil unions constitute second-class citizenship. As I discuss later in this book, the Vermont Supreme Court, the Vermont legislature, and gay-rights academics such as William Eskridge and Greg Johnson argue that civil unions are not second-class citizenship. I disagree, but reasonable people can conclude that civil unions are not second-class citizenship. Finally, the lead opinion in *Goodridge* is in part a plurality, not a majority, opinion. The fourth vote was provided by Justice John Greaney, who concurred "with the result reached by the court, the remedy ordered, and much of the reasoning in the court's opinion."[85] Because Justice Greaney did not specify with which parts of the lead opinion he agreed, there is no way to tell which portions of the lead opinion are majority and which are plurality. Massachusetts could "overrule" *Goodridge* by amending the state constitution, but such an amendment could not be finalized until November 2006 because it must be approved by the legislature in two consecutive sessions, and then sent to the voters for ratification.[86]

Reaction to *Goodridge* was swift and thunderous. The Reverend Louis Sheldon, chairman of the Traditional Values Coalition in Washington, D.C., declared that "Massachusetts is our Iwo Jima. For us, it's our last stand. We're going to raise the flag."[87] A syndicated columnist accused the court of "judicial tyranny" and of "arrogating imperious powers to itself;" the opinion itself was "intellectually fraudulent."[88] Another columnist asked whether "homosexuals comprehend that marriages involve responsibilities as well as privileges? Blood tests, for one thing. . . . Do homosexuals really want to take blood tests? Maybe gays aren't worried about [sexually transmitted diseases] anymore."[89] This columnist contended that the court's "insanity" will require invalidation of legal bans on incest and polygamy.[90] Another syndicated columnist explained that marriage "was established by God as the best arrangement for fallen humanity to organize and protect itself and create and rear children"; warned that "what is happening in our culture is an unraveling of all we once considered normal"; and urged the voters in 2004 to "pull the country back from the precipice," stating that "marriage defined should be the social-issue centerpiece of the coming [presidential] campaign."[91] Another columnist declared "it's now midnight in Massachusetts," as the state "now inches closer to a shameful reality, all because of the success militant homosexuals have had" in pushing their "aberrant agenda."[92] The official newspaper of the Catholic Archdiocese of Boston warned Democratic politicians that a "new political reality certainly requires careful consideration of the way Catholics cast their votes. Catholics need to seek out their candidates' views and positions on crucial issues, such as the definition of marriage."[93]

The Massachusetts high court resolved the *Goodridge* ambiguity on January 4, 2004. A majority of the justices explained that *Goodridge* required marriage. Civil unions would not suffice: Civil unions would be an "unconstitutional, inferior, and discriminatory status for same-sex couples. . . . Separate is seldom, if ever, equal." In other words, the Massachusetts court concluded that the only thing equal to marriage is marriage.

This tumult was all quite familiar to those of us living in Vermont in 2000. We'd been there before.

BATTLEFIELD VERMONT

On December 20, 1999, the Vermont Supreme Court made history. In Stan Baker's case,[94] the court held that the Vermont constitution guarantees same-sex couples the same legal benefits and protections now received as a matter of course by heterosexual couples who are married.

"Our common humanity" demands no less, the court ruled. The court then gave the legislature the first opportunity to fashion a mechanism to implement the guarantee of marital equality. The legislators had three basic[95] options. The legislature could simply open up the institution of civil marriage to include gay and lesbian couples or ignore the court's invitation and leave it to the judiciary to make real the right the court had just recognized.[96] Or the lawmakers could adopt a "third way"—between the extremes of doing nothing or everything—and create a parallel system that offers same-sex couples every legal benefit and responsibility of marriage without the name.[97] In choosing the third way, the Vermont legislature created the most comprehensive system of same-sex benefits in the nation.[98] The legislature called its concept "civil unions."

According to Vermont Law School Professor Greg Johnson, the Vermont statute created nothing less than "the most advanced domestic partnership in the world at the time."[99] The statute extends more than 300 benefits,[100] now granted automatically by law to married heterosexuals, to same-sex couples. The day after the Vermont Senate passed the bill, the *New York Times* called it "an American first"[101] and the *L.A. Times* noted that "supporters and opponents alike view it as the country's most comprehensive gay rights legislation— the boldest step in an expanding movement to extend legal benefits to gay and lesbian couples."[102]

Before Vermont, judicial victories for same-sex couples were soon followed by electoral defeats. The Hawaii Supreme Court, for instance, suggested in 1993 that the denial of marriage licenses to same-sex couples might violate the state constitution,[103] and an Alaska trial court ruled in 1998 in favor of same-sex marriage.[104] "The court victories in Hawaii and Alaska were erased by popular votes on [amendments to the respective state constitutions on] the same day (and by the same 2/3–1/3 percentage) in November 1998."[105]

The court decision in Stan Baker's case and its aftermath received extraordinary national and international media attention. Literally hundreds of substantial news stories on the Vermont events were published in newspapers outside of Vermont.[106] The decision in Stan Baker's case was a lead story on the top of the front page of the *New York Times* and the *Boston Globe*.[107] Both the *Times* and the *Globe* wrote editorials on the decision. The lead editorial in the *Times* was headlined "Vermont's Momentous Ruling."[108] The *Globe* called *Baker* a recognition of reality as well as an acknowledgment of "our common humanity."[109] The international press also followed the story closely.[110] The attention to Vermont has not been a one-time media event. Over the following years, more than a half-dozen state legislatures considered bills patterned after Vermont's civil unions statute.

The significance of this story reaches far beyond the geographical borders of the Green Mountain State. The Vermont events have been a catalyst for national developments on an issue of widespread national interest and importance.

This is a story that transcends regional boundaries as well as gay/straight categories. Vermont's story is—and will continue to be—America's story.

LIKE SPORES ON THE WIND

[The vast majority of the same-sex couples receiving civil unions in Vermont] do not live in Vermont. Once they're back home, legal issues are sure to rise as they separate, die, or try to file joint tax returns. One by one, state courts will be asked to recognize Vermont civil unions by applying that state's law or their own.

—*National Law Journal*, December 2000[111]

The civil unions legislation put Vermont on a collision course with other states and with an act of Congress. At least two states, Nevada and Nebraska, have passed measures explicitly refusing to recognize civil unions such as Vermont's.[112] At the time Vermont's bill was passed, 31 states and the federal government had enacted statutes or state constitutional amendments refusing to recognize same-sex marriages in those or any other states. Within six months of Vermont's enactment of its new law, the number of states banning recognition of same-sex marriage had risen to 35.[113] The number is now 37; Texas became the 37th when it banned gay marriage in May 2003.[114] (Interestingly, at the time the courts held state bans on interracial marriage unconstitutional, "30 states had laws and six states had constitutional provisions prohibiting African Americans and whites from marrying."[115] I'd guess that many of the 37 that bar same-sex marriage today were the same states that banned interracial marriage back then).

It isn't just the states that explicitly refuse to recognize same-sex marriage—federal law does as well. In 1996, an election year, Congress passed the "Defense of Marriage Act" or DOMA. The DOMA provided in part that "no state . . . shall be required to give effect to any public act, record or judicial proceeding in any other state . . . respecting a relationship between persons of the same sex that is treated as a marriage under the laws of such other state, . . . or a right or claim arising from such relationship."[116] The 1996 act also defined "marriage" and "spouse" for purposes of federal agencies and federal regulations.[117] For purposes of federal agencies, marriage is "only a legal union between one man and one woman as husband and wife."[118] For purposes of federal regulations, "the word 'spouse' refers only to a person of the opposite sex who is a husband and wife."[119] The federal DOMA "sailed through Congress by margins of 342 to 67 in the House and 85 to 14 in the Senate. DOMA was signed into law without a whimper by [President Bill Clinton] in a private ceremony."[120]

There is a strong argument that the DOMAs are unconstitutional,[121] but, before their legality can be tested, a state must recognize same-sex marriage or civil unions must be treated as the legal equivalent of marriage for purposes of interstate portability. The federal DOMA was enacted when many observers expected Hawaii to recognize same-sex marriage, but Hawaii declined to do so.[122]

Vermont's civil unions law will continue to have a national impact for two simple reasons: demographics and legal uncertainty. As of July 11, 2003, Vermont had recorded 5,786 civil unions, according to the state's public health statistics chief.[123] Eighty-five percent of these civil union licenses have been issued to *non-Vermont* residents.[124] This means that thousands of nonresidents come to Vermont, get "civilly unionized," and return to their home states to live. Inevitably, the resident states will have to decide what recognition, if any, they will give to the Vermont civil union.

For example, a lesbian couple from Georgia received a Vermont civil union. Back in Georgia, the couple raised a legal argument that Georgia should treat the Vermont civil union as a legal marriage.[125] The Georgia Court of Appeals refused to recognize the civil union.[126] The same thing happened in Connecticut; an appellate court refused to dissolve a Vermont civil union;[127] the Connecticut Supreme Court agreed to take up the issue, but the plaintiff died of HIV-AIDS before the court ruled. And in Texas, a couple sought to dissolve a Vermont civil union.[128] A Texas district judge initially agreed to grant the divorce, but the state attorney general stepped in. The Attorney General "feared granting the divorce would signal that the state recognized the union in the first place." He argued that "a court cannot grant a divorce where no marriage existed."[129] The judge agreed and reversed himself.[130] By contrast, a West Virginia family court judge did agree to use divorce laws to dissolve a civil union.[131] A Mississippi court ruled in favor of a lesbian couple from Vermont who sought to have both their names listed on the birth certificate of a boy adopted from Mississippi five years previously.[132] Same-sex couples in New Jersey and Indiana have filed a lawsuit seeking to overturn that state's ban on gay marriage.[133] And so on.

Likewise, legal uncertainty spawns litigation. Had Vermont simply authorized same-sex marriage, the duties of other states to recognize such marriages would have been uncertain enough. Perhaps, as Mark Strasser has argued, the Privileges and Immunities clauses of the Constitution would require other states to recognize Vermont same-sex marriages.[134] Perhaps the Constitution's Full Faith and Credit Clause would mandate such a result.[135] Perhaps "choice of law"[136] theory will require other states to recognize Vermont civil unions. How such legal guarantees interact with the federal and state "Defense of Marriage Acts" (assuming the DOMAs themselves pass constitutional muster),[137] and how the DOMAs might be affected by federal and state antidiscrimination laws, would have increased the indefiniteness of the portability of Vermont same-sex marriages. That Vermont adopted civil union—not same-sex marriage—magnifies the legal uncertainty.

The Supreme Court's 2003 decision in the Texas privacy case, *Lawrence v. Texas*, ratchets up the uncertainly yet another few notches. The right to privacy rationale of *Lawrence*—and the Court's denunciation of law that demeans the lives of gays and lesbians—raise serious doubts about whether the DOMA statutes are constitutional. On this score the Scalia/Rehnquist/Thomas dissent in *Lawrence* was right on target.

As Greg Johnson observed, the only certainty is that "until other states adopt civil unions or same-sex marriage, what we will likely see is a wave of full faith and credit litigation, as couples civilly united in Vermont sue for marital protections in other states."[138] "Wave" seems the operative metaphor. The *National Law Journal* reported in December

2000 that "gay and lesbian lawyers across the country were bracing for a wave of litigation over the status of same-sex couples whose relationships have been given a new status in the state of Vermont."[139]

During 2003, legislatures in Connecticut, Montana, and Rhode Island debated bills that would have authorized same-sex marriage.[140] In seven states, civil unions bills, patterned after Vermont's, were introduced.[141] Five died. As of this writing, civil unions bills were still pending in Massachusetts and California.[142]

The upshot is that "one by one, state courts will be asked to recognize Vermont civil unions by applying that state's law or their own."[143] Activists on both sides of the culture war know it. The facts on the ground—that the impact of Vermont's civil unions law would extend to every state in the nation—is precisely why the national partisans on both sides of the issue devoted so many resources to Vermont during the civil unions battles. Nonresident civil unions will spread the influence of the Vermont law like spores on the wind.

Gary Bauer and William Raspberry agree on virtually nothing. Bauer is an erstwhile Republican presidential candidate and founder of the conservative Campaign for Working Families. Raspberry is a nationally syndicated columnist, a liberal, and an African American. Bauer is a ferocious opponent of Vermont's civil unions law; Raspberry is an equally ferocious supporter of the statute. The two men agree, however, on the law's national significance. According to Bauer, "The Vermont legislature has taken a major step toward radically redefining our most important social institution and overturning 4,000 years of Judeo-Christian moral teaching."[144] Raspberry responded, "You know what? I agree with [Bauer]. The Vermont law is a prelude to a radical redefinition of marriage."[145]

"If there were any lingering questions about whether the nation was watching Vermont's civil union debate unfold, those questions were put to rest on Sunday [April 30, 2000] on Constitution Avenue."[146] That day was the culmination of the Millennium March on Washington, D.C., the fourth national march in the nation's capital in 31 years. Hundreds of thousands of people attended the march, which occurred only days after the Vermont civil unions bill was signed into law.

"As soon as Vermont's banner-carrying brigade inched its way into the parade lineup for the Millennium March on Washington, the roar went up from the crowd. 'Thank you Vermont!' was the common refrain among the thousands of gays and lesbians who lined the parade route. . . . The cheering was constant for the duration of the Vermont group's hour-long march from the Washington Monument to the Mall. . . . The roughly 125 Vermonters who marched behind the Vermont Freedom to Marry Task Force banner were treated as heroes for the cause."[147]

Among others praising Vermont at the rally was U.S. Representative Jerrold Nadler of New York. " 'Vermont stands as a beacon of hope to everyone in the nation who is truly interested in equality,' [Nadler] said. It appeared that nearly everyone at the march was aware of the law and its potential consequences for the rest of the country."[148]

National opinion magazines took predictable positions on the civil union law. The conservative *Weekly Standard* ran a cover story headlined "Who Lost Vermont?"[149] The issue included two lengthy denunciations of civil unions. The first urged that Vermont be "give[n] . . . to Canada" and bemoaned the "sad decline of the Green Mountain State."[150] The piece trashed the state supreme court justices as "all career government lawyers who couldn't get elected dogcatcher at most town meetings."[151] The other article, by David Coolidge, described the civil unions statute as the culmination of "the long march to legitimize homosexuality in Vermont" and warned other states that they may be "forced to follow" Vermont's example.[152]

From the opposite end of the political spectrum, *Mother Jones* magazine published a long love letter supporting same-sex marriage in general and Vermont's civil unions statute in particular.[153] The article praised *Baker* and the statute that followed as "a landmark victory in the decades-long nationwide struggle for legal recognition of gay relationships." The civil unions law was nothing less than a signal of "a sea change in American cultural politics. For the first time, the seemingly unstoppable antigay political juggernaut was halted—by a group of unlikely combatants in a rural state."[154]

The academic literature on the issue of same-sex marriage and civil unions was lively even before *Baker* and the civil unions law. It will continue to multiply in the wake of Vermont's civil unions law.[155] The Vermont law has already generated dozens of scholarly articles and several excellent academic books.[156]

Thus, understanding the Vermont events is crucial to understanding the issue of same-sex marriage in America. To outside observers, the

Vermont experience has been simplified into caricatures and sound bites: either a progressive state doing the right thing, or a victory for the culturally destabilizing forces of sexual permissiveness and promiscuity. Like most clichés, these contain a kernel of truth.

However, the Vermont experience was actually far more complex, and far more interesting. The truth, like the devil, is in the details. Any "lessons" from Vermont's encounter with the issue of same-sex marriage must be grounded in an accurate understanding of exactly what happened here during the year 2000. My aim in this book is to tell that story. Although Vermont has received widespread national attention, there has yet to be an inside account of what actually went on here. This is one of those stories in which you really needed to have been here—and to have taken good notes—to understand and appreciate what was occurring on the ground. I am not a native Vermonter (I've lived here only 15 years, barely a nanosecond in Green Mountain time), but I follow politics and culture here closely.

Rosa Parks once said, "I knew someone had to take the first step."[157] Vermont seemed an especially hospitable place to give comprehensive legal recognition to same-sex couples. In 1990 sexual orientation was included as a protected group under the state statute imposing increased penalties for crimes motivated by hatred of a particular group.[158] In 1992 Vermont enacted a civil rights statute that identified sexual orientation as a protected class under all the state's antidiscrimination laws.[159] The next year, the Vermont Supreme Court became the first court of last resort in the nation to rule that a lesbian can adopt her partner's children.[160] The following year, Vermont became the first state in the country to offer health insurance benefits to domestic partners of state employees.

It was in this context that the Vermont Supreme Court in *Baker* held that same-sex couples are constitutionally guaranteed marital parity with heterosexual couples. It was in this context that the Vermont legislature passed, and the governor signed into law, the most sweeping domestic partnership system in the nation and the world at the time.

There are two Vermonts. The first Vermont consists of people whose families have lived here for generations. With many exceptions, this Vermont tends to be conservative, traditional, and rooted in the values of rural America. The second Vermont consists of people like me: transplanted urbanites from places like Boston, New York City, or, in my case, Washington, D.C. With many exceptions, this Vermont tends to be liberal, nontraditional, and rooted in the ethos of the city. The political consequence of this influx of flatlanders has been the erosion of the state Republican party and the growth of the state Democratic and Progressive parties.

On many issues—the environment and banning billboards from the highways, for example—the two Vermonts coexist comfortably. Two recent issues of public policy have exposed the divisions between the two Vermonts. Both policy fights began with controversial rulings by the Vermont Supreme Court and ended with legislative enactments. One was school funding. The other was same-sex marriage.

The good news was that the legislature responded to *Baker* by enacting the sweeping civil unions statute. The bad news was the reason that Vermont did not simply open up its marriage laws[161] to include same-sex couples: That reason was what the politicians called political reality. And "political reality" was a polite term for homophobia.

Then-Governor Howard Dean illustrated Vermont's divided soul. On the one hand, Governor Dean emphatically rejected same-sex marriage. On the other hand, he worked hard to secure legislative enactment of civil unions.

Examples abound of the national hostility to same-sex marriage specifically and homosexuality generally. A poll published by *Newsweek* for the week ending March 20, 2000—as the same-sex marriage debate raged in Vermont—found that 57 percent of the general public are opposed to same-sex marriage; "50 percent say gays should not adopt; 36 percent say gays should not teach elementary school. Six in 10 gay men and women perceive 'a lot' of discrimination against homosexuals."[162]

A random survey of 71,570 military officers and enlisted personnel found widespread harassment based on sexual orientation in the military. "Eighty percent of service members questioned by the Pentagon's inspector general reported hearing antigay remarks during the last year and 33 percent said they heard them often or very often. . . . Antigay remarks and harassment are commonplace in the American military, especially in the form of offensive speech and gestures, and an overwhelming majority of service members believe their superiors and colleagues tolerate it 'to some extent.'"[163] The numbers were troubling: "While 80 percent reported hearing 'offensive comments' about gays, even more—85 percent—believed that the comments were tolerated within their units."[164] Thirty-seven percent said they had "witnessed or experienced some form of harassment" and, of these, in more than half "service members said they had witnessed or experienced that harassment in the form of graffiti, vandalism, threats, unfair discipline, discrimination in training or career opportunities or even physical assaults."[165] The survey was ordered after a gay soldier was beaten to death with a baseball bat at Fort Campbell, Kentucky.[166]

Gays "as a group are still among the most despised minorities."[167] In its most lethal form, such hostility has led to murder: "Hate crimes like the murder of Matthew Shepard and Pfc. Barry Winchell, beaten to death in his bunk at Fort Campbell, Ky., [in July 1999] shatter the most deeply cherished notions of security."[168]

Hostility towards gays and lesbians remains politically acceptable, unlike hostility towards African Americans. Consider two senators, Trent Lott and Rick Santorum. In 2002, Trent Lott waxed nostalgic about the good old days of Jim Crow America. Despite his serial apologies, Lott was roundly condemned by everyone from President Bush to the *Weekly Standard*. Lott had to step down as Senate Majority Leader. In 2003, Senator Rick Santorum equated gay love with bestiality and adultery.[169] Santorum claimed he was quoted out of context, but he did not apologize. President Bush remained silent. Santorum still holds his position as the #3 Republican in the U.S. Senate.

I don't mean to suggest that Vermont is immune from the nation's homophobia. It isn't. Homophobia is alive and well in Vermont, as I will demonstrate later in this book. Indeed, the post-*Baker* Vermont legislation was all the more remarkable because many, many Vermonters— probably more than a majority—opposed it; because a hefty percentage of such opposition was fierce; and because each and every senator and representative who voted for the bill did so in the knowledge that, within a matter of months, all of them would face reelection. More than a few legislators knew full well that they were risking political suicide in voting for the bill, but they voted for it anyway. How they, and how Vermont, came to that point is a fascinating case study in republican government at work trying to resolve one of the most emotionally contentious civil rights issues of our time. Vermont is a unique example of republican government in action, and it is that story I want to tell in this book. Along with a few others.

The developments in Vermont during the winter and spring of 2000 captured national and international attention because it was in *this* place, and at *this* time, that advocates of same-sex marriage won their first enduring victory. And it's a hell of a story. For reasons not entirely clear to me, Vermont has a special hold on the American imagination. Consider, as the AP's Christopher Graff has suggested, the Ben and Jerry's ice cream company.[170] Ben and Jerry's "is a tiny company with an insignificant share of the ice cream market."[171] "On the day [in April 2000] Unileaver bought Slim-Fast for $3.2 billion, and Ben and Jerry's for $326 million, it was the smaller purchase that captured the headlines and attention nationwide."[172] Why? "Quite simply because no one knows or cares who owns Slim-Fast. But they know Ben and they know Jerry . . . two real guys at the heart of the company; two guys who want to . . . make the world a better place, and that strikes a nerve with the public."[173]

Our lone member of the 435-person U.S. House of Representatives, Bernie Sanders, "strikes the same chord."[174] Why? Because Bernie Sanders is a Socialist and an Independent. And because "Bernie is the fighter for the little guy, taking on the powerful pharmaceutical industry or whoever is his enemy of the moment."[175]

In May 2001 Vermont U.S. Senator Jim Jeffords set off a political thunderstorm by switching parties from Republican to Independent.[176] Since Jeffords, a three-term Republican, would caucus with the Democrats, his change had the effect of transferring control of the Senate from Republican hands to Democratic. Jeffords's switch made the covers of *Newsweek, Time,* the *Nation,* and the *New Republic.*[177] *Newsweek*'s cover declared "Mr. Jeffords Blows Up Washington."[178] *Time*'s inner headline was "A One-Man Earthquake."[179] The *Nation*'s cover graphic depicted a Samson-like Jeffords bringing the pillars of the Senate down upon the heads of President Bush and (former) Majority Leader Trent Lott.[180] Jeffords explained that "in order to best represent my state of Vermont, my own conscience, and principles I have stood for all my life, I will leave the Republican party and become an Independent."[181] Jeffords's defection harmed him not one whit in Vermont. Independents and Democrats have been electing him for years. Republican leaders in the state have complained about him for years. A poll taken shortly after his announcement found that 66 percent of Vermonters polled said they agreed with Jeffords's decision and 27 percent disagreed.[182] Seventy percent rated Jeffords's job performance as "excellent" or "good."[183] In the end, Jeffords's defection didn't mean much. The Republicans retook control of the Senate and House in 2002.

And, for better or for worse, the presidential candidacy of former-Vermont Governor Howard Dean has placed the state into the national spotlight again. Dean has been characterized as a hard-left liberal, largely because of his strident opposition to the war in Iraq. Dean's surprisingly strong (but brief) candidacy has injected civil unions into the campaign; most of the nine Democratic candidates support civil unions.

Dean's candidacy in 2003 and Jeffords's defection in 2001, like civil unions in 2000, left much of the rest of the nation wondering what makes Vermont tick. The *Nation* editors wrote that "this small state of delicious anachronisms has once again worked its magic on the leaden cynicism of big-time power politics. Let's hear it for Vermonters, who send people of distinctive quality to speak for them in Washington. And let's hear it for Jim Jeffords and his truth-telling."[184] Writing in the same issue, Micah Sifry observed that "it's fitting that the first senator to become an independent in more than thirty years hails from Vermont, the state with the most advanced independent politics in the nation."[185]

Vermont has a well-earned reputation for independent thinking, for courage, and for being ahead of the national learning curve on issues of social justice. Vermont was a free and independent Republic from 1777, when the other colonies were still fighting for independence. After becoming the 14th state in the Union, in 1791, Vermont became the first (and, until the Civil War, remained the only) state to outlaw slavery by constitutional amendment[186] and to extend voting rights to all men regardless of property ownership. Vermont was the first state to call for direct election of its governor. Vermont was the first state to elect a woman as its lieutenant governor. Vermont's conservative U.S. Senator Ralph Flanders "had the courage to stand up in the U.S. Senate and call for an end to Joe McCarthy's red-baiting, taking a stand that for Flanders was steeled in the values of the Bill of Rights."[187]

Further, "Vermont is small enough to retain the sense of community lost elsewhere, and is unafraid to try the unconventional—to stand up for the little guy. . . . This state has always been seen as a bastion of common sense and a breeder of courageous people."[188] Vermont's legislature reflects these same traditions. Vermont's is truly a "citizen legislature. For eight months of the year, the 180 lawmakers live in their communities, tending to the jobs that are their primary vocation"[189] while a few are "primarily legislators," that "is still the exception. For the most part the lawmakers have real lives as farmers, teachers, bankers, business owners and lawyers. . . . The fact that lawmakers have real lives as citizens in their communities is a tremendous asset to the legislative process."[190]

For all of these reasons—all of these reasons why Vermont occupies a unique place in America's collective imagination—the national impact of *Baker* and its aftermath are magnified. If *we* can do it, without the sky falling in, then perhaps other states can and will. It won't be quick, of course, and it won't be easy. It took nearly a century—and a civil war that cost us more than 600,000 lives—for the rest of the nation to join Vermont in outlawing slavery.

ROADMAP

I would like to address three main things in this book. First, I would like to describe the *Baker* decision, to suggest that it is an utterly legitimate and appropriate instance of constitutional decision making, to catalog some of the homophobia that followed in the wake of the *Baker* decision, and to argue that protecting the civil rights of despised minorities is a central function of the judiciary. Second, and most importantly, I want to describe the political and cultural environment that resulted in the creation of civil unions. I want this book to tell a story. It is a story policymakers across the nation would be wise to understand. Wherever the rest of America is going with respect to same-sex marriage, Vermont got there first.

More precisely, I want to tell the *rest* of the story. Yale Law School Professor William Eskridge has superbly chronicled the legislative story of how the civil unions statute came to be passed.[191] I want to add the story of the war zone *outside* the legislative chambers, because those events drove events within the legislature, and to update the story to the present. Further, I disagree with Professor Eskridge's evaluation of the civil unions law.

Finally, I will evaluate the "third way" of civil unions. I conclude that Vermont's third way, although a giant step forward for gay rights, fails in the end: I believe that civil unions fail as a separate-but-equal version of same-sex marriage that stamps gay and lesbian couples with an unmistakable *badge of inferiority* and second-class citizenship.[192] In response to the fierce and widespread public opposition to granting same-sex couples any legal recognition, Vermont resurrected the old doctrine of separate-but-equal, along with the old myth that "separate" can ever be "equal." In *Brown v. Board of Education,* decided a half-century ago, the U.S. Supreme Court held that "separate educational facilities are inherently unequal."[193] This was so because legally mandated segregation stamped the segregated with a badge of inferiority. Similarly, denying committed same-sex couples the right to marry—while at the same time giving them the same bundle of legal rights associated with marriage—stamps those couples with an unmistakable badge of inferiority. In stressing to opponents that civil unions were not *marriage*—the statute itself defines marriage as a union between a man and a woman. This demarcation was at the core of the arguments made by the statute's legislative supporters—the new law sends same-sex couples the same message of second-class matrimonial citizenship that the separate-but-equal doctrine sent to racial minorities in the six decades before *Brown v. Board of Education.*

Some advocates for same-sex marriage agree that civil unions are an unacceptable resurrection of separate-but-equal.[194] However, I want to acknowledge at the outset that leading gay rights scholars and academics disagree with me entirely. Yale Law School Professor William Eskridge argues powerfully that civil unions will not relegate same-sex couples to a separate-but-equal status that would ultimately prove unequal. Eskridge asserts that gays and lesbians should support compromises like Vermont's statute without giving up on full marital equality. Compromises like civil unions will deliver legal rights and duties urgently needed by same-sex couples. They will also help create an environment in which same-sex couples are more likely, in the end, to win fully equal treatment of their relationships by the state.

Professor Eskridge, while conceding that civil unions are far from equal to civil marriage, argues that "it is greatly unfair to tag the civil unions measure as 'separate but equal'" and that *Baker* and civil unions bear closer kinship to *Brown v. Board of Education* than to the separate-but-equal case of *Plessy v. Ferguson.*[195] Vermont Law School Professor Greg Johnson contends that, far from stigmatizing same-sex couples with a badge of inferiority, civil unions liberate them to craft a new institution unburdened by the mess we heterosexuals have made of marriage; *vive la difference,* Johnson declares.[196]

Eskridge and Johnson may well be right. I may be wrong.

This is not a book aimed at a solely academic or legal audience. This is a book for the laity as well as for scholars. Anyone with a law degree can make the law mysterious, inaccessible, and incomprehensible. It is much harder to translate complicated and subtle legal concepts into a presentation accessible to nonscholars, without oversimplifying to a point that scholars will question the intellectual rigor of the project.

That is the razor's-edge I have tried to ride with this book. My experience translating the Byzantine law of capital punishment and *habeas corpus* law—some of the most arcane legal concepts in existence—prepared me well for this task, I think. I hope that the book will be of value to scholars and general readers alike.

A note on sources. I am acutely aware that this book is only a first draft of history and that, although parts of it are based on the best sources available at the time of this writing—newspaper accounts—those sources are imperfect. However, I believe the newspaper accounts upon which portions of this book depend are reliable enough to capture the essence of the events they describe. First, for the period covered here, I read, on a daily basis, the leading Vermont daily and weekly newspapers, *The Burlington Free Press, The Rutland Herald, The Valley News, The Herald of Randolph, The Times-Argus* of Barre and Montpelier, and the *Vermont Standard* of Woodstock. Such redundancy from newspapers with varying editorial positions on the issue at hand increased my confidence that I was getting it right. So did the high quality of the individual reporters on whom I rely. For a small, rural state, we have far better newspapers than what we are entitled to; gifted reporters, who could easily work at larger and more prestigious papers elsewhere, migrate here for the same lifestyle and quality of life reasons as do many other talented professionals.[197] Vermont has outstanding journalists for the same reason it has outstanding restaurants, bookstores, artists and writers: because there's something special about these mountains and these rivers and this air and this sky, and these qualities attract talented people to this place. Journalists like Christopher Graff and Jack Hoffman are experienced in covering Vermont politics. I have, at some point in the past, worked with most of the reporters whose work I cite in this book.

Finally, it might appear to some readers of my previous writings that this book is a departure from my typical focus on capital punishment.[198]

However, I have always seen capital punishment as a civil rights issue. I see the issue at hand in the same manner. Further, I think that my outsider status—I am neither gay nor a native Vermonter—might provide me with some insights missed by those combatants most closely involved. Finally, as I have discussed elsewhere,[199] I have great respect for feminist scholarship. Feminist scholars feel "able to venture into academic territory where we have no special claims to expertise. Feminists are notorious for not respecting the 'proper' boundaries of academic disciplines, and in our opinion that is all to the good."[200] Amen.

2   The *Baker* Decision

*A Legitimate Exercise
in Constitutional
Adjudication*

It was not integration we were fighting for, or segregation we were fighting
against, but something else. But what? I don't know, except that we had a
feeling of what it meant to be human.

—Julius Lester, 1981[1]

It was, as Vermont Supreme Court Justice John Dooley observed, "the most closely watched opinion in this court's history."[2] The
majority opinion observed that "our opinion provides greater recognition of—and protection for—same-sex relationships than has been recognized by any court of final jurisdiction in this country with the instructive exception" of Hawaii.[3]

The day the highest court in this state of "fewer people than cows" (according to the bumper stickers) became the first court of last resort in the
nation to rule that committed same-sex couples should receive the same
rights and benefits of heterosexual spouses, it was reported on the national network nightly news across America. A leading Vermont newspaper heralded *Baker v. State* with a *Japanese-Bomb-Pearl-Harbor*–size
headline,[4] and the newspaper devoted two full pages of space to excerpts
from the court's opinion.

If you haven't already read the opinions in *Baker*, you ought to. The
opinions have been dissected and analyzed exhaustively, but the best
defense of the *Baker* decision is in the court's eloquent and tightly reasoned opinion itself, along with Justice Dooley's concurrence and Justice Johnson's dissent.

THE RIGHT TO BE ORDINARY: FROM SEXUAL OUTLAWS TO . . . CIVIL MARRIAGE?

[I used to think there were] two kinds of people in the world, gay and straight. [Now I divide the world differently]: people who are parents, and people who aren't.

—Elizabeth Birch, a lesbian mother, 2000[5]

I must confess that, in a way, the entire conversation about same-sex marriage strikes me as somewhat dissonant. Heterosexuals have made a mess of marriage. One-half of marriages end in divorce; one-third of children are born out of wedlock; marriage rates are declining; domestic violence and child sexual abuse remain all too common.[6] I'm not sure why same-sex couples *want* access to this besieged institution.[7] For a long time, they didn't. Or, to put it more precisely, the gays and lesbians *I knew* didn't.

How times have changed. The two leading gay rights issues in the year 2000 were the rights of same-sex couples to marry and the rights of gays to be Boy Scouts.[8] Marriage and the Boy Scouts. Can there possibly be other American institutions that are so *straight*? So *ordinary*?

As described elsewhere,[9] I first encountered gay and lesbian activists in 1976. They, and I, were protesters at the Democratic and Republican National Conventions. That was only a few years after Stonewall, and the folks I met were radicals (a term I do not, and did not then, view as disparaging). In fact, "much of the political energy freed up by Stonewall was radical. The Gay Liberation Front was formed in New York within a month of the Stonewall riots. Nowhere was its radical philosophy more sharply expressed than in its attitude toward marriage: 'We expose the institution of marriage as one of the most insidious and basic sustainers of the system. The family is the microcosm of oppression.'"[10] I remember reading in college (not as assigned reading, but on my own) books by William Borroughs and others who viewed homosexuality itself as a declaration of rebellion and defiance against mainstream social institutions, including the institution of marriage.

"Many feminist lesbians long regarded marriage as an oppressive and patriarchal institution. Gay men long evinced little interest in marriage as well. Some had similar aversions to such an 'establishment' model; some chose other battles to fight for more basic acceptance.

Many gay men and lesbians also worried about sparking greater hostility from the conservative public—and success in pushing for marriage seemed so remote."[11]

As with all social movements, the people involved in the struggle for lesbian and gay equality are not homogeneous, and thus the struggle takes on different forms. Same-sex communities are as diverse as America. The same Stonewall revolt that radicalized much of the leadership of the gay movement also inspired individual same-sex couples to seek to marry. Within a year of Stonewall in 1969, a gay couple requested, and was denied, a marriage license.[12]

The *New York Times* reported that in "recent years, as public acceptance of gay and lesbian couples has grown, a national push for same-sex marriage has gained momentum, and it appears to have drawn its impetus not only from the gay rights advocates who organized it but from the most grassroots of levels: same-sex couples deciding they wanted, and would demand, the very same status as their straight counterparts."[13]

William Eskridge described the same-sex community's journey to seeking marriage:

> [The] 1980s saw a stealthy revival of the gay marriage issue. The revival was a product of several forces. One was the success of the gay rights movement in reducing discrimination against lesbian, gay, and bisexual employees, especially state and local government workers. Success in that arena bred dissatisfaction in another. Lesbian and gay employees with partners were being paid far less than similarly situated but married heterosexuals, because the latter had access to increasingly lucrative spousal health and insurance benefits. More important, gay men, lesbians, and bisexuals were themselves changing in the 1980s and changing in ways that made them more likely to settle down in a committed relationship. The "queer boomers" were aging, making more money than love, and settling down with partners. The guppie (gay urban professional) with a partner and a Porsche was replacing the free love advocate with a placard and a toke. The new Generation Xers were open to the diverse sexuality offered by gay liberation but more skeptical of its early barn-burning radicalism.
>
> The role of the AIDS epidemic is surely as complicated as it is significant. Its most apparent effect has been to scare gay and bisexual men into safer sex with fewer partners, but its deeper consequences are more important for the marriage issue. Commitment to another partner became a more attractive norm for those infected by the virus that leads to AIDS, as well as for those not infected. The need of people with AIDS for physical as well as emotional support brought many couples together and cemented more relationships than it tore apart. More important, AIDS

helped bring lesbians and gay men back together in a vigil of collective care for the suffering and dying. Whatever gravity gay life may have lacked in the disco seventies it acquired in the health crisis of the eighties. What it lost in youth and innocence it gained in dignity. Gay cruising and experimentation, noted by Cory as a permanent obstacle to gay marriage, gave way somewhat in the 1980s to a more lesbian-like interest in commitment. Since 1981 and probably earlier, gays were civilizing themselves. Part of our self-civilization has been an insistence on the right to marry.[14]

The landmark 1999 Vermont Supreme Court decision in *Baker v. State* came 28 years after "the first [reported] appellate decision in the United States on the issue of same-sex marriage."[15] In one of history's little quirks, that 1971 case was also called *Baker*. The Minnesota Supreme Court in *Baker v. Nelson* affirmed the denial of Jack Baker's and Mike McConnell's application for a marriage license.[16]

The Minnesota *Baker* decision "began its constitutional discussion with the premise that '[t]he institution of marriage as a union of a man and a woman, uniquely involving the procreation and rearing of children, is as old as the book of Genesis.'"[17]

Between the Minnesota *Baker* in 1971 and the Vermont *Baker* in 1999, "lawsuits by other same-sex couples" across the country had "steadily pressed constitutional objections to the law's exclusion of gay and lesbian couples from the institution of marriage. The plaintiffs lost in all the cases—until the Hawaii Supreme Court [in 1993] told the state that it was required to show a compelling reason to deny Ninia Baehr and Genora Dancel a marriage license."[18] After an amendment to the Hawaii Constitution nullified the court ruling (and after a victory in Alaska was also negated by a constitutional amendment) the focus shifted to Vermont.

The 1999 *Baker* decision occurred in a local context.[19] Pamela Gatos, when she worked as my student research assistant, and her daughter Brook Hopkins, interviewed Beth Robinson, one of the lead counsel for the *Baker* plaintiff's, about the roots of the case. Gatos and Hopkins reported:

> It is difficult to determine exactly when the work leading up to *Baker* and the civil unions bill began in Vermont. There were a number of "starting points" all of which were important in laying the groundwork for *Baker*.
>
> About ten years ago, the gay and lesbian community in Vermont began the work of getting the gay rights law passed. Following that, in 1993, the

Supreme Court decided the second parent adoption case, which was followed by the struggle to get the legislature to defend and codify that decision. Beth Robinson began to get involved with this work at that stage, but sees this previous groundwork as essential to *Baker*.

Another starting point was the Hawaii Supreme Court decision. Gays and lesbians had taken for granted that their relationships were relegated to second-class status. The Hawaii decision demonstrated that they should stand up and demand that they be treated as equals. Robinson sees the Hawaii decision as a watershed event on both sides. The Hawaii decision triggered a series of DOMA's, but also awakened the gay and lesbian community to the fact that marriage was worth pursuing. "There is more logic in going after marriage which is state sponsored discrimination, than going after employment discrimination laws. There is an irony that states are saying that states can discriminate and private employers can't."

In 1995 a same-sex couple approached Beth Robinson and Susan Murray wanting to be represented in a marriage case. Robinson and Murray felt it was not the right time. The groundwork had not been laid, the education had not been done, and the gay and lesbian community was not unified behind the issue. But they could not just say that it was not the right time—they had to make it *be* the right time.

In late 1995, the Vermont Coalition for Lesbian and Gay Rights, a state-wide umbrella organization, formed a committee to begin looking at gay and lesbian marriage. Robinson and Murray were a part of that committee that initially drafted a 45-page document of "speaking points" about same-sex marriage, which they used to train people to talk about the issue. They lead a seminar at the 1995 Queer Town Meeting (an annual event held in Vermont), which was the first organized introduction to this issue in Vermont.

This first year was spent examining the gay community's feelings about marriage. Was this really an issue they wanted to pursue? Were they just buying into the patriarchal model? But even so, weren't they really fighting about equality? The debate continued both on a philosophical and theoretical level, and on a strategic and practical level.

By the end of 1995, this committee had spawned a new organization, the Vermont Freedom to Marry Task Force, headed by Susan Murray and Beth Robinson, which declared its independence and went off on its own. At the 1996 Queer Town Meeting, there were 100 people at the seminar, and no one wanted to talk about whether or not marriage was a good idea. They all wanted to move forward and pursue marriage for gays and lesbians. This was the result of the grassroots effort by the Task Force, which initially focused its efforts on the gay and lesbian community, talking to groups and training speakers to unite the community around the issue. They went on to talk to churches, rotary clubs, and other community groups throughout the state.

This first phase was not directly related to any lawsuit or pending case, but was critical to what they would eventually achieve. One luxury they had when they began was that the issue had not yet been politicized. When the Task Force set up their booth at county fairs, a few people occasionally walked by and rolled their eyes, but until five months ago, they did not encounter the venom and hatred that has recently become so prevalent. The Task Force did not pay for any media until very recently, but rather focused on the grassroots work that "wins the hearts and minds" of Vermonters.

Robinson and Murray, being lawyers, were thinking about the legal aspect during this time. The Vermont Supreme Court was in flux, and 1996 was a presidential election year, but they began to lay the groundwork by talking with legislators and candidates. Through their work at the Task Force, many gays and lesbians in the state contacted Robinson and Murray for legal assistance, including the three couples who became the plaintiffs in *Baker*. The task force did not seek out couples, nor did they screen them. The couples did not know each other, and only one couple had been active in the Task Force previously. Robinson and Murray felt fortunate to have found the combination and diversity of people who became the plaintiffs.

Once Robinson and Murray realized that they were heading for litigation, they set up a meeting with Attorney General Amestoy. [Amestoy is now Chief Justice of the Vermont Supreme Court, and he wrote the main opinion for the court in *Baker v. State*. They talked generally about the issue, and that it would likely come up in Vermont, and offered him their research in hopes that the AG's office would support same-sex marriage. Amestoy was then appointed to the court, and they had to wait several months before Sorrell was appointed Attorney General and they could approach him. They later filed a motion to disqualify Amestoy—but it was denied. The Attorney General's office chose to fully oppose same-sex marriage, contrary to later allegations that they were actually in favor of it and did not make much of an effort to oppose it.

Prior to filing the suit in July 1997, each of the couples contacted their town clerks to alert them that they would be requesting marriage licenses. The clerks had letters prepared denying the licenses when they came in. Robinson and Murray asked Mary L. Bonuato from the Gay & Lesbian Advocates & Defenders (GLAD) in Boston to be cocounsel. She had expertise in gay and lesbian litigation that was valuable, but was sensitive to allowing Vermonters to be up front in Vermont. It was important that national gay groups not swoop in and take over. The three lawyers were a team—there was no designated lead council. They negotiated everything and did nothing without a consensus.

The constitutional amendment in Hawaii went to the voters in November of 1998, just a week before the oral arguments in *Baker*. That affected morale, and most likely the court's decision, as evidence by Justice Johnson's assertion that the court was engaging in political calculation by anticipating that if the court granted marriage it would cause the state to enact a constitutional amendment.

When Robinson and Murray first approached the legislature, they told them they were not asking them to legislate marriage for gays and lesbians. They only wanted the legislature to "play defense" by fighting against a constitutional amendment, DOMA, and other legislative attempts to undermine what they were trying to do in court. So when the court turned around and threw it to the legislature it caught them all off guard. That was not part of the plan. Fighting against something is very different than fighting for it.

The plaintiffs, the attorneys, and the Task Force were confident there was better than a 50-50 chance the court would decide to give marriage benefits to same-sex couples. If they had gotten marriage, there would have been a backlash, but it would have been against the court not the legislature. And that, Robinson believes, is what the court is there for.[20]

Baker v. State: "Our Common Humanity"

Genesis of a Civil Rights Case: The Baker Six

Legal cases are stories. The Vermont case *Baker v. State* was actually six stories, the stories of six people, six intertwined lives, three couples. Two of the braided lives that became the *Baker v. State* story were Nina Beck's and Stacy Jolles's, partners for "nearly a decade."[21]

In a way, the *Baker v. State* story had its genesis in a hospital emergency room. According to the *New York Times*, when Nina Beck—one of the *Baker* plaintiffs—"went into labor and frightening complications developed," Stacy Jolles—another *Baker* plaintiff—"tried to go into the emergency room with her. But she was stopped at the door, she said, and asked, 'who are you? Do you have any legal papers to be there?' "[22]

"Ms. Beck's son, Noah, was born with a heart defect" and died at age 2?.[23] But, as Jolles said on the day of the oral argument in *Baker*, "Noah is very much here with us today. He would want us very much to be married, and he would want us to pursue this to the end."[24]

Nina Beck and Stacy Jolles were one of the same-sex couples who initiated the *Baker* case. Lois Farnham and her partner of 27 years,[25] Holly Puterbaugh, were another. "Puterbaugh and Farnham led a quiet, private life until they decided to try to marry. They raised foster children and adopted a daughter. . . . Both teach . . . Farnham works as a health educator in Essex Junction. Puterbaugh teaches mathematics at the University of Vermont."[26]

The "Baker" of *Baker v. State* was Stan Baker. "A resident of Vermont for nearly 30 years, Baker is a direct descendant of Remember Baker, a lieutenant to Ethan Allen of the Green Mountain Boys."[27] Of course, lending his name to the landmark *Baker* decision guaranteed "Stan Baker a more memorable place in Vermont archives. 'It's a strange feeling' he said as his partner, Peter Harrington, stood at his side. 'I don't dislike it. I'm proud of it, but it's still strange sometimes.'"[28]

All three couples applied for civil marriage licenses, and all three couples were denied. The couples then filed a lawsuit "seeking a declaratory judgment that the refusal to issue them a marriage license violated the marriage statutes and the Vermont Constitution."[29] The trial court dismissed the lawsuits, ruling that the marriage statutes excluded same-sex couples and that such exclusion was constitutional because it "rationally furthered the state's interest in promoting 'the link between procreation and child rearing.'"[30] The Vermont Supreme Court heard oral arguments in the case on November 18, 1998.

The Oral Arguments

At the oral arguments in *Baker*, Beth Robinson, one of the two lead counsel for the same-sex couples "urged the justices to follow the lead of the California Supreme Court, which 50 years ago struck down statutes outlawing interracial marriage. 'The parallels between that case and this case are striking,' [Robinson] said. In 1948, proponents of the interracial ban used many of the same arguments as gay marriage opponents use today, she said."[31] Robinson argued that the California decision—the first in the nation allowing whites and African Americans to marry—was "controversial, courageous, and it was correct."[32] And, as Justice Denise Johnson pointed out, in response to the state's argument that no other state in the nation has recognized same-sex marriage, that "somebody has to be first, right?"[33] Nineteen years after the 1948 California decision, the U.S. Supreme Court, enforcing the federal constitution, invalidated all states' statutory bans on interracial marriage.[34]

Lawyers for the state tried to distinguish the ban on interracial marriage from the ban on same-sex marriage by asserting that the common law has always made a distinction between the latter but not the former. Justice Dooley replied: "What does that show, other than how long-standing the discrimination was?"[35]

Counsel for the government also argued that the Vermont legislature had already enacted legislation prohibiting discrimination against gays and lesbians, thus suggesting that homosexuals are "not a politically powerless minority."[36] Counsel for the same-sex couples disagreed: "It's puzzling to try to understand the state's argument. . . . To argue that things are fine now, that we don't have to worry about long-standing discrimination because we have an antidiscrimination statute, is to ignore the continuity of history. . . . We're dealing with a class of people who have been historically discriminated against."[37]

And not just in the past. A lawyer for the state warned that, if same-sex couples are allowed to marry, "social upheaval will soon follow. He raised the possibility of two brothers asking to be joined in holy matrimony. Polygamy was another threat, he said."[38]

The Decision
Three generations of imbeciles are enough.

— Justice Oliver Wendell Holmes, 1927[39]

A few days before the last Christmas of the twentieth century, the Vermont Supreme Court issued its decision in *Baker v. State*. The majority opinion, written by Chief Justice Amestoy for himself and Justices Morse and Skoglund, held that, under the Common Benefits Clause of the Vermont Constitution, same-sex couples were entitled to the same benefits now received by married heterosexual couples.

The Chief Justice began his analysis by noting that "there is no doubt that the plain and ordinary meaning of 'marriage' is the union of one man and one woman"[40] and that this "understanding of the term is well rooted in Vermont common law."[41] In enacting the marriage statutes, there was "a clear legislative assumption that marriage under our statutory scheme consists of a union between a man and a woman."[42] It was equally clear that, because "the marriage statutes apply expressly to opposite-sex couples," the "statutes exclude anyone who wishes to marry someone of the same sex."[43] The "fundamental question" then, is whether the common benefits clause of the state constitution allows the State of Vermont to "exclude same-sex couples from the benefits and protections that its law provide to opposite-sex married couples."[44]

The common benefits clause was part of the original Vermont Constitution of 1777, and the Chief Justice's opinion provides an excellent history lesson in that 223-year-old magnificent document. The framers of Vermont's 1777 Constitution obviously did not contemplate same-sex marriage. However, that is the beginning, not the end, of the analysis.

"Out of the shifting and complicated kaleidoscope of events, social forces and ideas that culminated in the Vermont Constitution of 1777, our task is to distill the essence of the motivating ideal of the framers," wrote the Chief Justice.[45] The challenge is to remain faithful to the historical ideal, while addressing the contemporary issues that the framers undoubtedly could never have imagined."[46]

Thus, the Common Benefits Clause captures certain core principles. "Chief among these is the principle of inclusion. At its core, the Common Benefits Clause expressed a vision of government that afforded every Vermonter its benefit and protection and provided no Vermonter particular advantage," the Chief Justice explained.[47] Citing *Dred Scott*, the Chief Justice reminded us that "the past provides many instances whence the law refused to see a human being when it should have."[48]

But not today, not now, not here. "The extension of the Common Benefits Clause to acknowledge plaintiffs as Vermonters who seek nothing more, nor less, than legal protection and security for their avowed commitment to an intimate and lasting human relationship is simply, when all is said and done, a recognition of our common humanity,"[49] the Chief Justice wrote. Tears came to my eyes when I first read those words: "our common humanity."

Thus, the majority opinion in *Baker* contained beautiful, inspirational rhetoric. What it didn't contain, oddly, was civil rights doctrine. Indeed, the *Baker* court was a landmark civil rights case that included little discussion of the animus that the law has historically directed toward homosexuals, and what discussion there was in the opinion was ambiguous.[50]

Rather, the *Baker* majority spoke of economics. The court viewed marriage as essentially being a cluster of economic and legal rights and benefits. Thus, the court was able to invalidate the exclusion of same-sex couples from the legal benefits of marriage while eliding the *reason* for the exclusion: prejudice based on sexual orientation.

This elision also allowed the *Baker* majority to recognize a constitutional right—the right to the economic and legal benefits of marriage—without also crafting a remedy. The *Baker* three-justice majority stopped short of saying that same-sex couples have a fundamental right to marry or that the existing civil marriage law must include gay and lesbian couples. Rather, the Chief Justice's opinion gave the legislature the first opportunity to craft a remedy to the right the court recognized in *Baker*. The *Baker* majority suggested two possible remedies: (1) extend the existing marriage laws to include same-sex couples, or (2) create some parallel system that would provide the same rights and benefits as marriage but that would be called something other than "marriage."

The *Baker* court held that the "judgment of the superior court upholding the constitutionality of the Vermont marriage statutes under [the Common Benefits Clause] is reversed. The effect of the court's decision is suspended, and jurisdiction is retained in this court to permit the legislature to consider and enact legislation consistent with the constitutional mandate described herein."[51] Earlier, the court had said "we hold that the current statutory scheme shall remain in effect for a reasonable period of time to enable the legislature to consider and enact implementing legislation in an orderly and expeditious fashion."[52]

The *Baker* majority opinion recognized that the judiciary is "not the only repository of wisdom."[53] The opinion is "characterized by a sort of judicial humility."[54] The *Baker* majority cited *Dred Scott* as an example of how judges can get it spectacularly wrong. The court could have cited other such shameful instances, such as the Japanese internment cases, Justice Holmes's remark in *Buck v. Bell* quoted at the beginning of this chapter, *In re Debs, Plessy v. Ferguson, and Bowers v. Hardwick*. Quoting Cass Sunstein, the *Baker* majority opinion reasoned that "when a democracy is in moral flux, courts may not have the best or final answers. Judicial answers may be wrong. They may be counterproductive even if they are right. Courts do best by proceeding in a way that is catalytic rather than preclusive and that is closely attuned to the fact that courts are participants in the system of democratic deliberation."[55] Christopher Graff astutely read these words to mean that the "justices believe they are right. But they are well aware that to endorse same-sex marriages today could well spark a reaction that would trample the rights of gays and lesbians."[56]

The decision seems fair enough, but not in a civil rights case. That, indeed, was the main point of the separate opinions in *Baker*. Justice Dooley joined in the majority's holding and mandate, and he was clear that his opinion "is a concurrence and not a dissent."[57] For Justice Dooley, "this is a civil rights case" and as such ought to have been decided under civil rights principles.[58] Although the marriage statutes are facially neutral with respect to sex, "no doubt the requirement that civil marriage be a union of one man and one woman has the effect of discriminating against lesbian and gay couples, like the plaintiffs in this case, who are unable to marry the life partners of their choice."[59] Justice Dooley was sharply critical of the majority's rejection of the tiered review approach used in equal protection clause cases (and by the Vermont Supreme Court in common benefits clause cases) in favor of a "balancing" or "sliding scale" approach.

Justice Johnson wrote a concurring and dissenting opinion. Like Justice Dooley, Justice Johnson viewed *Baker* as a civil rights case: "[T]his is a straightforward case of sex-discrimination," because "the marriage statutes establish a classification based on sex."[60] Although classifications based on sex are typically subject to heightened judicial scrutiny, Justice Johnson did not believe it "necessary to reach the question in this case," because the classification at issue in *Baker* failed even under an easygoing rational basis test:

> The State treats similarly situated people—those who wish to marry—differently, on the basis of the sex of the person they wish to marry. The State provides no legally valid rationale for the different treatment. The justifications asserted by the State for the classification are tautological, wholly arbitrary, or based on impermissible assumptions about the roles of men and women. None of the State's justifications meets the rational-basis test under the Common Benefits Clause. Finding no legally valid justification for the sex-based classification, I conclude that the classification is a vestige of the historical unequal marriage relationship that more recent legislative enactments and out own jurisprudence have unequivocally rejected. The protections conferred on Vermonters by the Common Benefits Clause cannot be restricted by the outmoded conception that marriage requires one man and one woman, creating one person—the husband. As this Court recently stated, "equal protection of the laws cannot be limited by eighteenth-century standards."[61]

Justice Johnson "would grant the requested relief and enjoin defendants from denying plaintiffs a marriage license based solely on the sex of the applicants."[62] She remarked that the majority's remedy "abdicates this court's constitutional duty to redress violations of constitutional rights" and took the majority to task for sending the *Baker* plaintiffs' constitutional rights to "an uncertain fate in the political cauldron" of the legislature.[63] Quoting from the 1963 U.S. Supreme Court decision in *Watson v. City of Memphis*, Johnson emphasized that the "basic guarantees of our Constitution are warrants for the here and now and, unless there is an overwhelming compelling reason, they are to be promptly fulfilled."[64] This is so even if such fulfillment be controversial or unpopular: "The Vermont Constitution does not permit the courts to decline to adjudicate a matter because its subject is controversial, or because the outcome may be deeply offensive to the strongly held beliefs of many of our citizens."[65]

The majority opinion responded to Justice Johnson's dissent (and, in turn, Justice Johnson replied to the majority's response to her separate opinion). In answer to the dissent's argument that the majority had "abdicated" its "constitutional duty" in declining to mandate that a marriage license be issued to the *Baker* plaintiffs, the majority pointedly said that the dissent "appears to assume that we hold plaintiffs are entitled to a marriage license. We do not."[66] Further, the majority believed that the cases decided under *Brown v. Board of Education* (particularly *Watson v. City of Memphis*) were inapposite because "we do not confront in this case the evil that was institutionalized racism. . . . Plaintiffs have not demonstrated that the exclusion of same-sex couples from the definition of marriage was intended to discriminate against women or lesbians and gay men, as racial segregation was designed to maintain the pernicious doctrine of white supremacy."[67]

It is important to emphasize that *Baker* was about—and was only about—*civil* marriage as a legal institution. The court was not addressing, much less changing, marriage as a religious institution. A *Boston Globe* op-ed piece noted that the *Baker* decision "elegantly peels off that contentious verbal wrapper—'marriage'—to expose the hundreds of rights and obligations that pulse just underneath. In every American state, these range from the vast—such as the right to inherit our dead spouse's estate even if she never made a will, the guarantee that you can hold your beloved's hand in the hospital, the obligation to support each other, the right to court oversight if you separate—to the trivial, such as the ability to share a hunting license. It's that enormous civil package that the Vermont court insists must be open to same-sex pairs. The key word in that sentence is civil."[68]

Civil "marriage," as understood in *Baker*, "is an overstuffed suitcase of a word, with far too many meanings jammed into its two syllables. Most people believe that real marriage is whatever they [or their parents] have had, or what their religion says it should be—even if, in our wildly pluralistic society, civil marriage is baggy enough to include childless atheists and Mormons with nine kids, Catholics opposed to divorce, and thrice-married U.S. Representative Bob Barr."[69] The *Baker* court "clearly stepped away from the veil-trailing, bell-ringing M-word's visceral associations, insisting that the Vermont Constitution's commitment to inclusion—written in 1777—means that any two people who willingly take on responsibility for each other deserve all the recognitions and protections that government can offer."[70]

The Plain Language of the Constitution
John Marshall has made his decision; now let him enforce it.
—Attributed to President Andrew Jackson, 1822[71]

The *Baker* decision, a victory for same-sex couples, was controversial from the moment it was handed down. One lawyer who had filed a friend-of-the-court brief in *Baker*, advised the legislature simply to ignore *Baker* because, in his view, the *Baker* decision was a "bizarre and illegal attempt by the court to usurp the power"[72] of the legislature. This lawyer viewed *Baker* as a "revolutionary"[73] and lawless advisory opinion that the legislature simply ought to ignore.

This view of *Baker* puzzles me. It seems to me that *Baker* was a straightforward application of the plain language of the Common Benefits Clause of the Vermont Constitution. The Common Benefits Clause states

> That government is, or ought to be, instituted for the common benefit, protection, and security of the people, nation, or community, and not for the particular emolument or advantage of any single person, family, or set of persons, who are a part only of that community.[74]

How this language applies to same-sex couples is, as the *Valley News* newspaper aptly put it, a "no brainer."[75] The court simply ruled that heterosexuals are, like any other segment of Vermont society, not allowed to receive preferential treatment or special favors from the law. "If couples of opposite sex may apply for and receive all the benefits that come from state-issued marriage licenses, so, too, must people of the same sex," the court explained.[76] The court in *Baker* held simply that this constitutional language forbids the State of Vermont from depriving same-sex couples "of the statutory benefits and protections afforded persons of the opposite sex who choose to marry."[77]

To read the plain language of the Common Benefits Clause to include same-sex couples is hardly "bizarre" or "revolutionary" or even terribly activist.[78] Reading and following the plain language of the constitution is the most conservative form of constitutional decision making.[79]

The critics of *Baker* are also wrong, I believe, in arguing that the decision usurped the power of the legislature. Some have claimed that the *Baker* court offended the principle of separation of powers by "forcing" the legislature to either modify the existing marriage statutes or create a parallel system of domestic partnerships.[80]

This is a misreading of the *Baker* opinion. The majority opinion spoke only of the *"opportunity"* it was giving to the legislature to act and that it was suspending the effect of its ruling "for a reasonable period of time to *enable* the legislature" to act and to *"permit"* the legislature to act.[81] Nowhere did the majority opinion use imperative language with respect to the legislature. And, in responding to Justice Johnson's dissent, the majority acknowledged that "our colleague may be correct that a mandate *intended to provide the legislature with the opportunity* to implement the holding of this court in an orderly and expeditious fashion will have the opposite effect"[82] of crafting a remedy for the constitutional right articulated in *Baker*. Judicial authority "is not the only repository of wisdom,"[83] the *Baker* majority noted.

Thus, the court did not "require" the legislature to do anything. Rather, all the court did was give the legislature the first "opportunity"[84] to craft a remedy for the constitutional right recognized by the court in *Baker*. The legislature was free to do nothing, in which case the court would fashion its own remedy.

In his testimony before the legislature, the attorney who filed the friend-of-the-court brief made the argument that the *Baker* court somehow denigrated the authority of the legislature by giving the legislature the first *"opportunity"*[85] to fashion a remedy for the constitutional right recognized by the court in *Baker*. The witness seemed to believe that it would have been more respectful of legislative authority for the court to have, in the first instance, come up with its own remedy.

This argument strikes me as just plain silly. Whatever one might think of *Baker's* punt to the legislature, it cannot be said that the court has prevented legislative and citizen participation in sorting out a solution to the same-sex partner conundrum. To the contrary, the court encouraged its coordinate branches of government, legislative and executive, as well as the people to whom they are politically accountable, to register their opinions on the issue.

In short, neither the constitutional right recognized by the *Baker* court's plain reading of the constitution, nor the court's decision to give the legislature the initial opportunity to craft a remedy, seem to me in any manner inappropriate. Moreover, the critics of *Baker* also fail to recognize that in *Baker* the court was fulfilling a crucial function of the judiciary: the protection of the fundamental constitutional rights of despised minorities.

THE DUTY OF COURTS TO PROTECT THE CIVIL RIGHTS OF DESPISED MINORITIES

Much of the opposition to same-sex marriage in the culture at large is inspired by antihomosexual emotions. People who dislike homosexuals or their imagined conduct are likely to oppose same-sex marriage. There is little I can say to such people, for visceral distaste is not susceptible to argument based on reason and facts.

—William Eskridge, 1996[86]

The argument that *Baker* illegitimately usurped the power of the legislature misses the point that protecting the civil rights of despised minorities is exactly what courts are supposed to do. In fact, an important duty—if not *the* most important duty—of the judiciary is to protect discrete and insular minorities historically subject to discrimination by the majority within and without the usual legislative and political process.[87] The framers of our constitution intended judges to be insulated precisely so that they can protect unpopular minorities from the prejudices and bigotry of the majority. This is what courts are *for*.

Characterizing *Baker* as a civil rights case—as opposed to an eco-nomic dispute between optometrists and ophthalmologists, or between store owners and street vendors—makes a great deal of difference in the way legislators interpret the issue. Legislatures make classifications among groups all the time (the optometrists win and the ophthalmolo-gists lose, for instance), and such classifications should and do receive minimal judicial scrutiny. However, when legislatures make classifica-tions based on despised minorities of people, or when legislatures deny fundamental rights (including, I believe, the right to marry), then courts take a much harder look at the classifications set out by the legislature.

In *Baker*, the court was dealing with a despised minority and with a fundamental human right. The fundamental nature of the right to marry seems beyond serious dispute. Marriage is the basic unit of social organization in our society. The right to marry is obviously different from the right to obtain a peddler's license, in much the same way as the right to education claimed by the children in *Brown v. Board of Education* is distinguished from the denial of certain economic benefits. The *Brown* briefs contain a passage I've always admired:

These infant appellants are asserting the most important secular claims that can be put forward by children, the claim to their full measure of the chance to learn and grow, and the inseparably connected but even more important claim to be treated as entire citizens of the society into which they have been born. We have discovered no case in which such rights, once established, have been postponed by a cautious calculation of conveniences. The nuisance cases, the sewage cases, the cases of the overhanging cornices, need not be distinguished. They distinguish themselves.[88]

The Supreme Court heard and rejected these arguments against inter-racial marriage in *Loving v. Virginia*:

These statutes also deprive the Lovings of liberty without due process of law in violation of the Due Process Clause of the Fourteenth Amendment. The freedom to marry has long been recognized as one of the vital personal rights essential to the orderly pursuit of happiness by free men.

Marriage is one of the "basic civil rights of man," fundamental to our very existence and survival. To deny this fundamental freedom on so unsupportable a basis as the racial classifications embodied in these statutes, classifications so directly subversive of the principle of equality at the heart of the Fourteenth Amendment, is surely to deprive all the State's citizens of liberty without due process of law. The Fourteenth Amendment requires that the freedom of choice to marry not be restricted by invidious racial discriminations. Under our constitution, the freedom to marry or not marry, a person of another race resides with the individual and cannot be infringed by the State.[89]

At the end of the day, the only argument against same-sex marriage is that it is so evil that legitimizing it would infect and undermine opposite-sex marriage. Same-sex marriage can be wrong only if gays and lesbians are wrong or immoral or less than human.

And, as I will discuss in the next chapter, many Vermonters seem to believe that homosexuality is dangerously immoral and that homosexuals are evil, disease-carrying, promiscuous abominations in the eyes of God and nature.

3 Backlash Against Gays and Lesbians
A Despised Minority in Vermont

Almighty God created the races white, black, yellow, malay, and red, and he placed them on separate continents. And but for the interference with his arrangement there would be no cause for such marriages. The fact that he separated the races shows that he did not intend for the races to mix.

—Virginia trial court, *Loving v. Virginia*
(upholding state law banning interracial marriage), 1967[1]

THIS CHAPTER provides samples of the homophobic reaction of many Vermonters to the *Baker* decision. It provides neither a full catalog nor a complete history of the reaction to *Baker*. Much of that reaction was positive and supportive of the court and the civil rights of gay people, but I focus on this strongly homophobic response to *Baker*—as expressed in public hearings, letters to the editor, and the results of Town Meeting Day 2000—because it had a direct impact on the legislature's response to *Baker*.

THE LEGISLATIVE HEARINGS

In response to *Baker*, the Vermont House Judiciary Committee held hearings and heard from expert witnesses including a historian of marriage, family law practitioners, and professors of constitutional law and family law.[2] Opponents of *Baker* urged the legislature to begin the process of amending the constitution to, in effect, overrule *Baker*. Thomas McCormick described the *Baker* ruling "as inconsistent with the will of most Vermonters."[3] Hal Goldman, of a group called Take It to the People, "delivered the most stinging attack on the court. . . . [He] accused the court of usurping the power of the legislature, overturning longstanding legal precedent and creating ambiguous legal standards for the future that would have far-reaching negative effects."[4] Goldman said *Baker* "had no legal validity, and he urged the legislature to simply ignore the ruling."[5] His statement that the *Baker* decision attempts to set up the court as a "benevolent dictatorship"[6] drew an admonition from the committee's chairman that "his use of hyperbole probably hadn't made a good impression on the committee."[7]

In addition to such testimony, the House and Senate Judiciary Committee scheduled a joint public hearing for January 25, 2000. The House Committee announced

> The hearing will run from 7:00 to 10:00 P.M. in the well of the House. In anticipation of a very large audience, witnesses will be selected at random from sign-up sheets. Witnesses will be limited to two-minute presentations, and will not be permitted to transfer their time to another. Witnesses will be asked to address the question: "What should be the legislature's response to the *Baker v. State* decision?" The Committees will require the witnesses, and the audience, to observe traditional rules of civility and decorum.[8]

The hearings drew an overflow crowd of 1,500, and "the number would have been in the thousands more if a snowstorm had not kept many away."[9] About 100 people had an opportunity to speak for the allotted time. Approximately "200 supporters of traditional marriage gathered on the front steps of the statehouse for an impromptu 'prayer rally.'"[10]

Because of the snowstorm that limited attendance at the first public hearing, the Judiciary Committee held a second hearing on February 1. "An estimated 2,000 people packed into the meeting rooms and corridors of a stuffy statehouse. At least 1,500 others staged a vigil and protest rally outside."[11] Another estimate placed the *Baker* protest crowd at 1,000.[12] While "citizens inside [the statehouse] spoke from a range of perspectives, those outside repeatedly sounded the same call. Speaker after speaker said the legislature should follow 'God's law' and refuse to allow lesbians and gays to marry."[13] A dozen "supportive legislators" joined the protestors on the statehouse steps. By the second round of public hearings, opponents of same-sex marriage included an argument that had been mentioned only sporadically the first time around. Speakers now were urging the legislature to impeach the *Baker* justices.[14]

At the public hearings held by the legislature "those who spoke against gay marriage repeatedly cited a verse in Leviticus that calls sex between men 'an abomination.' 'God's words were that same sexual relations were indeed immoral,'"[15] the *New York Times* reported. The *Rutland Herald* wrote

Several of the speakers denounced homosexuality as immoral, and they cited passages from Leviticus to bolster their arguments homosexuality violated the laws of God.

Leslie Crane of Williston read a letter from his 18-year-old son, who was unable to attend the hearing.

"I am shocked that we as a state and a nation are entertaining the idea of a homosexual union," Crane said, reading from the letter. "I believe that if Vermont legalizes this unnatural behavior, I believe there will be a migration like none have ever seen. Such an influx of homosexuals will be detrimental to the moral and family values that surround us in Vermont."[16]

The hierarchy of the Vermont Catholic Church vocally opposed the extension of marriage or domestic partnership benefits to gays and lesbians. Vermont Bishop Angell "condemned domestic partnerships as 'step one toward full acceptance of same-sex marriage' and has even challenged the validity of the [Baker] ruling itself, saying in his call to arms to Catholics, 'There are many sound legal minds who question the Supreme Court's authority to even issue such mandates to the legislature.'"[17] Vermont's bishop also "circulated a news release signed by [the bishop] that warned lawmakers their vote would be remembered by Vermonters on Election Day in November."[18] At least one Catholic member of the House of Representatives said the "church instilled fear"[19] when it circulated the news release. (There is no small irony here; as one of my law school colleagues pointed out, Catholics were not warmly welcomed in Vermont.)

A confab of clergy resulted in one memorable photo opportunity in mid-February 2000. Twenty-two clergymen (and, yes, they were all men) stood on the steps of the statehouse, bundled up against the snow on the ground at their feet, posing for the camera, holding placards spelling out "Constitutional Amendment."[20] The photo's caption explained: "About 100 clergy of various denominations gathered to call on lawmakers to pass an amendment to the Vermont Constitution that would define marriage as being between one man and one woman."[21]

Then there was the Reverend of the Burlington Area Evangelical Association. In his legislative testimony, although saying he was not making a moral judgment, the Reverend "went on to denounce homosexuals and to suggest that a 12-step program akin to those used in treating alcoholism could cure them."[22] (Indeed, even former U.S. Senate Majority Leader Trent Lott has compared homosexuals to alcoholics and kleptomaniacs who, although suffering from a disease, can be converted or cured. The Republican leadership had no problem with these comments; it was only when Lott spoke nostalgically about segregated America that he got into trouble.)[23]

There were witnesses at the public hearings who testified in support of legal recognition for same-sex couples. Gays and lesbians testified about the abuse and discrimination they had experienced in Vermont.[24] Such testimony was all the more credible and believable because it occurred in the midst of the other witnesses who deemed homosexuality a sin and an abomination and who deemed homosexuals to be mistakes of nature and trespassers in the holy office of matrimony.

LETTERS TO THE EDITOR

Letters-to-the-editors of Vermont's newspapers also revealed a deep vein of antigay and antilesbian feeling and are the most compelling evidence in the present public record of the homophobia churned up in the wake of *Baker*. Other parts of this chapter rely on accounts from secondary sources (newspaper accounts of the legislative hearings and the like). Although my use of redundant newspaper accounts of the same events increases my confidence that these accounts are reasonably reliable and accurate, I am aware that my understanding of the events themselves is filtered through the reporters' coverage. In contrast, the letters to the editor are primary sources in the public realm. That is, I presume the letters as published are virtually identical to the letters actually received by the newspapers—this presumption seems to me a safe one. These letters are the raw, unmediated, unalloyed expressions of Vermonters (identified by their town of residence) over a period of roughly four months.

I should note two additional things about the letters that follow. First, many of them are brutal and painful to read for their hatred and malice toward gays and lesbians. Second, they are somewhat repetitious, but I quote from a large number of them to convey their cumulative impact in the public debate as well as their specific content. By presenting quotations from these letter here, in roughly chronological order, I hope to give you some idea of what Vermonters experienced in reading the daily newspapers. Further, although I quote from many letters here, these are only a fraction of the total of such letters published in Vermont newspapers since *Baker* was decided in December 1999. Of the scores of letters to the editor published in the newspapers over those four months after the *Baker* decision, roughly 80 percent of those were hostile.

One letter stated flatly: "Two men or two women getting married to each other is sick."[25] Another, published in the same newspaper on the same day, said the Vermont Supreme Court "made a power grab" and urged that the legislature to "reprimand the Supreme Court for its ruling" and to "begin new hearings to determine how to hold the court accountable."[26] Another warned that homosexuals not "shove it down my throat or flaunt it."[27] Another letter, written by a "sixth-generation Vermonter," published in the same newspaper on the same day, condemned Governor Howard Dean as "a transplant from New York City—dictating his agenda for civil union" and argued that "we must all band together and get rid of all people who voted for civil unions. Especially Dean—the New York City dictator."[28]

One letter, written (as the writer put it) "as a Christian," asserted that "homosexuality is a perversion, no less than pedophelia and bestiality, and to try to divert from that fact by labeling it love, is a type of perversion in itself"; that "scriptures state plainly that the practice of homosexuality is an abomination and will be punished"; and that the legislature should give homosexuality "no more sanction than any other perversion."[29]

One letter complained that "those people" (and it's not clear whether the writer means homosexuals, the Supreme Court justices, or both) "should not come here and try to force their shoddy, perverted standards on us" and compared civil rights for gays and lesbians to incest, "sadism," "child molestation," and "sex with animals."[30] One letter argued that "we must stay above animals" and that "even animals don't indulge in those practices of homosexuality."[31]ne letter began by asserting that "[l]ogic is not one of the strong suits among supporters of homosexuals," and went on to decry "hedonistic homosexuals," and the "quaint, narcissistic" notion that homosexuality is anything other than a choice (and that it is neither a "medical condition" nor an immutable biological condition, as allegedly asserted by "the secret homosexual agenda") and to argue that the "constitution should not be used to protect and promote pedophile William Gacey [an apparent reference to John Wayne Gacy]" (thus equating homosexuality with pedophelia) and to contend that "homosexual organizations are dedicated to the overthrow of American society."[32]

One letter condemned "homosexuality's unspeakable obscenities" and the "voluntary, unnatural choices of man; noted that "there does not exist in medical science a shred of evidence that the alimentary canal is functional as the reproductive canal"; argued that "they [i.e., homosexuals] . . . posit some type of immutable genetic dysfunction that impels you to use organs unnaturally"; and characterized the same-sex marriage debate as "a distraction intended to hide far more terrible consequences. Space prohibits detailing three succeedingly fearsome analyses. However, a good starting point might be the formation of the first gay liberation organization, with Stalin's approval, in 1948, by Communist Party USA member Harry Hay."[33]

One letter blamed AIDS on homosexuals, saying that "homosexuality is a perversion of nature and an unhealthy lifestyle choice for individuals that has brought upon us the AIDS epidemic."[34] Another letter asserted that "God says a marriage should consist of one man and one woman" and that recognizing same-sex marriage would "open the floodgates for marriage to include any and every arrangement"— including polygamy.[35]

One letter cited figures purporting to show the promiscuity of gay men: A study of "156 homosexual couples" over five years found that "none, zero of these relationships were monogamous. They had all had sexual relationships outside their relationship."[36] The letter then compared same-sex marriage with polygamy, sex with animals, and incest. If "same-sex couples are normal, then how about two wives to one man, or maybe three? . . . How about the man in Missouri who wants to marry his horse. . . . How about your father wanting to marry his daughter, or his granddaughter?"[37] Finally, the letter invited us to "look at the Roman Empire before it fell, [when] it was full of immorality. Vicious murder in the Coliseum, homosexuality on the theater stage, newborn baby girls being thrown to wild animals or sold into prostitution because their father[s] didn't want a girl. Corruption within America will lead this nation to ruin."[38]

One letter warned that "many criminals would be coming to this state if a gay marriage law were passed."[39] Another, published in the same newspaper on the same day, argued that the "Bible's message on homosexuality is neither unclear nor questionable. From cover to cover, it condemns it as a sin."[40] A third letter, also published in the same day, criticized as "self serving" the legislative testimony of "the homosexual community" including "blatant displays of public affection . . . and exploitation of a minor child."[41] The fourth and final letter on the subject published by that newspaper on that day "strongly recommend[ed]" that the legislature "disregard the directive of the Supreme Court."[42]

One letter simply mourned: "If God could shed tears, he would fill lake Champlain. Today, God is love, but the practice of homosexuality is evil, and God does not love evil."[43]

One letter called "homosexual relationships" a "danger to the common good and the stability of the state;" argued that "homosexuals might be loving people, but it is a disordered love; for them to be truly loving and happy they must seek God's love and forgiveness, stop their homosexual conduct, and trust in God's help to lead chaste lives."[44] The letter compared same-sex couples with bigamous couples, polygamous couples, and incestuous couples and argued that "it is not discrimination to deny marital rights to polygamous or incestuous relationships, which are also a danger to the state. That's why these relationships are crimes and punishable as criminal offenses. Like homosexuality, these are not individual human rights issues; these area not issues of beliefs, these are issues of immoral human conduct, of good versus evil. . . ."[45]

One letter urged Vermonters not to "sit idly by and let homosexuals have their perverted ways" and denounced homosexuality as "sodomy."[46] Another letter, published in the same newspaper on the same day, was written by a "dairy farmer in the beautiful state of Vermont." As such, the writer explained, "I know well the laws of nature, for I work with nature, for I work with nature from sun up to sun down. Marriage between one man and one woman is natural to life."[47] The dairy farmer "warned" legislators that allowing gay marriage would open the possibility of bigamous marriages, incestuous marriages, polygamous marriage—or whatever else the mind can imagine. Do you think this would not or could not happen? Who would have believed that this issue [of same-sex marriage] would have gone this far?"[48] A third letter, published in the same newspaper on the same day, exhorted the Vermont legislature to "just say no [to *Baker*]. Don't even bring forth a bill. It's unnecessary, except as a way to validate homosexual coupling in the public forum."[49] When I first read this letter, I thought the phrase "homosexual coupling" might have been an unintentional pun, but the writer used the phrase twice in his letter (and the line "homosexual coupling in the public forum") is accurate: I triple-checked from the letter as originally published in the newspaper).

One letter said in its entirety: "A principal function of the state's courts and legislators is to defend and uphold every piece of moral filth, every perversion, every abomination which human nature can devise, no matter how repulsive or revolutionary to the mind untrained in the law, so called. I hope this will go for combating the proposal of the Supreme Court of Vermont. . . . I must however, insist that the honorable assembly stop offering prayers in the august halls of . . . depravity, so as to avoid the appearance of hypocrisy. Even in virtue, they make a pander to vice."[50]

One letter, after quoting from Leviticus ("If a man also lie with mankind as he lieth with a woman, both of them have committed an abomination") urged Vermonters to "throw out this unlawful civil-union abomination, as it is clearly contrary to the law of God."[51] Another letter, published on the same Sunday in the same newspaper claimed that "if civil union is passed, it will be the death of this state" because "to say that morality should stay out of the legal process is to say that the salt should be removed from the sea. If such a thing were possible, all sea life would die. If we remove morality from the law, law and civilization will die—as Vermont would die if domestic partnerships for same-sex couples becomes the law."[52]

The letter went on: "Speaking of morality, if civil union is passed, many homosexuals will move to this state. We have a right to know about all sides of this issue if they are to be our neighbors. Why have we heard endless reports about Mathew Shepard [the young gay man murdered by gay-haters in Wyoming], but the press has ignored the abuse and murder of 13-year-old Jesse Dirkhising by two homosexuals in Arkansas in 1999?"[53]

The letter continued: "We have heard nothing about the arrest of the nine men in an international gay-pornography ring in Texas, who abused scores of teenage boys, videotaped them, sold the movies, and killed one of the boys."[54] Another letter, published on the same Sunday in the same newspaper, called homosexuality a sin and suggested that the sin has been the cause of many deaths of AIDS.[55] One letter, published in another newspaper on the same Sunday, argued that a domestic partnership law would "remove decency from our state. Vermont is the only place where a license will be granted, mainly for abnormal relationships based on sexual preference. How soon before they change our name to the Gay Mountain State. . . . I will remember in November."[56]

One letter asserted that, if same-sex unions are legalized, "ruination is inevitable. When husbands and wives have no reason to harness their energies in support of the home, then drug abuse, alcoholism, sexual promiscuity, job instability, and overly aggressive behavior can be expected to run unchecked throughout the culture. And the lack of focused energies."[57]

One letter described homosexuality as a "sinful lifestyle" and explained: "Our laws concerning murder, theft, and other wrongs say these things are wrong (and sinful) because the Bible says they are wrong. The Bible is very clear on homosexual behavior—it is wrong and sinful."[58] Another argued that "framing this debate as a civil rights struggle is just another ploy by an incredibly well-funded and organized group hell-bent on legitimizing their deviancy."[59]

One letter equated homosexuality with "sodomy" and rued that it was no longer a crime; explained that the letters writer's reaction to *Baker* was "one of extreme disgust and disbelief that those in the highest office in the state could fail so miserably in their duty to uphold the moral integrity of the family structure of the people"; predicted that "one day, centuries from now, perhaps people will be able to read the sequel to Sodom and Gomorrah! It could be entitled 'Sodom and Gomorrah and Vermont'"; called *Baker* (or homosexuality, the letter isn't clear) "a time bomb for democracy" and characterized homosexuality as "immoral or socially inappropriate."[60] Another letter, after comparing homosexuality with "sodomy . . . not to be practiced with man or with beast," called homosexuality a "felonious act" and questioned, "Why should this felonious act be equated with the honorable relationship between a man and a woman in marriage."[61]

One letter asserted that "homosexuality is a practice that even animals don't indulge in.[62] The letter said that "the Bible clearly condemns homosexuality as an abomination. The Bible also states that there are two classes of people: the Christians who live by the commandments of God and the heathen who don't."[63] The letter called for "a Constitutional amendment banning same-sex marriage."[64]

One letter claimed that the argument that this is a civil rights issue "is the equivalent of proposing laws to give civil rights to alcoholics, habitual gamblers, and drug addicts."[65] Another letter claimed that "this is not a civil rights issue but a blatant attempt to force us to accept a form of relationship that is in direct opposition to the higher laws of the Lord" and pleaded that we "not let the covenant of marriage be undermined and degraded."[66] Another letter called domestic partnerships "a sacrilege" that "profanes traditional marriage and families."[67] Another letter expressed "worry about the education for our children, and now we want to teach them that this alternative lifestyle is acceptable" and opined that the Vermont Supreme Court "should be impeached."[68]

One letter said the domestic partnership bill is "about supporting and promoting moral, social, physical, and psychological deviancy;" argued that "homosexuality should not be advocated in any way, shape or form;" asked if "isn't it enough that they [i.e., homosexuals] parade down Church Street, Burlington, every year, flaunting their abhorrent aberration"; asked "what on earth do those Kamikazes in Montpelier think they are doing"; and extended "kudos to all the upstanding Vermonters who have voiced their anti–gay marriage/domestic partnership/civil-union sentiments. Keep up the good work. We must remain vocal and involved in order to overcome groundswell of idiocy running through the statehouse at present."[69]

Another letter published in the same newspaper on the same day, began, "I am a licensed minister" and went on to assert that in the Bible "homosexuality of any kind is condemned" and that "when the State of Vermont legislates any law that orders Christians to accept on equal terms that two homosexuals living together have the same benefits as a man and a woman who have been joined in a biblical spiritual marriage, and then through our taxes we are going to be forced to support a union that the Bible condemns, then I believe that the state is interfering with our freedom to practice religion."[70] Another letter, published in the same newspaper on the same day, criticized Catholic legislators who support domestic partnerships: "It is truly a shame that your conscience was not formed in the faith you purport to practice. . . . I suppose you must be Catholics of convenience." The letter expressed hope that such legislators "will be looking for some good place to enjoy their retirement, for many of us are going to work hard to prevent their reelection, no matter what district they are from."[71]

One letter referred to same-sex marriage as "marriage only in the deluded imagination of persons with psychological aberrations about sex."[72] Another asked why we should "aid and abet people in unhealthy relationships by making those relationships legal? Why are we falling prey to the emotional tirades of the homosexual lobby?"[73] Another denounced homosexual acts as "aberrant."[74] Another explained that "the Bible is God's word, and it does not condone same-sex marriage—period."[75] One letter argued that same-sex unions violate what the writer called "natural law," compared gay unions to incest, and claimed that "if homosexual marriages are granted, homosexuals will be given special privileges to have unions that are not based on natural law that is the foundation of marriage laws in Vermont and the rest of the country."[76]

One letter consisted of a single, short sentence: "The State of Vermont's legislature has [in voting for domestic partnership] voted to endorse sodomy, condemning the entire state to the fires of hell."[77] Another letter, published in the same newspaper on the same day, asked what gave the court, legislature, and governor "the right to dictate how to raise a child in the state of sodomy? Why do we keep opening the stove's door to hell's fire? . . . I feel a certain twist to my stomach when I realize that our children live in a society where open-mindedness cripples our sense of morality . . . [and] where every sexual encounter is commonplace and deterioration of salvation was imminent."[78] Another letter, published in the same newspaper on the same day, observed that "two dogs and cats do not constitute a family. A family by definition is . . . [a] husband meaning a male and a wife meaning a female . . . and the children they rear."[79] Another letter, published in a different newspaper on the same day, argued that "most people find their [i.e., homosexuals] sexual practices reprehensible. I heard a boy describing their sexual activity as perverted sex, and I accept that definition."[80]

One letter reasoned that "the important reason" to oppose a domestic partnership bill "is that same-sex unions or marriage do not equate with the natural biological laws of life and nature. When a man and woman refuse to accept and ignore these natural laws of nature, all kinds of physical and mental problems occur—and we all know of the worldwide epidemic caused by this type of behavior."[81]

One letter began: "My opinions on the civil unions [or domestic partnerships] issue are closely held. I have a strong sense of the difference between right and wrong. I have a complete understanding of the natural order of mankind and all living things. In the past, it has been proven many times in the Bible and in history books whenever this code is broken by members of society, and the society as a whole does not resist, that it is ultimately destroyed by its own excesses and lack of discipline."[82]

The letter continued: "The constitution of this state was written by individuals who well understood the moral codes of natural laws of mankind. . . . I do propose [a constitutional amendment] to define families as a union between a man and a woman. . . . This would nullify the [Baker] decision defining gay couples as families and reverse the ability for them to adopt. . . . They are already afforded the same rights and liberties as any other citizens in our society and do not require any special protection. . . . This [domestic partnership bill] cannot be justified for any reason."[83]

One letter explained that "whatever you call it [i.e., marriage or civil unions] same-sex unions could profoundly damage traditional moral values. Denying thousands of years of civilization and the vote of the people . . . it's a sad day for Vermont."[84] Another letter, published in the same newspaper on the same day, asserted that "I have learned some alarming facts on the serious health consequences of homosexual behavior. Learning the facts and knowing the truths do not make me a bigot or prejudiced."[85] Another letter, published in the same newspaper on the same day, compared being a homosexual with being "a wife-beater, a drunk, a pedophile" and asked "why won't newspapers print the data from the Center for Disease Control showing that 83 percent of all white male AIDS cases (to 6/99) are among homosexuals?"[86] This letter concluded: "Male homosexual practice is unclean. It's not homophobic to steer clear of filth. It's common sense."[87]

One letter asserted: "I am against the civil unions bill. If the Supreme Court has put the legislators in the position to make a stand, then maybe we should go back to the judges who made that determination. Corruption starts with judges and lawyers."[88]

The letter also compared giving marriage benefits to same-sex couples with companies that "are now [giving] benefits to pets. What will be next?"[89] And: "I have gay friends. I love them for who they are. I tolerate their actions, but I do not accept their actions. Love the sinner, hate the sin."[90]

Another letter, published in the same newspaper on the same day, warned against the influx of homosexuals with AIDS: "I resent the idea that we will shoulder not only Vermont's homosexual population, but most assuredly our neighboring states' homosexuals as well . . . can you imagine the influx? . . . The state Department of Health's annual budget is $2.1 million to service Vermont's 162 HIV/AIDS patients today. That is very expensive health."[91]

One letter decried "homosexual behavior" as "abnormal" and attributed such abnormality to sexual abuse.[92] Another letter, published in the same newspaper on the same date, said that the date of the *Baker* decision "will go down in history as Vermont's day of infamy"; complained that "five unelected, political appointees [i.e., the Vermont Supreme Court] had made "socially acceptable the lifestyle and practice of free love, homosexuals, and lesbians;" demanded enforcement of the section of the Vermont Constitution "pertaining to this state's laws for the encouragement of virtue and prevention of vice and immorality;" and "opposed" the idea that his 48 years of marriage "have no more legal and social standing than the relationships of homosexuals and lesbians."[93] Another letter, published in the same newspaper on the same day, said: "I am unilaterally adamantly opposed to any legislation that covertly, overtly, or blatantly recognizes, enables, permits, promotes, or encourages homosexual or lesbian behavior. We ought not ever, ever give false hope to homosexual behavior."[94]

Yet another letter, published in the same newspaper on the same day, argued that "nature itself declares homosexuality unnatural [and deviant sexual behavior] because children are born as male and female. . . . If homosexuality is granted government approval, then bestiality, polygamy, incest, and all other forms of sexual behavior will have to be granted such approval as well. . . . Homosexuality is a choice, which disqualifies homosexuals from needing civil rights protection and makes their attempts at civil rights highly offensive."[95] Yet another letter, published in the same newspaper on the same day, asserted that "the good people of Vermont must now accept, condone, and reward what many consider to be perversion, unnatural, and historically repugnant behavior" and to "accept as normal a lifestyle so obviously unnatural"; the letter also predicted that "the exodus from our schools, spurred mostly by a desire to protect one's children from immorality that is taught in the public schools, will accelerate as parents seek to prevent their children from being exposed to the new morality," in addition to "the resulting bankruptcy of our health care system as homosexuals with AIDS come to Vermont."[96]

One letter said that "homosexuality is a perversion of nature and an unhealthy lifestyle choice for individuals and society that has brought upon us the AIDS epidemic."[97] Another letter, published in the same newspaper on the same day, observed that "when the government determines to call a sin a civil union, I speak up."[98] Another letter, published in the same newspaper on the same day, asserted that legislators who support domestic partnerships "defy nature, normalcy, morality, their constituents' voices, the Vermont Constitution, the U.S. Constitution, and God."[99]

One letter warned: "We cannot overlook the ill effects that legalizing homosexual unions will have on the citizens of Vermont. The numbers are there. Even a small influx of homosexual people to Vermont will mean that AIDS and other sexually transmitted diseases will become more common. . . . While homosexuals account for less than 3 percent of the population, they account for 50 percent of gonorrhea of the throat and syphilis."[100]

One letter stated that the bill to extend marriage-like benefits to gay and lesbian couples was "making me sick to my stomach."[101] Another letter called the bill "a mockery of God, his will, and his people" and argued that "since the representatives pretend we do not exist and trample on our beliefs, shouldn't we shout louder, pray harder, and tell them: Our God is the same, still as strong as when he canceled out whole cities for acts of sodomy and totaled all nonbelievers in floodwaters."[102]

One letter claimed that nature intended heterosexuality and only heterosexuality: "I believe that if nature observed its creatures to be using their natural reproductive instincts exclusively in a perverted, nonprocreative fashion, the obvious inference would be that they were sick, exactly as a farmer would believe his roosters to be sick if they all cohabited together, ignoring the chickens."[103]

The letter went on: "We all know that sickness of body as well as mind exists in nature and thus it is not unnatural to be sick. We're all sick at times. What is unnatural is to wish not to get well—or even more unnatural, to wish to become sicker."[104]

And on: "Nature may concede that those who generally use their procreative instincts as intended ought to nevertheless, tolerate the behavior of their deviant fellows. But then would it be in nature's interest to also submit that they ought to, while tolerating the illness, actively enable and promote more sickness? I doubt it. If the straight ones decide to condone as well as encourage deviance, they have to be infested with an even worse disease: 'dupism' or 'liberal logic.'"[105]

And on: "I believe that nature, although very subtle about many things, makes perfectly clear and obvious its intentions for this natural and purposeful instinct. Thus, simple common sense suggests nature's intentions do not include same-sex marriage. Whatever the real or imagined inconveniences that result are not the business of courts or politicians."[106]

One letter said that the writer "fails to see how one can in fact love God and still practice adultery and homosexuality, and still consider themselves a friend of God."[107] Another letter, published by the same newspaper on the same day claimed that homosexual couples "claim to be partners. They are not partners. What kind of partners do they want us to think they are? I don't want to judge or condemn them, but, for God's sake brothers and sisters, let's not agree to their whining."[108] Another letter, published in the same newspaper on the same day, expressed "grave concerns over the education part of the domestic partnership bill. How can this not be taken as a green light to promote homosexual activity to our children? . . . [They] are flat out recruiting our children."[109] Yet another letter, published in the same newspaper on the same day, asserted that "homosexuality is a compulsive behavior that results in grave harm" and claimed that "while homosexuals account for less than 3 percent of the population, they account for a much higher percentage of AIDS patients and people with sexually transmitted diseases."[110]

One letter complained that people "will support a deviant lifestyle and call it civil rights is pretty pathetic. That these deviant people can speak of Martin King, Jr. and John Fitzgerald Kennedy in the same breath as they speak of their rights is truly appalling," and continued that "it's about time Vermonters took a stand and abolished this sort of behavior" (i.e., homosexuality) and asked "when are we going to realize that we are walking into a trap, cleverly set by this deviant part of our population."[111]

One letter called same-sex marriage as an "oxymoron notion indefensible in reality. . . [It] is meaningless and unworthy of consideration into law."[112] Another letter asserted that the domestic union bill "would lead up to our children being taught that homosexuality is normal and healthy when evidence speaks that it is not. . . . [It would force people of faith] to accept these relationships as normal when our scriptures say it is not."[113]

One letter predicted that "if Jesus were here today, he would treat the people who are desecrating the holy ordinance of marriage as described in the Bible the same as he did the money-changers who were desecrating his holy temple."[114] Another letter compared homosexuals to "alcoholics, habitual gamblers, and drug addicts."[115] Another letter, referring to a bill to extend marriage benefits to same-sex couples, asked whether "there is a single decadent society in history that has survived?"[116]

One letter complained that "little children come home to two mothers and two daddies, and everyone wonders what is wrong with that," citing this as an example of how, "in the last 20 years, we as a nation have lowered our expectations and our moral to a point where 6-year-old children are killing each other."[117] Also, "gays and lesbians march in our nation's capitol naked, and we sit back and do nothing."[118] And: "this is not a case of any kind of discrimination; these people chose whom they love and with whom they have sex, and they choose this very sick lifestyle on their own. They know going into it what the laws were. . . . I have friends who are gay, and I have friends who are lesbians. They are good people, but at some point we must stop treading water and retake our fundamental standards and morality."[119]

Some letters had a distinctivly Armageddon-esque quality to them. One letter, a call-to-arms by four ministers requires quotation in full:

> As members of the Evangelical Pastor Association of Central Vermont, we wish to state that we are opposed to any move whatsoever that would undermine or alter the marriage laws of the state of Vermont which clearly view marriage as between a man and a woman.
>
> We further opposed the granting of special "domestic partnership" arrangements that are clearly intended to circumvent the Vermont statutes. We believe the Vermont Supreme Court decision is in fact flawed in its judgment and amounts to the judiciary overstepping its clear constitutional boundaries.
>
> We urge all Vermonters to see this problem for what it truly is, *an attempt by a few to gain special privilege under the ruse of law. We encourage Vermonters to use all legal and legitimate means at their disposal to send a clear message to their representatives not to tamper with our laws.*
>
> Rev. Paul Wright, Rev. James Proctor, Rev. Russell Roholoff, Rev. Jerry Smith, Rev. David Lee, Rev. Michael Lawis, Rev. Thomas Walker.
> Royalton, Randolph, Williamstown, and Chelsea.[120]

One letter asserted a belief in "the proof as stated in the Bible that woman and man were made for each other is clearly evident in their plumbing connections, which fit perfectly."[121] Another letter, published in the same newspaper on the same day, argued that "there is something stronger and more important and deeper than the constitution. In mankind's history, the fabric in which we live, marriage is between a man and woman. Call it natural law, God's law or whatever—it is what is right. Same-sex marriages . . . are wrong."[122]

Another letter, published in the same newspaper on the same day, claimed that "homosexuality has and always will be a perversion. . . . To legitimize a lifestyle that is unnatural, immoral, and unhealthy is unthinkable."[123] Yet another letter published in the same newspaper on the same day equated homosexuality with sodomy, substance abuse, and criminal behavior, and warned that, if the domestic partnership bill passed, "severe ramifications will be inflicted on our children's future world. It's confusing enough in today's world to decipher evil vs. good, right vs. wrong in our society. . . . We are opening a Pandora's box of immorality."[124] Still another letter, published by the same newspaper on the same day asked whether "we want to leave a legacy of sodomy and maple syrup for our children."[125] Still, another letter, published by the same newspaper on the same day, argued: "I am a Christian, and I do not believe homosexual behavior is normal. I do not believe it is the type of relationship that God would want us in. . . . I do have a deep-seated emotional reaction to homosexual behavior, just as I would to any other type of behavior that I have come to realize is not in alignment with God's plan. . . . I do not want their [homosexual] lifestyle forced upon my children who attend public schools."[126]

One letter asserted that legislators who supported domestic partnerships had "sold out to immorality and degradation," as opposed to "the citizens of the state who have overwhelmingly said no to this stupidity."[127] The letter went on: "I am heavily involved in tourism and the challenges to bring people into this state. I have seen this work undone by this [domestic partnership bill]. Who will want to come to a place that openly embraces this perversity? Already I've seen individuals from other states, homosexual men dressed in women's clothing and make-up, here soliciting in [a Vermont town]. I am sickened by this behavior. It's disgusting at best."[128]

Another letter, published in the same newspaper on the same day, argued that the writer's civil rights would be violated "if people are forced by government mandate to live amongst other people whose lifestyle they consider morally reprehensible, if not actually disgusting."[129] Yet another letter called homosexuality "disordered sexual behavior" and claimed that "the view that homosexual activity is equivalent to, or as acceptable as, [heterosexual marriage] . . . has a direct impact on society's understanding of the nature and rights of the family and puts them in jeopardy. Endorsement of same-sex unions will send a new moral message to Vermonters (and all Americans). . . ."[130] Another, published in the same newspaper on the same day, was written "on behalf of our family. . . . We have been living in Vermont all our lives. We have raised 12 children and have 37 grandchildren presently."[131] this family wrote that "we do have a right to protect moral issues. Marriage between a man and a woman should not change, nor should any change occur in the laws. . . . It is important to love everyone, but it does not mean that we have to agree with what they do or promote it when we know it to be incorrect in the eyes of the Lord."[132]

One letter called homosexuality "reprehensible conduct" and compared it to "similar lifestyles surrounding God's destruction of Sodom and Gomorrah"; argued that "homosexuality, like incest, is condemned by Almighty God" as an "abomination"; and accused clergy who support same-sex marriage as "defil[ing] God's natural plan for holy matrimony and of "trad[ing] God's truth into a lie" and accused legislators of being "opposed to morality."[133] Another letter, published in the same newspaper on the same day advised the legislature to "cease all activity which either allows homosexuals to pretend to marry or otherwise join together. If the General Assembly refuses to uphold our constitution, thus violating their oaths, we are in terrible trouble because they are liars."[134]

One letter asserted that same-sex couples ought not be allowed to adopt children: "Do you mean to say it's OK to take an innocent little baby, who is unable to speak for its own 'civil rights,' to be brought up by a gay or lesbian couple? Does an adopted child have rights?"[135] To dispel any doubt, the letter-writer explained, "I do not condone the sexual lifestyle of homosexuals and don't think the wonderful state of Vermont should take a stand to support it by law."[136] Another letter, published in the same newspaper on the same day, stated that "we do not want our beloved state to legitimize this deviant lifestyle."[137]

One letter claimed that "America in the year 2000 stands at a vital crossroads" because of "decay and pollution of public morality. Our biblical and moral foundations are crumbling at an alarming rate."[138] Another letter, published in the same newspaper on the same day, as-

serted that "the rate of homosexuals using children for their sexual plea-
sures is 30 times greater than for heterosexuals—and your child or
grandchild could be the target."[139] Another letter, published in a different newspaper on the same day, asked "why the need to legitimize homosexual behavior? Simple. The need is to undermine the American
ideal, as outlined in the Communist Manifesto."[140]

One letter began: "The sin of homosexuality is usually the final stage
of those civilizations that turn from God."[141] The letter continued: "It was
for this crime [i.e., homosexuality] that God burned Sodom off the map
and ordered the destruction of Jericho along with other Old Testament
cities. In recent years, the number of homosexuals in Western civilization
has increased dramatically. We are taught to love one another, but not to
the extent where we endorse the wrong ways of gay people."[142]

Another letter, published in the same newspaper on the same day,
was intended "to respond to the many Christians who have spoken in
favor of gay marriage. Calling oneself a Christian or a Jew and advocating for gay marriage or civil unions are mutually exclusive. Read
your Bible. In our eagerness to be seen as politically correct we are becoming morally bankrupt. . . . Evil flourishes where good men do or say
nothing."[143]

Another letter, published in the same newspaper on the same day,
reminded Senators and Representatives who supported domestic partnerships "of how ticked off you were after House legislation was enacted to protect gays [from discrimination in employment and hous-
ing], only to have them create a scene . . . kissing each other in the House
chamber. . . ."[144]

This letter asked: "Will we be comfortable with gays and lesbians
kissing each other in public? A flaunted civil union between two males
or two females living next door? Will our children understand? It is
common knowledge that children who grow up in single-parent families grow up looking at life differently . . . children need to be exposed
to both parents, not to two fathers or two mothers."[145]

Another letter, published in the same newspaper on the same day,
warned that "to reward homosexual behavior is to abandon the primary rules governing our relationships with one another. In fact, it is to
shoot down the rule of law altogether . . . If we are incapable of con-
trolling our behavior, how can we be held accountable for what we do?
Law is rendered meaningless."[146]

Another letter, published in the same newspaper on the same day, began: "Recently I attended an all-day seminar given by Harvest—a Pennsylvania group whose mission is to help those trapped in sexual addiction break free to a normal, joyous, healthy lifestyle. They regularly assist people mired in a homosexual mindset to recognize the reality of their choice, and the available options and steps to freedom."[147] The letter explained: "As a friend of former and current homosexuals, I know it is a lifestyle choice, and a trap for those who are emotionally hurting. Therefore, it is not an unchangeable civil rights issue, but rather a matter of public health and safety due to the well-documented consequences."[148]

The letter went on to describe some of these "well-documented consequences": "Gay men often spend the latter years of their shortened lives in diapers, due to misusing their bodies against nature's design. They account for approximately 3 percent of our population but account for 50 percent of gonorrhea of the throat, syphilis, and other sexually transmitted diseases. . . . One in three homosexuals is also a substance abuser."[149] One letter contended that "the status of marriage cannot and should not be granted to homosexual behavior. It creates a respectability . . . on a plane with traditional marriage."[150]

One letter decried that "Vermont has become the gay capital of the entire world. There are some legislators who claimed they voted their conscience [in supporting the domestic partnership bill]. My question is, how can you vote your conscience if their [sic] is an empty space between your ears?"[151] The "majority doesn't count anymore. It's the so-called minorities. That explains the problems with this country, and especially Vermont. Every small, or large, group that thinks they're being treated unfairly makes loud noises, with the help of greedy lawyers who try to change age-old laws that have always worked for everyone."[152]

The letter went on to praise those states that have laws or "campaigns going on against same-sex marriage. Even the federal government, in the one right thing they've done since World War II, does not recognize same-sex marriage. Fortunately, when I leave the state I fly, so no one will know I'm from Vermont—even though I was born here 76 years ago."[153] Another letter, published in the same newspaper on the same day, said that the day Vermont law recognized domestic partnerships would "be recorded as a day in infamy in the history of Vermont."[154]

One letter, written "as the presiding officer of more than 3,000 faithful members of the Church of Jesus Christ of Latter-Day Saints,"[155] asserted that "homosexual and lesbian marriage, by whatever label you substitute for its name, is not a civil right; it is a moral wrong" and that allowing homosexuals to marry "would only contribute to the degeneration of the family"; the Mormon President denounced rejected domestic partnerships: "I reject the concept of tagging homosexual relationships with a look-alike marriage label."[156] Another letter, published by the same newspaper on the same day, claimed that "homosexuality is an immoral practice (by choice, like adultery and fornication) and has been for thousands of years"; called domestic partnerships "an immoral proposal"; and argued that "Catholics who do not believe in the teachings of the church regarding the immorality of homosexuality are not truly Catholic."[157]

Numerous letters threatened legislators with political retribution for voting for domestic partnerships. One letter predicted that "you will see a much-changed political landscape in Vermont in the future, primarily because people like me are now, probably for the first time, aroused, alarmed, angry, and taking careful note of vote tallies, and vow to . . . take careful note of who voted on each side of this bill, and remember it when they vote in November. I intend to help them remember."[158] Another urged Vermonters to "remember the people in the [legislature] that we elected and didn't vote the way of the people. They must go. . . . Come election time, we must show [the Governor] that we do know what we are voting for and replace this tyrant."[159]

I shudder to imagine how it must feel to be a gay or lesbian Vermonter and to hear this venom directed against them by their fellow Vermonters. Actually, one need not imagine. Susan Murray, a lead lawyer in *Baker*, told the House Judiciary Committee how it feels. "It's really painful to hear people say, 'You're immoral, you're an abomination.'"[160] As she testified, Murray "was barely able to hold back her tears. . . . Several times Murray had to pause to fight back tears, and once she apologized for losing her composure."[161]

Or listen to the anguished howl of this Vermont mother:

> Many letters have been sent to the [newspaper] concerning the homosexual menace in our state. I am the mother of a gay son, and I've taken enough from you good people.
> I'm tired of your foolish rhetoric about the "homosexual agenda" and your allegations that accepting homosexuality is the same thing as advo-

cating sex with children. You are cruel and you are ignorant. You have been robbing me of the joys of motherhood ever since my children were tiny. My firstborn son started suffering at the hands of the moral little thugs from your moral, upright families from the time he was in the first grade. He was physically and verbally abused from first grade straight through high school because he was perceived to be gay. He never professed to be gay or had any association with anything gay, but he had the misfortune not to walk or have gestures like the other boys. He was called "fag" incessantly, starting when he was 6.

In high school, while your children were doing what kids that age should be doing, mine labored over a suicide note, drafting and redrafting it to be sure his family knew how much he loved them. My sobbing 17-year-old tore the heart out of me as he choked out that he just couldn't bear to continue living any longer, that he didn't want to be gay and that he couldn't face a life with no dignity.

You have the audacity to talk about protecting families and children from the homosexual menace, while you yourselves tear apart families and drive children to despair. I don't know why my son is gay, but I do know that God didn't put him, and millions like him, on this Earth to give you someone to abuse. God gave you brains so that you could think, and it's about time you started doing that.

At the core of all your misguided beliefs is the belief that this could never happen to you, that there is some kind of subculture out there that people have chosen to join. The fact is that if it can happen to my family, it can happen to yours, and you won't get to choose. Whether it is genetic or whether something occurs during a critical time of fetal development, I don't know. I can only tell you with an absolute certainty that it is inborn.

If you want to tout your own morality, you'd best come up with something more substantive than your heterosexuality. You did nothing to earn it; it was given to you. If you disagree, I would be interested in hearing your story, because my own heterosexuality was a blessing I received with no effort whatsoever on my part. It is so woven into the very soul of me that nothing could ever change it. For those of you who reduce sexual orientation to a simple choice, a character issue, a bad habit or something that can be changed by a 10-step program, I'm puzzled. Are you saying that your own sexual orientation is nothing more than something you have chosen, that you could change it at will? If that's not the case, then why would you suggest that someone else can?

A popular theme in your letters is that our state has been infiltrated by outsiders. Both sides of my family have lived in Vermont for generations. I am heart and soul a Vermonter, so I'll thank you to stop saying that you are speaking for "true Vermonters." You invoke the memory of the brave people who have fought on the battlefield for this great country, saying that they didn't give their lives so that the "homosexual agenda" could tear down the principles they died defending. My 83-year-old father fought in some of the most horrific battles of World War II, was wounded and awarded the Purple Heart. He shakes his head in sadness at the life his grandson has had to live. He says he fought alongside homosexuals in those battles, that they did their part and bothered no one. One of his best friends in the service was gay, and he never knew it until the end, and when he did find out, it matter not at all. That wasn't the measure of the man.

You religious folk just can't bear the thought that as my son emerges from the hell that was his childhood he might like to find a lifelong companion and have a measure of happiness. It offends your sensibilities that he should request the right to visit that companion in the hospital, to make medical decisions for him, or to benefit from tax laws governing inheritance. How dare he . . . these outrageous requests would threaten the very existence of your family, would undermine the sanctity of marriage.

You use religion to abdicate your responsibility to be thinking human beings. There are vast numbers of religious people who find your attitudes repugnant. God is not for the privileged majority, and God knows my son has committed no sin.

The deep-thinking author of a letter to the Forum on April 12 who lectures about homosexual sin and tells us about "those of us who have been blessed with the benefits of a religious upbringing" asks, "Whatever happened to the idea of striving . . . to be better human beings than we are?" Indeed, sir, whatever happened to that?[162]

I am not suggesting that the homophobic, venomous statements quoted over the previous pages were the views of all, or most, Vermonters. Within days of the *Baker* decision, the *Valley News*, a leading newspaper in Vermont, editorialized in favor of same-sex marriage.[163] The editorial, headlined *Our Common Humanity*, argued that, "if the legislature embraces the spirit" of *Baker*, "it will realize that the best way to ensure that gay couples enjoy all of the benefits of marriage is to allow them to marry."[164] The editorial recognized that sanctioning same-sex marriage would "push some residents of the state further and faster than they wish to go in this highly charged matter" but concluded that "we can muster no persuasive argument for showing a decent respect for the prejudices of mankind. Civil rights are not to be apportioned to minorities based on the comfort levels of majorities."[165] In late February 2000, in the midst of the firestorm of homophobia over *Baker*, the *Valley News* reaffirmed its editorial position in favor of allowing same-sex marriages.[166] The *Valley News* reiterated that "opening the institution of marriage to all committed couples is what's right," noting that "we are among those who believe that separate institutions are inherently unequal."[167]

The Reverend William Sloan Coffin,[168] Eugene Rayner,[169] Rama Schneider[170] and Professor Victor Nuovo,[171] among others, wrote eloquent newspaper op-ed pieces in support of same-sex marriage. So have writers of letters to the editor. Communities of faith also did not speak with one voice on this issue; some Vermont religious leaders testified in favor of same-sex marriage and domestic partnerships,[172] and, during the height of the debate in Vermont, the rabbis of Judaism's Reform Movement, meeting in North Carolina, declared that same-sex unions were "worthy of affirmation" through "Jewish ritual and that Reform rabbis who decided to officiate at same-sex ceremonies would have the support of the branch's rabbinical body."[173]

THE POLLS AND THE PETITIONS

The wide and deep hostility to *Baker* surfaced elsewhere in Vermont. An opinion poll published on January 25, 2000 (a month after the *Baker* decision was issued), found that a majority of Vermont voters polled disagreed with the decision, and "nearly half said they would like to see the ruling overturned by amending the Vermont Constitution to define marriage as a union between one man and one woman."[174] A later poll, published on March 2, found that 45% disagreed with *Baker*, 47% agreed, and 8% weren't sure.[175] Twenty-nine percent favored a constitutional amendment to overrule *Baker*.[176]

In addition, petitions opposing *Baker* attracted 25,000 signatures.[177] The petitions were presented to the House Judiciary Committee by a group of 68 House members who had formed a House Traditional Marriage Caucus.[178] One member of the House explained that "House Republicans and Democrats have banded together in the name of traditional marriage."[179] The State Chairman of the Vermont Republican Party called for a constitutional amendment defining marriage as the union of one man and one woman.[180] The Associated Press noted that, at least as of March 1, 2000, "clearly there is a lot of opposition in the House to granting additional benefits"—*any* additional benefits—"to gay and lesbian couples."[181] And, "in a possible preview of the floor fight to come," the Associated Press wrote on March 4, "the tax-writing Ways and Means Committee narrowly" endorsed the Judiciary Committee's proposed system of domestic partnerships.[182] The vote was a razor-thin 6-5. The committee's chairman "steadfastly opposes opening marriage statutes to gays and lesbians."[183]

Several organizations expressed support for "traditional marriage" and opposed both same-sex marriage and comprehensive domestic partnerships. Take It To The People was the largest and oldest such Vermont group. The Vermont Traditional Family Institute argued (on its Web site) that "homosexual activists intend to use the machinery of state and federal civil rights laws to persecute those who do not accept their lifestyle. . . . The legalization of homosexual marriage will give homosexual activists a weapon to persecute faith-based charities which receive public funding."[184]

Homophobia in Vermont predated *Baker*, naturally. A poll done five years before *Baker* "found that 55 percent of Vermonters opposed a new contract with state employees that provided health benefits to unmarried domestic partnerships. Only 36 percent said they approved."[185] In 1998, the annual Doyle poll[186] of Town Meeting participants "asked Vermonters if they thought the legislature should authorize same-sex marriages. The tally was reported from 9,300 people in 133 towns: 32 percent said yes, 61 percent said no, and 7 percent were undecided. A poll taken in late 1999, two months before the *Baker* ruling was issued, found that "47 percent of Vermonters surveyed said they disapproved, and 40 percent said they approved of allowing couples of the same sex to marry."[187]

In 1992—a full seven years before *Baker* was decided—the *Rutland Herald*'s fearless Robert Mitchell editorialized:

> Many Vermonters who weren't talking about it must have questioned the need for the antidiscrimination bill which has passed both houses of the Legislature and yesterday was reported to be awaiting Gov. Howard Dean's signature. If the need was doubted, all doubts would have been erased by the hate campaign that was unleashed against the leading supporters of the legislation last week—anonymous of course. People who engage in such hateful activities don't have the courage to identify themselves. Either that or they are too ashamed to do so.
>
> The hate campaign was conducted by telephone in many instances and was also characterized by deposit of desecrated American flags at the homes of a number of legislators who supported the legislation. The implication is that those protesting the rights bill believe there is something un-American or unpatriotic about being a homosexual or a lesbian, as though that had anything to do with an individual's sexual preference.

Sadly at least some of the hate campaign was linked to religious scruples or philosophy. According to some religious sects homosexuality is outlawed by Biblical precepts.

One of the leading targets, if not the leading target of the campaign, was Rutland's state Sen. David Wolk, a leading sponsor of the antidiscrimination bill. Over a period of several weeks he and his family were subjected to a barrage of abusive phone calls. They had to resort to letting their telephone answering service take the calls. Sen. Wolk said he had heard that the issue had been the subject of sermons in a number of churches before the vote on the bill, presumably involving the religious right.

A suitable demonstration of support for the legislation would be to gather as many legislators together as possible when Gov. Dean signs the bill. It shouldn't be difficult to collect an impressive array of backers for such a demonstration in spite of the hate campaign. Or perhaps, more to the point, because of it.[188]

The Associated Press's Christopher Graff has noted that the opposition to *Baker* echoed another debate from the mid-1980s: the opposition to the Equal Rights Amendment (ERA).[189] The successful campaign to defeat the ERA in Vermont in 1986 contained "misinformation" that "the ERA would give 'homosexuals and lesbians the right to marry,'"[190] along with the Catholic Bishop of Vermont "rallying his troops against evil," an "outsider agitator" (that is, Phyllis Schafly) who joined "the battle to ensure the evil is snuffed out here and doesn't spread past the borders," and "some in the Republican Party [who were] pushing to put the GOP on record against this evil."[191] The ERA was defeated in Vermont on November 4, 1986. The vote was 89,426 people in favor, and 95,587 against it.[192]

Town Meeting Day 2000

At Vermont's Town Meeting 2000, held on March 7, voters in at least 50 Vermont communities cast nonbinding ballots on the *Baker* options of same-sex marriage or domestic partnerships.[193] Statewide polls were also conducted during town meetings.[194]

On Town Meeting Day and Super Tuesday—the largest single primary day in American history (which was also Fat Tuesday, the climax of Mardi Gras in New Orleans)—I stayed up late to watch the election returns. I switched channels between CNN reports of George Bush beating John McCain for the Republican presidential nomination and Al Gore pasting Bill Bradley for the Democratic nomination and WCAX-TV updates on the results of the town meeting votes on same-sex marriage. By 11:00 P.M., 20 towns had reported in, and the news was not good: voters in all 20 towns had rejected same-sex marriage, and 16 of the 20 had rejected domestic partnerships as well. The newspaper headlines the next morning told the tale: *Same-Sex Marriage Is Opposed*,[195] and *Gay Marriage Loses at Ballot Box*.[196] A subheadline offered the only silver lining: *Only A Handful of Towns Hold Votes on Issue*.[197]

It was a slaughter. "Some question" related to same-sex marriage or benefits "was on the Town Meeting Day warning in more than 50 of Vermont's 246 communities"[198] In not a single community did a majority of citizens vote in favor of same-sex marriage.[199] Thirty-eight towns "voted against the creation of 'domestic partnerships' which would give same-sex couples the rights and protections of marriage without being called marriage. Only 11 towns—slightly more than one in five—voted to support domestic partnerships.[200] (One town was tied, 23-23).[201] Nearly four out of five Vermont towns rejected domestic partnership along with marriage.

In many towns, the margins were not even close on same-sex marriage. In those towns voting on the matter, "voters generally rejected the idea of same-sex marriage by margins of three or four to one."[202] In some communities the vote was 5-to-1 against.[203] Domestic partnership "fared better at the polls, though it did not win majority approval except in a few towns."[204]

The meetings themselves were sometimes heated. "'It's a sin,' said Dana Kittlell at Fairfield's town meeting, a gathering at which former state senator Francis Howrigan stood to describe gays as 'disease-spreading cornholers.'"[205] In Athens, a relatively poor and conservative town of 313 people in southern Vermont, 50 or so people showed up at Town Meeting. Citizens "denounced homosexuality"[206] and the town clerk "said she would quit as a matter of conscience before she would sign a marriage certificate for a gay or lesbian couple. 'They will have to find a new town clerk, I will no do it,' said [the clerk]."[207] Athens resident Walter Ryan, "a retired builder wearing a cowboy hat, who moved with his family to Athens from southern California 12 years ago for the rural life,"[208] said "I don't think they have any rights at all."[209] Ryan's son, Wayne, "had the harshest language for gays and lesbians."[210] Wayne Ryan urged against changing "the word 'marriage' to mean something as ill and foul as same-sex partners."[211]

After Wayne Ryan spoke, a dairy farmer said he would like to know how his Representative—David Deen—planned to vote.[212] Representative Deen said he planned to support the Judiciary Committee's comprehensive domestic partnership bill.[213] When "residents pressured [the Representative] to vote in accordance with their majority's wishes and against the bill, he refused. 'This is a matter of conscience for me,' he said. I get to exercise my conscience, and you all get to vote the first Tuesday in November every other year' 'We will,' inserted Walter Ryan, Wayne's father. 'You'll be out.'"[214]

On the vote itself, the town opposed gay marriage 35 to 17 and opposed domestic partnership 39 to 13. A *New York Times* reporter observed that "the town's opinions seemed to reflect the depth and breadth of [opposition to same-sex marriage or domestic partnerships] in Vermont—in particular because it spoke as a whole town and not merely a motivated few who ventured to a statehouse hearing to speak out."[215]

In the town of Williamstown, some voters "maintained that [homosexuality] had led to the fall of ancient Rome, which, [one resident said] had been brought down by 'licentiousness and libertine behavior.'"[216] Voters did speak in favor of same-sex marriage, but they did not carry the day in a single Vermont town.

Supporters of domestic partnerships did their best to spin the trouncing they had taken on Town Meeting Day. The day after Town Meeting Day, Governor Dean said that many Vermonters did not understand that the House Judiciary Committee's bill defined marriage as a union between a man and a woman.[217] "Dean said he had attended five town meetings . . . and the people he encountered were unaware that such a definition was contained in the bill. And he blamed the news media for not reporting that information to Vermont voters."[218] The *Rutland Herald* agreed that the Town Meeting Day votes were "not definitive" because, in part, "most of those who voted" were "probably not aware that the bill before the House" defined marriage as a union between a man and a woman.[219]

Supporters of same-sex unions also correctly pointed out that most Vermont towns did not address this contentious issue on Town Meeting Day. The only openly gay member of the legislature—who received a standing ovation at his Town Meeting in Hinesburg[220]—"cautioned against giving too much weight to the Town Meeting Day results."[221] He said "it was primarily put in towns where there was less likely to be support."[222]

However, exit polls from the primaries were also conduced on Town Meeting Day, and these polls were conducted across the entire state. These exit polls "mirrored results from a poll conducted Feb. 25–27 for the *Burlington Free Press* and WPTZ-TV that found 47 percent of Vermonters agreed with [the *Baker* ruling] while 45 percent disagreed."[223]

Many Vermonters praised what they called the "civility" of the debate on the appropriate response to *Baker*. It's unclear to me what those people meant by "civility," because it appeared to me that the civility of the debate was decidedly unilateral. The supporters of *Baker* were indeed civil. Many opponents—including political and religious leaders—were not civil, characterizing their opponents as abominations, sins in the eyes of God, defects of nature, or the moral equivalent of child-rapists, bigamists, polygamists, or people who have sex with animals. Such assertions are not "civil," even when made in a quiet and respectful voice, and these generally were not.

4 Vermont's "Third Way"

Civil Unions as an Alternative to Civil Marriage

Most of the time it was like having a ballroom full of dancers, dancing different steps, to music that wasn't quite right for any of them.

—Tom Kelly, Gruman Aircraft Co., on the Lunar Excursion Module, 1995[1]

IN THIS chapter I want to trace the legislature's response to *Baker*. Justice Johnson, dissenting in *Baker*, warned against sending the matrimonial rights of same-sex couples into an uncertain fate in the "political cauldron"[2] of the legislature. (This was, perhaps, an allusion to *Macbeth*).[3] "Cauldron" was, as it turned out, an apt image.

It might be worth mentioning that I wrote this chapter as the events described were unfolding. My daily ritual was to pick up my four daily newspapers each morning, read them, put them aside for the day, write up the day's events in the evening, and have them word-processed into the manuscript by Laura Gillen and Judy Hilts the following morning. If this chapter contains an aura of uncertainty about the post-*Baker* bill's immediate future—much as a diary would—that is why: As I wrote it day-by-day, I genuinely *was* uncertain about what would happen next.

The *Baker* decision suggested that the legislature had two options. Actually, as Professor Greg Johnson observed, there were five possibilities: One, the legislature "can do nothing and, as long as they try hard, the supreme court will not interfere. Two, they can stonewall, and the court could somehow force them to act. Three, they can create a domestic partnership law. Four, they can allow same-sex marriage. And, finally, they can eliminate marriage as a civil right, reserving marriage for religion, and they can instead institute a domestic partnership law for all, gays, lesbians, and heterosexual couples alike."[4]

The option of opening up the marriage statutes to include same-sex couples was rejected early on by the governor as wrong and by legislators as politically unrealistic. However, a comprehensive parallel system of domestic partnership was expected to pass the 30-person Senate with relative ease.[5] But, before the bill even got to the Senate, it had to make it through the 150-member House. In the House, "the bill's fate was touch and go all the way."[6]

THE HOUSE JUDICIARY COMMITTEE: THE "POLITICAL REALITY" OF FIERCE PUBLIC OPPOSITION TO SAME-SEX CIVIL MARRIAGE

[The idea of same-sex marriage in Vermont is dead], and I will use all the powers of my office to keep it dead.

—Vermont Governor Howard Dean, February 2000[7]

The early indications were not encouraging. As discussed in the previous chapter, the House Judiciary Committee held a series of hearings in January 2000 at which experts in various fields testified—including clerics, some of whom testified against homosexuality—about their views on *Baker* and how the legislature should respond to *Baker*. The first witnesses addressed how the *Baker* decision ought to be interpreted.

The two lead lawyers on *Baker* testified that the legislature should simply open up the marriage laws to include same-sex couples. Susan Murray and Beth Robinson "told the committee that gay and lesbian couples still would be denied some important tangible benefits if the legislature stopped short of allowing them to marry and instead created domestic partnerships."[8]

"Robinson and Murray both spoke passionately when they described some of the tangible benefits that are denied gays and lesbians. But they were most forceful in talking about the intangible benefits that same-sex couples would not get if the legislature followed the domestic partnership option. Being denied the right to marry, Murray said, gives gays and lesbians the feeling they are inferior. 'There's a message they get that they're second-class citizens.'"[9]

"There's an erosion of the spirit," Murray said.[10] This loss was best illustrated, Murray testified later, when she "asked the committee to imagine the reaction if people who were now married were given the status of domestic partners. 'There would be an uproar,' she said. 'Those husbands and wives would feel they'd lost something.'"[11]

Robinson added, "The word (marriage) itself is something. Everybody knows what it means. It's a powerful term."[12]

Beth Robinson "compared the current opposition to same-sex marriage to earlier prohibitions against interracial marriages."[13] "Robinson also told the committee that when states finally recognized that they were discriminating against mixed race couples, no one suggested that an alternative relationship be created for them that would provide equal benefits but still not allow them to marry."[14]

Witnesses also told the committee that the *Baker* court "left open the question of whether same-sex couples could be adequately protected through domestic partnerships or whether marriage would have to be the ultimate solution. The witnesses pointed out that the court said it was leaving that question to another day. In part, the answer to that question will depend on what alternative the legislature devises if it chooses not to approve same-sex marriage."[15]

Vermont Law School Professor Peter Teachout disagreed that *Baker* required marriage: Domestic partnerships would do. Teachout explained how the legislature could adopt a minimalist view of *Baker* that would still pass constitutional muster. Veteran Vermont reporter Jack Hoffman described Teachout's testimony:

> Peter Teachout, a professor at Vermont Law School who specializes in constitutional law, said he believed the court had clearly left open the possibility that an alternative system could meet the test.
>
> Teachout pointed out that there had been a sharp disagreement on the court over that very issue. Associate Justice Denise Johnson argued strongly in a dissenting opinion that the court should have ruled that the three couples should be granted marriage licenses. However, the four other justices joined with the majority decision that said the Legislature could amend existing law or create an alternative system, such as domestic partnerships.
>
> There was an argument among the justices over domestic partnerships, Teachout said, so it was clearly considered by the court.
>
> Teachout agreed with Robinson and Murray that domestic partnerships would not provide all the same benefits of marriage. One thing same-sex couples wouldn't get, he said, was that gateway to other states.
>
> Teachout also talked about the intangible benefits.
>
> "The other thing you don't get is that bestowal of legitimacy," he said.
>
> Teachout then explained that the legal question for the state and the Legislature, if it followed the domestic partnership option, was whether it could justify treating same-sex couples somewhat differently than heterosexual couples.

By providing the legal benefits and protections, Teachout said, the state could remove much of the discrimination against same-sex couples. What the Supreme Court would have to decide in the future, if domestic partnerships were approved, is whether there were adequate reasons to justify the benefits that would still be denied to same-sex couples.[16]

The committee (along with its Senate counterpart) also held two joint public hearings on the matter; these hearings drew overflow crowds. At the end of the public hearings, one astute political observer remarked that the legislators "appeared a bit shell-shocked."[17]

Then, on February 9, the House Judiciary Committee voted, 8 to 3, in favor in principle of granting same-sex couples the right to equal benefits, under a yet-to-be-determined system of domestic partnership, but not letting them legally marry. Members of the majority of the committee were clearly influenced by what they saw as the "political realities" of widespread public opposition to same-sex marriage. "Almost to a person, committee members said they had to recognize the political realities both within the statehouse and among the public."[18]

Following the House Judiciary Committee's initial vote, Governor Dean declared the civil marriage option dead and promised to use "the powers of this office"[19] to keep it dead. Meanwhile, 12 legislators signed a resolution to impeach the Vermont Supreme Court justices based on *Baker*.[20]

Republican Representative Thomas Little, Chairman of the House Judiciary, took the lead in drafting the bill. On March 1, 2000, the Committee overwhelmingly recommended a comprehensive domestic partnership bill (the committee called it "civil union" rather than "domestic partnership").[21] The 45-page bill (H 847) provided that same-sex couples could form "civil unions," register them with the government, and be entitled to the more than 300 legal rights and benefits now conferred upon married heterosexual couples as a matter of course, including health, medical, legal, insurance, parental, and other benefits.

It is important to note that the bill did more than confer legal rights and benefits. It also imposed the same legal obligations and responsibilities as marriage. "Under the law, couples who enter into legal unions will join not only their hearts, but also bank accounts, real estate holdings, and parental rights. If their unions fail, they will have to go to court, just like heterosexuals seeking divorce."[22]

Thus, "someone who enters into a civil union that involves a large inheritance faces the prospect of a judge giving half of it to the estranged partner in a dissolution proceeding. That one partner's income will count when the other is applying for welfare or a student loan. And that breakups that once happened in the privacy of a home could be played out in a public courtroom."[23]

The House Judiciary Committee's bill included a fact-finding provision stating that under Vermont law "marriage" is a union between a man and a woman: "Civil marriage under Vermont's marriage statutes consists of a union between a man and a woman. This interpretation of the state's marriage laws was upheld by the Vermont Supreme Court in *Baker v. State.*"[24]

This definition of marriage as an exclusively heterosexual institution was important to Governor Howard Dean's eventual decision to support the bill, and, therefore, to the bill's passage through the House of Representatives.[25] A Vermont newspaper reported that "Dean said he had become one of the proposal's biggest supporters since the House Judiciary committee added language defining marriage as a union between a man and a woman."[26]

The comprehensive civil unions bill passed 10-1, with five Republicans, four Democrats, and one Progressive voting in favor of it. The lone dissenter, Rep. William Mackinnon, dissented because the bill did not go far enough: It did not allow same-sex couples to marry.[27]

H 847 was indeed impressively comprehensive, and it would provide the most comprehensive system of its type in the United States.[28] It was for this reason that Rep. William Lippert, the only openly gay member of the committee, made the formal motion to recommend the bill, and both he and the lawyer for the *Baker* plaintiffs hailed the proposed legislation.[29]

It was also impressive that the committee did not hide behind the court's decision in *Baker.* Given the volatile political aspects of the same-sex union question, one could have understood the committee's choice had it decided to do nothing more than what the state's highest court had mandated: that the legislators just follow the constitutional law of Vermont. The committee didn't take that easy way out. To the contrary, Chairman Little said pointedly that his committee had passed H 847 because "it was the right thing to do."[30]

I admire the courage of the House Judiciary Committee members in voting for H 847. Many Vermonters, and many of their legislative colleagues, opposed granting *any* benefits or rights to lesbian and gay couples. After the vote, "a trio of priests from out of state collared reporters outside the hearing room to denounce the bill and homosexuality."[31] Randall Terry, an antiabortion and antigay activist and founder of Operation Rescue, "stood near the door scowling. 'The day of judgment is coming folks,' Terry said as the committee meeting ended."[32]

Terry did more than scowl. The day the House Judiciary Committee voted out its bill, "Terry tried hard to get attention in the committee" and "his actions prompted lawmakers to bring a sheriff's deputy into the room to keep order. Before the vote, he prayed, argued with legislators, and warned that judgment day was coming; afterward, he booed them and said 'shame, shame, shame.'"[33] Some legislators who agreed with Terry on the merits shunned both Terry and his tactics. One whom seems to shun neither is Rep. Nancy Sheltra. "We're talking about a sexual activity, not a lifestyle,'" Sheltra said after the vote; she was "visibly shaking with anger after the vote. 'The voters back home are going to be extremely irritated, agitated, and disgusted, and I believe some legislators will lose their positions as a result.'"[34]

At least one member of the House Judiciary Committee found herself shunned after her vote in favor of the bill. "'It was after I made my decision that people started to call and be more forceful than I've ever encountered,'"[35] Rep. Cathy Voyer said. "'People who used to speak to me on the street will walk by me and not even acknowledge my presence,' Voyer said. 'That bothers me.'"[36]

Notwithstanding the personal courage of the committee members, their well-intentioned bill demonstrates why the rights of disfavored minorities ought to be decided by courts, not by politicians or voters. Politics has been called the art of the possible, and politicians are masters of compromise. It is a sad testament to this fact that the only openly gay member of the committee—and a strong supporter of allowing same-sex couples to marry—was "disappointed that the vote was not unanimous. He said that Rep. Mackinnon's decision to accept nothing short of same-sex marriage was 'a failure to engage in the political process.'"[37]

In any event, it was questionable whether the comprehensive plan passed out of the committee would bear any resemblance to the plan ultimately passed by the full House and Senate. In a "possible preview of the floor fight to come,"[38] on March 3 the House Ways and Means Committee voted favorably on H 847, the Judiciary Committee's domestic partnership bill. Those members of the Ways and Means Committee voting in favor of H 847 included three Democrats, two Republicans, and a Progressive; those opposed included three Democrats and two Republicans.[39] However, the bill passed only by the thinnest of possible margins, 6-5.[40] The vote could not have been closer, even though the bill contained the language defining "traditional marriage" as "a union between a man and a woman."[41]

Already, alternative, less-comprehensive versions of civil unions were being discussed by legislators.[42] Indeed, Rep. Mackinnon voted against the committee's comprehensive domestic partnership bill because he believed it had enough support to pass the full House: "If you're going to be unsuccessful, I'd rather be unsuccessful at least trying to do the constitutionally correct thing, [i.e., grant full marriage rights to same-sex couples]."[43]

THE FULL HOUSE, THE MIGHTY DUCKS, AND THE IDES OF MARCH

One cloud is enough to eclipse the sun.

—Thomas Fuller (1608–1661)[44]

The Preliminary Vote

Eight days after Town Meeting Day 2000—and eight months before every member of the legislature would face the voters for reelection— the full House took up the issue of same-sex unions and the bill voted out of the House Judiciary Committee. On the eve of the full House deliberations, commentators gave wavering legislators pep talks in favor of the comprehensive version of domestic partnerships.[45] The *Rutland Herald* reminded its readers of Edmund Burke's dictum that "your representative owes you not his industry, but his judgment; and he betrays instead of serving you if he sacrifices it to your opinion."[46]

Two days before the full House voted on the civil unions bill, the Associated Press reported that "House leaders are counting votes to determine if the bill has any chance of passage."[47] The day before, the Associated Press reported that '[e]ven though there's not quite a majority in the House" in favor of the comprehensive civil unions bill, backers predicted "the bill would pass later this week."[48]

Still, supporters conceded that the situation was "unpredictable" because, in part, "there are expected to be such a wide variety of amendments that could substantially alter the bill."[49] One expected amendment would define marriage as one man and one woman and would "prohibit the state from recognizing same-sex marriages performed in another state."[50] Another amendment "that opponents plan to push is a broader reciprocal benefits system that would replace" domestic partnerships.[51] This system would provide fewer benefits to a greater number of people.

Legislators had been "deluged with tens of thousands of letters, phone calls, and e-mails."[52] Whether judged by letters, phone calls or e-mails, the pressure on legislators (from both sides) was remarkable: "For many lawmakers" the "pressure from folks at home [was] intense."[53] Rep. Susan Wheeler received calls "warning her not to vote for the civil union bill, or else. Wheeler said, 'People call up and don't give a name and say 'shame, shame, we're going to vote you out.' "[54]

Rep. Wheeler even received what she understood to be a threat: "A man who warned she'd better watch her back. 'I think that was a threat,' Wheeler said. 'I found that unnerving.' "[55] Another legislator reported receiving a phone call that "included an unpleasant gun threat."[56]

Leading the charge to defeat the civil unions bill in the House was the House Traditional Marriage Task Force, which had grown to 68 members on the eve of the House debate.[57] The day before the House took up the bill, Rep. Robert Starr, co-chairman of the caucus, warned his colleagues that they ought to listen to the people of Vermont.

"On the table before Starr were Town Meeting Day tabulations [of polls and votes] from 114 towns. . . . The message in the numbers was clear: 111 of 114 towns opposed same-sex marriage; 101 of 114 opposed domestic partnerships. . . . And most of the town votes weren't even close."[58] The Traditional Marriage Caucus claimed they had the votes to defeat the bill: "I believe we do have the votes to kill it," one representative said the day before the vote.[59] Supporters of the bill disagreed.[60]

Take It To The People was also ready for the fight—armed with little plastic yellow ducks. To bring home their point that the civil unions bill was marriage in everything but name—"if it looks like a duck, walks like a duck, talks and swims like a duck, then it must be a duck"—the organization had left "yellow rubber duck key chains" on "the desks of every House member"[61] earlier in the week. "The key chains looked like children's toys."[62] On the night of the vote, "several ducks could be seen . . . sitting demonstrably on opponents' desks."[63]

When the House began debating the bill, one of its leading opponents "counted 72 solid votes against it. He needed just a few more to kill the bill outright, and didn't think it would be hard to get them."[64]

It would come down to 10 or 15 undecided votes in the 150-member House. "I think it depends on who's sick. It's that close," said one representative.[65] "There was a handful of lawmakers from both sides who were out of the building because of illness [the day before the vote], and it was unclear whether they would be back in time for [the] planned debate."[66]

The rules of the Vermont House provide that every bill goes to a vote of the full House twice. During the initial vote, amendments can be offered. Then there is a vote on the bill itself, more debate and more amendments, and a final vote is held.

The full House took up the issue of same-sex unions at 9:00 A.M. on Wednesday, March 15. The chairman of the Judiciary Committee began the historic debate by outlining the bill clause by clause and explaining to his colleagues why the committee had proposed it.[67] It was, he said, a civil rights bill. The House then broke in caucuses. After reconvening, the process of debate, offering amendments, and voting began.

The House debated the bill for about ten hours on this day.[68] Several amendments were proposed and rejected. One amendment to the bill would have asked Vermonters to vote on whether to hold a constitutional convention. It was defeated, 103-45.[69] A second amendment would have posed questions to the voters during the general election in November 2000. It was rejected, 91-56.[70] A third amendment would have changed the bill to provide fewer benefits to a broader group of people. It was defeated, 118-29.[71] Finally, an amendment was offered that would have gone beyond the domestic partnerships bill and allowed same-sex couples to marry. It was resoundingly rejected, 125-22.[72]

One amendment passed, and it was significant. "Some who wavered were persuaded to support the bill after the House added this sentence: *'Marriage means the legally recognized union between one man and one woman.'*"[73] The findings of the bill already defined marriage as a man and a woman. That wasn't enough: The exclusion of same-sex couples from marriage (a version of the "Defense of Marriage Act," or DOMA) had to be a part of the bill itself.

The Judiciary Committee "met with the leadership of the Freedom to Marry Task Force for more than an hour in the early part of the day, discussing the need to concede what they called 'half a DOMA' in order to see the bill passed."[74] So, in order to keep the votes of House members who threatened to withdraw their support of the bill," the bill was amended to include the sentence explicitly denying the right of marriage to gay and lesbian couples.[75]

Politically, adding this explicit preclusion to the bill "won over"[76] the three sponsors of the amendment. "When [those three] came over, that helped us an awful lot," said a member of the Judiciary Committee.[77] Had this sentence not been added to the bill—a sentence leaving no doubt that domestic partnerships for same-sex couples were separate from (and, in my view unequal to) marriage as enjoyed by heterosexual couples—the domestic partnership bill might have gone down in flames.

Several legislators spoke of the political risks they were taking in voting for the bill. However, they said, this was a civil rights bill, and they were prepared to accept the political consequences of voting for a bill of which their constituents disapproved.[78]

The debate was at times passionate on both sides. One representative argued that "if this passes, it will mark the beginning of the end of life in Vermont as I have known it for 56 years."[79] Another said: "I truly feel sorry for the State of Vermont . . . we're really putting ourselves in a dangerous position of judgment from the Almighty God."[80]

One representative "told of the pain her family suffered as her two daughters 'tried to fit the mold' as they were growing up," saying "[t]hey did not choose to be different. . . . Their pain and their inability to fit the mold has been our pain as well. . . . Please help to remove the stigma.'"[81] Rep. Francis Books, the only African American member of the House, compared the issue at hand with the civil rights movement and argued that in both cases the judiciary was required to act to protect the civil rights of an unpopular minority—indeed, against the fierce protests of the majority public: "Thank goodness that there have been people in this country who have said we can't take a person and . . . deny their rights. . . . Please consider the human beings that you have decided to place a stigma on."[82]

The day's highest drama came when Rep. William Lippert spoke. The Associated Press's Ross Sneyd reported the following:

Bill Lippert has spent the past 10 weeks sitting in the House Judiciary Committee debating whether he should be given the same rights as the other 10 people around the table.

So, roughly eight hours into yesterday's debate over granting gays and lesbians the benefits of marriage through civil unions, when Lippert rose to speak, a hush fell over the House chamber.

At first, Lippert's voice seemed on the verge of breaking.

"I think it's important to put a face on this," said Lippert, a Hinesburg Democrat and the only openly gay member of the legislature.

And then he did.

"I've had the privilege of developing a deep, devoted, loving, caring relationship with another man," Lippert said, his voice gaining strength.

He described how, during the intense weeks of debate in the Judiciary Committee, he has endured more hatred from opponents of gay marriage or civil unions than he ever had before in his life.

But he said the hatred was misguided. He argued that gays and lesbians enriched Vermont, partly because they have endured discrimination and prejudice.

"Gay and lesbian people, gay and lesbian couples, deserve not only rights, they deserve to be celebrated," Lippert said. "Our lives, in the midst of historical prejudice and discrimination, are, in my view, in some ways miracles. . . . The goodness of gay and lesbian people, gay and lesbian couples, is a triumph against discrimination and prejudice.

"We deserve to be welcomed because, in fact, we are your neighbors, your friends, indeed, we are your family," he said.

Lippert praised his colleagues in the legislature who have stood with him in his struggle to end discrimination and to extend the rights, benefits, and privileges of marriage to same-sex couples.

"They got targeted, too," Lippert said. "For some, hate runs that deep, discrimination runs that far."

Besides discrimination, gay men have suffered through the epidemic of AIDS, Lippert said, caring for one another and continuing to form committed relationships.

"Don't tell me about what a committed relationship is and isn't," Lippert said. "I've watched my gay brothers care for each other. There is no love and no commitment greater than what I've seen and what I've known."

Almost before Lippert wrapped up his speech and sat down, Rep. Robert Kinsey, a conservative Republican from Craftsbury, was on his feet.

"I just heard the greatest speech I've heard in my 30 years," Kinsey said. "And that's why I'm glad to be a friend of the member from Hinesburg and that's why I'm glad to be on his side."[83]

The vote came down to the wire. Critical lawmakers—the undecided middle whose votes were necessary for the bill to pass—waited until the final minutes to decide how they would vote.[84]

At the end of a long day of soul-searching and realpolitik, the vote on the bill itself (which took place after 9:00 P.M.) was close but seemed solid.[85] The Judiciary Committee's comprehensive domestic partnership bill was approved by a margin of 11 votes: 79 to 68.[86]

Speeches and appeals to conscience accounted for some shift of the center of gravity in favor of the bill. One astute observer noted afterwards that "in the final hours of debate Wednesday, as undecided lawmakers began to make up their minds, the balance began to shift. It shifted because the House added a single sentence to the bill—and because the bill's most ardent supporters said words that touched their colleagues' souls."[87]

The Final Vote

The preliminary vote did not necessarily mean that the bill would pass the House. The bill's chief advocate explained that "there are people who will move along because they think it is the fairest thing to do, to allow a bill to get its most mature state of consideration but then who reserve the right to vote against it in the final vote. This was clearly a vote like that."[88] Indeed, "at least three lawmakers who voted yes [on the preliminary vote] were still undecided but wanted to keep the bill alive for more discussion the next day."[89]

The day after the House voted initial approval of the bill, the chamber debated it again and voted on it again. More hostile amendments were offered, and all were fended off.[90] One amendment would require anyone applying for a domestic partnership license to be tested for HIV, and a same-sex couple would "be allowed to enter a civil union only if they both tested positive or both tested negative."[91] Rep. Nancy Sheltra, a proponent of the amendment argued that testing was necessary to protect homosexuals "from their own epidemic of AIDS."[92] The amendment was defeated 136 to 2.[93] Rep. Sheltra "rose several times during the day to offer antigay rhetoric and statistics."[94]

After 17 hours of debate over the two days, the House prepared for the final vote.[95] The *Burlington Free Press* reported

> William Lippert didn't quite know what he was going to say when he stood up in the House chamber for one last speech Thursday night.

Lippert, a Democrat from Hinesburg and the only openly gay law-maker in Vermont, told his colleagues that they had nothing to fear from giving the rights and benefits of marriage to gays and lesbians.

"We are not a threat," Lippert said. "As you continue to get to know us, you will overcome your fear. . . ."

Then he recalled how, as a child, he would sit at the dinner table with his minister father and read the Bible. Plenty of Bible verses had been thrown around during the past two days as the House debated "civil unions" for same-sex couples, he said, but one verse stuck with him the most.

"Love thy neighbor as thyself," Lippert said. "We are your neighbors. We are worth loving. We will love in return. This is a good thing. Vermont does not have reason to fear."

As Lippert finished, many of his colleagues were in tears. No one else stood to speak. And the House voted 76-69 on a bill that would create civil unions.[96]

The margin of victory was smaller than on the previous day—seven votes as opposed to eleven—but the change was due to only a single defection. One lawmaker switched his vote from "yes" to "no."[97] Others missed the final vote for medical reasons, including a representative "who fell down the stairs at the House speaker's podium in the morning and broke her leg."[98]

As the final vote was tallied, the crowd erupted. The Speaker banged his gavel to no apparent effect. He banged it harder. He banged it until the gavel's head came off.

The House's action was a lead story on the front page of the *New York Times* for two consecutive days.[99] The *Times* also editorialized in favor of the vote.[100]

THE SENATE JUDICIARY COMMITTEE

I'm wondering how many times we have to say that [the civil unions partnership bill] is not marriage. . . . The House overwhelmingly rejected marriage. . . . It's now in the bill twice. . . . How many times do we have to say "No, [it's not marriage]"?

—Sen. Richard Sears, Chair, Senate Judiciary Committee, April 3, 2000[101]

Shortly after the final vote of the full House, supporters of the civil unions bill predicted that the Senate would follow suit.[102] However, "anyone who thought the Senate Judiciary Committee would simply rubber-stamp" the House bill "was wrong."[103]

If the Senate were to pass the bill at all, "it [was] likely to be modified along the way."[104] In fact, three factors made the bill especially vulnerable in the Senate. The first was numerical: Thirty Senators, as opposed to 150 members of the House of Representatives, presented a smaller and more focused target against which opponents could direct their resources. Second, the Senate, unlike the House, was empowered to propose amendments to the Vermont Constitution. Third, the Senators would be grappling with the bill closer to election time.

The first day that the Senate Judiciary Committee officially had the bill before them, two members of the six-member committee said they could not support a domestic partnership bill.[105] Instead, they said they would support a constitutional amendment prohibiting same-sex marriage. One of the two Senators explained: "I'm trying to articulate in a constitutional framework what I've heard from my constituents. . . . I'm sympathetic to domestic partnership. My constituents aren't. If there's a choice between what they want and what I want, they win."[106]

In an interview given during the committee's first week of hearings on the issue, the committee's chairman acknowledged that "the pressure has been tremendous on my committee."[107] The chairman noted that passage in the Senate was "not assured" and that "everyone has assumed there are 16 or 17 votes in the Senate . . . I don't assume that at all. I think it's not a done deal. I think it's unfortunate that the impression was left after the House vote, that it was law and just waiting for the governor to sign."[108]

Two post-*Baker* amendments to the Vermont constitution were proposed to the Senate Judiciary Committee. One amendment would add to the constitution a definition of marriage as a union between a man and a woman. This amendment, if enacted, would not overrule *Baker*. It would also not be inconsistent with the domestic partnership bill that passed the House. What it would do is prevent the supreme court (or the legislature) in the future from requiring that same-sex couples have a state-law right to marry.

Another proposed amendment to the Vermont constitution was intended to overrule *Baker*. Proposed by Senator Vincent Illuzzi, this amendment would define marriage as a man and a woman and also would change the constitution to allow the legislature—and only the legislature—to confer the rights and benefits associated with marriage.[109]

Lobbying against legal recognition of same-sex couples did not abate when the issue moved from the House to the Senate. "Public interest in the issue remain[ed] high, and the [Senate Judiciary Committee's] first meeting was thronged, primarily by people wearing white ribbons who describe themselves as supporters of traditional marriage between a man and a woman."[110] The "extent of the Senate's interest in modifying [the House bill], and the pressure some Senators feel to change it, become apparent for the first time [at the first meeting] in a cramped meeting room off the cafeteria."[111] Lobbying on the domestic partnership bill in the Senate had "been heavy and it appear[ed] to be growing ever more intense" as the Senate Judiciary Committee began studying the bill.[112]

The Ad War

The advertising campaign also intensified. One advertisement occupied an entire page of the newspaper.[113] Across the top of the page, a one-inch bold headline declared "House Passes Gay Marriage."[114] In somewhat smaller boldface type, the ad said that "The Following Legislators Voted Against Traditional Values" and then followed with a list of the House who had voted for the domestic partnership bill[115] (only 22 of the 76 listed in the ad actually voted for same-sex marriage). The bottom of the page of the *Burlington Free Press*'s version of the ad claimed that "The Future of Your Children and Grandchildren Is Now in the Hands of 30 Vermont Senators and the Governor. . . . You must call your Senator at home, telephone them at the State House, fax them or go visit them in person! . . . We need your help!"[116] The ad also included a graphic of a duck and a notation that the advertisement was sponsored by "Vermonters for Traditional Marriage, A Committee to Take It To The People."[117]

Take It To The People ran other ads as well. One half-page blared "We Don't Want Same-Sex Marriage/And We Won't Back Down."[118] And: "This *Is* Marriage's Eleventh Hour, and The People of Vermont Demand a Voice."[119] The ad declared:

> **Now, *we'll* vote *our* conscience.**
> A majority of Vermonters has said it loud and clear:
> We don't want homosexual marriage.
> We want the benefits of marriage to be kept solely for the union of one man and one woman.
> The Governor says we don't understand.

And last week, 79 Legislators defied the will of the people by voting to give homosexual and lesbian couples all the rights and benefits of marriage.

They said they were *voting their consciences.*

Well, now it's time that we claim the right to vote *our consciences* on this all-important question as well.

A Constitutional Amendment: The Only Way.

A vote by The People: It's a guaranteed part of the Constitutional Amendment process. And it's the *only* way we can make our voices heard.

But it *won't* happen unless we make it happen.

And time is short.

We must get the Vermont Senate to approve the Constitutional Amendment to Preserve Marriage NOW, then pass it to the House for approval—before this legislative session ends in a few short weeks.

Then, Vermonters can have their say.

If we fail, there won't be another chance until 2003.

And by then, it's safe to assume that marriage in Vermont, as we know it today, will be gone forever.

Don't doubt what you know. If you've already called your Legislators on this issue, *call again now.* Save marriage for our children's generation, and for those to come.[120]

The ad included a graphic of an hourglass winding down with the caption "Marriage: The Eleventh Hour."[121] The ad instructed readers to "cut out and tape this hour-glass symbol to the side of your home or car window, to show friends and neighbors you've taken a stand to save traditional marriage."[122] At least this symbol of Take It To The People didn't look like a children's toy.

These weren't the ads that had Governor Dean on TV sputtering— literally sputtering—with rage. Waving an advertisement that listed Dean's "name at the top of a newspaper advertisement" that "linked him with support for pedophelia, providing contraceptives to children, and public funding of artificial insemination for lesbians—an advertisement he called 'perfectly asinine.'"[123] The ads were placed in the *Burlington Free Press* and in the *Rutland Herald.*[124] "'What's Howard Dean's Next Item?,' the ad in the *Herald* headlined. It listed the status of the 'homosexual agenda,' including legalizing 'all forms of sexual expression: sodomy; pedophelia/sex with children.'"[125]

The Associated Press observed on March 24, 2000, that the "ad campaign was just the latest example of how the debate over granting the same rights and benefits of marriage is becoming increasingly nasty."[126] And "more ads [were] on deck."[127]

A week later, the same organization ran another advertisement. This ad, bordered in black (It looked a bit like a Florida death warrant) said:

WHAT HAS HOWARD DEAN PLANNED
FOR YOUR CHILDREN?

Paying for homosexual indoctrination
in your schools with your money!

He recommended giving $12,000 of your taxes to "Outright Vermont," to help them do an even better job in your schools to achieve the acceptance of homosexual behavior by the most innocent of our little children!

This is just some of what your $12,000 will do to your children:

Reeducation on gender identity, and asking kids to "come out."
Telling kids religious faith is ritualistic abuse.
Telling them that being normal is "heterosexism."
Telling the schools all the wonderful laws his administration supported
    to insure that homosexuals could have their way with your children.[128]

Randall Terry's group, called "Loyal Opposition" also ran ads. One half-page ad, headlined in huge white type on a black background, was headlined "Vermonters: Beyond the Rhetoric, Lie the Facts."[129] The following text appeared in boldface: "THIS BILL LEGALIZES HOMO-SEXUAL MARRIAGE! Do our legislators really think we are that stupid?... The following area Representatives refused to adhere to the will of the People of Vermont and brazenly rejected the wishes of their constituents and VOTED FOR HOMOSEXUAL MARRIAGE! Call them at home and voice your displeasure."[130] The ad then provided the home phone numbers of 15 Representatives—along with the home phone numbers of all 30 Senators. The ad went on (also in boldface): "THE FACT IS THIS. These representatives were put into office to represent you.... IF THEY WILL NOT CHANGE THEIR VOTE ON THIS ISSUE, WE MUST VOTE THEM OUT OF OFFICE IN NOVEMBER AND WE SHOULD TELL THEM SO NOW!!! CALL NOW!!! ... We can win this battle and preserve decency and morality, BUT NOW IS THE TIME FOR VIGOROUS ACTION TO BE TAKEN."[131]

The other side ran ads too. These ads were moderate in tone and accurate in content. The Vermont Freedom to Marry Action Committee, for instance, ran an advertisement headlined "The Truth About the Civil Union Bill."[132] The ad noted that the House bill was "a compromise between those who sought full inclusion for same-sex couples in the marriage laws and those who opposed extending any civil rights to gay and lesbian couples."[133] The heart of the ad was a series of five bullet points. The first bullet point was that the bill "Specifically excludes gay couples from marrying by saying that *'marriage means the legally recognized union of one man and one woman.'* "[134]

There was also the mail blitz. In a six-day period, the Lieutenant Governor and the Speaker of the House (both of whom had at one time supported same-sex marriage) had received 10,000 postcards advocating against same-sex marriage or domestic partnerships.[135] A spokesman for the organization that generated the postcards said he had printed "a million" and "may print more."[136]

A Williston minister, working with a Washington, D.C. group, mailed letters to more than 81,000 Vermonters.[137] I received the unsolicited mailing urging me to send in postcards opposing domestic partnership as well as same-sex marriage. One such letter came to my home on April 2:

Reverend D.A. Stertzbach
March 30, 2000

Dear Vermont voter,

As you read this, the Vermont Senate is planning to give homosexual couples the same legal status as marriage. God's sacred covenant between a man and woman will be replaced by Vermont's celebration of same-sex "unions."

Only your immediate action will stop them.

Since the Vermont Supreme Court stood morality on its head by insisting that our state give homosexuals rights reserved to married couples, politicians have thrown their hands up and cried out they have no choice but to do as the court instructs.

That's a cowardly lie.

Weak-minded politicians in the state House already caved in to the Supreme Court and radical Homosexual Lobby. But the Senate still must pass H. 847 (and the Governor sign), the so-called "Civil Union" bill creating a parallel marriage track.

If you will speak out now—by sending the enclosed postcards to your Senator and Governor Dean, or better yet writing a personal letter—we can derail this homosexual powergrab. You'll find your Senator's name printed just above your own on the enclosed envelope.

Instead of destroying traditional morality and teaching our children that homosexuality is just another "lifestyle choice," Senators should pass a Constitutional Amendment to define marriage as a union between a man and woman—and to explicitly ban any form of "Union" for homosexuals.

The Amendment must originate in the Senate, and requires four votes over four years, then the Governor's signature, and finally a popular vote.

It won't be easy, but it's the only answer that protects marriage—the fundamental building block of our society.

The radical Homosexual Lobby has wasted no time in ramming their radical agenda through the system in near-record time.

That's why your Senator needs to hear from you this week.

The first order of business is to reject the pro-homosexual "Civil Union" bill, H. 847.

You see, the court has no authority to write laws.

But most Senators need a good solid jolt of voter fury to stiffen their spines and convince them that if they do not reject pro-homosexual bills their jobs will be on the line.

Every politician fears the wrath of the voters.

If you and I can bury the Senate in an avalanche of outrage, we can stop the "Civil Union" bill dead in its tracks.

Then we can start working on the Constitutional Amendment.

But I can't do it alone.

Your help is absolutely vital to the project's success.

That's why I hope and pray that today—right now—you'll fill out the enclosed postcards and mail them to your Senator and to Governor Dean. I've enclosed extra cards for your friends, neighbors and family.

Even better, write a letter of your own expressing your outrage at what the radical homosexuals are trying to do.

Also please return the attached reply memo so I'll know how many cards and letters have been sent. That crucial information will help me lobby the politicians much more effectively.

And if at all possible, please consider making a contribution of $25, $50, $100—whatever you can afford—to help me put this lobbying program together and make it effective.

But most important, please sign and send your postcards or personal letters today. Thank you.

Sincerely,
/ss
Reverent D.A. Stertzbach

P.S. If you and I don't act now the Vermont Senate is going to create a system of "Civil Union" for homosexuals. Only your action will stop them.

Please sign and mail the attached postcards to your Senator and Governor Dean (or better yet send a personal letter) demanding that they reject the pro-homosexual bills and initiate a Constitutional Amendment to protect the sanctity of marriage. Let them know their jobs are on the line.

Your Senator's name is printed on the reply envelope just above your name.[138]

The letters to the editor continued as well. For example, on April 5, 2000, the *Valley News* newspaper published two letters on the issue. This was the first:

To the Editor:
Well, we have done it again—or I should say, our elected leaders have done it. They have chosen to degrade the lifestyle that has been established for thousands of years by telling homosexuals that their lifestyle is an OK thing to do. Our own governor has even said in public that he will support the bill being passed by our elected leaders in Montpelier.

It's pretty clear that we need new leadership. That our elected leaders will support a deviant lifestyle and call it civil rights is pretty pathetic. That these deviant people can speak of Martin King, Jr. and John Fitzgerald Kennedy in the same breath as they speak of their rights is truly appalling. Civil rights were granted to all the minorities many years ago. There is no civil rights being violated here; quite the contrary.

Many who have written to this paper have quoted the Scripture in support of disallowing these people the same rights enjoyed by people who have a "regular marriage." They make a good case. However, instead of quoting regular Scripture verses, why don't we simply look at the big page. And by this I mean Revelations, the last chapter of the New Testament. All these things are prophesied. We as a people can prevent these prophesies from coming to pass if we will clean up our act, to put it bluntly. If we would follow the steps of West Virginia and disallow all same-sex marriage, we would be a step ahead of the game.

If these people want to live together, that's their thing. But to expect the rest of the world to accept them as regular people is another. Wake up, people. What is wrong with good old-fashioned virtue? When are we going to realize that we are walking into a trap, cleverly set by this deviant part of our population?

It's clear to this writer who I am going to support for governor, and it will be Ruth Dwyer. She doesn't go for this stuff, either. It's about time Vermonters took a stand and abolished this sort of behavior. What sort of leaders do we have who will condone behavior that goes against the grain of all that we have been brought up to believe? I'll tell you what we have: A weak bunch of politicians who won't stand up for what they know is really right.

If the people of Vermont who claim to be real Vermonters stand up and be counted, we will vote out of office every one who voted "yes" on this bill. So, for all you real Vermonters, fight this bill on same-sex anything, and vote these people out of office, and that includes our governor. Are we mice, or are we real Vermonters?[139]

This was the other letter:

To the Editor:
I was born a Vermonter. More important, I was born an American. As I watch the government of Vermont working to tear at the very foundation on which the nation was built, I become angry. While I do oppose gay marriage in any form, this is not what I wish to write about. When I think abut the extreme sacrifices made by early patriots to give us the chance to establish a government by the people, I wonder how we can stand by while those in power undermine the system.

Ours is a system of checks and balances. It is for the people—not elected officials—to vote according to the dictates of their conscience. Elected officials are supposed to represent the people. Read the Vermont Constitution! The high court has set itself up as a governing body, while the legislature has decided to ignore the people. The job of the Supreme Court is to interpret the original intent of the framers of the law, not to respond to the mood of the interest groups and sway to the winds.

In the case of marriage, there can be no doubt that the original framers meant man and woman. Just read the state constitution and sense the mood of the authors, or study a little history. Worse, the court mandated that the legislature enact a law and even gave guidance about its wording. When the court makes laws (and in essence that is exactly what they are doing) we no longer have freedom. We are being governed by a few non-elected people who have an indefinite term of office. This is not the first time the court has mandated laws. Remember school funding. I would also have you note that when New Hampshire saw the success of the court mandate in Vermont, its court also tried it. Is this what we want—rule by the state Supreme Court?

I find it unbelievable that the legislature and the governor, in the face of the overwhelming public outcry, have vowed to pass legislation that we the people of the state of Vermont do not want. Who allowed these people to have so little fear of the populace? We did. We tolerated legislative action we did not want; we kept quiet.

Well, quiet time is over. Many people fought and died for this type of government. I've only one voice and one vote, but I will make it heard! If people want to change the marriage laws by constitutional amendment and the people vote to support that change, fine. But for the court to dictate to the legislature, the governor and the people is a vast breach of the trust placed in all of us by our founding fathers and patriots.[140]

Even before the March ad and postcard wars, the amounts of money lobbying spent by both sides of the same-sex unions debate "outstrip[ped] those reported by any of the hundreds of other companies and groups"[141] that filed their lobbying reports filed on March 24, 2000. Activists on both sides had spent more than $100,000.[142] Two opposition groups spent more than $40,000,[143] as did one organization supporting the House bill. By contrast, "for example, prescription drug prices were a big issue in the State Senate, but the Pharmaceutical Researchers and Manufacturers of America reported spending only $12,500."[144] These "reports didn't cover costs from March, when groups on both sides of the issue bought many newspaper advertisements urging people to call their legislators."[145]

Randall Terry said he planned to spend more than $10,000 in an ad campaign.[146] "Newspapers' ads are pretty effective in terms of getting people to actually call their legislators," Terry reportedly said.[147]

The Committee

Meanwhile, back in the legislature, the day after the House gave final approval to the civil unions bill, the Senate began working on its own response to *Baker*. Unlike the House, the Senate Judiciary Committee did not even consider whether same-sex couples ought to be allowed to marry. Within hours of the House vote, the President Pro Tem of the Senate had "ruled out same-sex marriage as a possibility. 'We are not going back to the marriage question.'"[148] The day after the House vote, the Senate Judiciary Committee made it official, deciding unanimously "to pursue the same course as the House. It will not draft a bill opening the marriage statutes to gay and lesbian couples. Instead, it will seek to create an equivalent legal status, which the House chose to call civil unions."[149]

In the Senate, as in the House before it, marriage was off the table as a concession to "political reality." Removing marriage as an option was designed to send a message to opponents of any kind of legal recognition of same-sex couples. The chairman of the Senate Judiciary "said he believed the [unanimous vote taking marriage off the table in the Senate] was an important statement to his own constituents and to opponents of gay marriage. 'I hope it tells them that whatever we're working on will be a domestic partnership bill, but marriage won't happen in the State of Vermont,'" said the chairman.[150]

This senatorial preemptive strike occurred while the Senate girded for combat. The day of the final House vote, the President Pro Tem of the Senate said, "I have a lot of anxiety about it. . . . I am very concerned about how this issue has torn the state apart. I want to bring people together, and I'm not sure I'll be able to do that."[151] The president expected the Senate to become "a clear target for opponents. 'I expect things to get much more intense as it comes over to the Senate. . . . I've told the members to get ready.'"[152] The Chairman of the Senate Judiciary Committee had taken other precautions as well: "I have asked that a member of the security staff be with us in the room when we meet" the chairman "told the other five members of the committee. He said he wasn't worried about the senators' safety but about preventing any disruptions that could slow their work."[153]

On its first day of hearings, the Senate Judiciary Committee received testimony from one of the plaintiffs in *Baker*. It was the first time any of the six *Baker* plaintiffs had "told lawmakers their views on how to grant same-sex couples the rights and benefits of marriage."[154] All but one of the plaintiffs were present during the testimony, which was described by the Associated Press's Ross Sneyd:

> Celebrating their eighth anniversary Wednesday, Nina Beck and Stacy Jolles spent their morning at the State House.
>
> Beck told the Senate Judiciary Committee in tearful testimony of their fervent desire for the state to legally recognize their relationship and therefore confer on their family the rights and benefits granted to opposite-sex couples.
>
> "Stacy and I have been through everything a couple can imagine," Beck told the senators as Jolles sat in the audience rocking their infant. "We share a deep love for each other, have shared in the joy of the birth of our two children, and the devastating grief at the loss of our firstborn. We survived that loss because of the strength of the bond between us and in no small part because of the vows we exchanged eight years ago."
>
> . . .
>
> Wednesday's testimony was the first time senators have been confronted so personally with the desire for legal recognition that same-sex couples are seeking.

Beck put that desire in the most human terms, detailing how she and Jolles met 10 years ago, fell in love, and ultimately had a religious commitment ceremony on March 22, 1991.

"But then, as now, despite our spiritual union, Stacy and I have no legal bond to each other," Beck said. "The ramifications of this are far-reaching and affect our lives every day."

Beck gave birth in 1995 to her and Jolles' first son. Beck detailed how they had to produce power of attorney papers when she had to be unexpectedly taken to the hospital during that first pregnancy.

"If we had been legally married, these privileges would have been granted automatically," Beck said.

She brought tears to the eyes of many in the hearing room when she explained how little Noah, at 2? years old, needed a heart transplant because of a rare heart disease. But the boy died after six weeks of hospitalization, just after the lawsuit was filed in which Beck and Jolles unsuccessfully sought a marriage license from the South Burlington city clerk.

Beck since has given birth to another son, Seth, whom Jolles cradled during the testimony. Jolles has had to formally adopt both boys to be recognized as their legal parent.

So Beck asked the committee to provide her and Jolles, and gay and lesbian families across the state, access to the rights that automatically flow to couples who may marry.

"Civil marriage can strengthen the fabric of our society as it protects and nurtures the bonds between a couple and a family," she said. "Civil marriage is currently the only construct by which these benefits are granted in our society. Without access to this system, we are denied any legal recognition of our unions and of our families. Without legal recognition, we are vulnerable."

It remains to be seen what the Legislature might offer Beck and Jolles. The House bill stops short of marriage, but would provide the benefits they seek. Their lawyers say they remain convinced that the only way to provide same-sex couples true equality would be to allow them to marry.

That prompted Sen. John Bloomer, R-Rutland, to question why the Senate was even considering the House bill. "If we're going to spend six weeks here to have nothing more than another civil suit, I would personally want to reevaluate the use of my time," he said.

Lawyer Beth Robinson said, however, that the Freedom to Marry Task Force would not sue if the civil unions bill were enacted into law.

"The freedom to marry community supports this bill as a step to equity," Robinson said.[155]

The Senate Judiciary Committee also heard from the Chairman of the House Judiciary Committee, the chief advocate for the House's comprehensive civil unions bill. The House chairman told his Senate counterparts that he "believ[ed] the [House] bill would satisfy the supreme court's mandate. Though society might look at married couples differently from those united by civil unions, he said, the committee's job was to address civil rights under law, not societal perceptions. It could take generations before Vermonters view marriages in the same light as civil unions, he said. 'Vermont needs some time to grow into that level of acceptance' [the House chairman] said. 'As the events of the last three months have shown, this is of paramount interest to Vermonters. Words are important. Symbols are important.'"[156]

In addition, the Senate committee received testimony by one of their colleagues who had proposed a constitutional amendment barring same-sex marriage.[157] The Senator argued that "civil rights should not be judged by lifestyle or sexual behavior" and that "the vast majority of . . . constituents support traditional marriage and feel threatened by level recognition of same-sex unions."[158] The committee also heard from Take It To The People, which reminded the Senators about the results of the Town Meeting Day votes.

The Judiciary Committee also heard from Vermont Law School Professor Gil Kujovich, an expert on constitutional law. Senator Vincent Illuzzi pressed Kujovich on whether he supported the *Baker* decision.[159] "Kujovich responded that it was within a reasonable legal interpretation of the Common Benefits Clause. Senator Illuzzi came back with, 'do you, or do you not, support the *Baker* decision?' Kujovich firmly stated, 'I do not have a position.'"[160]

Kujovich also warned the Senators that any legal differences between civil unions and marriages would render the former vulnerable to constitutional challenge. Such vulnerability would be increased if the differences between unions and marriages were motivated by animus toward homosexuals.[161] He counseled that the legislation would be safer if justified by the protection of traditional marriage rather than by hostility toward same-sex couples.[162]

The Senate Judiciary Committee, as had its House counterpart earlier, heard testimony from leadership of Vermont communities of faith and, as before, religious leaders did not speak with a single voice.[163] Vermont's Catholic Bishop Kenneth Angell reiterated "his strong opposition to conferring the rights and benefits of marriage on same-sex couples regardless of whether it's short of the full marriage that gays and lesbians sought. 'Do not let the court or anyone else push you around,' Angell told the Judiciary Committee. 'You have no duty, moral or constitutional, to weaken the institution of marriage. If the court thinks otherwise, then let the people overrule the court. This is the United States of America. We are not ruled by kings, whether on a throne or in a courtroom."[164]

Vermont's bishop also restated that the "Catholic church believes the only appropriate response to the court's ruling is a constitutional amendment defining marriage as a union between a man and a woman. Angell suggested an amendment that he said would restore to the legislature 'the rightful authority to regulate marriage, and to make your own best judgment about other questions.'"

The "Jericho Walk"

On April 6, 2000, the opponents of the civil unions bill converged on the statehouse. Organized by Rep. Nancy Sheltra—the House member who had tried to persuade her colleagues to amend the bill to require all homosexuals wishing to enter into a partnership to be tested for AIDS—the featured speakers were Randall Terry and Republican presidential candidate Alan Keyes.

The 150 demonstrators gathered on the Statehouse steps at 8:00 A.M.[165] A pastor said a prayer: "We're in spiritual warfare, a warfare not against flesh and blood but against principalities and the powers of darkness."[166] And, he prayed: "We are asking God to intervene. We are recognizing the need of him in our state."[167]

Keyes gave his speech to an enthusiastic "howling crowd."[168] Keyes "drew parallels between homosexuality and rape, pedophelia, and adultery. 'So shall we have to forgo all discrimination against all adulterers now? Shall we forgo all discrimination against people who exploit children? Shall we forgo all discrimination against rapists and people of this kind?'"[169] Keyes continued, "'When you've legitimized pedophelia, you've legitimized polyandry.' Polyandry is the practice of having more than one male mate at a time."[170] When Keyes gave a lecture later, he "was interrupted repeatedly with cheers and at least four standing ovations as he delivered roughly the same message to an overflow crowd approaching 400 people."[171] "Keyes came to Vermont at the request of [Senator John Bloomer], and state GOP chairman Patrick Garahan."[172] Randall Terry introduced Keyes to the crowd of protesters, "and the two men hugged before Keyes began his speech, warning about the moral decay the legislature was going to visit on the state and the nation."[173] For those who missed Keyes's remarks live, the Baptist Fellowship Church of Randolph showed a video of the event every week night—for 10 weeks—[174] while the legislature dealt with the domestic partnership bill.

Randall Terry "encouraged protesters to seek out senators and make it clear that a vote in favor of the bill would be a ticket out of office. 'I have a message for some of those senators,' Terry said. . . . 'Prepare for an early retirement. We will remember in November. You and Governor Dean can go play golf somewhere. . . . As long as evil people are in office in this building, you are going to continue to see evil legislation.'"[175]

The marchers—carrying a large sign reading "Stop Civil Unions: Impeach Supreme Court Judges"—[176] also did a "Jericho Walk." They "circled the state Supreme Court and governor's office and climbed the statehouse steps seven times, blowing a ram's horn [a *shofar*] with each circuit—an allusion to the biblical story of Joshua whose followers circled Jericho seven times and blew a ram's horn in order to bring the walls of that city tumbling down."[177] Although the walls of Montpelier remained intact, the sky did "fill with clouds" and an April snow "began falling."[178]

The news accounts of the protest rally included photographs. There were the thuddingly predicable shots of Rep. Nancy Sheltra wagging her finger and of Alan Keyes speaking into a microphone.[179] For me, however, the saddest photo was of a father standing on the steps of the statehouse with three of his young sons, John, Joel, and James.[180]

John, who appeared to be around twelve years old, carried a sign that read "Civil Rights??!!!! Not!!!" Son Joel, around eight or nine years of age, carried a sign that read "NO Same Sex Marriage." So did son James, who seemed about eight or nine years old. Next to James, a person held a sign that read "NO Gay Education in Our School."[181]

Car Wars

The militia is preparing to overthrow you faggot lovers—with any force necessary.

—A handwritten note, left on the car windshield of Rep. Marilyn Rivero[182]

Automobiles and their occupants seemed to be targets of choice for some opponents of civil unions. In April 2000, the Associated Press reported that "several lawmakers have turned in their House license plates, saying they are tired of rude gestures thrown their way since the civil union bill was passed."[183] The article reported that, within the preceding week, three members of the House had "traded in the plates that include the 'House' moniker in exchange for ordinary numbered plates."[184] One representative said "you get it at a traffic light; sometimes they yell at you. . . . You get a few fingers, you think, 'Jeez, what happens when I leave the car parked downtown for a few hours."[185]

The cars of "at least six lawmakers [had] been vandalized [in the first four months of the year]."[186] One member of the House of Representatives "came out of a cancer survivors' support meeting to find all the car windows smashed."[187]

Although it was not clear whether the vandalism was in response to the same-sex unions bill, the Sergeant-at-Arms of the House "said that in some cases, it was likely. 'It always happens to some degree, but it's kind of getting to the point where it's hard to say it's just a coincidence.'"[188] One House member, "an avid trout fisherman, said he removed the legislative license plates because he was concerned his car would be vandalized while parked near one of his favorite fishing holes."[189]

The abuse did not distinguish between supporters and opponents of the bill. Both "have been on the receiving end of insults and obscene gestures."[190] One opponent, who changed his House license plate, "joked that he would get a bumper sticker that said, 'Don't blame me, I voted no.'"[191] Ho, ho, ho.

Some legislators feared not only for their cars. "A few lawmakers" exchanged their legislative license plates because they were "worried about threats of violence."[192] A member of the House "returned to her car in a Burlington parking garage and found a threatening message attached to the windshield. 'The militia is preparing to overthrow you faggot lovers—with any force necessary,' the anonymous hand-lettered note read.'"[193]

The Bill

To grant homosexuals all the substance of marriage while denying them the institution is, in some ways, a purer form of bigotry than denying them any rights at all. It is to devise a pseudoinstitution to both erase inequality and at the same time perpetuate it. . . . There is in fact no argument for a domestic partnership compromise except that maintenance of stigma is an important social value.

—Editorial, *New Republic*, 2000[194]

On Tuesday, April 10, after hearing three weeks of testimony, the Chairman of the Senate Judiciary Committee presented two proposed drafts of the Senate bill.[195] The only difference between the bills was the name given to the marriage substitute. One bill called the system "civil unions," as the House bill had done. "The other would shift back to a system that some argued carries more meaning with the public: domestic partnerships."[196]

Other than the more politically palatable name change to "domestic partnerships," the proposed Senate bills would have an effective date of eight months later than the House bill. Most importantly, the Senate bill "would ban out-of-state gays and lesbians from entering into civil unions in Vermont if such arrangements were illegal in their home states."[197] The Chairman explained that moving the effective date would allow state agencies to issue the requisite regulations, and that the residency requirement would parallel a similar requirements in the state's marriage laws.[198]

Beth Robinson, one of the lead counsel for the *Baker* plaintiffs, objected to all three proposed changes. Changing the name from "civil union" to "domestic partnership" would not be appropriate because "'civil union is a term that a large percentage of gays and lesbians have embraced,'" she said.[199] Robinson "also objected to the idea of waiting [eight additional months] for the civil unions bill to take effect. During that delay, she said, same-sex couples would be denied some of the legal rights and benefits that the Vermont Supreme Court said were guaranteed by the state constitution. People could die or become ill in the next eight months and their partners would be without the legal protections the bill was meant to provide, she said."[200]

As to the proposed residency requirement, Robinson objected that it was discriminatory and unconstitutional. Robinson said "that the residency requirement would set up a situation where opposite-sex couples from other states were being encouraged to come to Vermont to get married, but same-sex couples were being told they were not welcome."[201]

Robinson "said the residency requirement would put Vermont in the position of upholding similar discrimination on behalf of other states.

Robinson said if other states still prohibited interracial marriage, Vermont would not want to deny such couples the right to marry here because it would violate the state constitution. The residency requirement, she said, 'seeks to make Vermont an agent of unconstitutional discrimination' by other states. 'It's unconstitutional. . . .'"[202]

By contrast, opponents hailed the residency requirement. A board member of Take It To The People said " 'there is welcome attention being paid to the issue of residency for civil unions'. . . . His organization has been concerned that out-of-state homosexual couples would flock to Vermont to get civil union licenses and then try to force recognition of their unions in other states."[203]

Then, in a move that surprised some observers, on Tuesday, April 11, the Senate Judiciary Committee voted to send to the full Senate a proposed constitutional amendment that was intended to overturn the *Baker* decision. The proposed amendment, offered by Senator Vincent Illuzzi, "would strip the power of the Supreme Court to rule, as it did [in *Baker*] that same-sex couples have a right to the legal benefits and protections of marriage."[204]

As discussed above, the committee had before it two proposed constitutional amendments. One would simply have defined marriage as a union between a man and a woman. This amendment, which would not have overruled *Baker*, was defeated unanimously by the committee.[205] Illuzzi's amendment was designed to overrule *Baker* by adding to the constitution language that the "General Assembly shall define the legal benefits and responsibilities associated with marriage. No provision of this Constitution shall be held to require that any such benefits and responsibilities be extended by the General Assembly or the judiciary to any grouping of people other than one man and one woman."[EN[206]

Oddly, the committee voted to send the proposed amendment to the full Senate without a recommendation that the Senate either adopt it or reject it.[207] " 'I feel like I've fallen into Alice in Wonderland,' a visibly angry [Senator John Bloomer] said. 'It's very absurd for us to be introducing a proposal and then voting it out adversely.' The committee ultimately decided against making an adverse recommendation, which would have meant it was suggesting that the Senate reject the amendment."[208]

The committee's vote to send the amendment to the full Senate was 5-1, and that vote "came after hours of acrimonious debate within the committee, as well as plenty of hallway huddles and note-passing as Senate President Pro Tempore Peter Shumlin tried to orchestrate a way to bring the measure to the Senate floor with a minimum of fighting. 'I was trying to find a way to get a constitutional amendment out of a committee that did not want to amend the Constitution,' Shumlin said later. 'I'm trying to get everything on the table' by the day the full Senate would take up the issue." Thus, the committee voted 5-1 to "have the proposed constitutional amendment debated in the full Senate— even though four of the six committee members don't support the amendment."[209]

Until the day of the committee vote, "it appeared the committee would not vote to bring a constitutional amendment to the floor because most members opposed both [of the proposed amendments]. However, some Republicans threatened to try to force a vote. Rather than have a fight over that, Senate leaders agreed to bring out a proposal that could be debated in the full Senate."[210]

"Then the jockeying began over which proposal to debate. Some Republicans [had] been maneuvering to have a vote just on adding the marriage definition to the Constitution. They believe if Democrats vote against such an amendment, it [would] show that they really support same-sex marriage. Democrats, on the other hand, would like to have a vote on Illuzzi's amendment. That vote, they believe, [would] reveal the people who are opposed to providing legal benefits to gay and lesbian couples."[211]

The same day the Senate Judiciary Committee decided to send to the full Senate the proposed constitutional amendment to overrule *Baker*, four senators and four representatives held an open public meeting in Franklin County.[212] "More than 500 people filled the Bellows Free Academy audience" in "a raucous and emotional meeting that at times became openly hostile" and in which "people frequently jeered and cheered."[213]

"One opponent threatened civil disobedience if gays and lesbians were afforded equal rights."[214] A town clerk "said civil unions were the same as marriage and it would 'violate [his] conscience' to issue a license for it."[215] (Another town clerk said he would happily issue such licenses.)[216]

At the meeting, "emotions ran so high—especially among opponents of rights for same-sex couples—that several times the audience had to be admonished the rights of others to speak."[217] Rep. William Lippert "felt compelled to interrupt the proceedings to ask for cooperation. 'I apologize; I'm not from this community,' he said, as the audience hushed to dead silence. 'It is very difficult for all the people . . . to respond when something you say is jeered or cheered."[218]

As one representative defended his vote for the civil unions bill, "he was interrupted several times and booed."[219] A senator was "cheered heartily by his supporters" when he said he supported a constitutional amendment."[220]

In the end, the bill voted out of the Senate Judiciary Committee contained none of the proposed changes. The name remained "civil unions."[221] The residency requirement was deleted.[222] With the exception of a few areas, the effective date was actually moved up to July 1. The Senate bill was functionally identical to the House bill.

The vote was 4-2.[223] Committee member (and Senate Republican Leader) John Bloomer and Vincent Illuzzi voted against the bill. Senator Bloomer said, "The bill is very close to the House bill, and it's very close to marriage, so I can't support it. . . . As elected officials, we're supposed to be responsive to our constituents. My constituents are not supportive of the bill, because they believe it's too close to marriage."[224]

The vote split along party lines. All four Democrats on the Committee voted for the bill, and both Republicans voted against it.[225] A Take It To The People lobbyist noted the partisan nature of the vote: "I think the majority spoke. . . . It happened to be all Democrats. I think it's becoming more and more strange why it's always Democrats."[226]

The Senate's minor changes to the House bill, while insignificant to the substance of the proposed legislation, were significant politically. If the Senate simply adopted the House's version, then the bill would not go back before the House.[227] However, if the Senate changed the bill in any way, then the revised bill would need to win majority approval by the House.[228] Given the narrowness of the House's initial approval (by only a four-vote margin), and the fragility of the House coalition that produced that narrow victory,[229] sending a revised bill might well not survive a House vote.

THE FULL SENATE

Shadow Boxing

The Senate Judiciary Committee's 4-2 vote on the bill occurred on a Wednesday. The original plan had been for the full Senate to take up the bill, and the proposed constitutional amendment, the following Monday.

However, on Friday, April 14, when the Senators tried to schedule the upcoming debates and votes, "lawmakers exploded in a bitter parliamentary battle—and they didn't even discuss the merits of the issue."[230] It was "a partisan clash over scheduling. In what Democratic leadership called political gamesmanship, Republicans tried unsuccessfully to delay debate. . . . 'The issue here is purely politics.'" said the Senate President Pro Tem.[231]

The "heated debate" ended in a Republican Senator "throwing his calendar in frustration onto the floor of the chamber."[232] The calendar-throwing Senator "didn't get the full week [of delay] he wanted," although "he did win one more day; instead of taking up the [Constitutional] amendment and the civil unions bill on Monday, as originally planned, the Senate would hold off until Tuesday."[233]

"The one-day delay was a compromise between the two sides after Democrats were faced with having to make appearances for a weekend session just to block Republicans' attempts at a delay."[234] Senator John Bloomer had "hinted during the debate" that the weekend sessions might be used by "'the right people and the wrong people showing up.'"[235] Another Senator had "warned, along with other Republicans, that he would attempt during the weekend sessions" to further delay the final debate and vote. The two sides "were at an impasse until late in the afternoon [on Friday] when the Tuesday compromise was forged."[236]

On that same Friday the 14th, the *Burlington Free Press* polled all 30 Senators on how they would vote on the civil unions bill and on the two constitutional amendments likely to be proposed on the floor of the full Senate.[237] According to the *Free Press*'s Friday poll, the bill would pass and both constitutional amendments would fail—if the bill remained unchanged and if Senators did not change their minds during the floor debate.

The *Free Press*'s Friday nose-counting found that 17 of the 30 Senators would vote for the bill, 11 would vote against, and two were undecided. The bill needed 16 votes to pass. The newspaper also found that the proposed constitutional amendment to define marriage as one man and one woman would fail: 15 Senators oppose it, 11 support it, and 4 are undecided.[238] The amendment would require 20 votes (of the 30-person Senate to pass). The more comprehensive Illuzzi amendment, aimed at overruling *Baker*, would "fail by a wider margin. Twenty Senators oppose it, five favor it, and five are undecided."[239]

The *Free Press* poll also highlighted how partisan the issue had become. Every single Senator who planned to vote against the bill was a Republican.[240] With only two exceptions, all of the Senators who intended to vote for the bill were Democrats.[241]

Even before the full Senate began debating the bill, opponents were working to defeat it when it came back to the House for consideration of the minor changes the Senate Judiciary Committee had made to the House bill. "Only four [House] members would have to switch their votes to defeat the bill."[242]

A leader of the House Traditional Marriage Caucus said Friday the 14th that "we have a group of [House] names from which there is a potential to defeat the bill. . . . It's real. It's going to take some work, but it's real."[243] A lobbyist for Take It To The People echoed that their strategy was to try to reach those House members who voted for the bill but who also wanted a constitutional amendment.[244]

Senate President Pro Tem Peter Shumlin responded "that even if the House delivered a credible threat of defeating the bill if no constitutional amendment were proposed, the Senate would not listen. 'The Senate isn't going to be intimidated on a question of basic principles, like the Vermont Constitution,' Shumlin said. He added that there would be nowhere close to the two-thirds majority needed to pass a constitutional amendment in the Senate."[245]

I'm writing these words on the Saturday April 15, the weekend before the full Senate takes up the bill and the constitutional amendments. It's midafternoon, and I'm in the hammock in my backyard, wearing shorts and a t-shirt, under a flawlessly blue Vermont sky. There's a gentle wind out of the west, and it's ruffling my pages of yellow legal paper. My neighbors to the left are mowing their lawn; my neighbors in back are setting up a swing set for their two young daughters; I hear music from the house to the right, which means their daughter is home from college for the weekend. It's hard to imagine that, less than an hour north of here, people in Montpelier are strategizing for their endgame push to defeat the civil unions bill. But I know they are.

I remember days like this from when I was a South Florida capital public defender. Occasionally, I'd be able to take a Sunday off from the work to walk along the coastline of the Atlantic Ocean or the Gulf of Mexico. I'd walk along the beach, under an equally beautiful but different sky than we have in Vermont. It was hard for me to imagine, during those walks along the beach, that my regular day job was to try to protect the basic human right—the right to live—of my clients, some of whom were African American, all of whom were poor, and all of whom were hated by pretty much everyone else in Florida. Against that hatred there was my law office and the law itself. Often I felt simply impotent in the face of the hatred and the perversions of law and justice caused by the hatred. It was hard for me to imagine that many, many people hated my clients and wanted them killed. But they did.

The newspaper headlines on the day before the Senate debate were militaristic in metaphor. The *Burlington Free Press* announced "Senators Prepare for Battle."[246] The *Valley News* declared "Senate Girds for Civil Union Vote."[247]

Both headlines were above the same Associated Press story. The story began: "To a casual observer, the bitter politicking last week over scheduling in the Senate probably looked rather petty. But in the highly charged political atmosphere surrounding the debate over same-sex marriage benefits, even if it is petty it can carry a lot of weight. . . . And politics are what it's all about."[248]

Going into the debate, "as several senators pointed out, everyone's mind [was] pretty well made up."[249] Still, "how the issue" played "itself out over the next few days could determine the success or failure of the initiative."[250] And the political strategy was "getting ever more complicated."[251]

The opponents of the bill continued to use a strategy of (1) linking the bill to the two proposed constitutional amendments, and (2) getting the Senate to change the House bill in any way, so as to require a House vote on the Senate version—a House vote that would kill the bill if the fragile House coalition did not hold.

The Associated Press noted that the outcome of the Senate votes on constitutional amendments "could help to determine the votes not only in the Senate, but also in the House. . . . 'We've been counting heads [in the House] and we think we can kill the Senate-passed bill when it comes back to us if it doesn't come with a constitutional amendment. . . . He might be right. Only four [House] lawmakers would have to change their votes for the bill to die in the House."[252] Similarly, in the

Senate, "leaders know there are some senators who may not vote for the bill if they can't also vote in favor of the constitutional amendment proposals."[253]

The obvious solution was for the Senate to forgo its minor changes to the House bill, thus eliminating the need to send the revised bill back to the House for a vote. However, the Senate does not like to rubber-stamp House bills. The Chairman of the Senate Judiciary committee "has been frustrated throughout the process that he might be unable to introduce any Senate ideas into the bill. 'It's unfortunate that in some quarters, people think the House did perfect work,'" the chairman said.[254] In a few days, one House opponent predicted, "we'll see how clever the Senate is."[255] Senator Jeb Spaulding said, the day before the Senate began debate, "I think, given the natural concerns around this issue, it wouldn't look too good to look like a rubber stamp."[256]

Part of this was Senatorial pride, and part of it was a belief that the House majority would hold. The day before the Senate took up the bill, the President Pro Tem "said he would be willing to reconsider his position [about not simply adopting the House version] if there was some possibility that the House votes were no longer there. 'If you can prove to me that the House absolutely cannot pass our bill, I'm all ears,' he said. 'But I think there's more blustering than fact.'"[257]

There may or not have been "facts"—the House leaders were "trying to determine how certain" the votes were, but they had "no solid answers" as of the night before the Senate debate[258]—but there certainly was "bluster." The evening before the debate, the two Republican gubernatorial candidates, speaking to about 50 Republicans at a Rutland County Holiday Inn, "suggested . . . that the controversial civil unions bill could be the springboard that finally catapults the GOP back into power in state government."[259] Both candidates, Ruth Dwyer and William Meub, "solidified what is shaping up to be one of the central Republican themes in the coming election."[260] During the hour-long event, which included brief speeches by the candidates and a question-and-answer period, Candidate Meub said "it's important that we can get a message out . . . what's important is that we learn how to win. It's going to be important to get control of the House, get control of the Senate, and get control of the governorship."[261]

The *Baker* issue would not be the only issue in the campaign, Meub and Dwyer indicated, but clearly they saw it as a wedge issue with which to reach voters. There is, of course, a long history of demagoging such issues.[262]

As the Senate "girded" for "battle," the little yellow ducks returned to Vermont. The day before the Senate began debate, Take It To The People ran another in its series of duck ads. This one was more accurate than its other ads saying that the legislature was about to pass a marriage bill; these half-page ads called civil unions "a big step to Gay Marriage."[263] The ads featured a graphic of a giant goofy-looking duck called "civil union" about to step on the Vermont statehouse." Six days earlier, Take It To The People had run another half-page ad calling for a constitutional amendment "preserving traditional marriage."[264] This ad asked "Who can help the Senators get out of the box?" and answered "We the People!!"[265] The ad showed a duck (dubbed "civil union" astride the top of a box. The box was marked "Baker v. Vermont, Vermont Supreme Court, Return Guaranteed," and "To: Senate Judiciary Committee."[266] The duck was trying to keep the lid on the box, mashing the arms of the judiciary committee members trying to reach out of the box (the arms were labeled with the names of the six members of the committee.[267] (I know I'm not doing justice to this graphic. You sort of have to have seen it.)

I knew the Senatorial arithmetic. The civil unions bill needed 16 votes to pass. The Montpelier bookies were saying that the bill had 17 or 18 votes. Still, as the Senate plodded ahead, I kept thinking of an old Dizzy Dean saying: "The game was closer than the score indicated."

The Preliminary Vote

The weather on the day the Senate began debating the civil unions bill was gray and overcast. All day, the sun threatened to break through the clouds. All day, the spring rain threatened to drench the Green Mountain State. By nightfall, it had neither rained nor shone.

The first order of business was the proposed constitutional amendment to define marriage as a union between a man and a woman. The amendment's sponsor, Senator Julius Canns, argued that "our vote today can preserve or degrade the institution of matrimony"[268] and warned that "all of the United States and the world will judge our decision today."[269] The senator, whose ancestors were white, African American, and Native American, also argued that this was not a civil rights issue: "'I don't feel this is a civil rights case. . . .' He asked senators not to confuse race and sexual orientation. 'They are asking for rights because of their sexual habits.'"[270] The proposed amendment failed 17-13.[271]

Next came the proposed constitutional amendment to overrule *Baker*. The amendment's sponsor, Senator Vincent Illuzzi, called *Baker* an "unprecedented interpretation" and asked "Do you really believe that the 1777 authors intended to provide same-sex couples with the privileges and benefits of marriage?"[272] The Senate Democratic leader responded that "hundreds of people have told me with such indignation, shouldn't the majority rule? And the answer is no, not in America. Not in America when it comes to protecting the rights of the minority."[273] This proposed amendment was defeated 21-9.[274]

The debate on the civil unions bill itself was more sober than in the House. Only three senators spoke in opposition of the bill.[275] One senator argued that "their sexual orientation runs counter to the natural law. Their family unit runs counter to the natural law and if their sexual orientation became the standard, mankind would cease to exist."[276] He "suggested that extending legal benefits to gay and lesbian couples would encourage homosexuality and make homosexuality more acceptable." He also "said he had not seen any evidence to prove that homosexuality was anything other than a chosen lifestyle. Until evidence shows that it is not a matter of choice, [he said] he believes gays and lesbians should be disqualified from receiving the rights and benefits of marriage."[277]

Outside the Senate Chamber, visitors filled the hallway:

> At the top of the curving stairway leaving to the Vermont Senate, Nicole Christian of Northfield stood with a brightly colored sign: "Friendship does not equal marriage! Get real!"
>
> "What does that mean?" asked Virginia Renfrew, a lobbyist for the Vermont Coalition for Lesbian and Gay Rights.
>
> The question triggered a 10-minute debate between the two women— a continuation of a debate that has gripped Vermonters since the state Supreme Court ruled in December that denying the benefits of marriage to same-sex couples was a violation of the Vermont Constitution.
>
> Christian said that marriage is a union between a man and a woman, and that the idea of gays and lesbians marrying is a "sham." Renfrew told her that "the issue is around gays and lesbians in committed relationships."
>
> Christian: "I'm committed to my friends. I'll get up at 3 A.M. for my friends. . . . I'm committed to my sister."

Renfrew explained that she had been married, but eventually divorced and came to grips with her true nature as a lesbian. "I allowed myself to overcome what society was teaching me, that I was a sinful person."

Christian replied, "So you think God made a mistake when he created you?" She added a moment later that benefits for same-sex couples would force those with moral objections to "support your lifestyle."

Renfrew: "I support your lifestyle. I pay taxes." And so it went until the two agreed on one thing: Neither was going to change the other's mind.

□

Every now and then, the crowd in the hall outside the House chamber would clap and cheer when they could hear on the speaker a senator say something they agreed with. This didn't settle well with the speaker of the House, Michael Obuchowski.

In the relative calm of the foyer outside his office down a back hall of the Statehouse, the Rockingham Democrat caught up with Capitol Police Chief David Janawicz and asked him to restore and maintain decorum.

When the civil unions bill passed the House, Obuchowski banged his gavel so hard in a bid to quell the cheering that its head flew off.

"What we do here is not a sporting event," the speaker said in his office moments after speaking with Janawicz. "At the General Assembly, an expression of support is by voting for or against, not by clapping or other such things."[278]

Inside the small Senate chamber—"so white and elaborately detailed that it resembles a wedding cake"[279]—"several senators who voted against the bill said they were doing so because their constituents opposed it."[280] Senator John Bloomer "said he was following the wishes of his constituents, who he said were strongly opposed to the civil unions bill. His e-mail messages and letters were running 2-to-1 against the bill, he said. 'I'm not saying Rutland County is right,' he said, 'but that is where my constituents are.'"[281]

In midafternoon, my law school colleague and friend, Laura Gillen, mentioned that her senator, Mark MacDonald, was wavering in his support for the bill. Laura was e-mailing every Democrat in her district to encourage support for their senator. Another colleague and friend, Laura Davidson, had had a long talk with MacDonald the previous weekend.

MacDonald, who represented one of the most conservative areas in the state ("My people don't like change," he had said), had decided the night before that "he would oppose the civil unions bill and began to call constituents and tell them so.[282] One of them called back to ask the social studies teacher of 23 years: 'What are you going to tell the kids when you get back to school?' That stopped MacDonald cold."[283]

It "made little political sense" for MacDonald to vote for the bill; in fact, it would be more like political suicide.[284] Besides, MacDonald knew that the bill would pass even without his vote. His fellow Democrats said they would understand if he voted no. "Noting that they had enough votes to pass the plan without his support, some Democrats even advised MacDonald to break ranks for the sake of his political future."[285]

However, at 4:25 that afternoon, "MacDonald put up his hand, put politics aside, and voted his conscience."[286] MacDonald "said he made his decision [the night before] after talking with numerous friends. One of them asked, 'What are you going to tell the kids when you go back to school?' MacDonald teaches social studies to Randolph eighth-graders, who sometimes ask him about what's happening in Montpelier."[287] Before the Senate roll-call vote, "MacDonald stood on the Senate floor and told his colleagues that he 'could vote against this bill and then go [through Williston] and people would slap me on the back and say I was a good fella! But he could not get those eighth-grade students back in Randolph out of his head."[288] So MacDonald voted yes.

The debate and vote were over by 5:00 P.M. The bill passed by nearly a 2-1 margin, 19 votes yes to 11 votes no.[289] The vote also divided along party lines. "All 17 Democrats and two Republicans voted in favor of the measure. Eleven Republicans voted against it."[290]

Things were a bit rushed in the Senate. The Judiciary Committee chairman did not have to sign the bill. He signed a post-it note, slapped the post-it on the bill, and headed out.

Most significantly, the bill given preliminary approval was the *Senate's* version, of the bill, not the House's version, thus setting the stage for another showdown vote in the House. House and Senate leaders spent the evening after the preliminary vote "considering the possibility that the Senate version of the bill would fail if it were presented to the House."[291] The Speaker of the House "and his leadership team spent Tuesday [the day of the Senate vote] counting and recounting votes, trying to determine if vote switches or possible absences next week would change the outcome" in the House.[292]

In a way, the decision rested with Senator Richard Sears, the Chairman of the Senate Judiciary Committee.[293] The President Pro Tem of the

Senate "said he would accede to Sears's wishes on the matter—and
Sears said he did not want to vote for the House bill."

"'I am hoping to sleep on it,' Sears said. But, he added, 'I oppose it.' "[294]

The Final Vote

Thank you for your letter asking me to support civil unions. I am proud to say
that I cast my vote in support of [the civil unions bill] and the rights of all
Vermonters. In doing so, I think of the advice of a friend, an old Vermont
farmer: "Treat your land as though you'll live on it forever and your neighbor
as though you'll die tomorrow." Vermonters are my neighbors and this land
my home. I can do nothing but to vote accordingly.

—Vt. Senator Elizabeth Ready, in a letter to constituents[295]

After the preliminary vote, the Vermont bishop lamented that "traditional marriage has suffered a grievous blow."[296] A statement released
by the diocese also said that "if, as we strongly suspect, the defeat of a
constitutional amendment is against the heart-held desires of a majority of Vermonters, it is not only marriage that has been poorly served; it
is democracy itself that has been wounded."[297]

The final Senate debate was "short but heartfelt."[298] Again, Senator
Julius Canns took issue with the notion that same-sex marriage was an
issue of civil rights and he denied that gays and lesbians were victims
of discrimination. Canns, who described himself as a mixture of three
races—white, black, and Native American—gave an "angry speech" in
which he "lashed out at people who would say that gays and lesbians
faced the kind of discrimination he had endured."[299] While serving "in
the Marine Corps, he said, he drank from whites-only water fountains
and was prepared to fight anyone who challenged him. . . . 'I fought
where you folks never have been,' he said, jabbing a finger in the air.
'This is not a civil rights problem. This is a sex problem.' "[300]

Senator Sears disagreed. Sears "said he found himself targeted by
virulent opponents who told him he was headed for hell because he
supported giving benefits to same-sex couples. The experience, he said,
made him sympathize with gays and lesbians who were asking him for
rights. 'For a few months of my life, I have learned a little bit about what
it's like to be discriminated against,' Sears said. 'I began to realize what
these folks have put up with all their lives.' "[301]

The final Senate vote was the same as the preliminary vote the day
before. Nineteen senators voted yes. Eleven senators voted no.[302]

It was an emotional time, in part because some senators voting for the bill knew that that vote might well cost them the next election. "You see senators in tears—they know this vote may well be their last,"[303] said Senate President Shumlin. "'I've never seen a vote that required more courage.' Individual seats and the slim Democratic majority in both chambers is at stake, Senator Shumlin said. 'I've worked very hard to be in the majority,' he said. 'I recognize that today's action jeopardizes that, and I know my fellow senators recognize we jeopardize that. But there comes a time when you have to stand up for what you believe in, and this is it.'"[304]

The *LA Times* noted the day after the Senate vote that "supporters and opponents alike view it as the country's most comprehensive gay rights legislation—the boldest step in an expanding movement to extend legal benefits to gay and lesbian couples."[305] The *New York Times* called it "groundbreaking" and "an American first."[306]

For antiabortion and antigay jihadist Randall Terry, it was over. He conceded defeat after the Senate vote, he "cleaned out his storefront, made plans to leave town [the day after the vote], and said he will go on vacation to Italy next week. 'It's very simple,' Terry said. 'We lost.'"[307]

For the bill, and for same-sex couples, it was not quite over. The bill was in what the *Burlington Free Press* aptly called a "stretch run."[308]

Now it was back to the House.

RETURN TO THE HOUSE OF REPRESENTATIVES

The final Senate vote was on Wednesday, April 19. The final House vote was scheduled for the following Tuesday. In between was Passover and the Easter weekend.

The Easter Uprising

In the days between the final Senate vote and the upcoming House vote, opponents of the bill continued to predict that they had the votes in the House to kill the bill. However, these predictions were undermined by public admissions that their earlier statements had been more bluster than fact. Rep. George Schiavone, co-chairman of the House Traditional Marriage Caucus, had claimed, before the preliminary Senate vote, that his group "had enough votes to defeat the legislation if it was sent back to the House without a constitutional amendment."[309] After the Senate vote, Rep. Schiavone admitted that his "initial announcement was a ploy to grab attention rather than a declaration based on an actual head count. 'That was a little bit of hype,' he said referring to the press conference the caucus had held [the week before] announcing they had clinched enough votes to stop the bill in its tracks."[310] Still, Schiavone said the caucus expected "to gain at least two more votes with the return" of two representatives who had been "absent due to illness when the House cast its final vote on the bill."[311] One of the two representatives identified by the caucus confirmed that he would vote against the bill."[312]

The day after the Senate's final vote, about "200 Vermonters crowded into a public hearing in [the small rural town of Jericho] to question lawmakers about their controversial endorsement" of the bill.[313] One of the first members of the audience said, "I, for one, feel very betrayed. . . . I think we have been betrayed by the people who have been elected to represent us."[314] Another person, who identified herself a Native American, opined that "the legislature was poised to pass an immoral law. 'I think this is a moral issue. This is not a civil rights issue.'"[315] One audience member "told the lawmakers that the civil union plan threatened traditional families and family values," to which Rep. William Lippert responded with a request that the audience member consider *his* (same-sex) family: "I believe in family values, but include my family.'"[316]

The program closed when Senator James Leddy read—as he had read on the floor of the Senate—a letter from 78-year-old Helena Blair: "'I can only say that God blessed us with eight children, and my God made no mistake when he created homosexuals and when he gave us our son,' Helena Blair wrote Leddy. 'Please support the civil union bill.' Then a white-haired woman stood up and surprised Leddy and the crowd when she announced, 'I'm Helena Blair.' To that, many in the crowd responded with a standing ovation."[317]

On Saturday, April 22, I received at home a postcard. The front side of the card declared, in bold black letters, "VERMONT ALERT: Last Chance to Stop Homosexual 'Marriage'! Insist Your Representative(s) Vote Against 'Civil Union' Bill H.847." The back of the postcard said

VERMONT VOTER ALERT:
    If you're like most people in Vermont, you oppose marriage-like status for homosexual acts. However, if you don't take action, Vermont will never be the same.
    By the time you get this postcard, the Vermont State Senate may have passed a bill to give homosexual "couples" similar legal status as mar-

riage. Politicians are ready to cave in to the radical Homosexual Lobby and pass a so-called "Civil Union" bill with marriage-like status.

This minute, if possible, call your Vermont State Representative(s) and insist he/she vote against the so-called "Civil Union" bill H.847. You must be firm. Many politicians in Montpelier think if they give the radical Homosexual Lobby what they want (marriage-like status) and then pass a Constitutional Amendment defining marriage in a traditional sense, everyone will be happy.

You need to strongly communicate that if the so-called "Civil Union" bill passes the Constitutional Amendment idea is worthless. Insist your Representative(s) vote against "Civil Unions" in every procedural substantive vote.

You should find your Representative's name & phone number on the other side of this postcard just above your address. Please call right away. For each Representative listed on the other side there will be two phone numbers. The first number will be a number to the State Capitol, and the second will be his/her home or business number. Please call both phone numbers for each of your Representatives.

Eugene A. Delgaudio, Executive Director Public
Advocate of the United States[318]

Also, on Saturday, the *Rutland Herald* newspaper published a letter from Joe Tildon. Tildon's letter explained his recent resignation from his positions of Chairman of the Rutland City Democratic Party and Vice-Chairman of the Rutland County Democratic Party.[319] Tildon wrote: "As a conservative Democrat, I am strongly right-to-life. I believe natural life begins at conception and ends with natural death. I believe abortion for abortion's sake is murder. I believe the main purpose of marriage is the procreation of human life, God's way of continuing the process of creation. I believe that true constitutional law must have its foundation in the moral law."[320]

Tildon went on: "Consequently, same-sex marriage is impossible both theologically and biologically. It does not and cannot exist. People, through one means or another, select their states in life. Each state has its benefits and obligations, that is, the married state, the single state, and the same-sex state of life. This is not a case of civil rights or of civil rights being denied because one selects a style of life different from regular marriage. Each state has its benefits and its obligations."[321]

Tildon explained that on Town Meeting Day "on March 7, the citizens of this state had an opportunity to voice their opinions on same-sex marriage and that which amounts to the same thing, civil union.

Seventy-six of our legislators were deaf to wishes of the people who elected them and voted otherwise."[322]

"With that vote on March 15 and 16 in the House of Representatives, democracy died and anarchy took over," Tildon wrote. "The wishes of the few superceded the will of the majority. Thus I feel that I can no longer support the direction in which the Democratic leadership appears headed and it is with a heavy heart and deep sorrow that I have stepped down from my positions of leadership within the local Democratic Party."[323]

Tildon ended with a prayer: "May almighty God have mercy on Vermont."[324]

Easter Sunday provided no respite from the antihomosexual letters to the editor. One letter published that Sunday condemned same-sex couples as "abnormal relationships based on sexual preference" and vowed "we will remember in November."[325] Another Easter Sunday letter asked why the supreme court and the governor were "promoting the homosexual agenda? Are a majority of them part of the gay rights movement?"[326] The letter branded the domestic partnership bill "unconstitutional, for our laws are based on the law of God. God's law has been known and recognized by civilization for 6,000 years, and whenever civil laws were changed to suit human desires catastrophes happened. For proof, read history."[327]

The letter continued: "The law that survived is the same since the beginning—whether it is Judaism, Christianity, or even the uneducated natives, who were here before us. . . . [God] controls the universe, [and] sex belongs between a man and a woman. And, by the way, when the word love is spoken, it should not mean sex. We should be compassionate with homosexuals, for many of them are that way because of our tolerance and the liberal education that has gone on, mostly since the 1960s."[328]

The letter gave a warning: "I urge all legislators to pay close attention to what they are doing. Recall 1776 when the average citizens decided that the government was getting too much into dictating. Don't think it can't happen again. There could be another Tea Party."[329] Finally: "May God guide us to see the light."[330]

Also on Easter Sunday, the *Valley News*'s Jim Kenyon published an article on Take It To The People's targeting of 16 House members because the group had "potential swing votes" on Tuesday.[331] The group was "feverishly trying to persuade them to change their positions, or at the very least skip the vote" in hopes of sparking an uprising against the bill.[332]

Take It To The People's endgame effort included an e-mail sent to it's members, "urging them to make phone calls or even home visits to those listed. Of the 150 House members, these 16 would 'benefit from extra attention, as they might be convinced to change their vote (or have the flu) if they were given sufficient reason or experience continued pressure,' the e-mail stated."[333]

Bill supporters claimed their votes would hold.[334] However, "nothing is guaranteed on a vote of this magnitude, said [one representative]. 'This is all kind of hyperbole until your name is called on Tuesday.'"[335]

Legislators on both sides "worked through the holiday weekend to fortify their positions" for the anticipated Tuesday vote.[336] By the day before the expected vote, the Associated Press was reporting that although "the House's final vote could come as early as Tuesday, . . . legislative leaders caution that schedule could change."[337]

The day before the scheduled House vote, supporters of the bill ran full-page ads in Vermont newspapers. Accompanying three photos of same-sex couples, the advertisements declared "We Are Not a Threat. We are your friends, family, and neighbors."[338] The ads went on: "Gay and lesbian Vermonters work hard at our jobs, pay our taxes, contribute to our communities, follow our own diverse religious beliefs, and strive to be responsible citizens. Most of all, we treasure the families we have formed, and the lifelong commitments we share with our partners. We don't want special treatment. We just seek the same legal rights for our families that our heterosexual neighbors already have."[339]

Fat Tuesday

[. . .] this day shall live in infamy throughout the world.

—Vt. Rep. Henry Gray, April 25, 2000[340]

The day before the final House vote, opponents worked "to change lawmakers' minds and plotted parliamentary moves to keep the civil unions bill bottled up. . . . 'We feel confident that the House will give the will of the people its due consideration,' said David Rice, a lobbyist for Take It To The People, the largest Vermont group opposed to civil unions."[341] Legislators "opposed to the bill might try to delay it through parliamentary moves, in which they would ask the 150-member House to table the bill indefinitely, or perhaps table it until after the November election."[342] The Speaker of the House observed: "We'll find out tomorrow. They'll all be heard."[343]

The morning of the vote brought full-page newspaper ads by Take It To The People. Featuring a graphic of a smug-looking duck (eyes closed to slits, satisfied grin on its face; actually, the aquatic creature appeared a bit orgasmic) floating in a pond, the ads declared that "Civil Union Is Gay Marriage—A Duck Is a Duck." The ad's headline said: "Thank You To These Legislators For Protecting Traditional Vermont Family Values. All members of the House should vote to postpone action on H.847 until after November. Give the people time to consider and understand this legislation." The ad then listed the names and districts of 70 House members the organization wished to "thank."[344]

When the Speaker of the House banged his gavel at "a few minutes after 10:00 A.M. to signal the beginning of the work day, lawmakers were already sitting at their desks."[345] Then followed three hours of debate, and then the final vote. It was over before the House broke for lunch.

"In a series of mournful and sometimes angry speeches, lawmakers opposed to civil unions said the bill would dilute traditional marriage by putting it on an equal footing with homosexual relationships."[346] One representative said, "This is a sad, dark day for the state of Vermont, and may God help us all."[347]

Rep. Nancy Sheltra "said in a graphic speech that she couldn't support any bill which condoned same-sex relationships, which she believes are an affront to God. 'If you care anything about humanity,' she asked, 'why would you encourage anal sex and STDs and AIDS on part of our society?"[348] "Another representative warned, 'What we are trying to do is against the law of nature and against God's law.' A third called the civil unions bill 'social rape' and a sign of 'moral rot,' and a fourth said gays 'choose to engage in unnatural and unhealthy acts.'"[349]

Rep. Neil Randall "told his colleagues that passing this bill will lead to the 'spread of disease.' He went on to describe homosexuality as an addiction. 'Like alcoholism, you cannot be cured unless you first admit you have a problem,' Randall said."[350] Randall also "predicted that the nation will be 'appalled' by Vermont's action, and that the state will suffer economically. . . . 'Our lady of liberty weeps. The crumbling of that foundation is based on moral rot,'" Randall said.[351]

Rep. George Schiavone warned his colleagues that a majority of Vermonters opposed the bill and would remember at election time six months hence. "Stop shoving this bill down the throats of our people," Schiavone said.[352] "Our people are coughing and gagging and choking on this bill" and could "throw it up and throw us out."[353]

Rep. Henry Gray predicted in his floor speech that "if this bill passes, this day shall live in infamy throughout the world. . . . This is not the case of civil rights. But this is a case of sexual preference."[354] Some lawmakers "handed their colleagues bumper stickers reading 'Don't blame me. I voted NO.'"[355]

As had been the case during the previous House debate on the bill, Rep. William Lippert "listened as a few House members denounced homosexuality as "unnatural" and a perversion."[356] Again he responded: "'We are not a burden on society,' he said. 'We are not sinful. We do not engage in unnatural behavior. We do not ask for special privileges.'"[357] Passing the bill, Lippert said, "would mean that the state was saying that my family, me and my partner, are a family of worth in the state of Vermont.'"[358] And: "'May we be the last generation of gay and lesbian Vermonters who have formed our committed relationships without the possibility of a law that grants us our rights, benefits, and responsibilities.'"[359]

The day of the final House vote it was a spectacularly beautiful spring day outside. After a week of overcast skies, rain, snow flurries, and sleet, Tuesday, April 25, was so bright and sunny that it hurt the eyes.

I checked in with Vermont Public Radio periodically throughout the day, but there was no news about the bill. At exactly 2:22 a fax came in from the law school. It was written by Laura Davidson, and passed along to me by Laura Gillen. It said

> Yeah! Yippee! And Hallelujah!!!
> I couldn't stand the suspense and called the Secretary of the Senate. The House passed the Senate's version of the Civil Union bill, 79 to 68!!!!!!! Thanks everyone for your support and hard work in helping to make this happen!
>
> I'm going to go give someone a hug right now. Email just isn't a satisfying enough medium for my current level of enthusiasm!!!
>
> Laura[360]

Despite the predictions of the bill's opponents, the vote this time was even more lopsided than the 76-69 vote a month previously. None of the earlier "yes" votes switched. "In the end, only four votes were different. Two lawmakers who had been absent in March [were present in April] (one for the bill, one against it), and two others who had voted 'no' in March voted 'yes' in April."[361]

One of those two switches was the biggest surprise of the day. Recall that Rep. Bill Mackinnon had voted against the bill in the House Judiciary Committee and on the two previous votes by the full House. Mackinnon opposed the bill because it did not go far enough. He wanted same-sex couples to have the right to marry. As recently as the weekend before the final House vote, Mackinnon, notwithstanding heavy pressure to vote for the bill, remained firm in his refusal to vote for a bill that created a separate but equal marriage substitute for gay and lesbian couples.

What turned Mackinnon around was the "thank you" ad that Take It To The People ran the Tuesday of the final vote. Mackinnon's "stubborn opposition to half-measures melted on Tuesday after he was named in [the] newspaper advertisement that thanked the bill's opponents for upholding traditional marriage. Several lawmakers said that had sent him over the edge."[362]

Thus Take It To The People succeeded where "months of pressure from the bill's supporters" had failed.[363] Their final ad switched Bill Mackinnon from a stubborn opponent to a grudging supporter of the civil unions bill.

GOVERNOR HOWARD DEAN

[one *Baker* plaintiff turned to another] and offered a new version of the traditional proposal: "CU me!"

That she could not say "marry me" reflects the gap between the civil unions . . . and actual marriage.

—*New York Times*, April 26, 2000[364]

Governor Howard Dean "hadn't planned to sign the civil unions bill at all on Wednesday,"[365] April 26. However, he "learned in the late morning that the House had adjourned for the day much earlier than expected—meaning the bill could officially be transferred to his desk."[366]

Around "noon, House clerk Donald Milne picked up the bill—a thick sheaf of papers annotated with rubber stamps and ballpoint pens, held together with a black binder clip—and walked it over to the governor's statehouse office. Dean's attorney, Janet Ancel, signed for the document. That launched a flurry of phone calls and huddled meetings among the governor's staff. An hour later, spokeswoman Susan Allen emerged to announce there would be a news conference at 2:00 P.M.

"At 1:40 P.M., as six police officers stood watch outside Dean's office, he said a few words about the bill and signed it into law. The staffers who had gathered burst into applause, which could be heard clearly through the heavy office door."[367]

Thus, "a bare 24 hours after the House gave its final approval, Governor Howard Dean signed the civil unions bill" into law.[368] Governor Dean "signed the bill privately, in his statehouse office, surrounded by about a dozen members of his staff. Uncharacteristically, on a bill of any significance, the governor did not invite in advocates of the bill, its legislative authors, or the media to witness and record the signing."[369] The governor explained that he signed the landmark bill privately "because he did not want to give the appearance of celebration on an issue that has divided the state. 'In politics, bill signings are triumphal,' he said. 'They represent the overcoming of one side by the other. These celebrations, as the subject matter of the bill, will be private.' "[370]

Dean made these remarks at a news conference held about half an hour after the private signing. Also at the press conference, Dean spoke passionately about why he signed the bill.[371]

The governor's signature on the civil unions bill did not mean that the legislative response to *Baker* was over. The year 2000 was an election year, and every member of the House and Senate would be up for reelection in November. And what the legislature made in early 2000 could be unmade—by a new group of legislators—in early 2001. Opponents of *Baker* made clear that *Baker* would be a defining issue in the November 2000 state elections in Vermont.

It took less than a week after the initial House vote for the first political candidate in the House "to surface out of the controversial vote"[372] over same-sex unions. "Representative Joyce Barbieri's vote in favor of [the civil unions] bill has motivated another Wallingford resident to declare his candidacy for the Vermont House. . . . [He] said he decided to run after Barbieri voted for the bill."[373] The challenger reasoned that " 'I think a representative should represent the people that elect them, especially on an issue like this. . . .' An overwhelming majority of Wallingford voters"[374] opposed domestic partnership as well as marriage for same-sex couples. The challenger personally opposes both, and so do the constituents he wants to represent: " 'Seventy-five percent of the people of Wallingford do not want to have anything to do with a gay marriage bill, and she [the incumbent] voted against her constituency.' "[375]

Randall Terry claimed to have "recruited 13 candidates to challenge lawmakers who had voted for" the bill.[376] Terry had also conducted workshops for potential candidates.

It promised to be an adventuresome election season.

THE LAWYERS

On May 18, 2000—after the governor had signed the bill but before the law went into effect—my research assistant Pamela Gatos and her daughter Brook Hopkins interviewed Beth Robinson, one of the lead counsel for the *Baker* plaintiffs. Three days after the interview, Gatos and Hopkins described the meeting in a memo:

> The plaintiffs and their attorneys in *Baker* as well as the Vermont Freedom to Marry Task Force fully expected the Vermont Supreme Court to rule in favor of same-sex marriage. When the decision came down and the legislature was given the opportunity to handle the issue, however, the gay and lesbian community needed to come up with a strategy. Would they support a domestic partnership bill or would they stand for nothing less than marriage? They eventually decided to support the civil unions bill, but this decision was not made out of a necessity to compromise. It was a decision that was made after a careful and thoughtful risk analysis of all the other options and a consciousness that winning the civil unions battle did not mean that the war for gay and lesbian equality was over.

> Because of their previous research and work, the Vermont Freedom to Marry Task Force was confident that they had enough supporters in the Senate to block a constitutional amendment prohibiting same-sex marriage, and possibly enough votes to pass marriage. They were a little more worried about the full House. They were prepared to risk losing a marriage bill in the House and to go back to court.

> Robinson and Murray went to the legislature asking for marriage and spent the first five or six weeks in House Judiciary making their argument. The committee gave them a good faith nod, and if the vote had been by secret ballot it probably would have been for marriage. One of the sur-

prising things for the legislators at the public hearings was the number of gays and lesbians who came forward and talked about their lives. These people could never have done that if they could not have gone back to their jobs the next day confident they would not get fired.

When the House decided to write a civil unions bill, Robinson and Murray, the Vermont Freedom to Marry Task Force, the plaintiffs, and the gay community as a whole had to decide if they were going to support the bill or fight against it in hopes of achieving marriage in the future. At first, they were strongly inclined to fight the bill and go back to court. Robinson claimed she was philosophically ready to fight the civil unions bill. When the language was worked out, however, they realized that they could not fight a bill that went farther than any other state in protecting and recognizing gay and lesbian relationships. The Task Force recognized that it would be extremely difficult to convince the Vermont gay and lesbian community that sending the issue back to the court was a good strategy especially considering the possibility of long delays and a constitutional amendment similar to that in Hawaii. The Vermont gay and lesbian community was strongly, if somewhat surprisingly, unified throughout the entire process and the Task Force did not want to risk fracturing this unity. They decided to support the bill—a decision that greatly improved its chances of passage.

Because most of the testimony by gay and lesbian people before the house indicated that they wanted marriage and would be dissatisfied with the second-class citizenship status of domestic partnerships, the decision to support the civil unions bill required a drastic rhetorical shift. The Task Force's message was that they recognized civil unions as a second-class citizenship but that it was a step in the right direction and that the fight for marriage was not over. (This harmed them politically because opponents pointed to their message that the fight was not over to prove that civil unions was just a way to sneak marriage in later.)

Although the Task Force decided to accept the civil unions compromise, they were not prepared to accept everything the House and Senate might offer to ensure its passage. Robinson described their reaction to the amendment that would outlaw the recognition of same-sex marriage from other states. The Task Force, the plaintiffs, and the attorneys were divided on this issue. Half wanted to fight the bill if this amendment were passed, and half wanted to accept the amendment. In the end, they decided to stand their ground and come out against the amendment.

Murray speculates that although the civil unions bill is an important step towards same sex marriage, the momentum for fighting for marriage will wane. She recognizes that Vermont set a precedent for other states in adding an extra step between no recognition of gay and lesbian relationships and marriage. She doubts that any state will enact same-sex marriage before implementing a comprehensive domestic partnership bill. She is not hopeful that Vermont will adopt same-sex marriage before other states have at least taken steps toward providing domestic partnership benefits to gay and lesbian couples.

The decision to dismiss the suit was made for several reasons. The plaintiffs are tired, the attorneys are tired, and the gay and lesbian community is tired. It is unlikely that the court would find the civil unions bill unconstitutional considering what the state has been through in recent months. Additionally there would be a potentially damaging political backlash if they were to go back before the court after fighting so hard for civil unions.

Robinson indicated that despite Governor Dean's adamant opposition to gay marriage, his work on the civil unions bill was productive. Perhaps more admirable was Dean's speech after signing the legislation into law. Murray was happy that he seemed to "get" that the purpose of the court case and that the bill was symbolic. It was not solely about benefits. Dean recognized that the bill sends a message to gay and lesbian teenagers who are considering suicide, and friends and relatives of gay and lesbian people that the State of Vermont officially supports homosexual relationships.

The passage of the civil unions bill elicited an understandably mixed reaction from Vermont's gay and lesbian community. They were pleased to have such a comprehensive bill but disappointed that their original goal of marriage was not realized. The non-Vermont gay and lesbian community's response to the bill has been overwhelmingly positive, however. This is demonstrated by the Vermont delegation's celebrity status at the recent Millennium March as well as personal encounters that Robinson has had with many out-of-state gay and lesbians. Robinson maintains that it is important to keep both perspectives in mind. The civil unions bill has gone farther than any other state in protecting and promoting gay and lesbian couples and is, therefore, a cause for celebration. Gays and lesbians must also remember, however, that it relegates them to second-class citizenship and that they must not be afraid to continue to demand marriage.[377]

REVOLT OF THE CLERKS

The civil union certificates themselves would be issued by town clerks. "A survey conducted by the Vermont Municipal Clerks and Treasurers Association in April (2000) found that 32 of that group's member clerks would not issue the certificates," even though such action could subject them to a civil rights lawsuit.[378] Thirty-six clerks said they were undecided about whether they would issue the certificates.[379] Eighty-nine said they would issue them.[380]

On May 25, 2000, town clerks across the state received a letter from Rep. Nancy Sheltra and other opponents of the civil unions statute. Sheltra wrote: "You as a town clerk have been put in a situation by the passage of the civil unions legislation which may totally compromise your beliefs."[381] The mailing also contained a survey asking the clerks "whether they would refuse to issue civil union certificates for same-sex couples."[382] Sheltra's "jihad" would be spearheaded by a new organization, called Standing Together to Reclaim the State (STAR).[383]

The town clerk of Tunbridge announced she would resign her position of nine years rather than issue civil unions certificates.[384] To the Tunbridge clerk, "a Christian and mother of four the new legislation represents a stark contradiction of her religious connections."[385]

By contrast the Topsham town clerk chose defiance. Calling civil unions "endorsed perversion," the Topsham clerk "says she will not personally issue civil union licenses to same-sex couples and she is asking residents whether the town should defy state law by not making the licenses available at all."[386] In a memo "sent on town letterhead to every Topsham household" in June 2000, the clerk "tells voters she will not issue the licenses and asks if they should defy the law, resign, or appoint a willing assistant to do the paperwork."[387] As of June 25, 2000, "most of the responses so far have urged defiance of the law."[388]

The Betting Pool

Four weeks before the civil unions law would go into effect, opponents—including the ubiquitous Rep. Nancy Sheltra—filed a lawsuit seeking to declare the statute "null and void" and seeking an injunction against its taking effect.[389]

The lawsuit alleged that 14 members of the House of Representatives engaged in a betting pool on the day the bill received preliminary approval. The complaint asserted that the "betting pool gave lawmakers a conflict of interest, and that 14 supporters should have been disqualified from the voting on the measure."[390] With those 14 members disqualified, "the outcome of the vote in the House would have been different, and the bill would have been defeated."[391]

Each of the 14 legislators "bet one dollar.[392] Thus the pool concerned $14. The winner donated the $14 jackpot to charity."[393]

The betting pool originated with Rep. Ann Seibert. Seibert "said she had made an error of judgment but called the lawsuit silly. 'Anyone who thinks that would have changed the vote really has no grasp on reality,' Seibert said."[394]

The suit sought an injunction blocking the law from going into effect. Oral arguments were heard on June 24, 2000, a week before the statute's effective date. A lawyer for the 11 plaintiff-legislators specified that "on the very floor where the law making it a crime to gamble and act as a bookie 14 Representatives participated in a betting pool and violated the law that would subject the citizens of Vermont to incarceration."[395]

On Monday, June 26, 2000, the trial court denied the injunction.[396] The judge's order found that the plaintiffs had "failed to demonstrate that they will suffer irreparable harm between now and the time a decision is rendered on the validity of the civil union bill"[397]

The next day, the plaintiffs were back in court with a renewed request for injunctive relief.[398] The idea was to add two town clerks as plaintiffs, who said they would be harmed if forced to issue civil union licenses. Counsel for the plaintiffs asserted that "these town clerks object to (issuing civil union licenses) on moral and religious grounds."[399]

The trial judge denied the injunction around noon on Saturday, June 30, less than 12 hours before the new law would go into effect.[400]

Vows and Cat Calls

Their names were Carolyn Conrad and Kathleen Peterson.[401] Just after midnight on June 30/July 1, minutes after the new law went into effect, they became the first couple to receive a civil union license in Vermont.[402]

Ted Sweet, my research assistant, interviewed Conrad and Peterson. His report follows:

To: Professor Mello
From: Ted Sweet
Date: July 14, 2000
Re: Meetings with Kathleen Peterson and Carolyn Conrad

On July 9th 2000 and again on July 14th 2000 I met with Kathleen Peterson and Carolyn Conrad to discuss their historical civil union which took place on July 1st 2000 at approximately 12:01 A.M. in Brattleboro, Vermont. The first interview took place telephonically and the second meeting took place at the "Moles Eye," a local eatery in Brattleboro. The tone of the conversation was casual dialogue rather than question and answer, in order to facilitate speaking candidly about all the issues and subissues concerning this matter.

Due to me showing the sincerity of recording Kathleen and Carolyn's comments, my first two meetings were not tape recorded. Although the meetings were not tape recorded, extensive notes were taken and their comments are [as presented below] recorded verbatim in my handwritten notes.

Questions and Responses

Ted: Currently, how do you feel since you received your civil union?

Kathleen   Extremely happy!

Carolyn: Now I can introduce Kathleen as my "wife" and know that it has legal foundation to it. We feel good about the whole event in general. Annette Cabby, the town clerk, was very supportive and opened her office at midnight to issue the license, and we had friends and supporters on hand for support also.

Ted: Many historians state that Rosa Parks was handpicked to be sitting on the bus in 1964 in Alabama, an event that was the catalyst for the Civil Rights movement. Were you two picked to be the first recipients of the civil union by any gay group or movement?

Carolyn: No. Before we decided to undergo our civil union we called the Freedom to Marry Task Force and asked if there was anybody in particular that they have deemed to be first and they told us there was no such couple picked.

Ted: Is it difficult for gay people to come out of the closet and proclaim publically that they are gay?

Kathleen: It depends on who you are surrounded by. If you are surrounded by very supportive people, then it is something that one can consider. On the other hand some parents are freaked out by this revelation and some even "disown" their own children. You will also find some friends you had before will no longer consider themselves friends.

Ted: Is it safe for a person to state they are gay?

Kathleen: Outing is publicly stating that you are gay.

Ted: So, are they any safety issues?

Kathleen: Yes. There are a lot of mean people in this world and the right to make your own decision concerning your sexual orientation should be a person's personal choice.

Ted: What do you think about the Take Back Vermont program that is blossoming in the wake of the civil union bill passage?

Kathleen: I do not feel that these people speak for the state of Vermont in general. I feel they are a small voice that has media attention and therefore it seems larger than it really is. I do believe that there are people out there with animosity regarding same-sex civil unions, but I do not feel it is a majority stance.

Ted: Do you feel that the state will have a large migration of gay people come to Vermont in response to the passage of the civil unions bill?

Carolyn: No. There just aren't as many jobs in Vermont as there are in, say, California. People from San Francisco will not relocate to Vermont and give up a $80,000 a year job to make $20,000 a year here.

Ted: Why do you think people feel so strongly against the same-sex civil union bill here in Vermont?

Carolyn: I think some people view gays and lesbians as a group that is "evil" or has an "agenda." They think that gays are after something they have. I've heard some people say that this civil union bill will bankrupt the state. Little do these people know that gays pay taxes much like they do and we pay for our health insurance programs also.

Ted: Why do you think some people hate gays as they do?

Kathleen: People hate what they do not know. Fear of the unknown.

Ted: What would you say to gay couples who are not utilizing the same-sex civil union bill?

Carolyn: That it is their own choice, much like couples who do not wed in traditional relationships. Whether it is a civil union or marriage, it is an event that two people must think over carefully before undergoing.

Ted: If and when the first dissolution or divorce comes after the granting of a same-sex civil union occurs, do you expect any negative backlash to be hurled at the gay community?

Kathleen: Of course. But if people look at [it] in perspective (straight couples divorce at a 50% rate) they shouldn't make any comment at all.

Ted: Would you two be willing to come to our school and speak or be part of a panel concerning civil unions?

Kathleen: Ted, we would be glad to!

Carolyn: Of course, we would have to check our schedules but most definitely.

Ted: On behalf of Professor Mello and Vermont Law School, I thank you.[403]

At 12:00 midnight, sharp, as friends counted down the final seconds, the town clerk issued the license.[404] After one quick question, the document was signed.[405]

The couple then made a quick walk to Wells Fountain in downtown Brattleboro.[406] There they exchanged their vows and entered history.

As the women left the town hall with their license, they passed by a group of protestors from the Rutland Church of Christ.[407] One man shouted, "It's a sad day in Vermont" as the two women left the hall.[408] He proved he was half right.

THE NOVEMBER 2000 ELECTION

Vermonters are caught up in a civil war over civil unions.

—*New York Times*, Nov. 2, 2000[409]

"Take Back Vermont" and "Execute the Fag"

Gay and lesbian couples flocked to Vermont to be joined in civil union. A handful of Vermont residents sought civil union licenses, but the vast majority (85%) of couples taking advantage of the law were non-Vermont residents, which we call "flatlanders" (even if they live at the top of the Rockies). The *New York Times* reported in late July 2000 that "in Brattleboro, of the first 68 people who handed in their certified civil union licenses, only three were residents, and some couples came from as far as London, California and Georgia."[410] The *Boston Globe* observed that most civil union ceremonies were performed for out-of-state residents and that most were "quickie" ceremonies.[411]

I was unsurprised that relatively few Vermont residents were using the new law. For residents, the signs of opposition to the new law were everywhere. I mean "signs." Literally.

The signs proclaimed "Take Back Vermont," and they were everywhere.[412] One perceptive observer wrote in late July that during his 38-mile bicycle ride, he saw at least a dozen of the signs.[413] He noted that the signs were largely the work of opponents of the civil unions law, and he observed that "the signs might as well say GAYS NOT WELCOME."[414]

It's difficult to capture in words the impact the "Take Back Vermont" signs must have had on gays and lesbians in Vermont. One gay man described it to me this way: "You never know where the things would pop up. You're driving down the road, and suddenly you're ambushed by the 'Take Back Vermont' bumper sticker on the rear bumper of the car in front of you. You walk into a convenience store, and there they are. You can't go more than a mile or two before being assaulted by lawn signs. They're everywhere."

The ubiquitous "Take Back Vermont" signs did cause a bit of unintended comedy. Many nonresidents who were visiting the state during leaf season (and perhaps including some of those flatlander gays and lesbians who came here for a civil union) misunderstood the political import of the signs. The Associated Press reported that the "Take Back Vermont signs are driving tourists to stock up on maple syrup. Some leaf peepers have mistaken the political message for a marketing campaign"[415] to remind them to stock up on Vermont products before heading home. The governor even had a moment of comic relief as he described a "Louisiana woman who congratulated the state tourism department for the clever marketing strategy."[416]

There was nothing funny about the "Exacute[sic] the Fag" graffiti painted on the fence of a gay man in Brookfield.[417] The message "was crystal clear despite the misspelling," the Associated Press reported.[418] More ominously, the Associated Press noted that such hate-filled incidents were "happening more and more around Vermont."[419]

Direct hate mail was sent to tens of thousands of Vermonters. One letter claimed that "there is an active movement within state government that could expose our children to the gay sex life. . . ."[420]

An alarmist mailing from Rep. Nancy Sheltra was sent to Vermont legislators. The mailing consisted of an envelope stamped "Sensitive Material Enclosed: This is pornographic material which you supported with your vote."[421] Inside was a safe-sex brochure distributed by a local group called "Outright Vermont," which works to promote tolerance of gay and lesbian school children.[422] Anti–civil union clergy picketed the Burlington Outright office claiming their tax dollars were being used for pornography and the supposed "recruitment of our youth." One Outright employee received two death threats at the office. One intruder told the Outright employee "think about how you're going to eliminate yourself. If you don't do it, I will." A second intruder threatened to kill the Outright employee and "all fags."[423]

I heard the words "fag," "queer," and "dyke"[424] used in anger more often in the first two months of the new law than in the previous 12 years combined. Such epithets, the Associated Press wrote, used to be considered "ill-mannered at best" in "civil conversation. The anger over civil unions appears to have erased that unwritten rule in Vermont, at least for the time being."[425]

Children who were perceived by their classmates to be gay or lesbian, or who supported the civil union law, felt especially under attack.[426] One teacher wrote

> Some teachers say they've noticed a nastier edge in school, too. The Vermont Department of Education says that harassment of kids who are perceived to be gay has increased this fall. And administrators, for whatever reason, don't always step forward to protect them. At one local Vermont high school, students who've started a discussion group for gay and straight kids routinely find their signs either ripped down or defaced. "Join the Gay Straight Alliance" was changed to "Join the Gay Killer Alliance." An administrator's response: Don't put up the signs. "I told you this was going to happen," he reportedly told the students.
>
> It's no better for kids across the river. "I used to work in New York City," a mother in Lebanon told me the other day. "I do think of this as a safe place. But when I look at my son, I know it's not a safe place." Her 15-year-old son, Ben, who's gay, has been tormented in school for years. Recently a group of boys threatened to kill him. A few nights later, they followed him home. Ben stood on his front porch, waiting for his father to open the door, praying that he'd get there before the pack did. "Faggot!" they jeered from the car. One youth was within inches of Ben when his father opened the door.
>
> In the hallways, and even in class, teachers often seem not to hear the deafening chorus of "Faggot!" that greets Ben everyday. "Are you listening to this?" Ben asked one teacher, whose class is particularly abusive. The teacher said nothing, so Ben just said: "I've got to go" and headed down the hallway to the guidance counselor's office. "She talked to some of the teachers," Ben said. "But I never saw any results."
>
> "I've never heard teachers say: 'Don't use that language,'" agrees Victoria, a senior at a local Vermont high school. "They just say 'Be quiet.' They seem a lot more cautious about saying anything."
>
> Sarah, 17, another New Hampshire high school student, is open about being a lesbian. She told me she's routinely pushed into lockers, threatened, and was once thrown down a half flight of stairs. That she could handle. What Sarah couldn't handle was a substitute teacher who handed her a note, telling her that she'd burn in hell if she didn't repent. Sarah went home and swallowed 37 sleeping pills. Miraculously, she survived. "But if it had been the beginning of my freshman year," Sarah told me, "I would have put a gun to my head that night."[427]

Campaign Slugfest

The signs and the hate were partly the result of the fact that 2000 was an election year. During the legislature's consideration of the civil unions bill, opponents had threatened political retribution if the bill became law. When it did, opponents roared into action to make good on their promise.

In November 2000, the governor and every member of the legislature would stand for election. Opponents of the civil union law were determined to make the election a referendum on the new law. As the election season heated up, so did the rhetoric of organizations like Take Back Vermont, Vermont Speaks, Vermonters for Traditional Marriage, and Who Would Have Thought.

There promised to be no shortage of political demagogues willing to trade on the fear and bigotry of the kinds of letters quoted earlier in this essay. Ruth Dwyer, a candidate for the Republican nomination for governor, was an example. In a campaign speech given days before the full House voted on the domestic partnership bill, Dwyer "warned of a new threat to Vermont's way of life, this time to its cultural values."[428] Dwyer called the bill " 'the most radical social legislation in the country . . . It's so damaging to force something on the people . . . [passage of the bill] would tear the state apart.' "[429] This last bit—about the issue "tearing the state apart"—had the ring of a self-fulfilling prophecy. Soon after the House vote, Dwyer tore into two legislators who voted yes: At that meeting, "Dwyer 'made her position very clear,' and was 'relatively uninhibited' in criticizing the votes for civil union, acknowledged [one of the representatives who were on the receiving end of Dwyer's comments]. 'She feels it's a strong issue.' "[430]

Indeed, six months before the party primary and eight months before the general election, opposition to *Baker* was "shaping up to be the Republican's key issue in the upcoming election" for governor.[431] "The civil unions bill may even spell the end for Republicans who voted for it."[432]

Speaking to a standing-room-only crowd of Franklin County Republicans at the Abbey Restaurant, both candidates for the Republican nomination for governor used *Baker* and the post-*Baker* bills to attack the Vermont Supreme Court, the attorney general, and Governor Dean.[433] Candidate Ruth Dwyer charged the governor with arm-twisting to secure the votes needed in the House: "The civil union bill would not have passed the House without deal-making. . . . That's how Howard Dean leads. . . . The governor is very willing to threaten people, bribe people . . . to get a vote."[434] Dwyer "suggested that Republicans take their anger to the polls in November."[435]

Dwyer's opponent agreed. In addition to criticizing the governor and the House, William Meub, a lawyer, "attacked the attorney general's office for failing to mount a strong enough case before the Vermont Supreme Court in *Baker*."[436] Meub argued that the attorney general's office didn't make "a single argument" about "the history of what marriage is all about. There wasn't a single argument made that those rights were there to protect wives. . . . The legislature routinely gives legislation that favors one group over another group."[437]

A member of the House Judiciary Committee that drafted the domestic partnership bill was present at the meeting. He was reminded at the meeting that his vote could cost him his seat: " 'I think you'll see the consequences this fall,' warned an audience member. 'That may be,' [the representative] responded, defending his position."[438]

Two weeks after the civil unions bill was signed into law, the chairman of the Vermont Republican Party sent a fund-raising letter to 3,000 to 4,000 state Republicans.[439] The letter argued that "call it what you will—same-sex marriage or civil union—this is a universally bad and dangerous idea that's wrong for Vermont! . . . In the name of common sense, an overwhelming majority of Republican House members voted NO to civil unions."[440]

This was an interesting pitch letter, given that 15 Republicans—including the bill's chief architect, the Chairman of the House Judiciary Committee—voted for the bill. The GOP chairman's fund-raising letter was only criticizing *Democrats* who supported the bill: " 'When we support Republicans, we are going to support all Republicans. We are not going to distinguish based on who voted for or against this bill.' Asked whether Republicans who supported the bill lacked the 'common sense' mentioned in his letter, [the chairman] said that was not the case. 'It's only the Democrats who lacked common sense,' he said, half-jokingly."[441]

The race for governor was a three-way slugfest. The Progressive Party—a force to be reckoned with in Vermont politics—selected Anthony Pollina as its standard-bearer. Pollina believed in same-sex marriage, although civil unions was a short compromise he could live with. Pollina's presence struck fear into Democrats for the same reason Ralph Nader's candidacy for President terrified national Democrats. Many feared that Pollina would do to incumbent Democratic Governor Dean what Nader ended up doing to Al Gore: siphoning off enough votes to give the election to the Republican (absent Nader, by any reasonable measure, Gore would have won Florida and therefore the presidency).

The Democratic candidate for governor was a foregone conclusion. Incumbent Democratic Governor Howard Dean would seek reelection. Dean had signed the civil union bill into law, and it was clear from the outset that his Republican opponents would make civil unions an issue in the election.

The question in the Republican primary was how stridently their candidate would push the anti–civil union sentiment. On this score the choice was clear. Bill Meub, a lawyer, opposed civil unions but he did so moderately. His primary opponent, Ruth Dwyer, was what we in the south call a fire-eater and a baiter.

Dwyer was a firebrand. For example, in late August, when asked by an interviewer "whether Dwyer thought the NEA [the nation's largest teachers' union] is promoting a homosexual agenda in Vermont," Dwyer responded: "The NEA itself promotes that agenda."[442] When asked again "whether she believed any Vermont schools were doing that," Dwyer replied: "Sure. I wouldn't be surprised."[443] Two newspapers editorialized against Dwyer's comments.[444]

Ruth Dwyer's message played well even to some Democratic leaders. The *Rutland Herald* noted that "displeasure over Vermont's new civil unions law has prompted some Democrats to publicly break ranks with their own party"[445] and endorse Dwyer for governor. Longtime Democrat Rep. Oreste Valsangiacomo led the charge. "What I'm going to say is SOS. Save our state, Ruth. Save our state."[446]

When the votes in the Republican primary were counted, Dwyer had won. Civil unions would be the central issue in the governor's race. The civil unions issue dominated the gubernatorial debates.[447]

The same was true of the races for the Vermont House and Senate. The Democrats held slim margins in both chambers. The Republicans saw civil unions as their chance to gain control. The civil unions issue transformed election cakewalks into cliffhangers. The local headlines tell the story: "Civil Unions Change Political Allegiances,"[448] "Candidates Civil Union Views Could Decide Orange-2 House Primary,"[449] "Civil Unions a Primary Issue,"[450] "Primaries Promise to be Volatile in Vermont,"[451] "Civil Unions Issue Tops Agenda in Orange District 4,"[452] "Civil Unions Dominate Debate for House Seats,"[453] "Challengers Pin Hopes on Civil Unions,"[454] "Gubernatorial Hopefuls Show Divide on Civil Unions,"[455] "Civil Unions Drive Politics in Orange-2,"[456] "Anger

Ripples through a State Once Known for Its Tolerance."[457] A *New York Times* article was headlined "Gay Law Roiling Vermont Elections" (Oct. 25, 2000), and an Ellen Goodman column in the *Boston Globe* was headlined "Vermonters Are Caught Up in a Civil War over Civil Unions" (Nov. 2, 2000).

In the Republican primaries, five legislators who supported the civil union statute were defeated at the polls.[458] Four other Republicans and one Democrat who voted for the bill won their contested primaries.[459]

Although the primaries were a mixed bag, on two points there was strong agreement. This election was all about civil unions.[460] And a lot of voters were very, very angry.[461] Newspapers called for civility, but there was little civility as the general election approached.[462] Instead the political discourse became even more rancorous and downright weird. One respected senior legislator asserted that the *Baker* decision was in fact the product of a grand conspiracy between the governor and Chief Justice of the Vermont Supreme Court. Indeed, so this conspiracy theory runs, the governor appointed the Chief Justice in 1997 so as to further the homosexual agenda.[463]

Three weeks before the election, presidential candidate Pat Buchanan came to Vermont to applaud the anti–civil union forces. Buchanan said that Vermont was a significant battleground in America's culture wars, and he predicted to foes of civil unions: "If you can win a victory here in November, that will resonate all across America."[464] Buchanan wasn't the only candidate for national office to address the same-sex union issue during the 2000 presidential campaign. During the only vice presidential debate, both candidates were asked about same-sex unions.

Election Night

For the nation, the November 7, 2000, election was the presidential campaign that wouldn't end—until the U.S. Supreme Court, 5-4, handed the prize to George W. Bush rather than Al Gore. For my wife Deanna and I, it was an early night. The Progressive candidate didn't do to Governor Dean what Ralph Nader did to Al Gore; Howard Dean bested Ruth Dwyer for governor, and Dwyer conceded defeat early in the evening. The Democrats held their majority in the state Senate. The Senate only barely—by a two-vote margin—remained in Democratic control.[465]

However, in the House, which had been in Democratic hands for 14 years, the Republicans took over. And they took over big: 83 of the 150

House seats.[466] Seventeen legislators—mainly House Democrats who had voted for the civil unions statute—were defeated.[467] These numbers, combined with the retirement of a number of Democrats, gave the House to the Republicans by a 16-seat margin.[468] The *Rutland Herald* called it a "GOP rout."[469] Voter turnout was more than 300,000, a state record.[470]

Three days after the election, a state trial judge issued a final decision in the lawsuit seeking to invalidate the civil unions statute.[471] The court dismissed the lawsuit for lack of "standing" by the plaintiffs and for lack of subject-matter jurisdiction.[472] The Vermont Supreme Court affirmed.[473]

Opponents of the civil union statute promised to push for repeal. Push they did.[474] The House of Representatives even voted to repeal the civil union statute.[475] However, the Senate refused even to take up the matter; given the political reality of Howard Dean as governor and a Democratic majority in the Senate, the efforts in the House had a doomed feel about them. Still, it was nasty; one proposal sought to declare same-sex relationships as a "health hazard."[476]

There were sideshows, however. In the House, there were only 47 votes for outright repeal.[477] The House did pass, by the thinnest of margins (the Speaker had to break a 69-69 tie) a bill to water-down civil unions by creating a wider system of benefits for more than same-sex couples.[478] The Senate refused even to take up the issue. The 2001 legislature session ended with the statute intact.

The smart money in the state capital was calling this the "last hurrah" for the anti–civil unions forces. My elected representative, Michael Kainen, concluded that "the issue is dead."[479] Kainen continued, "the last election cycle was the high-water mark. Even people I know who are anti–civil union . . . don't want the legislature to take any more time on it."[480]

AFTER: THE SEPTEMBER 11 TERRORIST ATTACKS

I haven't heard anybody complaining about civil unions since September 11. It puts fights like that in perspective.

—Vermont Governor Howard Dean, December 2001[481]

Four months after the first anniversary of Vermont's enactment of civil unions, the terrorists struck.[482] The September 11, 2001, attacks transformed America in ways we are only beginning to realize. In Vermont, the attacks seem to have vaporized much of the political opposition to civil unions. As Howard Dean noted, you don't hear much talk about civil unions anymore.

Maybe this is so because one of the heroes of United Airlines Flight 93 was gay.[483] Mark Bingham was a strapping 220-pound, six-foot-five rugby player. He led the attack on the hijackers and thus possibly saved the U.S. Capitol from destruction. "The al Qaeda planners subsequently interviewed on al Jezeera television made it clear that United Flight 93 was headed for the U.S. Capitol dome."[484] By pure dumb luck, the aircraft was 41 minutes late taking off.[485] That 41-minute delay meant that the passengers of Flight 93 knew what the passengers of the other fatal flights did not: that this was a suicide run, not a typical hijacking.[486] The passengers, including Mark Bingham, fought back. They paid with their lives, but their courage saved unknown numbers of people on the ground.

What if Flight 93 had left on time? "It would likely have hit the Capitol when the House of Representatives was in morning business, with sizable numbers of members on the floor, in nearby meeting rooms or on the capitol grounds."[487] The dome itself "is cast iron; had the plane hit it, the burning jet fuel would have caused molten cast iron to rain down on the building and the grounds, causing mass devastation. It is no exaggeration to say that we might have lost a couple hundred House members, with perhaps another hundred or so sent to burn units."[488] In other words, these members of Congress owe their lives to a gay man. (Maybe they could remember that as they consider a constitutional amendment banning gay marriage. And where was Senator Rick Santorum on September 11, 2001?)

Maybe Vermonters stopped talking about civil unions after September 11 because many gays and lesbians were murdered, many in the line-of-duty, by the terrorists on that deadly day. Even President Bush and typically antigay members of Congress were willing to recognize gay families posthumously, through the tragedy. The Mychal Judge Act of 2002, which allowed federal death benefits to be paid to the same-sex partners of firefighters and police officers who die in the line-of-duty, was sponsored by a Republican typically opposed to gay causes.[489] President Bush signed the bill at 6:00 P.M. on a Monday evening, just after a major speech on the Middle East; the White House sent out the news of the signing in a one-sentence e-mail.[490] Still, Bush signed it.

Or maybe September 11 proved to Vermont homophobes that America has *real* enemies. Our enemies are the people who carried out the terror attacks. Not the gay couple that lives down the street.

The September 11 attacks' moratorium on gay-bashing wasn't limited to Vermont. Shortly after September 11, televangelist Jerry Falwell blamed the attacks on "the pagans and the abortionists and the feminists and the *gays and lesbians* . . . all of them who have tried to secularize America, I point the finger in their face and say, 'You helped this happen.'"[491] Falwell's idiotic comments were condemned across the political spectrum, with Republicans from President Bush on down speaking forcefully against the preacher's remarks. However, two years later, when Senator Rick Santorum equated gay love with bestiality, nary a Republican criticized him. Nor were Supreme Court Justices Scalia, Thomas, and Rehnquist taken to task for making the same equation, dissenting in the 2003 Texas privacy case.[492] By 2003, politics seemed to have returned to normal: Republicans could again bash gays, and Democrats were calling Bush a liar and a warmonger.[493]

Regardless of the reasons, the issue of civil unions was low-key in the November 2002 Vermont elections.[494] The operative word during the run-up to the election was "calm."[495] The election itself seemed, as one headline put it, to "Assure Survival of the Civil Union Law."[496] The Associated Press reported that "instead of losing the Senate to an anti–civil union majority such as has controlled the House [for the previous] two years, supporters of the law gained in the House and widened their majority in the Senate."[497]

Howard Dean didn't run for governor in 2002; he decided to run for President instead. Vermont elected a Republican governor, Jim Douglas, and he doesn't seem to like the *Baker* decision. Although the governor said he won't apply a "litmus test" in filling vacancies on the Vermont Supreme Court, he did say that *Baker* showed insufficient judicial restraint.[498] Democrats and the *Rutland Herald* editorial page criticized the governor's remarks.[499] The homophobes in Vermont have shifted their sights to public school teachers who "promote" the "homosexual agenda."[500] A Vermont church withdrew from the Vermont Conference of the U.S. Church of Christ rather than accept a conference decision to be "open and affirming" toward gays and lesbians.[501]

By the close of the 2003 session of the Vermont legislature, civil unions had ceased to exist as a meaningful political issue.

A QUIET BIRTHDAY PARTY

Christopher Graff, a writer for the Associated Press, observed in April 2003 that "if not for the fact that Howard Dean is running for President, the third anniversary of his signing of the civil unions bill would have passed without notice. Civil unions have become an accepted part of Vermont life."[502]

Civil unions are here to stay. When the courts of Alaska and Hawaii had granted legal recognition to gay and lesbian couples, the people reversed the court decisions.[503] In Vermont, the court in *Baker*, and then the legislature with the civil union statute, extended marriage benefits and duties to same-sex couples. In November 2000, the people reelected the governor whom had signed the bill and the Senate that had passed it. Unlike Alaska and Hawaii, the people of Vermont did not reverse the court decisions to give gays and lesbians access to the benefits and burdens of marriage.

5 The Choice

What's Wrong With Vermont's Civil Marriage Substitute

[M]ost Negroes are fighting against the system of segregation rather than for the immediate opportunity to have their own children educated in integrated institutions. They do not want to go to "white" schools so much as they want to avoid being forced to attend "colored" schools. As one elderly Negro phrased it with respect to bus integration: "The seats at the back are just as good as those at the front. Most Negroes still sit in the back, even though we got the buses integrated. But we didn't fight for seats, we wanted to get rid of those signs."

—J.W. Pealtason, 1961[1]

I BELIEVE that even the sweeping system of marriage-like benefits created by the Vermont civil unions statute is still insufficient. That statute, for all its comprehensiveness, and for all the goodwill and courage of those who voted for it, legislators still created a separate and *un*equal system of matrimony. As we all should have learned from the sad history of separate-but-equal in the context of race, legally mandated "separate" is inherently "unequal" when the law marks the segregated class with a badge of inferiority. Vermont's new legal system of Jim Crow marriage for same-sex couples does just that.

Before rolling into my argument, I want to express my uneasiness about making it. Leaders of the Vermont gay and lesbian community strongly supported the civil unions law. The lead lawyers for the *Baker* plaintiffs pushed hard for civil unions. At least two of the most courageous and thoughtful gay rights scholars disagree with virtually all I am about to assert. Yale Law School Professor William Eskridge, in his brilliant book, *Equality Practice: Civil Unions and the Future of Gay Rights*, demonstrated that the civil unions law does not assure full equality with marriage. Civil unions are unequal in status, unequal in their interstate portability, and unequal as regards benefits and obligations afforded by federal law.[2] Still, Eskridge rejects the notion that *Baker* and civil unions resurrect the separate-but-equal doctrine of *Plessy v. Ferguson*: "I am a classic liberal and a gay person who supports legal recognition of same-sex marriage. My last book criticized the twentieth-century legal regime that created an 'apartheid of the closet'. . . . Yet I do not believe the civil unions law creates an apartheid. . . . Nor do I believe the analogy to *Plessy* holds up. Formally, the law neither separates citizens nor equalizes their entitlements. Functionally, the law ameliorates rather than ratifies a sexuality caste system. The racial apartheid adopted by southern state legislatures and upheld in *Plessy* was very different from the new institution suggested in *Baker* and adopted by the Vermont legislature. Similarly, it is greatly unfair to tag the civil unions measure as 'separate-but-equal.'"[3]

Vermont Law School Professor Greg Johnson goes even further: "Was it a mistake to support civil unions? I don't think so, because it gave same-sex couples rights they badly needed. But on top of that, what is wrong with being different? The presumption behind Mello's position may be that no lesbian or gay couple could possibly want something other than what heterosexual couples have, that marriage is the pinnacle, the summit, the only form of state recognition worth pursuing—the key to equality and happiness. I would hope that the struggle for same-sex marriage is about more than imitation and emulation. Civil unions give the lesbian and gay community a chance to be different, a chance to celebrate its identity . . . *vive la difference.*"[4]

I agree with Johnson and Eskridge that *Baker* and civil unions were great leaps forward for same-sex couples, both required great courage. No one who lived in Vermont in 2000, as Johnson did, or who interviewed the legislative leaders, as Eskridge did, could fail to marvel at the guts of some Vermont legislators. I am extremely reticent to conclude that these acts of courage resulted in nothing more than a separate-but-equal marriage *lite*. Still, in the end, that is my reluctant conclusion. I might well be wrong, and Johnson and Eskridge might well be right. For months now I've been asking myself, who am I, a heterosexual, to disagree with gay men and scholars like Johnson and Eskridge? My answer is that scholars have a duty to ask uncomfortable questions out loud.[5] Thus, I will argue that civil unions are problematic, but I do not aim to make a brief for same-sex marriage. That has been done admirably by William Eskridge,[6] Barbara Cox, and others.

My argument will proceed in stages. First, I will address two assertions, made by opponents of same-sex marriage: that sexual orientation is a "choice" and that recognizing same-sex marriage would undermine the institution of traditional heterosexual marriage. Second, I will argue that civil unions stamp same-sex couples with a badge of inferiority; that civil unions are *un*equal to marriage, in ways tangible and intangible; and that Vermont's new law resurrected the discredited doctrine of separate-but-equal. Third, I will suggest that the Vermont legislature should have opted for marriage—and true equality—rather than civil unions. Civil unions were as controversial and contentious as marriage would have been. The legislature bought into what Martin Luther King called the "myth of time," that is, the idea that justice will be more palatable if it comes slowly and in stages. Finally, I argue that eventually the Vermont Supreme Court should recognize same-sex marriage.

Prejudice, the Courts, and the Choice about Whom We Love

The life of the law has not been logic: It has been experience.

—Oliver Wendell Holmes, 1881[7]

The avalanche of homophobia that swept Vermont following *Baker* demonstrated that prejudice based on sexual orientation was real in Vermont. The *Baker* court was an eminently legitimate act of the judiciary: to protect the civil rights of despised minorities. As I've suggested, this is what courts are *for*—and it's why the civil rights of minorities ought not be decided by majority vote.

The *Rutland Herald,* in a lead editorial published the Sunday before Town Meeting Day 2000, made the same point indirectly. The newspaper asked, and then answered, a rhetorical question: If "constituents do not want [same-sex marriage or a comprehensive domestic partnership scheme], why should [legislators] approve it? The short answer, of course, is that all civil rights questions have tended to languish in the court of public opinion, since *the majority view causes discrimina-*

tion in the first place. It would be strange if the current case proved any different."[8]

Stuart Matis's Knees: Is Sexual Identity a "Choice"?

The demonization of gays and lesbians as immoral beings presupposes that people *choose* to be gay or lesbian. On the premise that sexual orientation is a "choice," many Vermonters—Take It To The People, for instance[9]—deny that this is a civil rights issue at all.

Some Vermont political leaders, and many ordinary Vermonters, see homosexuality as a "choice" (a "lifestyle choice," as some put it a bit scornfully) made by gays and lesbians. One representative argued, "I think the argument that this is a civil rights issue is completely bogus. I see choice in sexual preference."[10] During the Senate floor debate on the civil unions bill, Senator John Crowley "said he had not seen any evidence to prove that homosexuality was anything other than a chosen lifestyle. Until evidence shows that it is not a matter of choice, Crowley said, he believes gays and lesbians should be disqualified from receiving the rights and benefits of marriage."[11]

Senator Crowley alluded to an interesting issue. On whose shoulders rests the burden of proof that homosexuality is or is not a choice? The senator would place the burden on lesbians and gays to prove that they are telling the truth that they did not "choose" their sexual orientation. But I believe the burden of proof is on people like Senator Crowley to prove that homosexuality is *not* a choice. In the absence of such proof, I believe the witness of every gay and lesbian person I know that they did not choose their sexual orientation. Because I do not believe that all these gays and lesbians are lying about this point, I believe that opponents like Senator Crowley have not carried their burden of proof.

I also trust my own experience and instincts in concluding that sexual orientation—homosexual or heterosexual—is not a "choice." I certainly have no memory of "choosing" to be heterosexual. That's just the way I am. That's the way I've always been. I don't presume to know what "makes" people gay or lesbian—or what makes people homophobic bigots, for that matter.[12] Maybe it's genetics. Some inconclusive scientific data suggests it is.[13] Maybe it's environment. Some inconclusive scientific data suggests it is. Maybe it's hormones. Some inconclusive scientific data suggests it is.[14] Maybe it's a combination. Maybe it's none of the above. I confess to feeling uncomfortable about the question of whether homosexuality is *caused*, even in part, by genetics or biology or anything else that suggests homosexuality is somehow abnormal.

I do not believe anyone chooses their sexual orientation, however. What person with half a brain would *choose* to be gay or lesbian in the United States? When being gay means second-class citizenship? When it means, for many people, having to hide an essential part of their being from their families, their co-workers, their employers, and their classmates? When, according to Vermont schoolteacher, and select board member Michael Quinn, "suicide is the Number 1 cause of death among gay and lesbian youths of Vermont"?[15] When "half a dozen teachers" at a Vermont high school "have made their rooms safe havens for homosexual students"?[16] After the lynching of Matthew Shepherd, who would *choose* to be gay? And, as the recent rhetoric suggests, Vermont is not immune from the hate and prejudice that enabled the murder of Matthew Shepherd.

Wait, the opponents of same-sex marriage insist, gays are not discriminated against: They are equally free to marry a member of the opposite sex or to remain celibate.[17] There is, as one newspaper editorialized, an *Alice in Wonderland* quality to this line of argument.[18]

The first of these contentions reminds me of the fallacious argument that interracial marriage bans were not discriminatory because whites and African Americans were treated the same: Each was free to fall in love an marry someone of their same race. Or the argument that airline policies denying employment to flight attendants who become pregnant did not constitute sex discrimination because the policy applied to men and women equally: Any person, regardless of their sex, who became pregnant lost his or her job. (Wink wink.)

The "celibacy option" strikes me as psychologically unrealistic and simply cruel. If, as I believe, sexual orientation is not a choice—neither homosexuals nor heterosexuals choose their sexual orientation—then the celibacy alternative would deny homosexuals one of the most important and intimate ways of expressing human love. Passion and love are at the core of what it means to be alive, and to be human.[19]

Heterosexuals would impose on gays a celibacy they would not impose on themselves. This is the definition of an unjust law. Martin Luther King, Jr. wrote that "an unjust law is a code that a majority inflicts on a minority that is not binding on itself. This is difference made legal."[20]

People who advocate the celibacy option—and who argue that sexual identity is a choice—ought to tell it to the parents of Stuart Matis. Matis was gay. He was celibate until the day he died at age 32—he committed suicide. As a devout Mormon, "as a pious churchgoer, Stuart Matis prayed and worked to change his sexual orientation. He died trying."[21]

"Even as a young boy, friends recall, Matis cherished his Mormon identity and the church's moral demands."[22] The Church of Mormon treats homosexuality as "an 'abominable' sin"; the church "requires gays and lesbians to remain forever celibate," and Matis "didn't dare consider intimacy with men he met, and apparently remained celibate his whole life."[23]

From age 7, "Matis began harboring a terrifying secret: He realized he was attracted to boys. For the next 20 years he kept the secret from everyone he knew and prayed fervently to God to make him heterosexual. . . . Though he deeply loved his family, he showed little outward affection, fearing he would blurt out his secret. 'He would punish himself if he had a [homosexual] thought,' [said a childhood friend]. 'He wouldn't allow himself to go to a friend's birthday party or [wouldn't] watch his favorite TV program.' Instead, he would sit in his room and read scripture."[24]

As a college student at Brigham Young University, Matis spent "hours in the library looking for a technique for becoming straight. . . . A church therapist instructed him to suppress his sexuality or to undergo 'reparative' therapy to become a heterosexual."[25]

At age 31, Matis told his parents he was gay. "To Matis' surprise, his family accepted his homosexuality."[26] His church did not. "Matis was especially frustrated by the church's energetic efforts to pass Proposition 22, California's ballot initiative banning same-sex marriage. The YES ON PROP 22 signs that dotted his Santa Clara neighborhood, many placed there by church members, were a reminder of his failure to find acceptance as a Mormon and gay man."[27]

On February 22, 2000, Matis wrote a suicide note to his family, "explaining why he couldn't continue to live," left the note no his bed, "drove to the local Mormon church headquarters, pinned a DO NOT RESUSCITATE note to his shirt, and shot himself in the head."[28]

"'Mother, Dad, and family, I have committed suicide,' Matis's note began. 'I engaged my mind in a false dilemma: either one was gay or one was Christian. As I believed I was Christian, I believed I could never be gay.' Stuart Matis struggled his whole life to resolve that dilemma.

The people who dressed him for burial were struck by the sight of his knees, deeply callused from praying for an answer that never came."[29]

Eleven days after the celibate gay Mormon man blew his brains out, California "overwhelmingly" approved the law banning same-sex marriage.[30]

At bottom, the argument by heterosexuals that gays choose their sexual orientation—or that they choose to act upon their sexual orientation and to express their passion and love for a person of the same sex—is a thinly disguised criticism of homosexuality itself. The only reason to deny gays and lesbians the freedom of intimate expression of their love is because homosexuality itself is immoral, wrong, or at least inferior to heterosexual love. To deny people in love the freedom to make love can only be justified if the love itself is somehow wrong.

Susan Murray, one of the lead lawyers who brought the *Baker* lawsuit, told the House Judiciary Committee that "to talk about sexuality in terms of choice was to imply that it was better to be a heterosexual than a homosexual."[31] Beth Robinson, the other lead counsel in *Baker*, also addressed the choice issue in her legislative testimony. "Robinson pointed out that people have a choice about their religious faith. But the fact that a person's faith is chosen doesn't make it any less valid, she said."[32] It also doesn't make bans on interfaith marriage any less invalid.

In the end, heterosexuals arguing that homosexuals ought to just . . . act like them, brings to mind Henry Higgins's famous lament in *My Fair Lady*: "Why can't a woman be more like a man?" I think of Rex Harrison's refrain whenever I hear straights bemoan the simple fact of life that gays *aren't* straight. It seems weird to have to say that *gay people are gay*.

Sure, they can pretend they're otherwise. Many do. Many must—because of the prejudices that others impose on them. They have always pretended. Gays are masters at pretending. They've had to be. It's a basic survival skill.

Gays can pretend, they can pass. That's not the point. The point is *they shouldn't have to*. No human being should have to deny such a basic constituent of their personhood, their humanity.

Would Same-Sex Civil Marriage Undermine "Traditional" Civil Marriage?

The woman from California was making small talk, "You live in a wonderful state." My Vermont Law School colleague agreed: Vermont is a wonderful state. The California woman went on: "I got married because of same-sex civil unions in Vermont. My boyfriend and I had been living together forever. But, when we saw how hard gay people were *fighting* for the right to get married—a right I've always taken for granted—it made me realize how important marriage really was."[33]

The existence of same-sex marriage could *strengthen* traditional, heterosexual marriage, by reminding us heteros that marriage really is a privilege worth fighting for. Recall the California woman discussed at the beginning of this book. Gay marriage could strengthen traditional marriage in another way as well: competition. Conservative columnist William Safire explained:

> Rather than wring our hands and cry "abomination!" believers in family values should take up the challenge and repair our own house.
>
> Why do too many Americans derogate as losers those parents who put family ahead of career, or smack their lips reading about celebrities who switch spouses for fun? Why do we turn to the government for succor, to movie porn and violence for sex and thrills, to the Internet for companionship, to the restaurant for Thanksgiving dinner—when those functions are the ties that bind families?
>
> I used to fret about same-sex marriage. Maybe competition from responsible gays would revive opposite-sex marriage.[34]

Opponents of same-sex marriage argue the opposite, of course. They predict that gay marriage would undermine heterosexual marriage. However, opponents of gays and lesbians misunderstand not only the people who are the objects of their scorn, they also misunderstand the nature of the *civil* institution they would deny gay and lesbian couples.

Same-sex marriage does not undermine traditional marriage any more than golf undermines bowling. I have demonstrated that the only reason the Vermont legislature rejected marriage in lieu of civil unions was the political reality of homophobia. I believe the maintenance of the legally required stigma of same-sex couples is not a legitimate governmental interest. Rather, I assert that Vermont's separate-but-equal system of marriage ought to be held unconstitutional for precisely the same reasons that *Brown v. Board of Education* held separate-but-equal public schools unconstitutional, and for the same reason the post-*Brown* cases held separate-but-equal buses, swimming pools, golf courses, and libraries unconstitutional: Such legally mandated segregation marks the segregated with an unmistakable badge of inferiority. Indeed, the only real reason for the segregation is to make that mark.[35]

It seems to me that opponents of same-sex marriage are overly preoccupied with the "sex" and not concerned enough with the "marriage." Sexual intimacy is a part of marriage, but it is not the only part and, in my own experience, it is not the most important part. My marriage is mostly about a day-to-day caring, a thousand little things and words and gestures, spoken and unspoken. And even when I think of physical intimacy, it's not sex that comes to mind. It's cuddling on the couch after a long and lousy day at work. It's my wife reaching for my hand as we stood side by side on the Gettysburg battlefield. Heterosexual marriage isn't all about sex. Same-sex marriage would be little different, I imagine.

An editorial cartoon by Danziger captured this point perfectly. The cartoon included two identical frames. It was nighttime, with a crescent moon in the otherwise pitch-dark bedroom window. The pillow talk dialogue ran like this:

> Did you let the cat out?
> No, I thought you did.
>   No, I told you I didn't.
> I thought you said you were going to take care of that.
>   I never promised I would.
> You never do anything.
>   I never do anything? What do you mean?
> You know what I mean.
>   I certainly do not know what you mean. How would I know. . . .
> Oh, You're impossible.
>   I'm impossible? You're impossible!
> Well, no sex for you. . . .

That is the left frame of the bifurcated cartoon. The right frame is identical: same dark room, same window, same crescent moon, same pillow talk. The cartoon's caption was "Heterosexual and Homosexual Marriage Contrasted."

"Traditional" heterosexual marriage would lose nothing by allowing same-sex couples into the marriage club. The right of civil marriage is not a zero-sum game, in which granting gays the right to marry means that the heterosexual right to marry is devalued. By adding to the rights of same-sex couples, nothing is subtracted from heterosexual couples. The *Boston Globe* made this point well. "Heterosexuals and gays do not compete for rights; they share them."[36] In fact, same-sex unions "no more undermine traditional marriage than sailing undermines swimming."[37]

Most anti–same-sex marriage commentators don't even try to marshal evidence that gay marriage would undermine heterosexual marriage. Jeff Jacoby, a thoughtful columnist, did try:

> Well, here's a shred of evidence: The *Boston Globe* reports that in the three years since Vermont extended near-marriage status to same-sex civil unions, nearly 5,700 gay and lesbian couples have registered their relationship. Of those couples, close to 40 percent, or more than 2,000, include at least one partner who used to be married.
>
> Just a shred—but a jarring one. Of course, it doesn't mean that Vermont's civil union law broke up 2,000 straight couples. It *does* mean that where there used to be 2,000 traditional marriages, there are now 2,000 ruptured ones—and 2,000 gay or lesbian unions in their place. Were some of those marriages doomed from the outset? Probably. But it's also probable that some of them weren't. In another time or another state, some of those marriages might have worked out. The old stigmas, the universal standards that were so important to family stability, might have given them a fighting chance. Without them, they were left exposed and vulnerable.[38]

As Jacoby conceded, this was only a "shred" of evidence. In fact, it's even less. Most of those civil unions were obtained by out-of-staters. The evidence of civil unions' impact on marriage *in Vermont* points in the opposite direction. Steve Swayne crunched the numbers for an op-ed piece:

> Traditionalists . . . say that giving gay couples the benefits of marriage cheapens and undermines marriage. These accusations, if true, are . . . serious. . . . Our Vermont experiment, however, suggests that they are false.
>
> Take cheapen, for example. No one can prove that my civil union with my partner of 11 years devalues my neighbor's marriage. It's an opinion, and a silly one, for it masks a rather dim view of marriage. According to vital records reports from Vermont's Department of Health, there were fewer divorces in Vermont in 2001 (the first full year of the civil union law) than in 1999 (before there was a single civil union), but in 2000 and 2001, the number of divorces was significantly greater than the number of civil unions. Gay couples getting hitched demean marriage more than straight couples getting unhitched? I don't buy it.
>
> As for undermining marriages, 6,056 marriages were performed in Vermont in 1999, 122 more than in 1998. In 2000, the first year civil unions were available, 6,271 marriages were performed in Vermont, 215 more than in 1999.
>
> Then there's the 2001 report, which found that 5,983 marriages were performed in Vermont, 288 less than in 2000. We'll have to wait for the 2002 report to see if 2001 was an anomaly (perhaps due to the terrorist at-

tacks?) or part of a long-term trend. If the latter, traditionalists may have ammunition to argue that, as gay rights expand, marriage contracts. Still, I wager that none of the folks who got married in 2000 and 2001 feel that the civil union law weakens their marriages.

There's another interesting statistic in the reports. "The percentage of civil (marriage) ceremonies increased to 58.9 percent in 2001. This percent has increased every year since 1990 when it was 47.2 percent." More and more couples are choosing a justice of the peace or a judge instead of a minister or rabbi to get married. This is as true for first-timers as for people who are getting married for the second or third time. In 2001, for example, more first-time Vermont bridges opted for civil ceremonies than for religious ones. (The flip-flop for grooms happened in 2000.)

This statistic should concern traditionalists more than same-sex marriage. It says that more and more straight couples are separating the legal aspects of marriage from the liturgical ones, which is precisely what the courts are doing.

Civil marriage in Vermont is now more popular than religious marriage, and I suspect that other states (and Canada) have also seen an increase in the number of civil ceremonies and a decrease in the number of religious ceremonies.[39]

Reading about Randall Terry lobbying in Montpelier,[40] I felt like I was back home in Virginia, hearing how interracial marriage was an "abomination" and a crime against nature and God. Some Vermont opponents of civil unions didn't like Terry, and they told him to go home.[41] I wonder why Terry's openly homophobic rhetoric made them so uncomfortable. I suspect it's because Terry blew their cover as avowed nonhomophobes. They don't hate gays; they just believe in "legislature's rights" and the protection of what they call "traditional marriage."

This is all very familiar to me. During the battles over racial desegregation when I was growing up in Virginia,[42] the rallying cry wasn't "we hate Blacks." The rallying cry—especially by lawyers—was "states' rights." The banner of "state's rights" (as well as the Bible and nature and all the rest) were used in the 1960s to justify segregation, as they had been used in the 1860s to justify slavery.

Likewise, the argument in support of the "traditional family"[43] boils down to bigotry against gays and lesbians. Same-sex marriage will not affect heterosexual marriages at all—the latter will remain unaffected by the inclusion of homosexual couples, *unless,* and only unless, same-sex couples are so immoral and evil that they would somehow pollute "traditional" marriages by their mere presence.

The argument that same-sex civil marriages would undermine or infect heterosexual marriages is nothing more than bigotry decorated in legalistic doubletalk. Take It To The People is simply a homophobic hate group—albeit a genteel one, not unlike the White Citizens Councils and other "respectable" segregationists in the Jim Crow South. Substitute *race* for *homosexuals* in their position, and what they are becomes clear. Homophobia enshrouded in "traditional family values" is still homophobia. As between the two, Randall Terry and Take It To The People, I much prefer the open and honest bigotry of Randall Terry. I prefer bigotry raw, not diluted by the base alloys of hypocrisy and lawyerly doublespeak.

Many opponents of same-sex marriage—those opponents I think of as genteel homophobes and bigots—deny that they are homophobes or bigots. They purport to hate the sin but love the sinner (although they would deny extending any marriage-like benefits to homosexuals, not to homosexuality).

These people are most readily identifiable by their buts. As in, "I don't loathe homosexuals, *but* homosexuality is an abomination [a sin, an evil, a perversion of nature, the moral equivalent of child rape, sex with animals, polygamy, bigamy, and so on]." Sometimes the *but* is silent, but it's always there. To choose one random example from today's newspaper, a letter to the editor began by saying that "[t]his whole debate on same-sex union has nothing to do with hate or malice toward our gay brothers and sisters."[44] After a silent *but*, the next two sentences in the letter were: "[The debate] does have a lot to do with Jesus Christ saying, 'Go, and sin no more, your past sins are forgiven you.' Many people have died of AIDS."[45] Then, after suggesting that AIDS might be God's judgment against gay people, the letter concluded, "Is there a message in the above statements [about Jesus' admonition to sin no more and AIDS]? Maybe, just maybe."[46]

Opponents of same-sex marriage also assert that they aren't attacking gays and lesbians; they're just trying to protect the institution they call "traditional" marriage. I think people who make this argument are deluding themselves, and they're deluding themselves in exactly the same way that opponents of interracial marriage deluded themselves into thinking they weren't racist.

Gay-bashers even try to don the cloak of victimhood: They assert that their rights are being violated by people like me calling them homophobes and bigots and by forcing them to live in a state that provides same-sex couples with the benefits of marriage. These poor, discriminated-against, put-upon heterosexuals remind me of my white classmates in Virginia who claimed that *their* civil rights were violated by having to share school buses and classrooms with African Americans.

Actually, the grievances of the Vermont homophobes are even less credible than the racist complaints of my junior high school classmates. My classmates did indeed have to share buses and classrooms and lunchrooms with African Americans in close proximity. But the Vermont homophobes do not even need to do that: They need not even be in close quarters with gay or lesbian couples. Rather, their complaint is that their civil rights are violated by simply *knowing* that, somewhere else in Vermont, there are same-sex couples who are living their lives as civilly unionized couples.

The civil rights of these homophobic Vermonters are not violated by having to live in a state that recognizes civil unions or same-sex marriages. It is they who would deny gays and lesbians the civil right to marry. The homophobes will remain free to hate homosexuals, to teach their children to hate homosexuals, to exclude homosexuals from their homes and their social circles. No law—and no court—has jurisdiction over the hatred in individual human hearts. But the courts do have jurisdiction over the laws, and the *law* should countenance no inequality between heterosexual marriage and gay marriage. Any distinction that marks same-sex couples with a badge of inferiority—which is to say, in the present climate, any distinction—should be struck down for the same reasons that Jim Crow separate-but-equal public schools, public buses, public swimming pools, public golf courses, and public lunch rooms were struck down by the courts in the aftermath of *Brown v. Board of Education*.

Amid the dehumanizing rhetoric of the debate over same-sex marriage, it is important to remember the *people* who brought the *Baker* case. The plaintiffs in *Baker* were three same-sex couples who had lived together in committed relationships for periods ranging from 6 to 27 years. Two of the couples had raised children together. Each couple applied for a Vermont marriage license, and each was denied.

The *Baker* plaintiffs underscore the basic truth of the *Baker* ruling and the same-sex marriage debate: that gays and lesbians are people, too. The *Baker* plaintiffs reinforce the reality that gays and lesbians are *already* part of families all across Vermont and America. They are already part of the day-to-day of life here in Vermont and, indeed, everywhere.

The "Right To Be Ordinary"

Anna Quindlen has observed that the right being sought by same-sex couples is, in essence, the "right to be ordinary."[47] She wrote that sometimes it's difficult to "put your finger on the tipping point of tolerance. It's not usually the Thurgood Marshalls and the Sally Rides, the big headlines and the major stories. It's in the small incremental ways the world stops seeing differences as threatening. It's the woman at the next desk, the guy behind the counter at the deli. And it's finally happening for gays and lesbians. They're becoming ordinary."[48] Same-sex marriages, or civil unions in Vermont, would be much like my own marriage and the marriages of other heterosexual couples. "Happy families and happy friends watched happy people pledge their love. Big deal. Ho-hum. Yawn. . . . [And,] by the way, hurray."[49]

BADGES OF INFERIORITY

I was told by a fairly conservative member of the [House Judiciary] Committee that, if this were not an election year, the vote would have been 11-0 for *marriage.*

—Sen. Ben Ptashnick, 2000[50]

The *Baker* decision recognized a constitutional right but gave the legislature first crack at creating a remedy. The court suggested that the legislature could either extend the right of civil marriage to same-sex couples or create a comprehensive system of "domestic partnerships" that would be the functional equivalent of marriage but that wouldn't use the *m* word. The court retained jurisdiction in the case.

Witnesses before the House Judiciary Committee instructed the legislators how they might take a minimalist approach to *Baker.* According to Jack Hoffman, then-Chief of the Vermont Press Bureau, Vermont Law School Professor Peter Teachout, in his testimony in the Vermont legislature

> [O]ffered some arguments the state might make if the legislature approved domestic partnerships and that new system were challenged in court.
>
> Tradition was one, he said. Because marriage had traditionally been a union of one man and one woman, the state could argue that the parallel

arrangement was justified as long as domestic partners had almost all of the same benefits.

Teachout also said that if Vermont became the only state to allow same-sex marriage, it could attract gay and lesbian couples who wanted to marry—and might later want to divorce. If it appeared that would place an added burden on the Vermont courts and other state institutions, that could be another justification for creating domestic partnerships instead, according to Teachout.[51]

As is probably clear from the previous discussion in this book, I think my colleague is wrong on both counts. First, the claim that same-sex marriage undermines traditional marriage is a thinly disguised critique of homosexuality itself: Same-sex marriage could only destabilize heterosexual marriage if it is inherently so evil or immoral that its very *existence* undermines heterosexual marriage. The contention that marriage has always excluded gays is no more persuasive than the contention that the laws that long discriminated against African Americans in general and interracial marriage in particular justified the discrimination: The law did indeed discriminate for a very long time, but that fact damns the law; it doesn't justify the discrimination.

Teachout's second rationale for the legality of a separate-but-equal marriage substitute—that allowing same-sex marriage would draw hordes of homosexuals to Vermont, swamping our courts with their unions and divorces—seems to me equally unpersuasive. I doubt that many gays would migrate to Vermont and stay, for the same reasons relatively few heterosexuals do so: The winters are brutal and last nine months; good jobs are scarce, and they don't pay well; good housing and schools are difficult to find. Actually, the homosexual hordes argument supports allowing them to *marry*. If they can marry here, then that marriage might well prove portable: They can take it home with them. By contrast, civil unions would probably not be portable: If they get one here, it's only good here, so they'll be more likely to stay here.

Neither of these two arguments in favor of excluding same-sex couples from marriage passes muster even under an easygoing constitutional "rational basis" test, because they are both animated by an intent to deny such couples full equality with heterosexual marriage. Because gay people are a despised minority in Vermont—and because the right at issue is the fundamental right of civil marriage—these two argu-

ments should fail under "strict scrutiny" or under any other meaningful level of heightened judicial review.

I don't want to minimize the importance of the civil unions law. It
was a giant step forward for gay and lesbian couples. However, at the
risk of being churlish, I do believe that the statute (and the court's affirmation of the statute) illustrate why the remedy of a parallel system of
marriage-like benefits ought not be held to pass constitutional muster.

As comprehensive as the parallel system is, it remains a separate-but-
equal substitute for marriage. And the reason for the separateness—the
only reason for the separateness—was the strong public sentiment
against the recognition of same-sex marriage. The post-*Baker* legislative
activity suggests that Justice Johnson was prescient in her warning that
the *Baker* majority had left the plaintiffs "to an uncertain fate" in the "political cauldron"[52] of the legislature.

Prejudice based on sexual orientation directly influenced the legislature's response to *Baker*. The recognition of the "political reality" of
opposition to same-sex couples was evident from the very beginning
of the process that culminated with passage of the civil union bill. "Almost to a person, [House Judiciary Committee] members said they had
to recognize the political realities [that is, that marriage was not a vi-
able option politically] both within the statehouse and among the public."[53] That was why the House Judiciary Committee's first action was
to take marriage off the table—a move hailed by Governor Dean's declaration that the marriage option was dead and that he promised to
use "all the powers of this office" to keep it dead.[54] A *Time* magazine
story about the House bill began by noting accurately that "Vermont
isn't about to legalize gay marriage. That's what state lawmakers were
insisting . . . after its House of Representatives passed legislation allowing 'civil unions' for same-sex couples. And that's what the bill
says. It specifically defines marriage as a union between a man and a
woman."[55] The magazine also noted that the issue has generated "a
firestorm of protest."[56]

Likewise, Senator Vincent Illuzzi, "who was once a supporter of benefits for same-sex couples," reportedly said that "public opposition to
same-sex marriage and to the civil unions bill passed by the House had
led him to reverse his position" and introduce a bill calling for amendment of the State Constitution.[57] "He had introduced a bill that would

provide some legal benefits to same-sex couples as well as relatives. . . . Illuzzi said he had worked for three months to generate support for his bill, but couldn't" so he "put aside that proposal and in its place offered a constitutional amendment that he said reflected the wishes of his constituents."[58] Illuzzi explained: "I'm trying to articulate in a constitutional framework what I've heard from my constituents. . . . I'm sympathetic to domestic partnership. My constituents aren't. If there's a choice between what they want and what I want, they win."[59]

Legislators in both the House and Senate who voted for the civil unions bill stressed that it was *not* a marriage bill. A member of the House said "emphatically" that the bill passed was "'definitely not gay marriage—I think we all very clearly got the message that people did not want gay marriage.'"[60] Another "said that the bill 'is very clearly not a marriage bill. We put in the bill that marriage is between a man and a woman.'"[61]

As discussed above, members of the House Judiciary Committee were explicit that they were bowing to "political reality" in opting for civil unions rather than marriage. That "political reality" was homophobia in Vermont. Also in response to the political reality of the unpopularity of homosexuals, the committee's bill included a fact-finding (later added to the substantive provisions of the bill itself) that defined marriage as a union between a man and a woman—thus making clear that same-sex couples were being relegated *by law* to second-class matrimonial citizenship. Without this stipulation, the governor would not have worked hard to persuade the legislature to pass the bill. Even with the governor's efforts, the civil unions bill passed the full House by a margin of 79 to 68.[62] An amendment to the bill that would have expanded marriage to include same-sex couples was massacred in the full House, 125 to 22.

Similarly, in the Senate, Senator Richard Sears, the bill's leading advocate—responding to a colleague's claim that the bill would "degrade the institution of matrimony"—stressed that "the bill included language to make it clear that marriage would only be between a man and a woman. A constitutional amendment wasn't necessary, he said."[63] Another Senator, Jeb Spaulding, noted that the bill was a compromise with those who saw it as a threat to traditional marriage: "Soon after the supreme court ruling Spaulding had urged the legislature to allow gays and lesbians to marry. While he still supports that, he said the civil unions bill provides some comfort for people who want to protect tra-

ditional marriage because it does define marriage as a union between a
man and a woman."[64]

The importance of the legal distinction between heterosexual marriage and same-sex civil unions was also suggested by the heated response to an advertisement that accused them of having voted for same-
sex marriage. On March 21, a subsidiary of Take It To the People ran an
ad in the state's two largest newspapers, the *Burlington Free Press* and
the *Rutland Herald*. The ad declared "House passes gay marriage" and
"The following [76] legislators voted against traditional Vermont family values."[65] The ad then listed the 76 House members who voted for
the domestic partnership bill.

However, as the Associated Press reported, the House "took pains to
make [domestic partnership] a separate and distinct legal structure in
the face of reluctance to broaden the marriage statutes themselves. . . .
That's why House members who voted for the bill were so upset" with
the ads.[66] Top leaders in the House criticized the ad's failure to distinguish between heterosexual marriage and same-sex unions as "false
and misleading."[67] The Speaker of the House noted: "All we're asking
is to be accurate, not misleading."[68]

Similarly, the *Rutland Herald* railed against the ad's equation of the
civil unions bill with marriage. In the lead editorial published on the
Sunday following the ad's appearance, the newspaper called the ad a
"lie" because the ad was "based on a hidden assumption: that same-sex
marriage and [domestic partnerships/civil unions] are the same
thing."[69] But "the House did not pass same-sex marriage. The House
passed a bill creating civil unions."[70] The ad's equating of marriage with
partnerships "rely on lies and distortion" and are part of a "cloud of
misinformation swirling around the House," editorialized the *Herald*.[71]

Representative Cathy Voyer called "a blatant lie"[72] an ad that chided
her and other Representatives for voting for "homosexual marriage."[73]
Representative Voyer "noted that she and most of the other lawmakers
mentioned [in the ad] had actually voted against an amendment to the
House bill on civil unions that explicitly would have opened the state's
marriage statutes to include same-sex couples.[74]

The governor concurred. Governor Dean, in a newspaper op-ed
piece published on March 29, responded to the ads and defended domestic partnerships for same-sex couples as he had all along: Civil
unions were not marriage. "Some opponents of the legislation have

campaigned on what this bill is not," the governor reemphasized.[75] "The bill is not a gay-marriage bill. The bill defines marriage as a union between a man and a woman."[76]

The history of the post-*Baker* statute suggests that the bill was, in no small part, passed out of a desire to exclude same-sex couples from marriage. One potent argument made in support of the civil unions bill was that, if the legislature did not act, the supreme court might well impose marriage as a remedy for the constitutional right recognized in *Baker*. That, in fact, was a realistic reading of the *Baker* decision, and it underscores the "political reality" that undermined the proposition that the statute was not quite a law enacted to extend civil rights to gay and lesbian couples. The statute was, at least in part, a way to prevent same-sex couples from inclusion into the institution of marriage. But for the fact that the statute explicitly was *not* marriage, the bill never would have passed the legislature—partly because the governor was adamantly opposed to allowing same-sex couples to marry.

Some legislators who voted against civil unions and marriage were frank that their constituents influenced their votes. A House member "said that constituent opinion influenced his vote. He received an estimated 300 e-mails, calls, and letters, and only 22, he said, were 'for.' 'That's about a 15:1 ratio,' he said, 'and you can't ignore that.' [He] said the Doyle poll results also helped him gauge public opinion."[77] Another echoed these sentiments.[78]

As a case study in how "political reality" warped the legislature's response to *Baker*, consider the case of Representative William Mackinnon. Mackinnon, a Democrat, believed that true equality for same-sex couples required the right to marry. Mackinnon voted against the civil unions bill "because he firmly believes that the only proper solution is 'an inclusive civil marriage.' Mackinnon says he remains convinced that one type of union for all couples, be they hetero- or homosexual, 'is the constitutionally correct thing to do.' 'I think that history will bear me out on that,' he said, adding that he thought a future court may find this [domestic partnership] bill 'untenable.'"[79]

Based on his convictions, Mackinnon voted against the civil unions bill in the House Judiciary Committee. That earned him a rebuke from William Lippert, the only openly gay member of the committee and the House: Mackinnon's view was "shortsighted and not supportive of the gay and lesbian community in Vermont."[80]

Then the pressure on Mackinnon to bend to "political reality" really began in earnest. The House Majority Leader tried to persuade Mackinnon to vote for the bill when it came before the full House. So did Mackinnon's colleague from his district. So did Governor Dean, who "called Mackinnon into his office for a private conversation, but gave up after 35 minutes."[81]

That wasn't all. An important fundraiser in Mackinnon's district (who also happened to be vice-chair of the state Democratic Party), wrote a letter to the leading local newspaper arguing that Mackinnon's position "undercut" support for the bill.[82]

Mackinnon didn't budge. He voted against the bill in the full House because it did not allow same-sex couples to marry. "It's widely thought that his vote against civil unions will cost him his seat on the Judiciary Committee next year. There's also a possibility that Democrats will try to throw Mackinnon overboard by finding an opponent to run against him in the September primary."[83] The thoughtful commentator Steve Nelson rose to Mackinnon's defense,[84] but Nelson's voice was virtually the only public dissenter to the chorus of condemnation heaped on Mackinnon.[85] (As discussed in the previous chapter, Mackinnon eventually voted for the bill when it returned to the House following Senate action, after being thanked for his "no" vote by Take It To The People).

In the aftermath of *Baker*, a number of people stated that the civil unions option was inappropriate because it would create a separate-but-equal system of marriage. There was, however, little exploration of precisely what was wrong with separate-but-equal. My intent in this section is to nail down (1) exactly *why* the separate-but-equal doctrine was struck down by the U.S. Supreme Court in *Brown v. Board of Education* and post-*Brown* cases, and (2) why the reasoning of *Brown* and its progeny apply with full force to Vermont's civil unions.

It seems to me that the only true remedy for the constitutional right recognized in *Baker* is to grant same-sex couples the right to marry. The alternative is some form of separate-but-equal marriage substitute. But, as I thought we'd learned in 1954 in *Brown v. Board of Education*,[86] separate is inherently unequal—and unmistakably inferior—when it comes to fundamental human rights like education (and civil marriage) and even when it comes to such mundane things as eating a cheeseburger and drinking a Coke at a Woolworth lunch counter in North Carolina, or riding a crosstown bus in Montgomery, Alabama, or staying at a motel in Atlanta.

In 1896, in the infamous decision *Plessy v. Ferguson,* the Supreme Court upheld the constitutionality of separate-but-equal facilities for African Americans and whites. Homer Plessy, who was one-eighth African American and who was a resident of New Orleans had been forced *by law* to ride in the segregated section of a train coach. With a lone exception, the Supreme Court Justices unanimously upheld the right of the southern government to segregate Mr. Plessy, solely because of his race, from the white passengers in that train. The Supreme Court explained: "If one race be inferior to the other socially, the Constitution of the United States cannot put them on the same plane."[87]

Only John Marshall Harlan (the first Justice Harlan) dissented in Homer Plessy's case. Harlan wrote: "Our Constitution is color-blind, and neither knows nor tolerates classes of citizens. . . . [The] thin disguise of 'equal' accommodations for passengers in railroad coaches will not mislead anyone, nor atone for the wrong this day done."[88] That day lasted for more than half a century—and *Plessy v. Ferguson* provided the rigid segregation in the South during the tragic era of Jim Crow, the era of the tragic fiction that facilities racially segregated *by law* can ever be "equal."

Plessy remained the law of the land for nearly six decades, until 1954 and *Brown v. Board of Education,* when the Court decided that segregation imposes on African Americans a badge of inferiority. In its first brief to the Court arguing that separate-but-equal was an oxymoron, the United States government (as Anthony Lewis recently reminded us) asserted that "the curtain which fences Negroes off from other diners [in railroad dining cars] exposes, naked and unadorned, the caste system which segregation manifests and fosters. A Negro can obtain service only by accepting, or appearing to accept, under the very eyes of his fellow passengers, white and colored, the caste system which segregation signifies. . . . This [is a] message of humiliation."[89]

This "message of humiliation," this badge of inferiority, was exactly what was wrong with the separate-but-equal doctrine, according to the Court in *Brown.* The unanimous opinion in *Brown* explained that segregation is especially hurtful "when it has the sanction of the law; for the policy of separating the races is usually interpreted as denoting the inferiority of the Negro group."[90]

The *Plessy v. Ferguson* Court had said that "the underlying fallacy" of the African American plaintiff's complaint was its "assumption that the enforced separation of the two races stamps the colored race with a badge of inferiority. If this be so, it is not by reason of anything wrong in the act, but solely because the colored race chooses to put that construction on it."[91] In other words, racial minorities are simply being hypersensitive in inferring inferiority from the white majority's choice to segregate African Americans from the race of their former masters and owners.

The reply to *Plessy's* disingenuous reasoning is simple: Even a dog knows the difference between being tripped over and being kicked. The unanimous *Brown* Court put it more artfully: "In the field of public education the doctrine of 'separate-but-equal' has no place. Separate educational facilities are inherently unequal."[92]

Denying committed same-sex couples the right to civil marriage sends the same message of humiliation and second-class citizenship to gays and lesbians. The *New Republic* was quite right that any civil unions regime would be nothing more than separate-but-equal treatment of an unpopular minority: "To grant homosexuals all the substance of marriage, while denying them the institution, is in some ways, a purer form of bigotry than denying them any rights at all. It is to devise a pseudo-institution to both erase inequality and perpetuate it. . . . There is in fact no argument for a domestic partnership compromise except that the maintenance of stigma is an important social value—that if homosexuals are finally allowed on the marriage bus, they should still be required to sit in the back. . . . Equality is equality. Marriage is marriage."[93]

It has been argued that the *Brown v. Board of Education* invalidation of separate-but-equal is distinguishable from the case at hand because *Brown* was a school case and this is a civil marriage case. This argument is breathtakingly ahistorical. It ignores the entire—and successful—post-*Brown* history of the civil rights movement to desegregate the whites-only South.

Brown was an education case, but it was not limited to that factual context. *Brown's* principle that separate *meant* unequal was applied to everything from buses to restaurants to bathrooms to water fountains. *Brown* wasn't just a legalistic holding: It was a statement of human worth and morality that transcended the narrow dispute before the Court. The whites-only South was not limited to schools, and neither was the reach of *Brown*.

Take the laws mandating segregated buses in Montgomery,

Alabama, for example. During the Montgomery bus boycott led by Martin Luther King, Jr. in 1955 and 1956, the law requiring segregated public transportation in Alabama was challenged in court.[94] Lawyers for the segregationists argued that *Brown's* ban on separate-but-equal applied only to schools, not buses. Lawyers for the desegregationists argued that it did apply.

The case attacking Montgomery's segregated buses—called *Browder v. Gayle*—was heard by a panel of three federal judges. The court decided that, under *Brown*, a separate-but-equal system for transportation also was unconstitutional but that "in their private affairs, in the conduct of their private businesses, it is clear that the people themselves have the liberty to select their own associates and the persons with whom they will do business, unimpaired by the Fourteenth Amendment."[95] In other words, people have the freedom to discriminate in their *private* affairs and business, but in *public* spheres discrimination is unconstitutional.

"There is, however, a difference, a constitutional difference, between voluntary adherence to custom and the perpetuation and enforcement of that custom by law." Judge Rives observed that the separate-but-equal concept, on which *Plessy v. Ferguson* was based, "had its birth prior to the adoption of the Fourteenth Amendment in the decision of a Massachusetts State Court relating to public schools." "The separate-but-equal doctrine," Rives continued, "was repudiated in the area where it first developed, that is, in the field of public education.[96]

"We cannot in good conscience perform our duty as judges," Rives concluded, "by blindly following the precedent of *Plessy v. Ferguson* when . . . we think that *Plessy v. Ferguson* has been impliedly, thought not explicitly, overruled." The court held that "the statutes and ordinances requiring segregation of the white and colored races on the motor buses . . . violate the due process and equal protection of the law clauses of the Fourteenth Amendment to the Constitution of the United States."[97]

In 1960, in *Boynton v. Virginia*, the Supreme Court outlawed segregation in interstate bus terminals. In 1961, a challenge to segregation of bus and train terminals in Jackson, Mississippi, reached the Supreme Court. The Court's response was unsigned and blunt: "We have settled [in *Boynton*] beyond question that no state may require racial segregation of interstate or intrastate transportation facilities. The question is no longer open; it is foreclosed as a litigible issue."[98]

And it wasn't only Jim Crow buses in Alabama, as any student of *Brown* should know. Richard Kluger—author of *Simple Justice*, the magnificent book about *Brown v. Board of Education*—noted that "it became almost immediately clear that *Brown* had in effect wiped out all forms of state-sanctioned segregation."[99] In the spring of 1955, the Fourth Circuit, following *Brown*, held that Baltimore, Maryland could no longer segregate its bathing beaches or public recreation facilities.[100] The Supreme Court affirmed the Fourth Circuit, "on the same day it reversed a Fifth Circuit opinion upholding separate-but-equal golf courses for Blacks in Atlanta. That year, courts in Michigan and Missouri cited *Brown* as authority for ending segregated housing at municipally run developments."[101]

In the dozen years after *Brown* was decided "the Warren Court handed down decision after decision that followed the path of *Brown*. Segregation was outlawed in public parks and recreation areas, on or at all interstate—and intrastate—commerce facilities waiting rooms and lunch counters as well as the carriers themselves, in libraries and courtrooms and the facilities of all public buildings, and in hotels, restaurants and other enterprises accommodating the public."[102]

Law professors complained that the Court seemed to be so casual about extending *Brown* beyond the school setting. "How could the negative psychological effects of separate schools on student motivation to learn be invoked to justify the ending of Jim Crow busses, beaches, and golf courses?" the professors asked.[103] The Court didn't care. It continued to broaden "the premise of *Brown* to hold that all forms of racial segregation were discriminatory and therefore humiliating and therefore a violation of equal protection."[104]

Thus, separate-but-equal is illegal even when applied to such prosaic and mundane matters as riding a bus, playing golf, swimming on a public beach, or ordering lunch at a terminal lunch counter. One could argue, I suppose, that state-sanctioned civil marriage is distinguishable from state-sanctioned segregation of city buses. Indeed, they are: Marriage is far more important, and the badge of inferiority imposed on same-sex couples by separate-but-equal civil unions is far more dehumanizing, degrading, and humiliating.

The bus and lunch counter segregation cases are germane to the matter at hand even beyond the simple historical point they demonstrate about *Brown*'s extension beyond the school context. Governor Dean, and many Vermonters, find same-sex marriage "uncomfortable" (as our Governor put it). But, in the 1950s and 1960s, many southern whites found it just as "uncomfortable" to sit beside an African American person at a Greyhound lunch counter or on a bus. The courts correctly held that such "uncomfortableness" is not a legally or morally sufficient reason for separate-but-equal segregation. And, today, the vast majority of southern whites no longer feel uncomfortable about sharing pubic accommodation with African American people. They just got used to it— as most Vermonters would, in time, get used to the idea and reality of same-sex marriages in their midst.

Segregated buses were unlawful because they were required *by law* to be segregated, and because that law stamped African American riders with a badge of inferiority. As Dr. King's Montgomery bus boycott proved, however, segregated buses weren't the only transportation in town. African Americans wishing for integrated travel were free to arrange their own, by private means. By contrast, the State of Vermont has an exclusive monopoly on the issuance of civil marriage licenses: Unlike the citizens of Montgomery, Alabama, for same-sex couples in Vermont, the state is the only bus in town. And that bus will probably be segregated—continues to be segregated. Ever after civil unions, heterosexual couples ride in the front, and same-sex couples ride in the back. The reason—the only reason—for the separate-but-equal treatment is to mark same-sex couples with a badge of inferiority.[105]

Lawyers are masters at drawing distinctions. But, if the basic principle of *Brown*—that separate is inherently unequal—applies to Rosa Parks's right to sit in the front of a dusty cross-town bus in Montgomery, Alabama, then it seems to me that the only thing equal to marriage is marriage.[106] Opponents don't like the back-of-the-bus analogy. But it's actually a strong analog that shows precisely what's wrong with any version of steerage-class parallel system of marriage-like benefits to same-sex couples.

African American–only seats were generally equal to whites-only seats. The fare to get on the bus was the same. The bus itself was the same. The bus route was the same. The seats themselves were the same. The view might not be as good in the last row as in the first, but it's not much worse than the view from the third row or the fourth row or the fifth. A law that segregated African Americans in the front of the bus would be no less wrong—and no less unconstitutional—than the laws that required them to sit in the back of the bus. Notwithstanding the fact that the African Americans–only part of the bus was really equal to the whites-only part of the bus, the segregation itself was constitutionally and morally wrong because the *legally mandated* segregation itself marked the segregated people as inferior.

Any parallel matrimonial system of civil unions will, by its very existence, be separate—and therefore unequal—in the same way as the segregated bus. However, the civil unions bill enacted into law contained language that explicitly created a second-class matrimonial citizenship status for same-sex couples. The bill said that "civil marriage" in Vermont "consists of a union between a man and a woman."[107] The bill also distinguished between the terminology for the rites and rituals that symbolize the two classes of unions, heterosexual and same-sex. Marriages of heterosexuals are "solemnized." Unions of homosexuals would be "certified" by judges or clergy members.[108]

Governor Dean left no doubt that the legislative distinction between heterosexual marriages and gay civil unions was central to the political palatability of the unions bill. Responding to critics who "claimed that the House bill ignores the will of the majority," Dean "said that the House Judiciary Committee responded to the public's concern when it rejected a bill that would have supported same-sex marriage."[109] The governor explained, the Judiciary Committee "eliminated same-sex marriage because they heard from the public, so I think they are listening to the public."[110] As for the governor himself, the legal distinction between "traditional" heterosexual marriage and same-sex couples was critical to his own support for the House bill: "Dean said he had become one of the proposals' biggest supporters since the House Judiciary Committee adding language defining marriage as a union between a man and a woman."[111] The governor—who soon after *Baker* was decided stated his opposition to same-sex marriage—was pleased when the House Judiciary Committee rejected the marriage option. Governor Dean promised to use "the powers of [his] office"[112] to ensure that the marriage option remained off the table.

Even the comprehensive civil unions scheme signed into law will not be truly "equal" to marriage. Civil unions are unequal to marriage in terms of both tangible and intangible benefits. William Eskridge has noted that "in at least one sense, civil unions flunk the separate-but-equal rule . . . that is their lack of interstate portability."[113] Further, civil unions don't count as "marriages" for purposes of federal law (tax law, Social Security law, immigration law, etc.).[114]

The intangible benefits have to do with "a sense of belonging, a sense of being part of the community."[115] The *Valley News* recognized that marriage "confers a certain community status as defined by society. Establishing a parallel institution is a way to create an instrument for providing homosexual couples with everything but the social status that other couples enjoy."[116]

It is these intangibles (which aren't so intangible to the people who are denied them based on sexual orientation) that make me so uncomfortable with marriage substitutes such as civil unions.[117] The only reason for the creation of a complicated parallel system of civil unions—rather than simply opening up marriage to include same-sex couples—is to mark same-sex couples with a badge of inferiority. As the members of the House Judiciary Committee made clear, the only reason they opted for the cumbersome civil unions option, rather than choosing the more straightforward option of same-sex marriage was the "political reality." That "political reality" is the homophobia that swept the state in the wake of the *Baker* decision.

Eileen McNamara, a *Boston Globe* columnist, got it exactly right: "Domestic partnerships proposals are no more than a political dodge, an unconscionable sop to bigots who will tolerate homosexuality only if it can be segregated in some parallel universe. But gay and lesbian people do not live in a parallel universe. They live in this one."[118] "Why," McNamara wrote, "should our brothers, sisters, aunts, uncles, sons, and daughters be relegated to faux marriages simply to appease those who can live more easily than they can with discomfort."[119]

A gay man, writing in a letter to the editor of the *Rutland Herald*, made clear that the badge of inferiority is inherent in civil unions: "Separate-but-equal is a doctrine built on fear. It's purpose is to institutionalize and ensure the simple reality that 'separate' remains unequal; otherwise, no justification exists for 'separate' at all."[120]

LOVING

[Those who drew and ratified the Due Process Clauses of the Fifth Amendment or the Fourteenth Amendment] knew times can blind us to certain truths and later generations can see that laws once thought necessary and proper in fact serve only to oppress. As the Constitution endures, persons in every generation can invoke its principles in their own search for greater freedom.

—*Lawrence v. Texas*, 2003[121]

I'm a Southerner—a Virginian, actually. I grew up in Virginia, a state that, until the late 1960s, outlawed interracial marriages. The rhetoric in support of that particular piece of racist legislation—and the general culture of tolerance for racism that made such a law possible—have an eerie resonance to me today, as I listen to the homophobic rhetoric in favor of denying gays and lesbians the right to civil marriage. I've heard it all before: Marriage is a sacred institution; interracial marriage violates the Bible and God's will.

During the first 10 years of my life, interracial marriage was against the law—it was a criminal offense—where I lived. It was a Virginia case, *Loving v. Virginia*,[122] that the Supreme Court used as a vehicle to strike down such miscegenation laws.

In June 1958, Richard Loving, a white man, and Mildred Jeter, an African American woman, were married in the District of Columbia, where interracial marriages were legal. Soon after their wedding, the Lovings, who had both been residents of Virginia, returned to Virginia and set up their household in Caroline County.[123] A state grand jury indicted the Lovings for violating Virginia's ban on interracial marriages. The Lovings "pleaded guilty to the charge and were sentenced to one year in prison; however, the trial judge suspended the sentence for a period of 25 years on the condition that the Lovings leave the state and not return to Virginia for 25 years."[124] The judge's opinion explained:

> Almighty God created the races white, black, yellow, malay, and red, and he placed them on separate continents. And but for the interference with his arrangement there would be no cause for such marriages. The fact that he separated the races shows that he did not intend for the races to mix.[125]

Following their guilty plea, and pursuant to their sentence, the Lovings left Virginia. They moved to Washington, D.C., and sued to invalidate Virginia's miscegenation laws.[126]

In the U.S. Supreme Court, the Assistant Attorney General for the Commonwealth, R.D. McIlwaine III, of Richmond, argued the following:

> *McIlwaine:* We start with the proposition, on this connection, that it is the family which constitutes the structural element of society; and that marriage is the legal basis upon which families are formed. Consequently, this Court has held, in numerous decisions over the years, that society is structured on the institution of marriage; that it has more to do with the welfare and civilizations of a people than any other institutions; and that out of the fruits of marriage spring relationships and responsibilities with which the state is necessarily required to deal. Text writers and judicial

writers agree that the state has a natural, direct, and vital interest in max-
imizing the number of successful marriages which lead to stable homes
and families and in minimizing those which do not.

It is clear, from the most recent available evidence on the psycho-soci-
ological aspect of this question that intermarried families are subjected to
much greater pressures and problems than are those of the intramarried,
and that the state's prohibition of interracial marriage, for this reason,
stands on the same footing as the prohibition of polygamous marriage, or
incestuous marriage, or the prescription of minimum ages at which people may marry, and the prevention of the marriage of people who are
mentally incompetent.

[Chief Justice Earl] Warren: There are people who have the same feeling
about interreligious marriages. But because that may be true, would you
think that the state could prohibit people from having interreligious marriages?

McIlwaine: I think that the evidence in support of the prohibition of interracial marriages is stronger than that for the prohibition of interreligious
marriages; but I think that . . .

Warren: How can you say that?

McIlwaine: Well, we say that principally . . .

Warren: Because you believe that?

McIlwaine: No, sir. We say it principally on the basis of the authority
which we have cited in our brief.[127]

Bernard Cohen, arguing as a friend-of-the-Court, refocused the Justices on the human dimensions of the case before them:

If the framers had the intent to exclude antimiscegenation statutes, it
would have taken but a single phrase in the Fourteenth Amendment to
say, "excluding antimiscegenation statutes." The language was broad.
The language was sweeping. The language meant to include equal protection for Negroes. That was at the very heart of it, and that equal protection included the right to marry, as any other human being had the
right to marry, subject to only the same limitations.

And that is the right of Richard and Mildred Loving to wake up in the
morning, or to go to sleep at night, knowing that the sheriff will not be
knocking on their door or shining a light in their face in the privacy of
their bedroom, for "illicit cohabitation."

The Lovings have the right to go to sleep at night, knowing that should
they not awake in the morning their children would have the right to inherit from them, under intestacy. They have the right to be secure in
knowing that if they go to sleep and do not wake in the morning, that one

of them, a survivor of them, has the right to Social Security benefits. All of these are denied to them.

The enormity of the injustices involved under this statute merely serves as indicia of how the civil liabilities amount to a denial of due process to the individuals involved. As I started to say before, no matter how we articulate this, no matter which theory of the due process clause, or which emphasis we attach to it, no one can articulate it better than Richard Loving, when he said to me: "Mr. Cohen, tell the Court I love my wife, and it is just unfair that I can't live with her in Virginia." I think this very simple layman has a concept of fundamental fairness, and ordered liberty, that he can articulate as a bricklayer, that we hope this Court has set out time and time again in its decisions on the due process clause.[128]

Peter Irons described the outcome in *Loving v. Virginia*:

On June 2nd, 1967, Richard and Mildred Loving celebrated their ninth wedding anniversary. Ten days later, the Supreme Court added a present. The Lovings—and their kids—could sleep without any worries that Sheriff Brooks would drag them out of bed.

Like the *Brown [v. Board of Education]* case, *Loving v. Virginia* was unanimous. And like *Brown*, Chief Justice Warren spoke for the Court. His opinion was short and blunt. Virginia's law against racially mixed marriages violated two provisions of the Fourteenth Amendment. The equal protection clause bans racial laws that do not serve a "permissible state objective." The state's only purpose, Warren said, was "to maintain White Supremacy." The law also violated the due process clause, which protects the right of liberty. That right includes the "fundamental freedom" to marry, without restriction on race.

The Lovings were thrilled with their anniversary present. "I feel free now," Mildred said. "It was a great burden." Rich was relieved. "It's hard to believe. Now I can put my arm around my wife in Virginia."

Racial attitudes change slowly, but they have changed with the law. Fifty years ago, nine out of ten Americans opposed mixed marriages. Recent polls show only one in four are still opposed, most of them older. There are now a million interracial couples in the United States, including Supreme Court justice Clarence Thomas and his wife.

Rich Loving died in 1975, but Mildred still lives in the white cinderblock house he built. She still meets some hostile people, but attitudes, she says, have really changed. "The Old South is going away." Sheriff Brooks is one person whose attitude hasn't changed. "I'm from the old school," he says, "I still think the law should be on the books." Rich Loving had this advice for his kids about who to marry: "I'd leave it up to them, let them decide for themselves." His daughter Peggy married a man of mixed race. She's proud of both her parents for the stand they took. Thanks to the Supreme Court, Peggy and her family don't have to worry about Sheriff Brooks any more.[129]

The arguments made in favor of the Virginia ban on interracial marriage were eerily similar to the arguments today in favor of banning same-sex marriage. Susan Murray, one of the lead lawyers in *Baker*, testified before the House Judiciary Committee that interracial marriage had been called "unnatural," citing "a quotation from a U.S. Senator who opposed interracial marriage 'simply because natural instinct revolts as it is wrong.' And she said a U.S. Representative from Georgia warned that interracial marriage, 'necessarily involves degradation' of traditional marriage."[130]

Some have suggested that civil unions are not materially different from civil marriage, that it's only a label.[131] But when *the law* does the labeling, labels matter. During the oral arguments in *Baker*, Chief Justice Amestoy "posed a hypothetical that all marriage might be thrown out and replaced with some kind of domestic partnership status."[132] Counsel for the same-sex couples rejected the idea, and Justice James Morse responded, "so the label is everything?"[133]

Once again, the interracial marriage ban is instructive here. What if the U.S. Supreme Court in 1967, rather than ruling that whites and African Americans have the right to marry, ruled instead that states could create systems of domestic partnerships for interracial couples while retaining marriage for white couples only?

We instinctively recoil from this suggestion, because today we instinctively know that racism is wrong. It wasn't always so. Throughout much of the South, when I was growing up there, racism was as accepted and acceptable as is homophobia in 2003.

Sadly, although most Vermonters instinctively feel that racism is wrong, many Vermonters do not instinctively feel—in their gut—that prejudice based on sexual orientation is wrong. Here, today, it is acceptable in public discourse, for some Vermonters to call other Vermonters "abominations," "immoral," "evil," "crimes against nature." If we substitute "Black" or "Jew" for "gay" in today's rhetoric, we'd call it hate speech and condemn it. Yet, it's acceptable to use such hate speech against gays and lesbians. Why is that, do you think?

I teach Vermont state constitutional law and federal constitutional law at Vermont Law School. It's sometimes hard to get students to see as relevant old constitutional chestnuts that seem like embarrassing remnants of an atavistic past. One of these is separate-but-equal. Now, all of a sudden, separate-but-equal has become the statutory law of Vermont, at least for a while, until the Vermont Supreme Court says in the gay context what the U.S. Supreme Court has said in the public school and virtually every context with respect to race: When separation is mandated by law, and when that separation constitutes a badge of inferiority, separate is inherently unequal.

UNLIKELY HEROS

All segregation statutes are unjust because segregation distorts the soul and damages the personality. It gives the segregator a false sense of superiority, and the segregated a false sense of inferiority.

—Martin Luther King, Jr., *Letter from Birmingham City Jail*, 1963[134]

Legislatures are not known for their courage in the face of highly vocal, mobilized, and well-funded special interest groups, no matter how unrepresentative and bigoted those special interest groups might be. And people like Randall Terry, as well as groups like Take It To The People, are nothing if not loud and intimidating.

Maybe it was possible for the Vermont legislature to resist such intimidation and do right here. But I doubted it. Legislatures are masters at compromise, and elected legislators will feel a strong temptation to try to placate the homophobics and haters, even at the expense of the basic human rights and civil rights of Vermont's gay and lesbian people. Legislatures are notoriously flaccid, and I expected that our legislature would listen to the lawyers and pass a statute giving gays and lesbians the minimum of rights required by the *Baker* decision. This they did. They resurrected the separate-but-equal doctrine, and they enacted a civil unions law that gave rights while unmistakably relegating same-sex couples to second-class citizenship. They did this, in part, because lawyers told them that although separate-but-equal may not be a good thing, here is how you can get away with it anyway, maybe, depending on the judicial will and courage of the Vermont Supreme Court.

Although I can think of few courageous *legislatures*, I can certainly think of courageous *legislators*. Representative David Deen, Senator Mark MacDonald, Representative William Mackinnon, Representative Thomas Little, Representative William Lippert, Representative Michael Kainen, and Senator Benjamin Ptashnick, are some homegrown examples. Given the unpopularity of same-sex unions—and the evidence demonstrated that many Vermonters polled disfavored even civil unions[135]—it would have taken moral and political courage for the Vermont legislature to enact, and for Governor Dean to sign, a same-sex marriage bill.

Governor Dean found the issue "uncomfortable," and he favored civil unions only when it was made clear that such unions were not "marriage." He might even have vetoed a same-sex marriage bill.

Governor Dean's tepid response to *Baker*—and his public determination to place the full power of his office behind opposition to same-sex marriage—reminded me of President Eisenhower's refusal to use the moral power of his office to increase public understanding of *Brown* and the justice of racial desegregation. Eisenhower decried "extremists on both sides"—thus equating the NAACP with the White Citizen's Councils—and opined: "Well, I can say what I have said so often: It is difficult through law and through force to change a man's heart."[136]

This missed the point. The point of erasing legally mandated badges of inferiority isn't to erase prejudice in the hearts of men and women. It's to erase prejudice *in the law*. It's to erase *the law's* sanctioning of such prejudice.

I also don't necessarily agree with the idea that changing the law has no effect on changing the hearts of people. History suggests that changing the law can begin the much harder process of transforming people's attitudes of bigotry and prejudice. What President Eisenhower failed to understand post-*Brown*—and what Governor Dean failed to understand post-*Baker*—was that "the law itself and changes made under it give legitimacy to the social order that follows and brings about a change in attitudes. In Montgomery [Alabama], for example, white bus passengers changed their attitudes after they changed their seats."[137] After the *courts* forced them to change their seats.

"Burke Marshall understood the point very well. 'But laws *can* change the hearts of men,' he would say, stressing that it was the law that made change possible."[138] Howard Dean made clear that, when it comes to changing public hostility on same-sex *marriage*, the Vermont Supreme Court was on its own: It could expect no help from Vermont's chief executive.

I am intrigued by one thing. Take It To The People suggested that perhaps the legislature should have done nothing—should simply have ignored *Baker*. There are old names for this, old words from the South's opposition to *Brown v. Board of Education*: "interposition," "nullifica-tion," and (as it was called in my Virginia) "massive resistance." These doctrines, first articulated by John C. Calhoun in the 1830s and disin-terred by the segregationists of the 1950s and 1960s, held that the state could "interpose" its sovereignty against perceived "illegal federal en-croachment" (as a ballot initiative in Texas in 1956 put it).[139] A resolu-tion, enacted by the Alabama legislature in the mid-1950s, stated that the Supreme Court's decisions on racial desegregation "are as a matter of right, null and void, and of no effect."[140]

If the legislature had simply ignored *Baker*, that would have made it a no-brainer for the Vermont Supreme Court to do what it should have done in the first place: recognize that gays have a right to the "common benefit" of civil marriage, and that marriage is marriage is marriage.

In the end, I think it will be up to the Vermont Supreme Court. That would be unsurprising and appropriate. As I've said, this is what courts are *for*: to protect discrete, insular minorities from the bigotry of the ma-jority. That's why courts are antimajoritarian, antidemocratic institu-tions: to protect historically oppressed and discriminated-against mi-norities from the prejudices of the majority.

Both the *Baker* majority opinion and Justice Johnson's dissent recog-nized explicitly that courts sometimes must make decisions that prove unpopular. That's part of the job: to enforce the constitutional law with-out fear or favor. Reading Justice Johnson's dissent, I was reminded of a line from Holmes: "To think great thoughts you must be heroes as well as idealists."[141]

"ALL DELIBERATE SPEED" AND THE "MYTH OF TIME"

[It would be] different but equal

> —Governor Howard Dean, responding to the charge that civil
> unions would be separate-but-equal to marriage, 1999[142]

As mentioned earlier, the U.S. Supreme Court did not, in its landmark 1954 decision in *Brown v. Board of Education*, issue a decree ordering compliance with its holding that public school segregation was uncon-stitutional. In fact, the Court asked the parties for another round of briefs and oral argument on the issue of implementation. Fully aware of the emotional impact its ruling would have in the South, and wishing to move cautiously and reasonably, the Justices directed the parties to address several questions: (a) Should the Supreme Court issue a decree that African American children should forthwith be admitted to schools of their choice? (b) should the Supreme Court permit an effective gradual adjustment to be brought about from existing segregated systems not based on color distinctions? (c) assuming the Court would permit gradual desegregation, should the Supreme Court itself formulate detailed decrees? or (d) should the Court remand the cases to the lower courts with directions and, if so, what directions?[143]

Southerners saw the opportunity to evade *Brown*. The Arkansas Attorney General argued for the Justices to do what the Vermont justices did in *Baker*: to leave it to the legislature, to "the Congress for full implementation."[144] Southern legislatures were confident—and with good reason—that southern senators could filibuster any bill implementing *Brown*. South Carolina asked the Court to leave it to the lower courts, while conceding that there would be no integrated schools "perhaps not until 2015 or 2045."[145]

By contrast, Thurgood Marshall, arguing for the African American plaintiffs in *Brown*, urged the Court to issue firm instructions to the lower courts—including a "time limit,"[146] a fixed date, either September 1955 or September 1995,[147] or at any rate *some* fixed date by which time the lower courts must abolish segregation.

Marshall argued, "What is needed is a firm hand. . . . A District Court properly instructed by this Court will supply that firm hand. . . . If no time is set, they [the defendants] are going to argue in any event the same way they have argued here, which is nothing."[148] Marshall also called the Court's attention to the actual children on whose behalf the suits had been brought. Each of them had a "personal and present right" not to be discriminated against.[149]

The Southerners won this round of *Brown*, of course. The Supreme Court did not fix a specific date for desegregation. The Court only ordered desegregation with "all deliberate speed," leaving the lower federal court judges to make *Brown* a reality, which they did, eventually but heroically. But it took a long time. A *very* long time. I don't think that long time reduced the rancor; it might well have magnified it.

Vermont Law School Professor Gil Kujovich praised the Vermont Supreme Court for moving slow on same-sex marriage.[150] I am troubled when heterosexuals argue that gays and lesbians ought to settle for less than the full equality enjoyed by us heteros. I am troubled for the same reason I distrusted whites in the South of my youth who argued that African Americans ought to wait. It's easy to exhort others to wait for the full rights of citizenship you already enjoy. In thinking about *Baker* and the legislative response to *Baker*, it is well for us to remember the words of Thurgood Marshall about the "personal and present" rights of the African Americans in *Brown* not to be discriminated against.

That academics would urge gay and lesbian couples to go slow on same-sex marriage ought to surprise no one. As chronicled in Carol Polsgrove's important book *Divided Minds: Intellectuals and the Civil Rights Movement*,[151] white intellectuals, with a few exceptions, advised African Americans to be patient—even after the *Brown* decision and the 1964 Civil Rights Act and 1965 Voting Rights Act—rather than risk the anger and violence of white Southerners. It took the lunch-counter sit-ins, and the publication of James Baldwin's essay *Letter from a Region of My Mind*, to give patronizing white academics a sense of African American anger.

It is also well to remember what was wrong with the *Plessy v. Ferguson* separate-but-equal doctrine struck down in *Brown*: the badge of inferiority the doctrine marked upon African Americans. The words of Martin Luther King, Jr. in *Letter From Birmingham City Jail,* bear repeating and emphasizing: "*All segregation statutes are unjust because segregation distorts the soul and damages the personality. It gives the segregator a false sense of superiority, and the segregated a false sense of inferiority.*"[152]

Dr. King, in this same letter, also wrote of what he called the "myth of time."[153] After noting "I guess it is easy for those who have never felt the stinging darts of segregation to say, 'Wait,'" King explained his rejection of the myth of time, the idea that King was moving too fast towards desegregation, that if only he would be patient and wait, all would be well in the end.[154] King wrote that the myth of time grew "out of a tragic misconception of time. It is the strangely irrational notion that there is something in the very flow of time that will inevitably cure all ills. Actually, time is neutral. It can be used either destructively or constructively. I am coming to feel that the people of ill will have used time much more effectively than the people of good will. We will have come to repent in this generation not merely for the vitriolic words and actions of the bad people, but for the appalling silence of the good people."[155]

The *Baker* court's majority opinion included stirring words about "our common humanity." Yet that same court opinion seemed to leave open the possibility of a separate-but-equal system of domestic partnerships. I have to wonder how long same-sex couples in Vermont will have to wait for their common humanity and ours to be fully recognized.

Opponents of civil unions claim that such unions are the first step down the road leading to marriage. I hope they're right in this prediction, but I doubt it. I oppose civil unions precisely because I do *not* believe they will end in marriage.

Like the U.S. Supreme Court in *Brown I,* the Vermont Supreme Court in *Baker* recognized an important constitutional right. But, as there was a *Brown II* that mandated desegregation "with all deliberate speed," so will there be a follow-up litigation in the wake of the post-*Baker* statute.

Baker was truly a courageous decision, but the job is only partly complete. To finish the task will require at least as much, if not more courage, from our highest court.

SIMPLE EQUALITY AND SIMPLE JUSTICE

It's about time Vermonters took a stand and abolished this sort of behavior [that is, homosexuality].

—A letter to a Vermont newspaper, April 5, 2000[156]

The *Baker* litigation was about *people,* Vermont people. Nina Beck, 44, and Stacy Jolles, 41, are raising a son, Seth, who was one-month-old at the time of the *Baker* decision (the couple's first child, Noah, died soon after the *Baker* lawsuit was filed).[157] Lois Farnham, 51, has been with her partner, Holly Puterbaugh, for more than 27 years.[158] Stan Baker, 53, had been with his companion, Peter Harrington, for six years.

The question on the table in *Baker* was whether the State of Vermont would allow a despised minority in its midst equal access to the institution that is at the foundation of orderly family life: the right to civil marriage. The alternative—a domestic partnership scheme—would attempt to create a separate-but-equal institution for same-sex couples, which, as discussed earlier, would not truly be equal to civil marriage.

I have not always agreed with the Vermont Supreme Court's interpretations of the state constitution. I wasn't sure that *Brigham v. State,*[159] the court's school funding case, was an appropriate exercise in constitutional adjudication. I wasn't sure about *Brigham* because the parties in *Brigham* were not in need of special judicial protection from the prejudices of the majority population: They were not despised for who they are. They were not discrete and insular minorities historically subject to discrimination within and without the legislative process.

However, as I've said, the court got it right in *Baker,* when it mattered the most. Notwithstanding the rhetoric of the court's critics, *Baker* was not a radical decision. Chief Justice Amestoy is no revolutionary.

The Chief Justice is, however, a hero, an unlikely hero in the tradition of the Fifth Circuit and Federal District Court judges in the Deep South who implemented *Brown v. Board of Education* in Alabama, Mississippi, Louisiana, Georgia, and the other states comprising the old Confederacy.[160] For all its shortcomings and missed opportunities, for all its invitation to disinter the long-discredited doctrine of separate-but-equal, the Chief Justice is a hero for his court's unanimous recognition of our common humanity. And not just the Chief Justice. The entire *Baker* court, all five of them. They're all heroes.

Those southern federal judges in the era of *Brown*—white men all, enforcing the civil rights of African Americans—paid a dear and terrible personal price for their determination to follow the law in the teeth of racial hatred. Their lives were threatened, their families were shunned, their children were ostracized and ridiculed by their classmates at school—and by all the same sorts of people who believed, as fervently and as zealously as the homophobes of Vermont, that the Bible and God and nature decreed separation of the races.

Many argue that same-sex couples ought to be happy with whatever the legislature (and the people of Vermont, a majority of which oppose even civil unions, according to the town meeting votes and polls) choose to give them. Gays and lesbians ought to wait for marriage until the people come to accept it.

This argument also harkens me back to *Brown v. Board of Education.* As discussed above, the *Brown* Court did not order immediate compliance with its mandate; it only required states to desegregate their schools with "all deliberate speed." As we now know, "all deliberate speed" dragged on for two decades. In the end, the judiciary had to tell the segregationists that enough was enough.

I expect the same to be true of *Baker*. Many people (among them the editorial writers at the *Rutland Herald*) saw the outpouring of opposition to same-sex marriages as a reason to settle for less than marital equality.[161]

The opposite seems true to me. The ugly homophobia unleashed in Vermont by *Baker* (and here again I include the genteel apologists as well as the honest bigots) proves to me that only the *courts* can do simple justice here. If same-sex couples in Vermont have to wait until the people and politicians decide to grant them the basic human right of civil marriage, I have no doubt they will have to wait as long as the African American schoolchildren of Alabama had to wait to share a classroom with their white peers.

History teaches that people fear those different from themselves, and that people fear change. The inclusion of every group of outsiders, into the full benefits of American citizenship, has always come at a cost of social dislocation. For African Americans, America had to fight the bloodiest war in the nation's history, wait another century, and then fight another war in the courts and on the streets of places like Birmingham, Alabama. The Bible and the laws of God and nature were deployed to justify slavery, then the separate-but-equal doctrine, then Jim Crow. For women, it took the courts and Congress. Once again, the Bible and nature were trotted out to justify the unjustifiable.

Difference and change—so many people, even here in tolerant Vermont, seem to fear these things that perhaps I am being unfair to the opponents of same-sex marriage. Prejudice seems to be as much a part of some people as being gay is to other people. Part of me feels I ought to be more tolerant of other people's prejudices and bigotry.

Perhaps it's because I'm getting old, but I find myself less and less tolerant of racism, anti-Semitism, sexism, and homophobia. I've been hearing the same lame excuses for them all my life, and I'm tired of it. Rosa Parks sat down because she was tired and she "responded to one who inquired about her tiredness with ungrammatical profundity: 'My feet is tired but my soul is rested.'"[162] I'm standing up because my soul is tired.

Homophobia is neither new nor surprising. What did surprise me—naively, in retrospect—was that Vermont was supposed to be different. I heard the homophobia in grade school, junior high school, high school, college, and law school in Virginia. I heard it when I worked in Alabama and practiced law in Florida. I didn't think I'd hear it here. Not in Vermont.

I must confess to an ineffable feeling of sadness in discovering, since the *Baker* decision, that Vermont is perhaps not really so different from the South—from my South—when it comes to gays and lesbians. In the years I've been living up here, I've listened to talk about how tolerant this place is, how very different it is from the bad old South of my childhood. I've heard, again and again, how Vermont was the first state to outlaw slavery; until the Civil War, Vermont remained the only state with a constitutional ban on slavery. Vermont was the first to elect an African American to its state legislature. Vermonters played heroic and crucial roles in the Civil War, particularly in the repulse of Pickett's charge on the third day of the battle of Gettysburg.

It's easy and safe to be smug and self-righteous and sanctimonious about race when in a state is as monochromatic as Vermont.[163] Vermont "historically has had both the smallest number and smallest percentage of minority residents in the nation."[164] According to 1997 census date, Vermont's population is 98.4 white.[165]

Well, there *are* gay and lesbian people in Vermont. More than straight Vermonters might think. Some are out of the closet. I suspect that many are not and, given the outpouring of hate this state witnessed during 2000, it's easy to see why they're not.

As a Jew, I have encountered anti-Semitism in Vermont.[166] And many African Americans I know would take strong issue with the notion that Vermont—or at least that many Vermonters—are in fact as enlightened on matters of race as we might like to believe. A 2003 study determined that African Americans were arrested by police at higher rates than whites in Vermont.[167] The study, which was conducted by the Vermont Center for Justice Research, reinforced other studies that have shown African Americans are incarcerated in numbers disproportionately high compared to their percentage of the state population.[168] I have heard countless anecdotes about racism against African Americans in Vermont. One person of color recently told me (and I am paraphrasing here): "Vermont is more racist than the South, because Vermont is still in denial. At least the South is open and honest about its racism, and has tried to do something about it. The North—including Vermont—remains in denial about is own racism."

Actually, Vermont's reputation for tolerance had taken a pounding even before the homophobic reaction to *Baker*. In February 1999, ten months before the *Baker* decision was issued, the state advisory committee to the U.S. Commission on Civil Rights issued a report finding "widespread" racial harassment in Vermont's schools.[169] Equally significant, the report found Vermont in denial of this widespread racism.

Some of this report bears quotation and emphasis. *"Racial harassment appears pervasive in and around the state's public schools,"*[170] the report said. *"Such harassment is "widespread and pervasive . . . and is a reflection of overall race relations in the state. . . .* The elimination of this harassment is not a priority among school administrators, school boards, elected officials and state agencies charged with civil rights enforcement."[171] Public schools were found to be unresponsive to reports of harassment—brought to their attention by parents of minority students. "The report faulted teachers, school administrators, and government agencies for either not doing enough to combat racism and, in some cases, even contributing to it," the Associated Press wrote.[172]

The report, and the investigation that produced it, were triggered by "a spate of incidents in Burlington and elsewhere, where minority students said they had been verbally taunted and sometimes physically attacked by white students," the Associated Press reported.[173] The report was also based on two community forums held in November 1997 in Burlington and Rutland. At the hearings, 18 parents and three students gave first-person accounts about racial harassment in Vermont's public schools.[174]

Those hearings "painted a picture of a system that was not only unresponsive to, but often in denial of, parents' complaints" of racial harassment and assaults, according to Diane Derby of the Vermont Press Bureau.[175] One parent was told by the school board that she was "overreacting" when she tried to meet with the board about her children being called "nigger" in class.[176]

"Another parent told of how her son, an African American, was subject to taunts and daily harassment from a student who would put trash on her son's cafeteria tray and then utter a racist remark about slavery."[177] Still another "mother testified that her daughter was called a whore, while her son came home crying and told her they were calling him racist names."[178] The mother of a Puerto-Rican boy told of how her son had been branded immediately as a gang member.[179] An adoptive mother of an African American girl "said she got a panicked call one day that her daughter had lice. The teacher claimed she had a different kind [of lice] than what they had seen before and it could infect the whole school. In reality her unusual lice was not lice at all but sand from the sand box. Their reaction was so out of proportion; my daughter is isolated and terrified.'"[180]

In light of the public disapproval of *Baker*—and the poisonous antigay rhetoric that swept across the state in 2000—it seems to me sadly significant that the Vermont civil rights report focused on the racist attitudes of Vermont's *school children.* These children presumably learned their racism at home, in their "traditional" heterosexual families. I wonder if it's the parents of these racist kids who are now disrespecting gays in general and *Baker* in particular.

It is also significant that the racial harassment report spoke to racists attitudes in *1999.* Not 1989 or 1979 or 1969 or 1959, but 1999. The same year *Baker* was decided.

Of course, the 1999 report on racism in Vermont's schools—and the report's conclusion that the *"widespread and pervasive"* harassment in the schools "is a reflection of overall race relations in the state"181—did not appear in a vacuum. Notwithstanding Vermont's reputation for racial tolerance, shots were fired into the home of an African American clergyman in Irasburg in 1968.[182] Then-Governor Phil Hoff sparked a firestorm of opposition for his program to bring hundreds of African American children from Harlem to live with Vermonters.[183]

Yet, it is the "Niggerhead" incident that is most germane. Chris Graff, Montpelier Bureau Chief for the Associated Press, described what happened:

> For a century a mountain and pond in Marshfield carried the name Niggerhead. In 1966 the U.S. Board of Geographical Names dropped the names from its maps and called on the state of Vermont to change the names, saying the term "nigger" was derogatory.
>
> In 1967 the state Library Board, which had jurisdiction over place names, voted 6-1 that it "deemed no action necessary." The dissenter was James Holden, chief justice of the state Supreme Court.
>
> A year later an aide to Hoff, who was then governor, appealed to the state Board of Civil Affairs/Rights and again the matter came before the state Library Board, which again refused to take action.
>
> In 1970, a group called the "Committee to Abolish Niggerhead" formed and began orchestrating a campaign to change the names. Letters of support poured into the state, such as one from Shirley Files in the state archives in the secretary of state's office show this was an extremely contentious debate. One woman from Rutland wrote to the governor, "I suggest that the name be changed to 'White Trash.' This will show that white people do not feel sorry for themselves and perhaps the black people can take a lesson from this.
>
> A woman in Brookfield noted the dictionary defined niggerhead as 'tussocks of grass sedge standing out of a swamp," referred to blacks as "them" and "foreigners" and wrote: "I just can't have sympathy for any people who are so sensitive they even got Kake Walk outlawed because they thought it was poking fun at them. What a sad world this would be if no one could stand being laughed at."

A sheet opposing the name change detailed the many definitions of niggerhead, including "to describe a milk can," and concluded: "In view of the very widespread and accepted use of this word throughout the English language, it is a question whether the current disenchantment with the word by a relative minority should outweigh its broad acceptance in American and British dictionaries."

Gov. Deane Davis was silent. In 1970 an aide to the governor wrote to a person seeking a change in the name that "as the matter was thoroughly reviewed in due process in the last several years, it is not felt timely to open the matter again."

The state Library Board met again on the issue in April of 1971. But when Otis McRae, a black man and the leading advocate of the name change, referred to the racist attitudes of states leaders, particularly the governor, board members told him to "Shut up." He refused and the board walked out.

The Marshfield selectmen then sought to end the controversy by petitioning the board to change the name. Davis agreed, writing: "While I think this issue has been blown out of all proportion, nevertheless, if there are those, as there appear to be, who feel that the existence of the name is to some extent insulting or degrading, I personally feel that it would be better to clear the deck and come up with a brand new name. Emotions have run high on this matter and the continuance of the controversy would appear to indicate the existence of more racism in Vermont than I believe there can possibly be."

Both the mountain and pond took the name Marshfield.[184]

And now we hear the same excuses for inequality as were used by the South of my youth. Now we have newspapers editorializing, in the twenty-first century that "it isn't as easy to counter opposition to same-sex marriage" as it was to "counter racism in the civil rights era. The views of many opponents are shaped by ideas of sexuality taught by their religions. These moral teachings . . . have a legitimacy that racism does not have."

Well, no. Actually, it wasn't so "easy" during the civil rights era—not for the fighters on the front lines, although doubtless it *was* easier for the editorial writers of Vermont newspapers. For a long time in the South, hate and the threat of violence were in the air, palpable things. Those who spoke as the elected representatives either averted their eyes or made excuses for the unconscionable. Most people went on with their daily routines, living their lives in uncomfortable silence, ignoring the injustice around them, leaving the fight to others. And the Bible was read to justify racism, just as easily as it is today used to justify homophobia.

WHERE THE BUCK STOPS: THE VERMONT SUPREME COURT

I write today as a Vermonter to ask something very personal—I need your help to secure my right to marry the man whom I love more than anyone else in the world, and I am afraid.

Do you know what it means to have someone threaten you or your life? I do.

—A gay Vermonter, 2000[185]

It was a noble and idealistic hope that the *Baker* court expressed in inviting the legislature to have the first opportunity to craft a remedy for the constitutional right recognized in *Baker*. It was an act of faith that the people's elected representatives would do the right thing. It also was an act of faith that the people themselves would allow their elected representatives to do right.

It was not a forlorn hope. If any legislature would do right on this issue, it was Vermont's, with it's well-deserved tradition of tolerance and inclusion. Even if that hope failed to be realized, it does not follow that the *Baker* majority was wrong in extending it in the first place.

In the end, though, I believe the legislature did not—could not, was institutionally unable to—realize that hope. Robert E. Lee said, on the field at Gettysburg following the repulse of Pickett's charge, that he failed because he "asked more of men than they were able to give."[186] Here, I think, the *Baker* court asked more of politically accountable legislators than they were able to give. And we now know more than we did in December 1999 when *Baker* was decided. We now know that gays are in fact a despised minority in Vermont. We now know that homophobia in this state is both broad and deep. This is sad, but useful, knowledge to have when the issue returns to the Vermont Supreme Court.

The End of Baker
A page of history is worth a volume of logic.

—Oliver Wendell Holmes, 1921[187]

The *Baker* majority was explicit that it was *not* holding that there is *no* constitutional right of same-sex couples to marry. That issue the court saved for another day: "While some future case may attempt to establish that—notwithstanding equal benefits and protections under Vermont law—the denial of a marriage license operates per se to deny constitutionally protected rights, that is not the claim we address today."[188]

The issue will not, however, return to the Vermont Supreme Court in *Baker* itself. On May 10, 2000, the Associated Press reported that the three same-sex couples in *Baker* "[would] ask that their case be dismissed by the Vermont Supreme Court, their lawyer said."[189] According to attorney Beth Robinson, the couples decided that they would ask to withdraw the lawsuit when the civil unions law goes into effect on July 1. "'We're all kind of committed to the notion of trying to deal with healing,'" Robinson explained.[190] Indeed, given Robinson's and her co-counsel's active role in advocating for the civil unions bill, they would have had a difficult time arguing in the Vermont Supreme Court that the bill the lawyers themselves worked to pass was in fact unconstitutional.[191]

Professor Greg Johnson has written bluntly that the lawyer's decision to drop the *Baker* lawsuit was wise: "If the plaintiffs had gone back to the Vermont Supreme Court, they would have lost, and not by a 3-2 margin, or even 4-1, but 5-0."[192]

I'm not quite so pessimistic. Still, it would be very difficult for the *Baker* court to invalidate the comprehensive civil unions system adopted by the legislature. At significant political risk, the legislature did what the *Baker* court suggested: It enacted a parallel system of benefits that looks a lot like marriage. I have difficulty imagining the court invalidating a remedy that the court itself had suggested. Still, I think the court should do exactly that.

Retrospective Justification

This is something material, something I can see, feel, and understand. This means victory. This *is* victory.

—Abraham Lincoln, upon receiving a captured Confederate battle flag, 1863

Some folks claim that the negative public reaction against gays and the court is evidence that the court was wrong in *Baker*. I think the opposite is true. Every homophobic letter to the editor; every signature of the 25,2000 who signed the petitions in opposition of extending to same-sex couples marriage or a marriage substitute; every antigay letter and statement by the leadership of Vermont's clergy; every rabid bit of gay-bashing by elected representatives like Nancy Sheltra—every one of these things authenticates, validates, and reinforces the premises central to the legitimacy of the *Baker* decision: that gays are a despised minority especially in need of *judicial* protection of their fundamental civil rights, including the basic human right of civil marriage.

The outpouring of homophobia in Vermont—the genteel homophobes as well as the rabid bigots—reinforces the fact that *Baker v. State* was a civil rights case brought on behalf of a minority people whose sexual orientation is feared and loathed by a significant portion of the majority population. It is now clear—if it wasn't clear at the time *Baker* was decided—that gays are indeed a despised minority in Vermont. It is the job of the courts to protect the civil rights of despised minorities. It is up to the Vermont Supreme Court today—as it was up to the judiciary in the civil rights era of the 1950s and 1960s—to enforce the fundamental civil rights of Vermont's homosexual minority.

Again, I don't mean to underestimate how hard it would be on the justices to hold that civil rights principles mandate the recognition of same-sex marriage. Judges are human beings, and—as the lower court judges in the South who implemented *Brown v. Board of Education* could attest—the condemnation of their friends and neighbors hurt.[193] However, as Justice Johnson noted in her *Baker* dissent, "constitutional rights may not be denied simply because of hostility to their assertion or exercise."[194]

Because *Baker* was a civil rights case, I think it should have been decided under civil rights principles. One such principle is that statutes that burden unpopular and disfavored minorities—including, in my view, gays and lesbians—be subject to strict judicial scrutiny. In order to pass constitutional muster under "strict scrutiny," the classification must serve a compelling state interest that cannot be satisfied by any other, less-restrictive means. Under "strict scrutiny," the justification for prohibiting same-sex marriages—the notion that such unions are so immoral that they would pollute and undermine traditional heterosexual marriages—should fail.

The homophobic reaction to *Baker* persuaded at least one member of the House of Representatives that this fight is indeed a matter of protecting the civil rights of a despised minority. Representative Derek Levin explained his vote in favor of the comprehensive civil unions bill: "The thousands of e-mails and letters filled with hatred and fear that were delivered to each of us at the statehouse towards gay and lesbian people was what convinced me. The threats of eternal damnation for each of us who might vote favorably on this convinced me. The hatred and physical threats in some of those letters directed at me convinced me. Echoes of the civil rights past convinced me."[195]

Perhaps these same things will convince a majority of the Vermont Supreme Court to acknowledge that *Baker* was a civil rights case brought on behalf of a despised minority and that the separate system of domestic partnerships is inherently unequal and thus unconstitutional. In any event, the Vermont Supreme Court might well not have the final say on the legality of any domestic partnership law. The federal courts could still invalidate the post-*Baker* statute under the Equal Protection Clause of the U.S. Constitution—as the U.S. Supreme Court invalidated an amendment to the Colorado Constitution that (1) pervasively denied rights of nondiscrimination to gays and (2) was enacted based on animus towards gays and lesbians. The rights recognized by *Baker* were grounded in the state Constitution, but those state-created rights cannot be denied in a way that offends the federal Constitution.

The 2003 Texas Privacy Case: Lawrence v. Texas

If the U.S. Supreme Court meant what it said in the 2003 Texas privacy case, the underpinnings of the opposition to same-sex marriage have been undermined. The majority opinion in *Lawrence* began:

> Liberty protects the person from unwarranted government intrusions into a dwelling or other private places. In our tradition the State is not omnipresent in the home. And there are other spheres of our lives and existence outside the home, where the State should not be a dominant presence. Freedom extends beyond spatial bounds. Liberty presumes an autonomy of self that includes freedom of thought, belief, expression, and certain intimate conduct. The instant case involves liberty of the person both in its spatial and more transcendent dimensions.[196]

The majority emphasized that the issue was about privacy, not sex: "The case should be resolved by determining whether [John Lawrence and Tyron Garner] were free as adults to engage in the private conduct in the exercise of their liberty."[197] The important question was *not* whether the "Constitution conferred a right upon homosexuals to engage in sodomy."[198] Framing the issue this way "fail[s] to appreciate the liberty at stake."[199] To reduce the lives of gays and lesbians to sex demeans the claim the individual put forward, just as it would demean a married couple were it to be said marriage is simply about the right to have sexual intercourse. The laws involved in *Bowers* and here are, to be sure, statutes that purport to do no more than prohibit a particular sexual act. Their penalties and purposes, though, have more far-reaching consequences, touching upon the most private of places, the home. The statutes do seek to control a personal relationship that, whether or not entitled to formal recognition in the law, is within the liberty of persons to choose without being punished as criminals.

This, as a general rule, should counsel against attempts by the State, or a court, to define the meaning of the relationship or to set its boundaries absent injury to a person or abuse of an institution the law protects. It suffices for us to acknowledge that adults may choose to enter upon this relationship in the confines of their homes and their own private lives and still retain their dignity as free persons. When sexuality finds overt expression in intimate conduct with another person, the conduct can be but one element in a personal bond that is more enduring. The liberty protected by the Constitution allows homosexual persons the right to make this choice.[200]

The *Lawrence* Court overruled a 1986 decision. That decision, *Bowers v. Hardwick*, upheld the ability of the state to criminalize "sodomy" between consenting adults, regardless of sexual orientation. The Texas sodomy statute in *Lawrence* was limited to gay conduct. The *Lawrence* Court could have struck down the Texas statute without overruling *Bowers* by "declaring the Texas statute invalid under the Equal Protection Clause." Rather, the court declared the following:

That is a tenable argument, but we conclude the instant case requires us to address whether *Bowers* itself has continuing validity. Were we to hold the statute invalid under the Equal Protection Clause some might question whether a prohibition would be valid if drawn differently, say, to prohibit the conduct both between same-sex and different-sex participants.

Equality of treatment and the due process right to demand respect for conduct protected by the substantive guarantee of liberty are linked in important respects, and a decision on the latter point advances both interests. If protected conduct is made criminal and the law which does so remains unexamined for its substantive validity, its stigma might remain even if it were not enforceable as drawn for equal protection reasons. When homosexual conduct is made criminal by the law of the State, that declaration in and of itself is an invitation to subject homosexual persons to discrimination both in the public and in the private spheres. The central holding of *Bowers* has been brought in question by this case, and it should be addressed. Its continuance as precedent demeans the lives of homosexual persons.

. . .

Bowers was not correct when it was decided, and it is not correct today. It ought not to remain binding precedent. *Bowers v. Hardwick* should be and now is overruled.[201]

BUT MAYBE I'M WRONG

The civil unions analysis I just completed above may be completely wrong. This is the flaw: Leading gay rights activists and scholars disagree with me. Far from viewing civil unions as a "badge of inferiority" or a resurrection of separate-but-equal, thinkers and leaders such as Greg Johnson,[202] William Eskridge,[203] and Beth Robinson strongly support civil unions. Greg Johnson argues that civil unions provide same-sex couples with a grand opportunity to sculpt their *own* identities as couples, unencumbered by the baggage associated with heterosexual marriage.[204] *Vive la difference,* he celebrates.[205]

There is truth in this. They may be right. And I want to join in the celebration of civil unions. I really do. But I can't. For me, the only thing equal to marriage is marriage.

Since June 2003, we have had something of a test environment against which to measure civil unions against same-sex marriage. From 2001 to June 2003, Vermont's civil unions law was the only easy option open, in the western hemisphere, to gay and lesbian couples. In June 2003 the appellate court of Ontario, Canada, recognized same-sex marriage.[206] Marriage licenses were issued that same day.[207] The Canadian government seems poised to embrace the court decision.[208]

It will be interesting to see whether Vermont remains the destination-of-choice for same-sex couples who want to get hitched. The vast majority of couples who have been "CU'd" in Vermont were out-of-staters, and most of them have come from a privileged group. Around 90% have been white; most have been college graduates in their 30s and 40s; and they typically earn above-average incomes.[209]

Will these couples continue to travel to Vermont for civil unions? Or will they travel an hour more to Canada, where they can get married? Canada, like Vermont, has no residency or nationality requirements for marriage.[210] Same-sex marriages in Canada are no more (or less) likely to be recognized by other states than are Vermont civil unions. Will civil unions decline in Vermont, now that true marriage is equally available in Canada?

What the court did in *Baker*, and what the legislature did in response to *Baker*, took courage. Courage is not, as Hemingway said, "grace under pressure"; that's acting. Courage is not pointless and risk taking; the *reasons* for taking the risks must justify those risks; American soldiers in Iraq are courageous, whereas Evel Knievel is not.

My favorite definition of courage is Tim O'Brien's 1969 memoir, which in turn takes me back to Plato and Aristotle.[211] O'Brien was looking for "proper courage," during his tour in Vietnam, the sort of courage "exercised by men who know what they do is proper."[212] Proper courage, O'Brien continues, is "wise courage. It's acting wisely, acting wisely when fear would have a man act otherwise. It is the endurance of the soul in spite of fear—wisely."[213]

Socrates, in the dialogue *Laches*, distinguished between "foolish endurance" and "wise endurance."[214] He said: "only the wise endurance is courage."[215] Building upon *Laches*, O'Brien argues that "men must *know* what they do is courageous, they must *know* it is right, and that kind of knowledge is wisdom and nothing else. Which is why I know few brave men. Either they are stupid and do not know what is right. Or they know what is right and cannot bring themselves to do it. Or they know what is right and do it, but do not feel and understand the fear that must be overcome."[216]

Aristotle defined courage as "what enables you to do what is right, habitually." Courage is partly experience and partly reflection on that experience. O'Brien's heroes in Vietnam "had been out long enough to know; experienced and wise . . . Realistic and able to speak the truth. Conceited? Never. And, most strikingly, each of the heroes *thought* about courage, *cared* about being brave, at least enough to talk about it and wonder to others about it."[217] The French have a phrase, *courage sans peur* (courage without fear), which highlights that you can do something with your heart (*coeur*), and then you can do this fearlessly.

The comprehensive civil unions law was a significant step forward on the road to the matrimonial equality. It was a proud step. But Steve Nelson, a columnist for the *Valley News*, is right that "our aspirations should be higher."[218]

Nelson continued, "I and others have compared this legislation to the separate-but-equal sins of our past. The civil unions bill may provide equivalent legal rights to Vermont's gay couples, but these rights are offered with condescension and reluctance. Although we are now out of the downpour of hatred that soaks most of America, subtle bigotry still hangs heavy over Vermont's hills. We have begrudgingly granted gay men and women rights they have been long denied, but they ought not to feel grateful and we ought not to feel righteous." The danger, he warned, "is that this compromise solution goes just far enough to mire us in moral complacency for decades to come."[219]

In its time, the *Plessy v. Ferguson* decision was doubtless hailed by "moderates" as an important victory in the ongoing struggle for full equality. After all, the doctrine did require that facilities be *equal* as well as separate. We must go slow, the moderates would have urged. We must take "political reality" into account.

However, partial victories like *Plessy* tend to become prisons. It took African Americans six decades to break free of the prison erected by the *Plessy* victory. I wonder how long gay and lesbian Vermonters and Americans will have to wait before being released from the victory of civil unions.

6   Conclusion

Three Years After

We will have to repent in this generation not merely for the vitriolic words
and actions of the bad people, but for the appalling silence of the good people.

—Martin Luther King, Jr., *Letter from Birmingham City Jail*, April 16, 1963[1]

VERMONT. THE People's Republic of Vermont, an oasis of pro-
gressivism and toleration of people's differences in America. I cheered
when the Vermont legislature decided that same-sex couples are qualified to adopt. I was glad that gay-bashing was punished as a hate crime.
I was proud that my adopted state had outlawed discrimination based
on sexual orientation. For me, the *Baker* decision was an occasion for
dancing in the streets.

I owe a debt of gratitude to the Vermont homophobes and haters
who came out of the woodwork after *Baker* was decided. My first reaction to the *Baker* decision was one of joy and complacency: joy that my
state's highest court had recognized "our common humanity" with my
gay and lesbian friends, students, colleagues, neighbors, and acquain-
tances; and complacency that the legislature, now or in the near future,
would include same-sex couples in the fundamental human right of
civil marriage. I was nagged by the doubts that the *Baker* court might
have set the stage for a resurrection of the loathsome separate-but-equal
doctrine, but I shrugged off these worries. This was Vermont in the year
2000, not Virginia in 1954. I thought how nice it was to be living here
(where such an act of simple justice would be taken as so obviously
right and noncontroversial) rather than Virginia (where it would be unthinkable).

Then the backlash set in. Even the legislative hearings didn't snap me
out of my blithe complacency; I took them as merely the sour-grapes
whinings of lawyers and zealots who had lost in *Baker*. It was the letters
to the editor—that relentless daily drumbeat, day after day after day, for

193

weeks and then months, in virtually every Vermont newspaper I'd read—that served as my wake-up call that the stories of gay baiting and homophobia I'd heard over the years from my gay students and friends were not simply isolated instances: They were specific manifestations of a generalized hostility to gays and lesbians that was broad, deep and strong in Vermont. By Town Meeting Day in March 2000, I was wide awake.

The public backlash forced me to think more deeply about the issues raised in *Baker* and its aftermath. But for that backlash, that would not have happened, and I would not have written this book.

I've wondered, over the years since *Baker*, what makes people so fearful of gay people. My mother, Mrs. Ida Goldberg Mello, taught me from before I remember that we Jews have the least excuse of any group to discriminate against others because of who they are: We, of all people, should know better. My Jewish mother also taught me that it was the height of stupidity—and of mental, intellectual, and moral laziness—to judge an individual by his or her membership in a group. Groups include both good and bad members, and I was obligated to take each person as an individual, one at a time.

It has now been three years since the civil union statute became the law of Vermont. As of July 11, 2003, Vermont had issued at least 5,786 civil union licenses.[2] Eighty-five percent of those have been issued to out-of-state couples.[3]

In years since Vermont's civil unions statute made history, I am pleased to report that the sky has not fallen. The Connecticut River has not turned to blood.[4] There have been no plagues of frogs, flies, boils, or locusts.[5] Our cattle have not fallen over dead.[6]

Actually, everyday life remains unchanged. The mountains are as majestic as ever. The air is crisp as ever. Winter is long as ever. My neighbors still buy their newspapers and milk at Ken's Country Store. People still mow their lawns. The local sheep seem unchanged. The main topic of conversation is still the weather.

There are a few changes, if you know where to look for them. Civil unions announcements appear occasionally in some local newspapers. Bed-and-breakfasts advertise civil union specials on gay and lesbian Web sites. An online outfit "has booked travel arrangements for couples from Russia, Indonesia, and Australia who are planning civil unions in Vermont."[7]

Behind closed doors, same-sex couples have more legal rights—but still less than my wife and I have. Hopefully, they feel safer and a bit more equal.

The battlefields over same-sex unions, and over gay rights generally, moved on. As of this writing (November 2003), Massachusetts is ground zero in the gay-marriage wars, as Vermont was in 2000. After Vermont allowed civil unions, Texas became the 37th state to outlaw same-sex marriages. Same-sex couples in Massachusetts, New Jersey, and Indiana sued to overturn those states' bans on same-sex marriages.[8] The legislatures of Connecticut, Montana, and Rhode Island considered and rejected bills to recognize gay marriage.[9] A Texas judge refused to divorce a gay couple who had obtained a civil union in Vermont. Canada legalized gay marriage. The U.S. Supreme Court struck down sodomy statues and recognized that same-sex couples have a constitutional right to privacy. Episcopalians in the Diocese of New Hampshire elected as their leader the first openly gay bishop anywhere in the world.[10] Wal-Mart, the nation's largest private employer, extended its antidiscrimination policies to protect gay and lesbian employees.[11] The *New York Times* now includes the quasi nuptials of gay and lesbian couples, transforming its "weddings" pages into "weddings/celebrations" pages.[12]

In Vermont, however, nothing much has changed. That fact may be the strongest argument in favor of same-sex marriage.

Appendix A

Vermont Supreme Court Decision for Baker v. State

Stan BAKER, et al.

v.

STATE of Vermont, et al.

744 A.2d 864 (1999)

Supreme Court of Vermont.

AMESTOY, C.J.

May the State of Vermont exclude same-sex couples from the benefits and protections that its laws provide to opposite-sex married couples? That is the fundamental question we address in this appeal, a question that the Court well knows arouses deeply felt religious, moral, and political beliefs. Our constitutional responsibility to consider the legal merits of issues properly before us provides no exception for the controversial case. The issue before the Court, moreover, does not turn on the religious or moral debate over intimate same-sex relationships, but rather on the statutory and constitutional basis for the exclusion of same-sex couples from the secular benefits and protections offered married couples.

We conclude that under the Common Benefits Clause of the Vermont Constitution, which, in pertinent part, reads,

> That government is, or ought to be, instituted for the common benefit, protection, and security of the people, nation, or community, and not for the particular emolument or advantage of any single person, family, or set of persons, who are a part only of that community. . . .

Vt. Const., ch. I, art 7., plaintiffs may not be deprived of the statutory benefits and protections afforded persons of the opposite sex who choose to marry. We hold that the State is constitutionally required to extend to same-sex couples the common benefits and protections that flow from marriage under Vermont law. Whether this ultimately takes the form of inclusion within the marriage laws themselves or a parallel "domestic partnership" system or some equivalent statutory alternative, rests with the Legislature. Whatever system is chosen, however, must conform with the constitutional imperative to afford all Vermonters the common benefit, protection, and security of the law.

Plaintiffs are three same-sex couples who have lived together in committed relationships for periods ranging from four to twenty-five years. Two of the couples have raised children together. Each couple applied for a marriage license from their respective town clerk, and each was refused a license as ineligible under the applicable state marriage laws. Plaintiffs thereupon filed this lawsuit against defendants—* the State of Vermont, the Towns of Milton and Shelburne, and the City of South Burlington—seeking a declaratory judgment that the refusal to issue them a license violated the marriage statutes and the Vermont Constitution.

The State, joined by Shelburne and South Burlington, moved to dismiss the action on the ground that plaintiffs had failed to state a claim for which relief could be granted. The Town of Milton answered the complaint and subsequently moved for judgment on the pleadings. Plaintiffs opposed the motions and cross-moved for judgment on the pleadings. The trial court granted the State's and the Town of Milton's motions, denied plaintiffs' motion, and dismissed the complaint. The court ruled that the marriage statutes could not be construed to permit the issuance of a license to same-sex couples. The court further ruled that the marriage statutes were constitutional because they rationally furthered the State's interest in promoting "the link between procreation and child rearing." This appeal followed.[1]

I. The Statutory Claim

Plaintiffs initially contend the trial court erred in concluding that the marriage statutes render them ineligible for a marriage license. It is axiomatic that the principal objective of statutory construction is to discern the legislative intent. *See Merkel v. Nationwide Ins. Co.*, 166 Vt. 311,

314, 693 A.2d 706, 707 (1997). While we may explore a variety of sources to discern that intent, it is also a truism of statutory interpretation that where a statute is unambiguous we rely on the plain and ordinary meaning of the words chosen. *See In re P.S.*, 167 Vt. 63, 70, 702 A.2d 98, 102 (1997). "[W]e rely on the plain meaning of the words because we presume they reflect the Legislature's intent." *Braun v. Board of Dental Examiners*, 167 Vt. 110, 116, 702 A.2d 124, 127 (1997).

Vermont's marriage statutes are set forth in chapter 1 of Title 15, entitled "Marriage," which defines the requirements and eligibility for entering into a marriage, and chapter 105 of Title 18, entitled "Marriage Records and Licenses," which prescribes the forms and procedures for obtaining a license and solemnizing a marriage. Although it is not necessarily the only possible definition, there is no doubt that the plain and ordinary meaning of "marriage" is the union of one man and one woman as husband and wife. *See Webster's New International Dictionary* 1506 (2d ed.1955) (marriage consists of state of "being united to a person . . . of the opposite sex as husband or wife"); *Black's Law Dictionary* 986 (7th ed.1999) (marriage is "[t]he legal union of a man and woman as husband and wife"). This understanding of the term is well rooted in Vermont common law. *See Le Barron v. Le Barron*, 35 Vt. 365, 366–71 (1862) (petition by wife to annul marriage for alleged physical impotence of husband); *Clark v. Field*, 13 Vt. 460, 465 (1841) (suit to declare marriage null and void on ground that husband and wife had not consummated marriage); *Overseers of the Poor of the Town of Newbury v. Overseers of the Poor of the Town of Brunswick*, 2 Vt. 151, 152 (1829) (dispute between towns over liability for support of family turned, in part, on validity of marriage where justice of peace had not declared parties husband and wife). The legislative understanding is also reflected in the enabling statute governing the issuance of marriage licenses, which provides, in part, that the license "shall be issued by the clerk of the town where either the bride or groom resides." 18 V.S.A. § 5131(a). "Bride" and "groom" are gender-specific terms. *See Webster's, supra,* at 334 (bride defined as "a woman newly married, or about to be married"; bridegroom defined as "a man newly married, or about to be married").

Further evidence of the legislative assumption that marriage consists of a union of opposite genders may be found in the consanguinity statutes, which expressly prohibit a man from marrying certain female relatives, see 15 V.S.A. § 1, and a woman from marrying certain male relatives, *see id.* § 2. In addition, the annulment statutes explicitly refer to "husband and wife," *see id.* § 513, as do other statutes relating to married couples. *See, e.g.,* 12 V.S.A. § 1605 ("husband and wife" may not testify about communications to each other under rule commonly known as "marital privilege," *see State v. Wright,* 154 Vt. 512, 525, 581 A.2d 720, 728 (1989)); 14 V.S.A. §§ 461, 465, 470 (referring to interest of "widow" in estate of her "husband"); *id.* § 10 (requiring three witnesses where "husband or wife" are given beneficial interest in other's will); 15 V.S.A. § 102 (legal protections where "married man . . . deserts, neglects, or abandons his wife").

These statutes, read as a whole, reflect the common understanding that marriage under Vermont law consists of a union between a man and a woman. Plaintiffs essentially concede this fact. They argue, nevertheless, that the underlying purpose of marriage is to protect and encourage the union of committed couples and that, absent an explicit legislative prohibition, the statutes should be interpreted broadly to include committed same-sex couples. Plaintiffs rely principally on our decision in *In re B.L.V.B.,* 160 Vt. 368, 369, 628 A.2d 1271, 1272 (1993). There, we held that a woman who was co-parenting the two children of her same-sex partner could adopt the children without terminating the natural mother's parental rights. Although the statute provided generally that an adoption deprived the natural parents of their legal rights, it contained an exception where the adoption was by the "spouse" of the natural parent. *See id.* at 370, 628 A.2d at 1273 (citing 15 V.S.A. § 448). Technically, therefore, the exception was inapplicable. We concluded, however, that the purpose of the law was not to restrict the exception to legally married couples, but to safeguard the child, and that to apply the literal language of the statute in these circumstances would defeat the statutory purpose and "reach an absurd result." *Id.* at 371, 628 A.2d at 1273. Although the Legislature had undoubtedly not even considered same-sex unions when the law was enacted in 1945, our interpretation was consistent with its "general intent and spirit." *Id.* at 373, 628 A.2d at 1274.

Contrary to plaintiffs' claim, *B.L.V.B.* does not control our conclusion here. We are not dealing in this case with a narrow statutory exception requiring a broader reading than its literal words would permit in order to avoid a result plainly at odds with the legislative purpose. Unlike *B.L.V.B.*, it is far from clear that limiting marriage to opposite-sex couples violates the Legislature's "intent and spirit." Rather, the evidence demonstrates a clear legislative assumption that marriage under our statutory scheme consists of a union between a man and a woman. Accordingly, we reject plaintiffs' claim that they were entitled to a license under the statutory scheme governing marriage.

II. The Constitutional Claim

Assuming that the marriage statutes preclude their eligibility for a marriage license, plaintiffs contend that the exclusion violates their right to the common benefit and protection of the law guaranteed by Chapter I, Article 7 of the Vermont Constitution.[2] They note that in denying them access to a civil marriage license, the law effectively excludes them from a broad array of legal benefits and protections incident to the marital relation, including access to a spouse's medical, life, and disability insurance; hospital visitation and other medical decision-making privileges; spousal support, intestate succession; homestead protections; and many other statutory protections. They claim the trial court erred in upholding the law on the basis that it reasonably served the State's interest in promoting the "link between procreation and child rearing." They argue that the large number of married couples without children, and the increasing incidence of same-sex couples with children, undermines the State's rationale. They note that Vermont law affirmatively guarantees the right to adopt and raise children regardless of the sex of the parents, see 15A V.S.A. § 1-102, and challenge the logic of a legislative scheme that recognizes the rights of same-sex partners as parents, yet denies them—and their children—the same security as spouses.

In considering this issue, it is important to emphasize at the outset that it is the Common Benefits Clause of the Vermont Constitution we are construing, rather than its counterpart, the Equal Protection Clause of the Fourteenth Amendment to the United States Constitution. It is altogether fitting and proper that we do so. Vermont's constitutional commitment to equal rights was the product of the successful effort to create an independent republic and a fundamental charter of government, the Constitution of 1777, both of which preceded the adoption of the Fourteenth Amendment by nearly a century. As we explained in *State v. Badger*, 141 Vt. 430, 448–49, 450 A.2d 336, 347 (1982), "our constitution is not a mere reflection of the federal charter. Historically and textually, it differs from the United States Constitution. It predates the federal counterpart, as it extends back to Vermont's days as an independent republic. It is an independent authority, and Vermont's fundamental law."

As we explain in the discussion that follows, the Common Benefits Clause of the Vermont Constitution differs markedly from the federal Equal Protection Clause in its language, historical origins, purpose, and development. While the federal amendment may thus supplement the protections afforded by the Common Benefits Clause, it does not supplant it as the first and primary safeguard of the rights and liberties of all Vermonters. *See id.* at 449, 450 A.2d at 347 (Court is free to "provide more generous protection to rights under the Vermont Constitution than afforded by the federal charter"); *State v. Jewett*, 146 Vt. 221, 224, 500 A.2d 233, 235 (1985) (state constitution may protect Vermonters "however the philosophy of the United States Supreme Court may ebb and flow"); see generally H. Linde, *First Things First, Rediscovering the States' Bill of Rights*, 9 U. Balt. L.Rev. 379, 381–82 (1980); S. Pollock, *State Constitutions as Separate Sources of Fundamental Rights*, 35 Rutgers L.Rev. 707, 717–19 (1983).

A. Historical Development

In understanding the import of the Common Benefits Clause, this Court has often referred to principles developed by the federal courts in applying the Equal Protection Clause.[3] *See, e.g., Choquette v. Perrault*, 153 Vt. 45, 51–52, 569 A.2d 455, 458–59 (1989). At the same time, however, we have recognized that "[a]lthough the provisions have some similarity of purpose, they are not identical." *Benning v. State*, 161 Vt. 472, 485 n. 7, 641 A.2d 757, 764 n. 7 (1994). Indeed, recent Vermont decisions reflect a very different approach from current federal jurisprudence. That approach may be described as broadly deferential to the legislative prerogative to define and advance governmental ends, while vigorously ensuring that the means chosen bear a just and reasonable relation to the governmental objective.

Although our decisions over the last few decades have routinely invoked the rhetoric of suspect class favored by the federal courts, *see, e.g., Choquette,* 153 Vt. at 51, 569 A.2d at 458, there are notable exceptions. The principal decision in this regard is the landmark case of *State v. Ludlow Supermarkets, Inc.,* 141 Vt. 261, 448 A.2d 791 (1982). There, Chief Justice Albert Barney, writing for the Court, invalidated a Sunday closing law that discriminated among classes of commercial establishments on the basis of their size. After noting that this Court, unlike its federal counterpart, was not constrained by considerations of federalism and the impact of its decision on fifty varying jurisdictions, the Court declared that Article 7 "only allows the statutory classifications . . . if a case of necessity can be established overriding the prohibition of Article 7 by reference to the 'common benefit, protection, and security of the people.'" *Id.* at 268, 448 A.2d at 795. Applying this test, the Court concluded that the State's justifications for the disparate treatment of large and small businesses failed to withstand constitutional scrutiny. *Id.* at 269–70, 448 A.2d at 796.

Ludlow, as we later explained, did not alter the traditional requirement under Article 7 that legislative classifications must "reasonably relate to a legitimate public purpose." *Choquette,* 153 Vt. at 52, 569 A.2d at 459. Nor did it overturn the principle that the justifications demanded of the State may depend upon the nature and importance of the benefits and protections affected by the legislation; indeed, this is implicit in the weighing process. It did establish that Article 7 would require a "more stringent" reasonableness inquiry than was generally associated with rational basis review under the federal constitution. *State v. Brunelle,* 148 Vt. 347, 351, 534 A.2d 198, 201–02 (1987); *see also Hodgeman v. Jard Co.,* 157 Vt. 461, 464, 599 A.2d 1371, 1373 (1991) (citing *Ludlow* for principle that Article 7 "may require this Court to examine more closely distinctions drawn by state government than would the Fourteenth Amendment"). *Ludlow* did not override the traditional deference accorded legislation having any reasonable relation to a legitimate public purpose. It simply signaled that Vermont courts—having "access to specific legislative history and all other proper resources" to evaluate the object and effect of state laws—would engage in a meaningful, case-specific analysis to ensure that any exclusion from the general benefit and protection of the law would bear a just and reasonable relation to the legislative goals. *Ludlow*, 141 Vt. at 268, 448 A.2d at 795.[4]

Although it is accurate to point out that since *Ludlow* our decisions have consistently recited the federal rational-basis/strict-scrutiny tests, it is equally fair to observe that we have been less than consistent in their application. Just as commentators have noted the United States Supreme Court's obvious yet unstated deviations from the rational-basis standard, so have this Court's holdings often departed from the federal test.[5] In *Colchester Fire District No. 2 v. Sharrow*, 145 Vt. 195, 198–99, 485 A.2d 134, 136-37 (1984), for example, the Court ostensibly applied a rational-basis test to invalidate a payment scheme for revenue-bond assessments. While acknowledging the broad discretion traditionally accorded the Legislature in taxation and other areas of public welfare, the Court nevertheless examined each of the district's rationales in detail and found them to be unpersuasive in light of the record and administrative experience. *See id.* at 200–01, 485 A.2d at 137 (record established no "plausible relationship between the method of bond assessment and its alleged purposes").

In *Choquette*, 153 Vt. at 51, 569 A.2d at 458, the Court again purported to apply rational-basis review under Article 7 in holding a fence-repair statute to be unconstitutional. Not content to accept arguments derived from a bygone agricultural era, the Court held that the policies underlying the law were outdated and failed to establish a reasonable relation to the public purpose in the light of contemporary circumstances. *See id.* at 53–54, 569 A.2d at 459–60; *see also Oxx v. Department of Taxes*, 159 Vt. 371, 376, 618 A.2d 1321, 1324 (1992) (income tax assessment violated Equal Protection and Common Benefits Clauses as applied); *Lorrain v. Ryan*, 160 Vt. 202, 215, 628 A.2d 543, 551 (1993) (statutory scheme denying right of spouse of injured worker to sue third-party tortfeasor for loss of consortium violated Equal Protection and Common Benefits Clauses).

The "more stringent" test was also implicit in our recent decision in *MacCallum v. Seymour's Administrator*, 165 Vt. 452, 686 A.2d 935 (1996), which involved an Article 7 challenge to an intestacy statute that denied an adopted person's right of inheritance from collateral kin. While employing the rhetoric of minimal scrutiny, our analysis was more rigorous than traditional federal rational-basis review. Indeed, although the State proffered at least a conceivable purpose for the legislative distinction between natural and adopted children, we held that the classification was unreasonable, explaining that "[a]dopted persons have historically been a target of discrimination," *id.* at 459, 686 A.2d at 939, and that however reasonable the classification when originally enacted, it represented an "outdated" distinction today. *Id.* at 460, 686 A.2d at 939. Thus, while deferential to the historical purpose underlying the classification, we demanded that it bear a reasonable and just relation to the governmental objective in light of contemporary conditions.

This approach may also be discerned in the Court's recent opinion in *Brigham v. State*, 166 Vt. 246, 692 A.2d 384 (1997), addressing an Article 7 challenge to the State's educational funding system. Consistent with prior decisions, the Court acknowledged the federal standard, *see id.* at 265, 692 A.2d at 395, even as it eschewed the federal categories of analysis. Indeed, after weighing the State's justifications for the disparate funding of education against its impact upon public-school students, the Court concluded: "Labels aside, we are simply unable to fathom a legitimate governmental purpose to justify the gross inequities in educational opportunities evident from the record." *Id.* at 265, 692 A.2d at 396.

Thus, "labels aside," Vermont case law has consistently demanded in practice that statutory exclusions from publicly conferred benefits and protections must be "premised on an appropriate and overriding public interest." *Ludlow*, 141 Vt. at 268, 448 A.2d at 795. The rigid categories utilized by the federal courts under the Fourteenth Amendment find no support in our early case law and, while routinely cited, are often effectively ignored in our more recent decisions. As discussed more fully below, these decisions are consistent with the text and history of the Common Benefits Clause which, similarly, yield no rigid categories or formulas of analysis. The balancing approach utilized in *Ludlow* and implicit in our recent decisions reflects the language, history, and values at the core of the Common Benefits Clause. We turn, accordingly, to a brief examination of constitutional language and history.

B. Text

We typically look to a variety of sources in construing our constitution, including the language of the provision in question, historical context, case-law development, the construction of similar provisions in other state constitutions, and sociological materials. *See Benning*, 161 Vt. at 476, 641 A.2d at 759. The Vermont Constitution was adopted with little recorded debate and has undergone remarkably little revision in its 200-year history. Recapturing the meaning of a particular word or phrase as understood by a generation more than two centuries removed from our own requires, in some respects, an immersion in the culture and materials of the past more suited to the work of professional historians than courts and lawyers. *See generally* H. Powell, *Rules for Originalists*, 73 Va. L.Rev. 659, 659–61 (1987); P. Brest, *The Misconceived Quest for the Original Understanding*, 60 B.U. L.Rev. 204, 204–09 (1980). The responsibility of the Court, however, is distinct from that of the historian, whose interpretation of past thought and actions necessarily informs our analysis of current issues but cannot alone resolve them. See Powell, *supra*, at 662–68; Brest, *supra*, at 237. As we observed in *State v. Kirchoff*, 156 Vt. 1, 6, 587 A.2d 988, 992 (1991), "our duty is to discover . . . the core value that gave life to Article [7]." Out of the shifting and complicated kaleidoscope of events, social forces, and ideas that culminated in the Vermont Constitution of 1777, our task is to distill the essence, the motivating ideal of the framers. The challenge is to remain faithful to that historical ideal, while addressing contemporary issues that the framers undoubtedly could never have imagined.

We first focus on the words of the Constitution themselves, for, as Chief Justice Marshall observed, "although the spirit of an instrument, especially of a constitution, is to be respected not less than its letter, yet the spirit is to be collected chiefly from its words." *Sturges v. Crowninshield*, 17 U.S. (4 Wheat.) 122, 202, 4 L.Ed. 529 (1819). One of the fundamental rights included in Chapter I of the Vermont Constitution of 1777, entitled "A Declaration of Rights of the Inhabitants of the State of Vermont," the Common Benefits Clause as originally written provided:

> That government is, or ought to be, instituted for the common benefit, protection, and security of the people, nation or community; and not for the particular emolument or advantage of any single man, family or set

of men, who are a part only of that community; and that the community hath an indubitable, unalienable and indefeasible right, to reform, alter, or abolish government, in such manner as shall be, by that community, judged most conducive to the public weal.

Vt. Const. of 1777, ch. I, art. VI.[6]

The first point to be observed about the text is the affirmative and unequivocal mandate of the first section, providing that government is established for the common benefit of the people and community as a whole. Unlike the Fourteenth Amendment, whose origin and language reflect the solicitude of a dominant white society for an historically oppressed African American minority (no state shall "deny" the equal protection of the laws), the Common Benefits Clause mirrors the confidence of a homogeneous, eighteenth-century group of men aggressively laying claim to the same rights as their peers in Great Britain or, for that matter, New York, New Hampshire, or the Upper Connecticut River Valley. *See* F. Mahady, *Toward a Theory of State Constitutional Jurisprudence: A Judge's Thoughts,* 13 Vt. L.Rev. 145, 151-52 (1988) (noting distinct eighteenth-century origins of Article 7). The same assumption that all the people should be afforded all the benefits and protections bestowed by government is also reflected in the second section, which prohibits not the denial of rights to the oppressed, but rather the conferral of advantages or emoluments upon the privileged.[7]

The words of the Common Benefits Clause are revealing. While they do not, to be sure, set forth a fully formed standard of analysis for determining the constitutionality of a given statute, they do express broad principles which usefully inform that analysis. Chief among these is the principle of inclusion. As explained more fully in the discussion that follows, the specific proscription against governmental favoritism toward not only groups or "set[s] of men," but also toward any particular "family" or "single man," underscores the framers' resentment of political preference of any kind. The affirmative right to the "common benefits and protections" of government and the corollary proscription of favoritism in the distribution of public "emoluments and advantages" reflect the framers' overarching objective "not only that everyone enjoy equality before the law or have an equal voice in government but also that everyone have an equal share in the fruits of the common enterprise." W. Adams, *The First American Constitutions*, 188 (1980). Thus, at its core the Common Benefits Clause expressed a vision of government that afforded every Vermonter its benefit and protection and provided no Vermonter particular advantage.

C. Historical Context

Although historical research yields little direct evidence of the framers' intentions, an examination of the ideological origins of the Common Benefits Clause casts a useful light upon the inclusionary principle at its textual core. Like other provisions of the Vermont Constitution of 1777, the Common Benefits Clause was borrowed verbatim from the Pennsylvania Constitution of 1776, which was based, in turn, upon a similar provision in the Virginia Declaration of Rights of 1776. *See* J. Shaeffer, *A Comparison of the First Constitutions of Vermont and Pennsylvania*, 43 Vt. Hist. 33, 33-35 (1975); J. Selsam, *The Pennsylvania Constitution of 1776: A Study in Revolutionary Democracy*, 178 (1936). The original Virginia clause differed from the Pennsylvania and Vermont provisions only in the second section, which was contained in a separate article and provided "[t]hat no man, or set of men, are entitled to exclusive or separate emoluments or privileges from the community, but in consideration of public services." *See* Virginia Declaration of Rights, art. IV (reprinted in 11 *West's Encyclopedia of American Law* 82 (1998)).[8]

Although aimed at Great Britain, the American Revolution—as numerous historians have noted—also tapped deep-seated domestic antagonisms. The planter elite in Virginia, the proprietors of Eastern Pennsylvania, and New Yorkers claiming Vermont lands were each the object of long-standing grievances. Selsam, *supra*, at 255–56; R. Shalhope, *Bennington and the Green Mountain Boys: The Emergence of Liberal Democracy in Vermont, 1760–1850* at 70–97 (1996); G. Wood, *The Creation of the American Republic, 1776–1787* at 75–82 (1969). Indeed, the revolt against Great Britain unleashed what one historian, speaking of Pennsylvania, has called "a revolution within a revolution." Selsam, *supra*, at 1. By attempting to claim equal rights for Americans against the English, regardless of birthright or social status, "even the most aristocratic of southern Whig planters . . . were pushed into creating an egalitarian ideology that could be and even as early as 1776 was being turned against themselves." Wood, *supra*, at 83. While not opposed to the concept of a social elite, the framers of the first state constitutions believed that it should consist of a "natural aristocracy" of talent, rather than an entrenched clique favored by birth or social connections. *See id.* at 479–80. As the preeminent historian of the ideological origins of the Revolution explained, "while 'equality before the law' was a commonplace of the time, 'equality without respect to the dignity of the persons concerned' was not; [the Revolution's] emphasis on social equivalence was significant." B. Bailyn, *The Ideological Origins of the American Revolution*, 307 (1967). Thus, while the framers' "egalitarian ideology" conspicuously excluded many oppressed people of the eighteenth century—including African Americans, Native Americans, and women—it did nevertheless represent a genuine social revolt pitting republican ideals of "virtue," or talent and merit, against a perceived aristocracy of privilege both abroad and at home.

Vermont was not immune to the disruptive forces unleashed by the Revolution. One historian has described Vermont on the eve of the Revolution as rife with "factional rivalry [and] regional jealousy." G. Aichele, *Making the Vermont Constitution: 1777–1824*, 56 Vt. Hist. 166, 177 (1988). Competing factions in the Champlain and Upper Connecticut River Valleys had long vied for political and economic dominance. *See id.* at 180. Echoing Selsam on Pennsylvania, another historian has spoken of "Vermont's double revolution—a rebellion within a rebellion" to describe the successful revolt against both Great Britain and New York by the yeoman farmers, small-scale proprietors, and moderate land speculators who comprised the bulk of the Green Mountain Boys. D. Smith, *Green Mountain Insurgency: Transformation of New York's Forty-Year Land War*, 64 Vt. Hist. 197, 197–98, 224 (1996); see also Shalhope, *supra*, at 169 (egalitarian ideology of American Revolution "resonated powerfully with the visceral feelings" of Green Mountain Boys and others in Vermont).

The powerful movement for "social equivalence" unleashed by the Revolution ultimately found its most complete expression in the first state constitutions adopted in the early years of the rebellion. In Pennsylvania, where social antagonisms were most acute, the result was a fundamental charter that has been described as "the most radical constitution of the Revolution." Wood, *supra,* at 84–85; *see also* Shaeffer, *supra,* at 35–36. Yet the Pennsylvania Constitution's egalitarianism was arguably eclipsed the following year by the Vermont Constitution of 1777. In addition to the commitment to government for the "common benefit, protection, and security," it contained novel provisions abolishing slavery, eliminating property qualifications for voting, and calling for the governor, lieutenant governor, and twelve councilors to be elected by the people rather than appointed by the legislature. *See* Shalhope, *supra,* at 171–72. These and other provisions have led one historian to observe that Vermont's first charter was the "most democratic constitution produced by any of the American states." *See id.* at 172.

The historical origins of the Vermont Constitution thus reveal that the framers, although enlightened for their day, were not principally concerned with civil rights for African Americans and other minorities, but with equal access to public benefits and protections for the community as a whole. The concept of equality at the core of the Common Benefits Clause was not the eradication of racial or class distinctions, but rather the elimination of artificial governmental preferments and advantages. The Vermont Constitution would ensure that the law uniformly afforded every Vermonter its benefit, protection, and security so that social and political preeminence would reflect differences of capacity, disposition, and virtue, rather than governmental favor and privilege.[9]

D. Analysis under Article 7

The language and history of the Common Benefits Clause thus reinforce the conclusion that a relatively uniform standard, reflective of the inclusionary principle at its core, must govern our analysis of laws challenged under the clause. Accordingly, we conclude that this approach, rather than the rigid, multitiered analysis evolved by the federal courts under the Fourteenth Amendment, shall direct our inquiry under Article 7. As noted, Article 7 is intended to ensure that the benefits and protections conferred by the State are for the common benefit of the community and are not for the advantage of persons "who are a part only of that community." When a statute is challenged under Article 7, we first define that "part of the community" disadvantaged by the law. We examine the statutory basis that distinguishes those protected by the law from those excluded from the state's protection. Our concern here is with delineating, not with labeling the excluded class as "suspect," "quasi-suspect," or "non-suspect" for purposes of determining different levels of judicial scrutiny.[10]

We look next to the government's purpose in drawing a classification that includes some members of the community within the scope of the challenged law but excludes others. Consistent with Article 7's guiding principle of affording the protection and benefit of the law to all members of the Vermont community, we examine the nature of the classification to determine whether it is reasonably necessary to accomplish the State's claimed objectives.

We must ultimately ascertain whether the omission of a part of the community from the benefit, protection, and security of the challenged law bears a reasonable and just relation to the governmental purpose. Consistent with the core presumption of inclusion, factors to be considered in this determination may include (1) the significance of the benefits and protections of the challenged law; (2) whether the omission of members of the community from the benefits and protections of the challenged law promotes the government's stated goals; and (3) whether the classification is significantly underinclusive or overinclusive. As Justice Souter has observed in a different context, this approach necessarily "calls for a court to assess the relative 'weights' or dignities of the contending interests." *Washington v. Glucksberg*, 521 U.S. 702, 767, 117 S.Ct. 2258, 138 L.Ed.2d 772 (1997) (Souter, J., concurring). What keeps that assessment grounded and objective, and not based upon the private sensitivities or values of individual judges, is that in assessing the relative weights of competing interests courts must look to the history and "'traditions from which [the State] developed'" as well as those "'from which it broke,'" *id.* at 767, 117 S.Ct. 2258 (quoting *Poe v. Ullman*, 367 U.S. 497, 542, 81 S.Ct. 1752, 6 L.Ed.2d 989 (1961) (Harlan, J., dissenting)), and not to merely personal notions. Moreover, the process of review is necessarily "one of close criticism going to the details of the opposing interests and to their relationships with the historically recognized principles that lend them weight or value." *Id.* at 769, 117 S.Ct. 2258.[11]

Ultimately, the answers to these questions, however useful, cannot substitute for "'[t]he inescapable fact . . . that adjudication of . . . claims may call upon the Court in interpreting the Constitution to exercise that same capacity which by tradition courts always have exercised: reasoned judgment.'" *Id.* (quoting *Planned Parenthood of Southeastern Pa. v. Casey,* 505 U.S. 833, 849, 112 S.Ct. 2791, 120 L.Ed.2d 674 (1992)). The balance between individual liberty and organized society, which courts are continually called upon to weigh, does not lend itself to the precision of a scale. It is, indeed, a recognition of the imprecision of "reasoned judgment" that compels both judicial restraint and respect for tradition in constitutional interpretation.[12]

E. The Standard Applied

With these general precepts in mind, we turn to the question of whether the exclusion of same-sex couples from the benefits and protections incident to marriage under Vermont law contravenes Article 7. The first step in our analysis is to identify the nature of the statutory classification. As noted, the marriage statutes apply expressly to opposite-sex couples. Thus, the statutes exclude anyone who wishes to marry someone of the same sex.[13]

Next, we must identify the governmental purpose or purposes to be served by the statutory classification. The principal purpose the State advances in support of the excluding same-sex couples from the legal benefits of marriage is the government's interest in "furthering the link between procreation and child rearing." The State has a strong interest, it argues, in promoting a permanent commitment between couples who have children to ensure that their offspring are considered legitimate and receive ongoing parental support. The State contends, further, that the Legislature could reasonably believe that sanctioning same-sex unions "would diminish society's perception of the link between procreation and child rearing . . . [and] advance the notion that fathers or mothers . . . are mere surplusage to the functions of procreation and child rearing." The State argues that since same-sex couples cannot conceive a child on their own, state-sanctioned same-sex unions "could be seen by the Legislature to separate further the connection between procreation and parental responsibilities for raising children." Hence, the

Legislature is justified, the State concludes, "in using the marriage statutes to send a public message that procreation and child rearing are intertwined."

Do these concerns represent valid public interests that are reasonably furthered by the exclusion of same-sex couples from the benefits and protections that flow from the marital relation? It is beyond dispute that the State has a legitimate and long-standing interest in promoting a permanent commitment between couples for the security of their children. It is equally undeniable that the State's interest has been advanced by extending formal public sanction and protection to the union, or marriage, of those couples considered capable of having children, that is, men and women. And there is no doubt that the overwhelming majority of births today continue to result from natural conception between one man and one woman. *See* J. Robertson, *Assisted Reproductive Technology and the Family*, 47 Hastings L.J. 911, 911–12 (1996) (noting the number of births resulting from assisted-reproductive technology, which remain small compared to overall number of births).

It is equally undisputed that many opposite-sex couples marry for reasons unrelated to procreation, that some of these couples never intend to have children, and that others are incapable of having children. Therefore, if the purpose of the statutory exclusion of same-sex couples is to "further [. . .] the link between procreation and child rearing," it is significantly underinclusive. The law extends the benefits and protections of marriage to many persons with no logical connection to the stated governmental goal.

Furthermore, while accurate statistics are difficult to obtain, there is no dispute that a significant number of children today are actually being raised by same-sex parents, and that increasing numbers of children are being conceived by such parents through a variety of assisted-reproductive techniques. *See* D. Flaks, et al., *Lesbians Choosing Motherhood: A Comparative Study of Lesbian and Heterosexual Parents and Their Children*, 31 Dev. Psychol. 105, 105 (1995) (citing estimates that between 1.5 and 5 million lesbian mothers resided with their children in United States between 1989 and 1990, and that thousands of lesbian mothers have chosen motherhood through donor insemination or adoption); G.

Green & F. Bozett, *Lesbian Mothers and Gay Fathers, in Homosexuality: Research Implications for Public Policy,* 197, 198 (J. Gonsiorek et al. eds., 1991) (estimating that numbers of children of either gay fathers or lesbian mothers range between six and fourteen million); C. Patterson, *Children of the Lesbian Baby Boom: Behavioral Adjustment, Self-Concepts, and Sex Role Identity, in Lesbian and Gay Psychology* (B. Greene et al. eds., 1994) (observing that although precise estimates are difficult, number of families with lesbian mothers is growing); E. Shapiro & L. Schultz, *Single-Sex Families: The Impact of Birth Innovations upon Traditional Family Notions,* 24 J. Fam. L. 271, 281 (1985) ("[I]t is a fact that children are being born to single-sex families on a biological basis, and that they are being so born in considerable numbers.").

Thus, with or without the marriage sanction, the reality today is that increasing numbers of same-sex couples are employing increasingly efficient assisted-reproductive techniques to conceive and raise children. *See* L. Ikemoto, *The In/Fertile, the Too Fertile, and the Dysfertile,* 47 Hastings L.J. 1007, 1056 & n. 170 (1996). The Vermont Legislature has not only recognized this reality, but has acted affirmatively to remove legal barriers so that same-sex couples may legally adopt and rear the children conceived through such efforts. *See* 15A V.S.A. § 1-102(b) (allowing partner of biological parent to adopt if in child's best interest without reference to sex). The state has also acted to expand the domestic relations laws to safeguard the interests of same-sex parents and their children when such couples terminate their domestic relationship. *See* 15A V.S.A. § 1-112 (vesting family court with jurisdiction over parental rights and responsibilities, parent-child contact, and child support when unmarried persons who have adopted minor child "terminate their domestic relationship").

Therefore, to the extent that the state's purpose in licensing civil marriage was, and is, to legitimize children and provide for their security, the statutes plainly exclude many same-sex couples who are no different from opposite-sex couples with respect to these objectives. If anything, the exclusion of same-sex couples from the legal protections incident to marriage exposes their children to the precise risks that the State argues the marriage laws are designed to secure against. In short, the marital exclusion treats persons who are similarly situated for purposes of the law, differently.

The State also argues that because same-sex couples cannot conceive a child on their own, their exclusion promotes a "perception of the link between procreation and child rearing," and that to discard it would "advance the notion that mothers and fathers . . . are mere surplusage to the functions of procreation and child rearing" Apart from the bare assertion, the State offers no persuasive reasoning to support these claims. Indeed, it is undisputed that most of those who utilize nontraditional means of conception are infertile married couples, see Shapiro and Schultz, *supra*, at 275, and that many assisted-reproductive techniques involve only one of the married partner's genetic material, the other being supplied by a third party through sperm, egg, or embryo donation. *See* E. May, *Barren in the Promised Land: Childless Americans and the Pursuit of Happiness*, 217, 242 (1995); Robertson, *supra*, at 911–12, 922–27. The State does not suggest that the use of these technologies undermines a married couple's sense of parental responsibility, or fosters the perception that they are "mere surplusage" to the conception and parenting of the child so conceived. Nor does it even remotely suggest that access to such techniques ought to be restricted as a matter of public policy to "send a public message that procreation and child rearing are intertwined." Accordingly, there is no reasonable basis to conclude that a same-sex couple's use of the same technologies would undermine the bonds of parenthood, or society's perception of parenthood.

The question thus becomes whether the exclusion of a relatively small but significant number of otherwise qualified same-sex couples from the same legal benefits and protections afforded their opposite-sex counterparts contravenes the mandates of Article 7. It is, of course, well settled that statutes are not necessarily unconstitutional because they fail to extend legal protection to all who are similarly situated. *See Benning,* 161 Vt. at 486, 641 A.2d at 764 ("A statute need not regulate the whole of a field to pass constitutional muster."). Courts have upheld underinclusive statutes out of a recognition that, for reasons of pragmatism or administrative convenience, the legislature may choose to address problems incrementally. *See, e.g., City of New Orleans v. Dukes,* 427 U.S. 297, 303, 96 S.Ct. 2513, 49 L.Ed.2d 511 (1976) (legislature may adopt regulations "that only partially ameliorate a perceived evil"); *Williamson v. Lee Optical of Okla., Inc.,* 348 U.S. 483, 489, 75 S.Ct. 461, 99 L.Ed. 563 (1955) ("The legislature may select one phase of one field and apply a remedy there, neglecting the others."). The State does not contend, however, that the same-sex exclusion is necessary as a matter of pragmatism or administrative convenience. We turn, accordingly, from the principal justifications advanced by the State to the interests asserted by plaintiffs.

As noted, in determining whether a statutory exclusion reasonably relates to the governmental purpose it is appropriate to consider the history and significance of the benefits denied. *See Glucksberg*, 521 U.S. at 710, 117 S.Ct. 2258 (to assess importance of rights and interests affected by statutory classifications, courts must look to "history, legal traditions, and practices"). What do these considerations reveal about the benefits and protections at issue here? In *Loving v. Virginia*, 388 U.S. 1, 12, 87 S.Ct. 1817, 18 L.Ed.2d 1010 (1967), the United States Supreme Court, striking down Virginia's antimiscegenation law, observed that "[t]he freedom to marry has long been recognized as one of the vital personal rights." The Court's point was clear; access to a civil marriage license and the multitude of legal benefits, protections, and obligations that flow from it significantly enhance the quality of life in our society.

The Supreme Court's observations in *Loving* merely acknowledged what many states, including Vermont, had long recognized. One hundred thirty-seven years before *Loving*, this Court characterized the reciprocal rights and responsibilities flowing from the marriage laws as "the natural rights of human nature." *See Overseers of the Poor*, 2 Vt. at 159. Decisions in other New England states noted the unique legal and economic ramifications flowing from the marriage relation. *See, e.g., Adams v. Palmer*, 51 Me. 480, 485 (1863) ("it establishes fundamental and most important domestic relations"). Early decisions recognized that a marriage contract, although similar to other civil agreements, represents much more because once formed, the law imposes a variety of obligations, protections, and benefits. As the Maine Supreme Judicial Court observed, the rights and obligations of marriage rest not upon contract, "but upon the general law of the State, statutory or common, which defines and prescribes those rights, duties, and obligations. They are of law, not of contract." *See id.* at 483; see also *Ditson v. Ditson*, 4 R.I. 87, 105 (1856) (marriage transcends contract because "it gives rights, and imposes duties and restrictions upon the parties to it"). In short, the marriage laws transform a private agreement into a source of significant public benefits and protections.

While the laws relating to marriage have undergone many changes during the last century, largely toward the goal of equalizing the status of husbands and wives, the benefits of marriage have not diminished in value. On the contrary, the benefits and protections incident to a marriage license under Vermont law have never been greater. They include, for example, the right to receive a portion of the estate of a spouse who dies intestate and protection against disinheritance through elective share provisions, under 14 V.S.A. §§ 401–404, 551; preference in being appointed as the personal representative of a spouse who dies intestate, under 14 V.S.A. § 903; the right to bring a lawsuit for the wrongful death of a spouse, under 14 V.S.A. § 1492; the right to bring an action for loss of consortium, under 12 V.S.A. § 5431; the right to workers' compensation survivor benefits under 21 V.S.A. § 632; the right to spousal benefits statutorily guaranteed to public employees, including health, life, disability, and accident insurance, under 3 V.S.A. § 631; the opportunity to be covered as a spouse under group life insurance policies issued to an employee, under 8 V.S.A. § 3811; the opportunity to be covered as the insured's spouse under an individual health insurance policy, under 8 V.S.A. § 4063; the right to claim an evidentiary privilege for marital communications, under V.R.E. 504; homestead rights and protections, under 27 V.S.A. §§ 105–108, 141–142; the presumption of joint ownership of property and the concomitant right of survivorship, under 27 V.S.A. § 2; hospital visitation and other rights incident to the medical treatment of a family member, under 18 V.S.A. § 1852; and the right to receive, and the obligation to provide, spousal support, maintenance, and property division in the event of separation or divorce, under 15 V.S.A. §§ 751–752. Other courts and commentators have noted the collection of rights, powers, privileges, and responsibilities triggered by marriage. *See generally Baehr v. Lewin*, 74 Haw. 530, 852 P.2d 44, 59 (1993); D. Chambers, *What If? The Legal Consequences of Marriage and the Legal Needs of Lesbian and Gay Male Couples*, 95 Mich. L.Rev. 447, passim (1996); J. Robbennolt & M. Johnson, *Legal Planning for Unmarried Committed Partners: Empirical Lessons for a Preventive and Therapeutic Approach*, 41 Ariz. L.Rev. 417, passim (1999); J. Trosino, *American Wedding: Same-Sex Marriage and the Miscegenation Analogy*, 73 B.U. L.Rev. 93, 96 (1993).

While other statutes could be added to this list, the point is clear. The legal benefits and protections flowing from a marriage license are of such significance that any statutory exclusion must necessarily be grounded on public concerns of sufficient weight, cogency, and authority that the justice of the deprivation cannot seriously be questioned. Considered in light of the extreme logical disjunction between the classification and the stated purposes of the law—protecting children and "furthering the link between procreation and child rearing"—the exclusion falls substantially short of this standard. The laudable governmental goal of promoting a commitment between married couples to promote the security of their children and the community as a whole provides no reasonable basis for denying the legal benefits and protections of marriage to same-sex couples, who are no differently situated with respect to this goal than their opposite-sex counterparts. Promoting a link between procreation and childrearing similarly fails to support the exclusion. We turn, accordingly, to the remaining interests identified by the State in support of the statutory exclusion.

The State asserts that a number of additional rationales could support a legislative decision to exclude same-sex partners from the statutory benefits and protections of marriage. Among these are the State's purported interests in "promoting child rearing in a setting that provides both male and female role models"; minimizing the legal complications of surrogacy contracts and sperm donors; "bridging differences" between the sexes; discouraging marriages of convenience for tax, housing, or other benefits; maintaining uniformity with marriage laws in other states; and generally protecting marriage from "destabilizing changes." The most substantive of the State's remaining claims relates to the issue of childrearing. It is conceivable that the Legislature could conclude that opposite-sex partners offer advantages in this area, although we note that child-development experts disagree and the answer is decidedly uncertain. The argument, however, contains a more fundamental flaw, and that is the Legislature's endorsement of a policy diametrically at odds with the State's claim. In 1996, the Vermont General Assembly enacted, and the Governor signed, a law removing all prior legal barriers to the adoption of children by same-sex couples. See 15A V.S.A. § 1-102. At the same time, the Legislature provided additional legal protections in the form of court-ordered child support and parent-child contact in the event that same-sex parents dissolved their "domestic relationship." Id. § 1-112. In light of these express policy choices, the State's arguments that Vermont public policy favors oppo-site-sex over same-sex parents or disfavors the use of artificial repro-ductive technologies are patently without substance.

Similarly, the State's argument that Vermont's marriage laws serve a substantial governmental interest in maintaining uniformity with other jurisdictions cannot be reconciled with Vermont's recognition of unions, such as first-cousin marriages, not uniformly sanctioned in other states. *See* 15 V.S.A. §§ 1–2 (consanguinity statutes do not exclude first cousins); 1 H. Clark, *The Law of Domestic Relations in the United States* § 2.9, at 153–54 (2d ed.1987) (noting states that prohibit first-cousin mar-riage). In an analogous context, Vermont has sanctioned adoptions by same-sex partners, *see* 15A V.S.A. § 1-102, notwithstanding the fact that many states have not. *See generally* Annotation, *Adoption of Child by Same-Sex Partners,* 27 A.L.R.5th 54, 68–72 (1995). Thus, the State's claim that Vermont's marriage laws were adopted because the Legislature sought to conform to those of the other forty-nine states is not only spec-ulative, but refuted by two relevant legislative choices which demon-strate that uniformity with other jurisdictions has not been a govern-mental purpose.

The State's remaining claims (e.g., recognition of same-sex unions might foster marriages of convenience or otherwise affect the institution in "unpredictable" ways) may be plausible forecasts as to what the fu-ture may hold, but cannot reasonably be construed to provide a rea-sonable and just basis for the statutory exclusion. The State's conjectures are not, in any event, susceptible to empirical proof before they occur.[14]

Finally, it is suggested that the long history of official intolerance of intimate same-sex relationships cannot be reconciled with an interpre-tation of Article 7 that would give state-sanctioned benefits and pro-tection to individuals of the same sex who commit to a permanent do-mestic relationship. We find the argument to be unpersuasive for several reasons. First, to the extent that state action historically has been motivated by an animus against a class, that history cannot pro-vide a legitimate basis for continued unequal application of the law. *See MacCallum,* 165 Vt. at 459–60, 686 A.2d at 939 (holding that although adopted persons had "historically been a target of discrimination," social prejudices failed to support their continued exclusion from intestacy law). As we observed recently in *Brigham*, 166 Vt. at 267, 692 A.2d at 396, "equal protection of the laws cannot be limited by eighteenth-century standards." Second, whatever claim may be made in light of the undeniable fact that federal and state statutes—including those in Vermont—have historically disfavored same-sex relationships, more recent legislation plainly undermines the contention. *See, e.g.*, Laws of Vermont, 1977, No. 51, §§ 2, 3 (repealing former § 2603 of Title 13, which criminalized fellatio). In 1992, Vermont was one of the first states to enact statewide legislation prohibiting discrimination in employment, housing, and other services based on sexual orientation. *See* 21 V.S.A. § 495 (employment); 9 V.S.A. § 4503 (housing); 8 V.S.A. § 4724 (insurance); 9 V.S.A. § 4502 (public accommodations). Sexual orientation is among the categories specifically protected against hate-motivated crimes in Vermont. *See* 13 V.S.A. § 1455. Furthermore, as noted earlier, recent enactments of the General Assembly have removed barriers to adoption by same-sex couples, and have extended legal rights and protections to such couples who dissolve their "domestic relationship." *See* 15A V.S.A. §§ 1-102, 1-112.

Thus, viewed in the light of history, logic, and experience, we conclude that none of the interests asserted by the State provides a reasonable and just basis for the continued exclusion of same-sex couples from the benefits incident to a civil marriage license under Vermont law. Accordingly, in the faith that a case beyond the imagining of the framers of our Constitution may, nevertheless, be safely anchored in the values that infused it, we find a constitutional obligation to extend to plaintiffs the common benefit, protection, and security that Vermont law provides opposite-sex married couples. It remains only to determine the appropriate means and scope of relief compelled by this constitutional mandate.

F. Remedy

It is important to state clearly the parameters of today's ruling. Although plaintiffs sought injunctive and declaratory relief designed to secure a marriage license, their claims and arguments here have focused primarily upon the consequences of official exclusion from the statutory benefits, protections, and security incident to marriage under Vermont law. While some future case may attempt to establish that—notwithstanding equal benefits and protections under Vermont law—the denial of a marriage license operates per se to deny constitutionally protected rights, that is not the claim we address today.

We hold only that plaintiffs are entitled under Chapter I, Article 7, of the Vermont Constitution to obtain the same benefits and protections afforded by Vermont law to married opposite-sex couples. We do not purport to infringe upon the prerogatives of the Legislature to craft an appropriate means of addressing this constitutional mandate, other than to note that the record here refers to a number of potentially constitutional statutory schemes from other jurisdictions. These include what are typically referred to as "domestic partnership" or "registered partnership" acts, which generally establish an alternative legal status to marriage for same-sex couples, impose similar formal requirements and limitations, create a parallel licensing or registration scheme, and extend all or most of the same rights and obligations provided by the law to married partners. *See* Report, *Hawaii Commission on Sexual Orientation and the Law* (Appendix D-1B) (1995) (recommending enactment of "Universal Comprehensive Domestic Partnership Act" to establish equivalent licensing and eligibility scheme and confer upon domestic partners "the same rights and obligations under the law that are conferred on spouses in a marriage relationship"); C. Christensen, *If Not Marriage? On Securing Gay and Lesbian Family Values by a "Simulacrum of Marriage,"* 66 Fordham L.Rev. 1699, 1734–45 (1998) (discussing various domestic and foreign domestic partnership acts); A. Friedman, *Same-Sex Marriage and the Right to Privacy: Abandoning Scriptural, Canonical, and Natural Law Based Definitions of Marriage,* 35 How. L.J. 173, 217–20 n. 237 (1992) (reprinting Denmark's "Registered Partnership Act"); *see generally* Note, *A More Perfect Union: A Legal and Social Analysis of Domestic Partnership Ordinances,* 92 Colum. L.Rev. 1164 (1992) (discussing local domestic partnership laws); M. Pedersen, *Denmark: Homosexual Marriage and New Rules Regarding Separation and Divorce,* 30 J. Fam. L. 289 (1992) (discussing amendments to Denmark's Registered Partnership Act); M. Roth, *The Norwegian Act on Registered Partnership for Homosexual Couples,* 35 J. Fam. L. 467 (1997) (discussing Norway's Act on Registered Partnership for Homosexual Couples). We do not intend specifically to endorse any one or all of the referenced acts, particularly in view of the significant benefits omitted from several of the laws.

Further, while the State's prediction of "destabilization" cannot be a ground for denying relief, it is not altogether irrelevant. A sudden change in the marriage laws or the statutory benefits traditionally incidental to marriage may have disruptive and unforeseen consequences. Absent legislative guidelines defining the status and rights of same-sex couples, consistent with constitutional requirements, uncertainty and confusion could result. Therefore, we hold that the current statutory scheme shall remain in effect for a reasonable period of time to enable the Legislature to consider and enact implementing legislation in an orderly and expeditious fashion.[15] *See Linkletter v. Walker,* 381 U.S. 618, 628, 85 S.Ct. 1731, 14 L.Ed.2d 601 (1965) (no constitutional rule impedes court's discretion to postpone operative date of ruling where exigencies require); *Smith v. State,* 93 Idaho 795, 473 P.2d 937, 950 (1970) (staying operative effect of decision abrogating rule of sovereign immunity until adjournment of next legislative session); *Spanel v. Mounds View School Dist. No. 621,* 264 Minn. 279, 118 N.W.2d 795, 803–04 (1962) (same). In the event that the benefits and protections in question are not statutorily granted, plaintiffs may petition this Court to order the remedy they originally sought.

Our colleague asserts that granting the relief requested by plaintiffs— an injunction prohibiting defendants from withholding a marriage license—is our "constitutional duty." 744 A.2d at 898 (Johnson, J., concurring in part and dissenting in part). We believe the argument is predicated upon a fundamental misinterpretation of our opinion. It appears to assume that we hold plaintiffs are entitled to a marriage license. We do not. We hold that the State is constitutionally required to extend to same-sex couples the common benefits and protections that flow from marriage under Vermont law. That the State could do so through a marriage license is obvious. But it is not required to do so, and the mandate proposed by our colleague is inconsistent with the Court's holding.

The dissenting and concurring opinion also invokes the United States Supreme Court's desegregation decision in *Watson v. City of Memphis,* 373 U.S. 526, 83 S.Ct. 1314, 10 L.Ed.2d 529 (1963), suggesting that the circumstances here are comparable, and demand a comparable judicial response. The analogy is flawed. We do not confront in this case the evil that was institutionalized racism, an evil that was widely recognized well before the Court's decision in *Watson* and its more famous predecessor, *Brown v. Board of Education*, 347 U.S. 483, 74 S.Ct. 686, 98 L.Ed. 873 (1954). Plaintiffs have not demonstrated that the exclusion of same-sex couples from the definition of marriage was intended to discriminate against women or lesbians and gay men, as racial segregation was designed to maintain the pernicious doctrine of white supremacy. *See Loving*, 388 U.S. at 11, 87 S.Ct. 1817 (holding antimiscegenation statutes violated Equal Protection Clause as invidious effort to maintain white supremacy). The concurring and dissenting opinion also overlooks the fact that the Supreme Court's urgency in Watson was impelled by the city's eight year delay in implementing its decision extending *Brown* to public recreational facilities, and "the significant fact that the governing constitutional principles no longer bear the imprint of newly enunciated doctrine." *See Watson*, 373 U.S. at 529, 83 S.Ct. 1314; *Dawson v. Mayor & City Council of Baltimore*, 220 F.2d 386 (4th Cir.), *aff'd*, 350 U.S. 877, 76 S.Ct. 133, 100 L.Ed. 774 (1955). Unlike *Watson*, our decision declares decidedly new doctrine.

The concurring and dissenting opinion further claims that our mandate represents an "abdicat[ion]" of the constitutional duty to decide, and an inexplicable failure to implement "the most straightforward and effective remedy." 744 A.2d at 897-98, 901-02. Our colleague greatly underestimates what we decide today and greatly overestimates the simplicity and effectiveness of her proposed mandate. First, our opinion provides greater recognition of—and protection for—same-sex relationships than has been recognized by any court of final jurisdiction in this country with the instructive exception of the Hawaii Supreme Court in *Baehr*, 852 P.2d 44. See Hawaii Const., art. I, § 23 (state constitutional amendment overturned same-sex marriage decision in *Baehr* by returning power to legislature "to reserve marriage to opposite-sex couples"). Second, the dissent's suggestion that her mandate would avoid the "political caldron" (744 A.2d at 898-99) of public debate is—even allowing for the welcome lack of political sophistication of the judiciary— significantly insulated from reality. *See* Hawaii Const., art. I, § 23; *see also* Alaska Const., art. I, § 25 (state constitutional amendment reversed trial court decision in favor of same-sex marriage, *Brause v. Bureau of Vital Statistics*, No. 3AN-95-6562 CI, 1998 WL 88743 (Alaska Super.Ct. Feb. 27,

1998), by providing that "a marriage may exist only between one man and one woman").

The concurring and dissenting opinion confuses decisiveness with wisdom and judicial authority with finality. Our mandate is predicated upon a fundamental respect for the ultimate source of constitutional authority, not a fear of decisiveness. No court was ever more decisive than the United States Supreme Court in *Dred Scott v. Sandford*, 60 U.S. (19 How.) 393, 15 L.Ed. 691 (1857). Nor more wrong. Ironically it was a Vermonter, Stephen Douglas, who in defending the decision said—as the dissent in essence does here—"I never heard before of an appeal being taken from the Supreme Court." *See* A. Bickel, *The Morality of Consent* 101 (1975). But it was a profound understanding of the law and the "unruliness of the human condition," *id.* at 11, that prompted Abraham Lincoln to respond that the Court does not issue Holy Writ. *See id.* at 101. Our colleague may be correct that a mandate intended to provide the Legislature with the opportunity to implement the holding of this Court in an orderly and expeditious fashion will have precisely the opposite effect. Yet it cannot be doubted that judicial authority is not ultimate authority. It is certainly not the only repository of wisdom.

> When a democracy is in moral flux, courts may not have the best or the final answers. Judicial answers may be wrong. They may be counterproductive even if they are right. Courts do best by proceeding in a way that is catalytic rather than preclusive, and that is closely attuned to the fact that courts are participants in the system of democratic deliberation.

> C. Sunstein, *Foreword: Leaving Things Undecided*, 110 Harv. L.Rev. 4, 101 (1996).

The implementation by the Vermont Legislature of a constitutional right expounded by this Court pursuant to the Vermont Constitution for the common benefit and protection of the Vermont community is not an abdication of judicial duty, it is the fulfillment of constitutional responsibility.

III. Conclusion

While many have noted the symbolic or spiritual significance of the marital, it is plaintiffs' claim to the secular benefits and protections of a singularly human relationship that, in our view, characterizes this case.

The State's interest in extending official recognition and legal protection to the professed commitment of two individuals to a lasting relationship of mutual affection is predicated on the belief that legal support of a couple's commitment provides stability for the individuals, their family, and the broader community. Although plaintiffs' interest in seeking state recognition and protection of their mutual commitment may—in view of divorce statistics—represent "the triumph of hope over experience,"[16] the essential aspect of their claim is simply and fundamentally for inclusion in the family of state-sanctioned human relations.

The past provides many instances where the law refused to see a human being when it should have. *See, e.g., Dred Scott*, 60 U.S. at 407 (concluding that African slaves and their descendants had "no rights which the white man was bound to respect"). The future may provide instances where the law will be asked to see a human when it should not. *See, e.g.*, G. Smith, *Judicial Decision Making in the Age of Biotechnology*, 13 Notre Dame J. Ethics & Pub. Policy 93, 114 (1999) (noting concerns that genetically engineering humans may threaten very nature of human individuality and identity). The challenge for future generations will be to define what is most essentially human. The extension of the Common Benefits Clause to acknowledge plaintiffs as Vermonters who seek nothing more, nor less, than legal protection and security for their avowed commitment to an intimate and lasting human relationship is simply, when all is said and done, a recognition of our common humanity.

The judgment of the superior court upholding the constitutionality of the Vermont marriage statutes under Chapter I, Article 7 of the Vermont Constitution is reversed. The effect of the Court's decision is suspended, and jurisdiction is retained in this Court, to permit the Legislature to consider and enact legislation consistent with the constitutional mandate described herein.

DOOLEY, J., concurring.

I concur in Part I of the majority opinion, the holding of Part II, and the mandate. I do not, however, concur in the reasoning of Part II. I recognize that to most observers the significance of this decision lies in its result and remedy. In the cases that come before us in the future, however, the significance of this case will lie in its rationale—that is, how we interpret and apply Chapter I, Article 7 of the Vermont Constitution. Moreover, in this, the most closely watched opinion in this Court's history, its acceptability will be based on whether its reasoning and result are clearly commanded by the Constitution and our precedents, and whether it is a careful and necessary exercise of the Court's limited powers. I do not believe that the majority's rationale meets this exacting standard, and I fear how it may be applied—or ignored—in the future.

This is a concurrence and not a dissent. I agree with the majority that the consequence of limiting marriage to a man and woman is the exclusion of these plaintiffs, and many persons similarly situated, from numerous rights, benefits, and duties that government and society provide to—and impose on—married persons. However we might have described marriage in relation to the very limited government that was created by our Constitution, the complexity of the current system of government-created benefits and burdens has made civil marriage a modern-day emolument, a government recognized and supported special status for which these plaintiffs are not eligible.

This is a civil rights case, very different from a claim of discrimination with respect to, for example, a peddler's fee, *see State v. Hoyt*, 71 Vt. 59, 42 A. 973 (1899), operation of partnerships, *see State v. Cadigan*, 73 Vt. 245, 50 A. 1079 (1901), or regulation of river pollution, *see State v. Haskell*, 84 Vt. 429, 79 A. 852 (1911). It is also very different from a claim that exemptions to a Sunday closing law unconstitutionally discriminated against large stores, the issue in *State v. Ludlow Supermarkets, Inc.*, 141 Vt. 261, 448 A.2d 791 (1982). The United States Supreme Court has recognized that discrimination based on race, alienage, national origin, or sex requires greater justification than economic discrimination, such as discrimination in the fees charged certain peddlers based on the type of goods they are selling. *See City of Cleburne v. Cleburne Living Center, Inc.*, 473 U.S. 432, 440–41, 105 S.Ct. 3249, 87 L.Ed.2d 313 (1985) (discussing the standards for scrutinizing various classifications). Compare *United States v. Virginia*, 518 U.S. 515, 532, 116 S.Ct. 2264, 135 L.Ed.2d 735 (1996) (sex), and *Loving v. Virginia*, 388 U.S. 1, 11, 87 S.Ct. 1817, 18 L.Ed.2d 1010 (1967) (race), with *Williamson v. Lee Optical of Oklahoma, Inc.*, 348 U.S. 483, 486–88, 75 S.Ct. 461, 99 L.Ed. 563 (1955) (economic regulation). Until this decision, we also recognized this distinction. As we stated in *Brigham v. State,* 166 Vt. 246, 265, 692 A.2d 384, 396 (1997): "Where a statutory scheme affects fundamental constitutional rights or involves suspect classifications, both federal and state decisions have recognized that proper equal protection analysis necessitates a more searching scrutiny. . . ."

The marriage statutes do not facially discriminate on the basis of sexual orientation. There is, however, no doubt that the requirement that civil marriage be a union of one man and one woman has the effect of discriminating against lesbian and gay couples, like the plaintiffs in this case, who are unable to marry the life partners of their choice. The majority proclaims that most decisions have concluded that lesbians and gay men are not a suspect classification, inferring that any conclusion to the contrary is wrong. *See* 744 A.2d at 878 n. 10. On this point, however, I believe the central analysis of *Ludlow* is critical:

> [A] state court reviewing state legislation is in a very different posture from the United States Supreme Court when it undertakes the parallel task. Rather than disposing of a case on the premise that its impact will presumably affect more than fifty varying jurisdictions, a state court reaches its result in the legal climate of the single jurisdiction with which it is associated, if federal proscriptions are not transgressed.

41 Vt. at 268, 448 A.2d at 795. Although our precedents mandate use of at least a close cousin of the federal equal protection test, we must, as we said in *Ludlow,* apply that test in our own "legal climate."

Vermont's legal climate differs considerably from that in other jurisdictions where courts have held that lesbians and gay men are not a suspect classification. Indeed, the federal analysis of the rights of lesbians and gay men almost always starts with *Bowers v. Hardwick,* 478 U.S. 186, 106 S.Ct. 2841, 92 L.Ed.2d 140 (1986), a decision that reflects a legal climate quite hostile to those rights. *Bowers* upheld a Georgia conviction for sodomy based on a sex act committed by two males in the bedroom of defendant's home. *See id.* at 196, 106 S.Ct. 2841. It held that, for due process purposes, individuals do not have "a fundamental right to engage in homosexual sodomy." *Id.* at 191, 106 S.Ct. 2841.

Federal courts considering equal-protection challenges have relied on *Bowers* to conclude that lesbians and gay men are not a suspect classification. They rationalize that if homosexual conduct can constitutionally be criminalized, homosexuals cannot constitute a suspect class. *See, e.g., Equality Found. of Greater Cincinnati, Inc. v. City of Cincinnati*, 128 F.3d 289, 292–93 (6th Cir.1997) (holding that under *Bowers* and its progeny, homosexuals do not constitute suspect class because conduct which defined them as homosexuals could constitutionally be proscribed); *Ben-Shalom v. Marsh*, 881 F.2d 454, 464–65 (7th Cir.1989) (citing *Bowers* and holding that because homosexual conduct may constitutionally be criminalized, homosexuals do not constitute a suspect class); *High Tech Gays v. Defense Indus. Sec. Clearance Office*, 895 F.2d 563, 571 (9th Cir.1990) (same); *Woodward v. United States*, 871 F.2d 1068, 1074–76 (Fed.Cir.1989) (same); *Padula v. Webster*, 822 F.2d 97, 102–03 (D.C.Cir.1987) (same); *see also* Opinion of the Justices, 129 N.H. 290, 530 A.2d 21, 24 (1987) (stating that for federal equal-protection analysis homosexuals do not constitute a suspect class, nor is there a fundamental right to engage in sodomy according to *Bowers*).

The majority errs in relying on these cases because the *Bowers* rationale applied in all of them is not applicable in Vermont today. Although Vermont, like all states, once criminalized sodomy, and had a "fellation" law, see *State v. LaForrest*, 71 Vt. 311, 312, 45 A. 225, 226 (1899) (holding sodomy a crime by virtue of 1 V.S.A. § 271—formerly V.S. § 898—and adopting common law so far as applicable in Vermont); 13 V.S.A. § 2603 (repealed 1977, No. 51, § 2), it repealed this law in 1977 and does not now prohibit, or otherwise restrict, homosexual conduct between adults, except on the same terms that it restricts heterosexual conduct. *See, e.g.*, 13 V.S.A. § 3252 (sexual assault); 13 V.S.A. § 3253 (aggravated assault); 13 V.S.A. § 2601 (lewd and lascivious conduct).

Since 1992, it has generally been the policy of Vermont to prohibit discrimination based on sexual orientation. *See* 1991, No. 135 (Adj.Sess.). This includes discrimination based on "female or male homosexuality." 1 V.S.A. § 143. Thus, I believe our "legal climate" is vastly different from that in *Bowers*, where, after considering that twenty-four states had criminalized sodomy between consenting adults, the United States Supreme Court concluded that there was no fundamental right, deeply rooted in the Nation's history, to engage in such conduct. My point here is simply that the rationale in federal decisions for withholding a more searching scrutiny does not apply in Vermont. The majority errs in relying on these decisions and the state court decisions applying the same federal analysis.

Chapter I, Article 7 of the Vermont Constitution actually contains three clauses, the most important of which is the second, which contains the prohibition on governmental actions "for the particular emolument or advantage of any single person, family, or set of persons, who are a part only of that community." This antiprivilege language, and variations on it, is contained in the vast majority of pre–Civil War state constitutions. *See, e.g.,* Conn. Const. of 1818, art. I, § 1; Ky. Const. of 1792, art. XII, § 1; Mass. Const., art. VI (adopted in 1780); N.H. Const., art. X (adopted in 1784); N.C. Const. of 1776, art. III; Ohio Const. of 1851, art. I, § 2; Va. Const. of 1776, Bill of Rights, § 4; Tx. Const. of 1845, art. I, § 2. At least in this century, the jurisprudence in Vermont is similar to that in most states. *See, e.g., Town of Emerald Isle v. State,* 320 N.C. 640, 360 S.E.2d 756, 764 (1987) (classification is not exclusive emolument if intended to promote general welfare and reasonable basis exists to conclude it serves public interest); *Primes v. Tyler,* 43 Ohio St.2d 195, 331 N.E.2d 723, 728–29 (1975) (statute violates constitution because no governmental interest justifies grant of special privilege and immunity); *Rosenblum v. Griffin,* 89 N.H. 314, 197 A. 701, 706 (1938) (classification is constitutional under New Hampshire or federal law if based on some reasonable ground); *City of Corbin v. Louisville & Nashville R.R.,* 233 Ky. 709, 26 S.W.2d 539, 540 (1930) (purpose of emoluments and privileges clause is to place all similarly situated citizens on plane of equality under law).

Oregon, like Vermont, has developed an independent state constitutional jurisprudence. Article I, Section 20 of the Oregon Constitution, adopted in 1859, provides that no law shall "grant [. . .] to any citizen or class of citizens privileges, or immunities, which, upon the same terms, shall not equally belong to all citizens." This provision is similar in purpose and effect to our Common Benefits Clause. *See* D. Schuman, *The Right to "Equal Privileges and Immunities": A State Version of "Equal Protection,"* 13 Vt. L.Rev. 221, 222–25 (1988). The Oregon Supreme Court has described that provision precisely how we today have described Chapter I, Article 7: "Antedating the Civil War and the equal protection clause of the fourteenth amendment, its language reflects early egalitarian objections to favoritism and special privileges for a few rather than the concern of the Reconstruction Congress about discrimination against disfavored individuals or groups." *State v. Clark*, 291 Or. 231, 630 P.2d 810, 814 (1981). Just as this Court has acknowledged in developing its Article 7 jurisprudence, the Oregon court has recognized that a privilege for a person or group of persons means discrimination against others. *See id.* at 814 (Article I, Section 20 of Oregon Constitution protects against adverse discrimination as well as against favoritism). Thus, while developing an independent state constitutional jurisprudence, the Oregon Supreme Court has looked to the decisions of the United States Supreme Court, but has adopted the federal analysis only where the court finds it persuasive. *See State v. Kennedy*, 295 Or. 260, 666 P.2d 1316, 1321 (1983); *see, e.g., Hewitt v. State Accident Ins. Fund Corp.*, 294 Or. 33, 653 P.2d 970, 976 (1982) (declining to adopt federal standard of intermediate scrutiny for sex-based classifications).

The Oregon Supreme Court, like this Court, has adopted the federal, tiered framework for analyzing equal-protection-type constitutional challenges. *See Hewitt*, 653 P.2d at 976 (following United States Supreme Court analysis that asks whether classification is made on basis of suspect classification, and if so, whether such classification is subject to strict scrutiny). Moreover, it has held, as we have held, that its state constitution "prohibits disparate treatment of groups or individuals by virtue of 'invidious' social categories" and that discrimination against a suspect class is subject to strict scrutiny. *Id.; see MacCallum v. Seymour's Adm'r*, 165 Vt. 452, 460, 686 A.2d 935, 939 (1996) (Article 7 protects against invidious discrimination). I point out the similarities between our Article 7 jurisprudence and Oregon's § 20 jurisprudence because this Court has not established the criteria for identifying suspect classifications, while the Oregon courts have. Because of the historical similarity, I find it useful to look to Oregon case law, and the United States Supreme Court decisions upon which it relies, in considering whether lesbians and gay men are a suspect classification under Article 7.

In *Hewitt*, the Oregon Supreme Court determined that sex-based classifications are suspect because (1) they focus on an immutable personal characteristic and thus "can be suspected of reflecting 'invidious' social or political premises, that is to say, prejudice or stereotyped pre-judgments," and (2) "[t]he purposeful historical, legal, economic, and political unequal treatment of women is well known." 653 P.2d at 977. Accordingly, the court held that sex-based classifications are inherently suspect, like the United States Supreme Court found classifications based on race, alienage, and nationality. *See id.* at 977–78 (citing *Loving v. Virginia*, 388 U.S. 1, 11, 87 S.Ct. 1817, 18 L.Ed.2d 1010 (1967) (race); *Graham v. Richardson*, 403 U.S. 365, 372, 91 S.Ct. 1848, 29 L.Ed.2d 534 (1971) (alienage); *Oyama v. California*, 332 U.S. 633, 646, 68 S.Ct. 269, 92 L.Ed. 249 (1948) (nationality)).

Although the Oregon Supreme Court has not addressed whether les-bians and gay men are a suspect classification, the Oregon Court of Appeals has recently done so. *See Tanner v. Oregon Health Sciences Univ.*, 157 Or.App. 502, 971 P.2d 435 (1998). In *Tanner*, the court held that Article I, Section 20 of the Oregon Constitution requires the Oregon Health Sciences University to extend health and life insurance benefits to the un-married domestic partners of its homosexual employees. *See id.* at 448. The *Tanner* court examined the *Hewitt* two-part test for defining suspect classes and determined that "immutability—in the sense of inability to alter or change—is not necessary" because alienage and religious affil-iation—which may be changed—have been held to be suspect classifi-cations. Thus, it held that defining a suspect class depends not on the immutability of a class-defining characteristic, but upon (1) whether the characteristic has historically been regarded as defining a distinct so-cially recognized group, and if so (2) whether that group has been the subject of adverse social or political stereotyping. *See id.* at 446. Apply-ing this test, the court concluded that the class of homosexual couples is clearly defined in terms of stereotyped personal and social character-istics; is widely regarded as a distinct, socially recognized group; and indisputably has "been and continue [s] to be the subject of adverse so-cial and political stereotyping and prejudice." *Id.* at 447. Thus, the court found that the plaintiffs, three lesbian couples, were members of a sus-pect class.

In this concurrence, I do not detail a suspect-classification analysis, but I can summarize my opinion by saying that I agree with the general framework adopted by the Oregon courts in *Hewitt* and *Tanner*. These decisions concerning Article I, Section 20 of that state's constitution are entirely consistent with the law we have developed under Chapter I, Article 7 of the Vermont Constitution, at least prior to this decision. I find *Hewitt* and *Tanner* far more persuasive than the majority's decision, which backtracks from the established legal framework under Article 7 and fails to provide any guidelines whatsoever for the Legislature, the trial courts, or Vermonters in general to predict the outcome of future cases.

I agree with the majority that the State cannot justify the denial of legal benefits and responsibilities of civil marriage to gay and lesbian couples. And I agree that the appropriate remedy is either to require the State to extend the option of receiving these benefits and associated responsibilities to these couples, or to require that it offer the opportunity for civil marriage on equal terms. I will briefly explain my disagreement with the majority's rationale for reaching the same result.

The majority's analysis under Chapter I, Article 7 proceeds in three steps: (1) there is one equality standard imposed by Article 7, and it applies to claims of civil rights discrimination and economic discrimination alike; (2) the equality standard is higher, that is, more active, than the standard imposed by the Equal Protection Clause of the Fourteenth Amendment for analyzing claims of economic discrimination; and (3) under the new standard, the denial of the benefits of marriage to lesbians and gay men violates Chapter I, Article 7. In the first two steps, the majority makes statements entirely contrary to our existing Article 7 jurisprudence. As to the third step, I find no standard in the Court's decision—it is entirely a matter of "judgment."

The first step in the Court's analysis requires overruling a long series of precedents holding that where a statutory scheme affects fundamental constitutional rights or involves suspect classifications, Article 7 requires "a more searching scrutiny." *Brigham,* 166 Vt. at 265, 692 A.2d at 396.[17] Among the decisions that have stated this standard are *L'Esperance v. Town of Charlotte,* 167 Vt. 162, 165, 704 A.2d 760, 762 (1997); *MacCallum,* 165 Vt. at 457, 686 A.2d at 936-37; *Benning v. State,* 161 Vt. 472, 486, 641 A.2d 757, 764 (1994); *In re Sherman Hollow, Inc.,* 160 Vt. 627, 628, 641A.2d 753, 755 (1993) (mem.); *Oxx v. Department of Taxes,* 159 Vt. 371,

376, 618 A.2d 1321, 1324 (1992); *Hodgeman v. Jard Co.*, 157 Vt. 461, 464, 599 A.2d 1371, 1373 (1991); *State v. George*, 157 Vt. 580, 588, 602 A.2d 953, 957 (1991); *Town of Sandgate v. Colehamer*, 156 Vt. 77, 88, 589 A.2d 1205, 1211 (1990); and *Choquette v. Perrault*, 153 Vt. 45, 51-52, 569 A.2d 455, 459 (1989).[18] The majority barely acknowledges the multitiered standard stated in those cases, and dismisses it as a "rigid" analysis. *See* 744 A.2d at 877–78. It is ironic that in a civil rights case we overrule our precedent requiring the State to meet a higher burden in civil rights cases, but still conclude, under the lower standard, that the State has not met its burden.

The effect of the majority decision is that the State now bears no higher burden to justify discrimination against African Americans or women than it does to justify discrimination against large retail stores as in *Ludlow*. I doubt that the framers of our Constitution, concerned with preventing the equivalent of British royalty, would believe that the inevitable line-drawing that must occur in economic regulation should be equated with the denial of civil and human rights. I do not believe that the new standard is required by, or even consistent with, the history on which the majority bases it.

The second step is also at variance with our Article 7 law, even as it seeks to rely upon it. The majority holds that Article 7 requires a more active standard of constitutional review than the Fourteenth Amendment, as interpreted by the United States Supreme Court, in the absence of a fundamental right or suspect classification. *See* 744 A.2d at 871–72. This means that in the future this Court is less likely to defer to the Legislature and more likely to find its acts unconstitutional than would the United States Supreme Court. Again, I find great irony in the fact that we are doing this unnecessarily in a case where the main theme of the State and many amici is that we must defer to the Legislature on the issue before us.

I agree that *Ludlow*, *Choquette*, and *MacCallum* contain important holdings about how equality challenges are addressed by a state court. *Ludlow* holds that we must look at justifications for distinctions that are realistic in view of Vermont's unique legal culture. *See Ludlow*, 141 Vt. at 268, 448 A.2d at 795. *Choquette* and *MacCallum* hold that such justifications must be relevant to contemporary circumstances and not be wholly archaic. See *Choquette*, 153 Vt. at 53-54, 569 A.2d at 460; *MacCallum*, 165 Vt. at 461, 686 A.2d at 940. None of these decisions demonstrate that "Vermont decisions reflect a very different approach from current federal jurisprudence," which is how the majority characterizes them. 744 A.2d at 870–71. Indeed, we have said over and over that the test, where no fundamental right or suspect class is involved, "is the same under the Equal Protection Clause of the Fourteenth Amendment to the United States Constitution" as under Article 7. *Lorrain v. Ryan*, 160 Vt. 202, 212, 628 A.2d 543, 550 (1993); *see Brigham*, 166 Vt. at 265, 692 A.2d at 395; *L'Esperance*, 167 Vt. at 165, 704 A.2d at 762. Although the majority seeks to rely on isolated statements from *Ludlow*, in fact, we are by this decision creating a new, more active standard of review in Article 7 challenges.[19]

We have wisely, in the past, avoided the path the majority now chooses, a path worn and abandoned in many other states. When Justice Hayes decried the failure of litigants to raise state constitutional issues, see *State v. Jewett*, 146 Vt. 221, 229, 500 A.2d 233, 238 (1985), he could not have been referring to challenges under state anti-emolument and equality provisions. In state after state, throughout the nineteenth and early twentieth centuries, state supreme courts routinely struck down economic and social welfare statutes under these provisions using an analysis similar to that employed by the majority in this case. *See* H. Gillman, *The Constitution Besieged: The Rise and Demise of Lochner Era Police Powers Jurisprudence*, 9 (1993). For example, in *Auditor of Lucas County v. State*, 75 Ohio St. 114, 78 N.E. 955, 957 (1906), the Ohio Supreme Court struck down an Ohio law that provided a stipend of $25 each quarter to adult blind persons because it was over-inclusive (including rich and poor) and underinclusive (including only some disabled persons). See also *City of Cincinnati v. Cook*, 107 Ohio St. 223, 140 N.E. 655, 656 (1923) (striking down ordinance that allowed parking in front of train station only with consent of supervisor of station, in part because it created "privilege or immunity" in those who were allowed to park); *Low v. Rees Printing Co.*, 41 Neb. 127, 59 N.W. 362, 368 (1894) (striking down eight-hour-day law because it exempted farm or domestic labor); *State v. Pennoyer*, 65 N.H. 113, 18 A. 878, 881 (1889) (striking down statute requiring licensing of all physicians, except those who resided in only one town between 1875 and 1879, because it imposed unequal burden on members of same class); *Millett v. People*, 117 Ill. 294, 7 N.E. 631, 636 (1886) (striking down statute requiring mine operators who tied wages to amount of coal extracted to keep scale at mine so coal could be weighed before managers had chance to separate unusable material); *In re Jacobs*, 98 N.Y. 98, 112-14 (1885) (striking down act addressing deplorable working conditions under which cigar makers labored in tenements by banning the manufacturing of cigars in those dwellings); *Ex parte Westerfield*, 55 Cal. 550, 551 (Sup.Ct.1880) (striking down law making it misdemeanor for bakers to force employees to work between six o'clock Saturday evening and six o'clock Sunday evening).

Most of these decisions reflect judicial attitudes prevalent in the era of *Lochner v. New York*, 198 U.S. 45, 25 S.Ct. 539, 49 L.Ed. 937 (1905), when the United States Supreme Court was routinely striking down economic and social welfare legislation. As the United States Supreme Court modified its jurisprudence to give primacy to the federal and state legislative role in economic and social welfare legislation, state courts did likewise, often on the basis that Fourteenth Amendment jurisprudence was equally applicable under state due process and equality provisions. See Gillman, supra, at 62. *See, e.g., Department of Mental Hygiene v. Kirchner*, 62 Cal.2d 586, 43 Cal.Rptr. 329, 400 P.2d 321, 322 (1965) (Fourteenth Amendment to federal Constitution and §§ 11 and 21 of Article I of California Constitution provide generally equivalent but independent protections in their respective jurisdictions); *People v. Willi*, 109 Misc. 79, 179 N.Y.S. 542, 547 (Del.Cty.Ct.1919) (methods of analysis under Fourteenth Amendment and state constitution are identical); *City of Chicago v. Rhine*, 363 Ill. 619, 2 N.E.2d 905, 908 (1936) (simultaneously analyzing federal and state equal protection claims); *Ex parte Caldwell*, 82 Neb. 544, 118 N.W. 133, 134 (1908) (upholding under state and federal constitutions statute prohibiting common labor on Sunday).

The Vermont Supreme Court never adopted an activist stance in reviewing economic and social welfare legislation, and history shows we chose the right course. We could have relied upon the looser and more activist language that prevailed in the federal cases in the early twentieth century—the same language that the majority relies upon today, 744 A.2d at 872 n. 4—to substitute our judgment for the Legislature, but wisely we did not. Unfortunately, we have now resurrected that approach. I can find no justification for the holding that Article 7 requires a more activist approach than the Fourteenth Amendment for reviewing social welfare and economic legislation. We were right in Lorrain, Brigham, and L'Esperance on this point and should adhere to those precedents.

Finally, concerning the third step of the majority's analysis, I question whether the majority's new standard is ascertainable, is consistent with our limited role in constitutional review, and contains appropriate judicial discretion. As Justice Johnson explains in her dissent, *see* 744 A.2d at 880 n. 13, the strength of the federal approach is that it disciplines judicial discretion and promotes predictability. *See* C. Sunstein, *Foreword: Leaving Things Undecided*, 110 Harv. L.Rev. 6, 78 (1996). Indeed, the Oregon courts have followed the federal approach in this area to avoid a balancing process "of pragmatic considerations about which reasonable people may differ over time," Kennedy, 666 P.2d at 1321, and "policy choices disguised as ad hoc evaluations based on comparison of incommensurables." Schuman, *supra*, at 227. The majority calls the federal approach "rigid" at one point, A.2d at 878, but then describes it, as applied in *Tanner*, as an invitation to subjective judicial decision making. 744 A.2d at 878 n. 10. The two criticisms are as inconsistent as any criticisms could be. I accept the former—rigid—as accurate, at least in comparison with the wide judicial discretion the majority claims here as an alternative. The latter—subjective judicial decision making—is, however, the least accurate criticism the majority could level.

Two points about the new standard are particularly troublesome for me. The majority now requires that legislative classifications be "reasonably necessary to accomplish the State's claimed objectives." 744 A.2d at 878. In our imperfect world, few legislative classifications are "necessary," and most legislation could be more narrowly tailored to the state's objective. I cannot square this standard with our limited role in constitutional adjudication. As I noted earlier, while language to this effect appears in *Ludlow*, it has never been used as the basis of one of our decisions until today.

More importantly, I cannot endorse, in this vitally important area of constitutional review, a standard that relies wholly on factors and balancing, with no mooring in any criteria or guidelines, however imperfect they may be. On this point, I agree with Justice Johnson. *See* 744 A.2d at 880–81 n. 13. I accept the majority's assertion that it has attempted to avoid a standard based on "personal notions" and that all constitutional adjudication requires reasoned judgment, but I do not believe that it has succeeded in properly applying the critical considerations it has identified. 744 A.2d at 879. Instead of mooring its analysis within the framework of fundamental rights and suspect classifications, the majority professes to make its new Article 7 standard "objective and grounded" by requiring courts, in balancing the competing interests, to "look to the history and 'traditions from which [the State] developed' as well as those 'from which it broke.'" 744 A.2d at 879. It is difficult to conceive that any persons sitting on this Court, whatever their philosophical persuasions, would be insensitive to the history and traditions from which Vermont developed, and those from which it broke, but how this standard will be applied to Article 7 challenges is not at all predictable. In the end, the approach the majority has developed relies too much on the identities and personal philosophies of the men and women who fill the chairs at the Supreme Court, too little on ascertainable standards that judges of different backgrounds and philosophies can apply equally, and very little, if any, on deference to the legislative branch.

The final irony in this decision for me is that the balancing and weighing process set forth in the Court's opinion describes exactly the process we would expect legislators to go through if they were facing the question before us free from the political pressures necessarily created by deeply held moral convictions, in both directions, of substantial members of their constituents. We are judges, not legislators.

For the above reasons, I concur in the mandate, but respectfully disagree with Part II of the Court's decision, the majority's rationale for reaching this mandate.

JOHNSON, J., concurring in part and dissenting in part.

Forty years ago, in reversing a decision that had denied injunctive relief for the immediate desegregation of publicly owned parks and recreational facilities in Memphis, Tennessee, a unanimous United States Supreme Court stated

The basic guarantees of our Constitution are warrants for the here and now, and, unless there is an overwhelmingly compelling reason, they are to be promptly fulfilled.

> *Watson v. City of Memphis*, 373 U.S. 526, 533,
> 83 S.Ct. 1314, 10 L.Ed.2d 529 (1963).

Plaintiffs come before this Court claiming that the State has unconstitutionally deprived them of the benefits of marriage based solely upon a discriminatory classification that violates their civil rights. They ask the Court to remedy the unlawful discrimination by enjoining the State and its municipalities from denying them the license that serves to identify the persons entitled to those benefits. The majority agrees that the Common Benefits Clause of the Vermont Constitution entitles plaintiffs to obtain the same benefits and protections as those bestowed upon married opposite-sex couples, yet it declines to give them any relief other than an exhortation to the Legislature to deal with the problem. I concur with the majority's holding, but I respectfully dissent from its novel and truncated remedy, which in my view abdicates this Court's constitutional duty to redress violations of constitutional rights. I would grant the requested relief and enjoin defendants from denying plaintiffs a marriage license based solely on the sex of the applicants.

The majority declares that the issue before this Court does not turn on the heated moral debate over intimate same-sex relationships and, further, that this Court has a constitutional responsibility to consider the legal merits of even controversial cases. *See* 744 A.2d at 867. Yet, notwithstanding these pronouncements, the majority elects to send plaintiffs to an uncertain fate in the political caldron of that very same moral debate.[20] And to what end? Passing this case on to the Legislature will not alleviate the instability and uncertainty that the majority seeks to avoid, and will unnecessarily entangle this Court in the Legislature's efforts to accommodate the majority's mandate within a "reasonable period of time." 744 A.2d at 887.

In 1948, when the California Supreme Court struck down a state law prohibiting the issuance of a license authorizing interracial marriages, the court did not suspend its judgment to allow the legislature an opportunity to enact a separate licensing scheme for interracial marriages.

See *Perez v. Lippold,* 32 Cal.2d 711, 198 P.2d 17, 29 (1948) (granting writ of mandamus compelling county clerk to issue certificate of registry). Indeed, such a mandate in that context would be unfathomable to us today. Here, as in *Perez,* we have held that the State has unconstitutionally discriminated against plaintiffs, thereby depriving them of civil rights to which they are entitled. Like the Hawaii Circuit Court in *Baehr v. Miike,* No. Civ. 91-1394, 1996 WL 694235, at *22 (Haw.Cir.Ct., Dec. 3, 1996), which rejected the state's reasons for excluding same-sex couples from marriage, we should simply enjoin the state from denying marriage licenses to plaintiffs based on sex or sexual orientation. That remedy would provide prompt and complete relief to plaintiffs and create reliable expectations that would stabilize the legal rights and duties of all couples.

I.

My dissent from the majority's mandate is grounded on the government's limited interest in dictating public morals outside the scope of its police power, and the differing roles of the judicial and legislative branches in our tripartite system of government. I first examine the State's narrow interest in licensing marriages, then contrast that interest with the judiciary's fundamental duty to remedy civil rights violations, and lastly emphasize the majority's failure to adequately explain why it is taking the unusual step of suspending its judgment to allow the Legislature an opportunity to redress the unconstitutional discrimination that we have found.

This case concerns the secular licensing of marriage. The State's interest in licensing marriages is regulatory in nature. *See Southview Coop. Housing v. Rent Control Bd.,* 396 Mass. 395, 486 N.E.2d 700, 704 (1985) ("Licensing is simply a means of regulating."). The regulatory purpose of the licensing scheme is to create public records for the orderly allocation of benefits, imposition of obligations, and distribution of property through inheritance. Thus, a marriage license merely acts as a trigger for state-conferred benefits. *See Priddy v. City of Tulsa,* 882 P.2d 81, 83 (Okla.Crim.App.1994) (license gives to licensee special privilege not accorded to others, which licensee otherwise would not enjoy). In granting a marriage license, the State is not espousing certain morals, lifestyles, or relationships, but only identifying those persons entitled to the benefits of the marital status.[21] See *People ex rel. Deukmejian v. County of Mendocino*, 36 Cal.3d 476, 204 Cal.Rptr. 897, 683 P.2d 1150, 1155 (1984) (licensing regulates activity based on determination of qualification of licensee).

Apart from establishing restrictions on age and consanguinity related to public health and safety, see 18 V.S.A. § 5142 (minors and incompetent persons); 15 V.S.A. §§ 1, 2 (consanguinity), the statutory scheme at issue here makes no qualitative judgment about which persons may obtain a marriage license. See *Leduc v. Commonwealth*, 421 Mass. 433, 657 N.E.2d 755, 756–57 (1995) (historical aim of licensure is generally to preserve public health, safety, and welfare). Hence, the State's interest concerning the challenged licensing statute is a narrow one, and plaintiffs have prevailed on their constitutional claim because the State has failed to raise any legitimate reasons related to public health or safety for denying marital benefits to same-sex couples. See *Commonwealth v. Bonadio*, 490 Pa. 91, 415 A.2d 47, 50 (1980) ("With respect to regulation of morals, the police power should properly be exercised to protect each individual's right to be free from interference in defining and pursuing his own morality but not to enforce a majority morality on persons whose conduct does not harm others."). In my view, the State's interest in licensing marriages would be undisturbed by this Court enjoining defendants from denying plaintiffs a license.

While the State's interest in licensing marriages is narrow, the judiciary's obligation to remedy constitutional violations is central to our form of government. Indeed, one of the fundamental principles of our tripartite system of government is that the judiciary interprets and gives effect to the constitution in cases and controversies concerning individual rights. See *Marbury v. Madison*, 5 U.S. (1 Cranch) 137, 163, 177–78, 2 L.Ed. 60 (1803); see also *Shields v. Gerhart*, 163 Vt. 219, 223, 658 A.2d 924, 927–28 (1995) (emphasizing "the preeminence of the Vermont Constitution in our governmental scheme," which includes right of citizens under Chapter I, Article 4 to find a certain remedy promptly and without delay).[22]

This power is "not merely to rule on cases, but to decide them." *Plaut v. Spendthrift Farm, Inc.*, 514 U.S. 211, 218–19, 115 S.Ct. 1447, 131 L.Ed.2d

328 (1995); see Records of the Council of Censors of the State of Vermont 431 (P. Gillies and D. Sanford eds., 1991) (supreme judicial tribunals are to regard constitution as fundamental law superior to legislative enactment; consequently, if enactment is repugnant to constitution, judges are bound to pronounce it inoperative and void). As this Court has stated on numerous occasions, when measures enacted pursuant to the State's police powers have no real or substantial relation to any legitimate purpose of those powers and invade individual "rights secured by the fundamental law, it is the duty of the courts to so adjudge, and thereby give effect to the Constitution." *State v. Morse*, 84 Vt. 387, 394, 80 A. 189, 191–92 (1911) (quoting *Mugler v. Kansas*, 123 U.S. 623, 8 S.Ct. 273, 31 L.Ed. 205 (1887)); *see Beecham v. Leahy*, 130 Vt. 164, 172, 287 A.2d 836, 841 (1972) ("It is the function of the judicial branch to pass upon the appropriateness and reasonableness of the legislative exercise of police power."). This Court emphasized in *Morse* that "in its last analysis, the question of the validity of such measures [enacted under the police powers] is one for the court." 84 Vt. at 394, 80 A. at 191.

The power of courts to fashion remedies for constitutional violations is well-established in both this Court's and the United States Supreme Court's jurisprudence concerning individual rights and equal protection. See *MacCallum v. Seymour's Adm'r*, 165 Vt. 452, 462, 686 A.2d 935, 941 (1996) (holding that statute denying adopted children right to inherit from collateral heirs violated Common Benefits Clause, and declaring plaintiff to be lawful heir of estate of collateral relative); *Medical Ctr. Hosp. v. Lorrain*, 165 Vt. 12, 14–15, 675 A.2d 1326, 1329 (1996) (determining that doctrine making husbands liable to creditors for necessary items provided to wives violated principle of equal protection when applied only to men, and choosing to abolish doctrine rather than to extend it to both men and women); *see also Heckler v. Mathews*, 465 U.S. 728, 740, 104 S.Ct. 1387, 79 L.Ed.2d 646 (1984) (when right invoked is that to equal treatment, "the appropriate remedy is a mandate of equal treatment"); *Davis v. Passman*, 442 U.S. 228, 241–42, 99 S.Ct. 2264, 60 L.Ed.2d 846 (1979) (within "great outlines" of Constitution, "judiciary is clearly discernible as the primary means through which these rights may be enforced"; unless Constitution commits issue to coordinate branch, "we presume that justiciable constitutional rights are to be enforced through the courts"). Particularly in civil rights cases involving discrimination against a disfavored group, "courts do not need specific [legislative] authorization to employ a remedy, at law or in equity, that is tailored to correct a constitutional wrong." *Aguayo v. Christopher,* 865 F.Supp. 479, 487–88 (N.D.Ill.1994) (finding unconstitutional on its face statute making citizenship available to foreign-born children of citizen fathers, but not citizen mothers, and issuing judgment declaring plaintiff to be a citizen).

Accordingly, absent "compelling" reasons that dictate otherwise, it is not only the prerogative but the duty of courts to provide prompt relief for violations of individual civil rights. See *Watson,* 373 U.S. at 532–33, 83 S.Ct. 1314 (defendants have heavy burden of showing that delay in desegregating public parks and recreational facilities is "manifestly compelled by constitutionally cognizable circumstances"). This basic principle is designed to assure that laws enacted through the will of the majority do not unconstitutionally infringe upon the rights of a disfavored minority.

There may be situations, of course, when legislative action is required before a court-ordered remedy can be fulfilled. For example, in *Brigham v. State,* 166 Vt. 246, 249, 269, 692 A.2d 384, 386, 398 (1997), this Court declared that Vermont's system for funding public education unconstitutionally deprived Vermont schoolchildren of a right to an equal educational opportunity, and then retained jurisdiction until the Legislature enacted legislation that satisfied the Court's holding. Plainly, it was not within the province of this Court to create a new funding system to replace the one that we had declared unconstitutional. The Legislature needed to enact legislation that addressed issues such as the level of state funding for public schools, the sources of additional revenue, and the framework for distributing state funds. See Act 60, 16 V.S.A. §§ 4000–4029. In finding a funding source, the Legislature had to consider whether to apply a flat or progressive tax on persons, property, entities, activities, or income. These considerations, in turn, required the Legislature to consider what state programs would have to be curtailed to make up for the projected additional school funding. All of these complex political decisions entailed core legislative functions that were a necessary predicate to fulfillment of our holding. *See Brigham,* 166 Vt. at 249, 692 A.2d at 386 (devising system for funding public education lies within prerogative of Legislature).

A completely different situation exists here. We have held that the Vermont Constitution entitles plaintiffs "to obtain the same benefits and protections afforded by Vermont law to married opposite-sex couples." 744 A.2d at 886. Given this holding, the most straightforward and effective remedy is simply to enjoin the State from denying plaintiffs a marriage license, which would designate them as persons entitled to those benefits and protections.[23] No legislation is required to redress the constitutional violation that the Court has found. *Cf. Watson*, 373 U.S. at 532, 83 S.Ct. 1314 (desegregation of recreational facilities does not present same kind of cognizable difficulties inherent in desegregating schools). Nor does our paramount interest in vindicating plaintiffs' constitutional rights interfere in any way with the State's interest in licensing marriages. Far from intruding upon the State's narrow interest in its licensing statute, allowing plaintiffs to obtain a license would further the overall goals of marriage, as defined by the majority—to provide stability to individuals, their families, and the broader community by clarifying and protecting the rights of married persons. *See* 744 A.2d at 884. *Cf. In re B.L.V.B.*, 160 Vt. 368, 372, 375, 628 A.2d 1271, 1274–75 (1993) (purpose of adoption statute read in its entirety is to clarify and protect legal rights of adopted persons, not to proscribe adoptions by certain combinations of individuals, denying children of same-sex partners security of legally recognized relationship with second parent serves no legitimate state interest).

The majority declines to provide plaintiffs with a marriage license, however, because a sudden change in the marriage laws "may have disruptive and unforeseen consequences," and "uncertainty and confusion could result." 744 A.2d at 886–87. Thus, within a few pages of rejecting the State's doomsday speculations as a basis for upholding the unconstitutionally discriminatory classification, the majority relies upon those same speculations to deny plaintiffs the relief to which they are entitled as the result of the discrimination. *See* 744 A.2d at 886–87.

During the civil rights movement of the 1960s, state and local governments defended segregation or gradual desegregation on the grounds that mixing the races would lead to interracial disturbances. The Supreme Court's "compelling answer" to that contention was "that constitutional rights may not be denied simply because of hostility to their assertion or exercise." See *Watson*, 373 U.S. at 535, 83 S.Ct. 1314. Here, too, we should not relinquish our duty to redress the unconstitutional discrimination that we have found merely because of "personal speculations" or "vague disquietudes." *Id.* at 536, 83 S.Ct. 1314. While the laudatory goals of preserving institutional credibility and public confidence in our government may require elected bodies to wait for changing attitudes concerning public morals, those same goals require courts to act independently and decisively to protect civil rights guaranteed by our Constitution.[24]

None of the cases cited by the majority support its mandate suspending the Court's judgment to allow the Legislature to provide a remedy. In *Linkletter v. Walker*, 381 U.S. 618, 622, 85 S.Ct. 1731, 14 L.Ed.2d 601 (1965), the issue was whether the decision in *Mapp v. Ohio*, 367 U.S. 643, 81 S.Ct. 1684, 6 L.Ed.2d 1081 (1961), extending the exclusionary rule[25] to the states through the federal due process clause applied to all state court convictions that had become final before *Mapp*. The Court declined to apply *Mapp* retroactively, stating that both defendants and the states had relied upon the decision that *Mapp* had overruled, that the fairness of the underlying trials had not been placed at issue, and that applying *Mapp* retroactively would severely tax the administration of justice in state courts. *See Linkletter*, 381 U.S. at 637–39, 85 S.Ct. 1731. After noting that it was not concerned with "pure" prospectivity because the exclusionary rule had been applied in *Mapp* itself, the Court held that new rules may be applied prospectively "where the exigencies of the situation require such an application." *See id.* at 622, 628, 85 S.Ct. 1731.

Unlike *Linkletter*, the issue here is not whether the majority's holding should be applied retroactively or prospectively, but rather whether the relief it has promised should be provided promptly by this Court or at some uncertain future time by the Legislature. Neither these plaintiffs nor any same-sex couples seeking the benefits and protections of marriage obtain any relief until the Legislature acts, or failing that, this Court acts again. Thus, the majority is not applying its holding on even a purely prospective basis. In any event, assuming that *Linkletter* continues to have vitality in cases involving civil rights violations, see *Fairfax Covenant Church v. Fairfax County Sch. Bd.*, 17 F.3d 703, 709, 710 (4th Cir.1994) (stating that Supreme Court has recently cast serious doubt upon practice of departing from traditional rule of retroactive application, which is "the rule inherent in the judicial function" of applying and interpreting law in real controversies), the "unforeseen consequences" alluded to by the majority cannot be considered "exigencies" warranting relief only at some unspecified future time.

The other two cases cited by the majority also concern whether court rulings should be applied prospectively or retroactively. In those cases, the courts weighed the potential consequences of a decision to abrogate common-law sovereign immunity—the doctrine declaring that the government is immune from lawsuits. *See Smith v. State,* 93 Idaho 795, 473 P.2d 937, 950 (1970) (applying decision to abrogate doctrine of sovereign immunity to cases before court but otherwise staying decision until adjournment of following legislative session to prevent undue hardship to government agencies that relied on doctrine); *Spanel v. Mounds View Sch. Dist. No. 621,* 264 Minn. 279, 118 N.W.2d 795, 803–04 (1962) (staying decision to abrogate sovereign immunity until following legislative session to prevent hardship to government agencies that relied on doctrine); *cf. Presley v. Mississippi State Highway Comm'n,* 608 So.2d 1288, 1298 (Miss.1992) (giving retroactive application to decision finding sovereign immunity act unconstitutional would pose fiscally disastrous consequences to state agencies). These courts simply acknowledged that retroactively applying their holding abrogating sovereign immunity, without affording the legislature an opportunity either to alter insurance coverage or enact an immunity statute, would have potentially disastrous fiscal consequences for the state. *See Hillerby v. Town of Colchester,* 167 Vt. 270, 293, 706 A.2d 446, 459 (1997) (Johnson, J., dissenting) (favoring quasi-prospective approach that would afford Legislature time to react to holding abrogating general municipal immunity). That is not the situation here, where no disastrous consequences, fiscal or otherwise, have been identified.

I recognize that the Legislature is, and has been, free to pass legislation that would provide same-sex couples with marital benefits. But the majority does not explain why it is necessary for the Legislature to act before we remedy the constitutional violation that we have found. In our system of government, civil rights violations are remedied by courts, not because we issue "Holy Writ" or because we are "the only repository of wisdom." 744 A.2d at 888–89. It is because the courts "must ultimately define and defend individual rights against government in terms independent of consensus or majority will." L. Tribe, *American Constitutional Law*, § 15.3, at 896 (1978).[26]

"[G]roups that have historically been the target of discrimination cannot be expected to wait patiently for the protection of their human dignity and equal rights while governments move toward reform one step at a time." *Rosenberg v. Canada*, Docket No. C22807 (Ontario Court of Appeals, April 23, 1998, at 17–18) (quoting *Vriend v. Alberta*, [1998] S.C.J. No. 29 (Q.L.), at para. 122). Once a court has determined that a discriminatory classification has deprived plaintiffs of a constitutionally ripe entitlement, the court must decide if the classification "is demonstrably justifiable in a free and democratic society, not whether there might be a more propitious time to remedy it." *Id.* at 18.

Today's decision, which is little more than a declaration of rights, abdicates that responsibility. The majority declares that plaintiffs have been unconstitutionally deprived of the benefits of marriage, but does not hold that the marriage laws are unconstitutional, does not hold that plaintiffs are entitled to the license that triggers those benefits, and does not provide plaintiffs with any other specific or direct remedy for the constitutional violation that the Court has found to exist. By suspending its judgment and allowing the Legislature to choose a remedy, the majority, in effect, issues an advisory opinion that leaves plaintiffs without redress and sends the matter to an uncertain fate in the Legislature. *Cf. In re Williams*, 154 Vt. 318–19, 321, 577 A.2d 686, 686–87 (1990) (statute requiring district court to hold hearings, issue findings, and advise local legislative bodies concerning alleged police misconduct violated separation of powers between judicial and legislative branches by requiring courts to give advisory opinions, upon which municipalities might or might not act). Ironically, today's mandate will only increase "the uncertainty and confusion" that the majority states it is designed to avoid. 744 A.2d at 886–87.

No decision of this Court will abate the moral and political debate over same-sex marriage. My view as to the appropriateness of granting plaintiffs the license they seek is not based on any overestimate (or any estimate) of its effectiveness, nor on a miscalculation (or any calculation) as to its likely permanence, were it to have received the support of a majority of this Court. Rather, it is based on what I believe are the commands of our Constitution.

II.

Although I concur with the majority's conclusion that Vermont law unconstitutionally excludes same-sex couples from the benefits of marriage, I write separately to state my belief that this is a straightforward case of sex discrimination.

As I argue below, the marriage statutes establish a classification based on sex. Whether such classification is legally justifiable should be analyzed under our common-benefits jurisprudence, which until today, has been closely akin to the federal equal-protection analysis under the Fourteenth Amendment. Therefore, the State must show that the classification is narrowly tailored to further important, if not compelling, interests. Not only do the rationalizations advanced by the State fail to pass constitutional muster under this or any other form of heightened scrutiny,[27] they fail to satisfy the rational-basis test as articulated under the Common Benefits Clause.[28]

"We have held that the Common Benefits Clause in the Vermont Constitution, see ch. I, art. 7, is generally coextensive with the equivalent guarantee in the United States Constitution, and imports similar methods of analysis." *Brigham,* 166 Vt. at 265, 692 A.2d at 395; see also *Lorrain,* 160 Vt. at 212, 628 A.2d at 550 (test under Common Benefits Clause is same as test under federal Equal Protection Clause). Where the statutory scheme affects a fundamental constitutional right or involves a suspect classification, "the State must demonstrate that any discrimination occasioned by the law serves a compelling governmental interest, and is narrowly tailored to serve that objective." *Brigham,* 166 Vt. at 265, 692 A.2d at 396. Otherwise, classifications are constitutional if they are "reasonably related to the promotion of a valid public purpose." *MacCallum,* 165 Vt. at 457, 686 A.2d at 937–38.

As the majority states, the marriage "statutes, read as a whole, reflect the common understanding that marriage under Vermont law consists of a union between a man and a woman." 744 A.2d at 869. Thus, the statutes impose a sex-based classification. *See, e.g., Brause v. Bureau of Vital Statistics*, No. 3AN-95-6562 CI, *6, 1998 WL 88743 (Alaska Super. Feb. 27, 1998) (prohibition on same-sex marriage is sex-based classification); *Baehr v. Lewin*, 74 Haw. 530, 852 P.2d 44, 64 (1993) (Levinson, J., plurality opinion) (same). A woman is denied the right to marry another woman because her would-be partner is a woman, not because one or both are lesbians. Similarly, a man is denied the right to marry another man because his would-be partner is a man, not because one or both are gay. Thus, an individual's right to marry a person of the same sex is prohibited solely on the basis of sex, not on the basis of sexual orientation. Indeed, sexual orientation does not appear as a qualification for marriage under the marriage statutes. The State makes no inquiry into the sexual practices or identities of a couple seeking a license.

The State advances two arguments in support of its position that Vermont's marriage laws do not establish a sex-based classification. The State first contends that the marriage statutes merely acknowledge that marriage, by its very nature, cannot be comprised of two persons of the same sex. Thus, in the State's view, it is the definition of marriage, not the statutes, that restricts marriage to two people of the opposite sex. This argument is circular. It is the State that defines civil marriage under its statute. The issue before us today is whether the State may continue to deprive same-sex couples of the benefits of marriage. This question is not resolved by resorting to a historical definition of marriage; it is that very definition that is being challenged in this case.

The State's second argument, also propounded by the majority, *see* 744 A.2d at 880 n. 13, is that the marriage statutes do not discriminate on the basis of sex because they treat similarly situated males the same as similarly situated females. Under this argument, there can be no sex discrimination here because "[i]f a man wants to marry a man, he is barred; a woman seeking to marry a woman is barred in precisely the same way. For this reason, women and men are not treated differently." C. Sunstein, *Homosexuality and the Constitution*, 70 Ind. L.J. 1, 19 (1994). But consider the following example. Dr. A and Dr. B both want to marry Ms. C, an X-ray technician. Dr. A may do so because Dr. A is a man. Dr. B may not because Dr. B is a woman. Dr. A and Dr. B are people of opposite sexes who are similarly situated in the sense that they both want to marry a person of their choice. The statute disqualifies Dr. B from marriage solely on the basis of her sex and treats her differently from Dr. A, a man. This is sex discrimination.[29]

I recognize, of course, that although the classification here is sex-based on its face, its most direct impact is on lesbians and gay men, the class of individuals most likely to seek same-sex marriage. Viewing the discrimination as sex-based, however, is important. Although the original purpose of the marriage statutes was not to exclude same-sex couples, for the simple reason that same-sex marriage was very likely not on the minds of the Legislature when it passed the licensing statute, the preservation of the sex-based classification deprives lesbians and gay men of the right to marry the life partner of their choice. If, as I argue below, the sex-based classification contained in the marriage laws is unrelated to any valid purpose, but rather is a vestige of sex-role stereotyping that applies to both men and women, the classification is still unlawful sex discrimination even if it applies equally to men and women. *See MacCallum,* 165 Vt. at 459, 686 A.2d at 939 (Constitution does not permit law to give effect, either directly or indirectly, to private biases; when government itself makes the classification, it is obliged to afford all persons equal protection of the law); *Loving v. Virginia,* 388 U.S. 1, 8–9, 11, 87 S.Ct. 1817, 18 L.Ed.2d 1010 (1967) (statute prohibiting racial intermarriage violates Equal Protection Clause although it applies equally to whites and blacks because classification was designed to maintain white supremacy.)[30]

Although Vermont has not had occasion to consider the question, most, if not all, courts have held that the denial of rights or benefits on the basis of sex subject the state's action to some level of heightened scrutiny.[31] This is so because the sex of an individual "frequently bears no relation to ability to perform or contribute to society." *Frontiero v. Richardson,* 411 U.S. 677, 686, 93 S.Ct. 1764, 36 L.Ed.2d 583 (1973) (plurality opinion). Moreover, in some cases, such as here, sex-based classifications "very likely reflect outmoded notions of the relative capabilities of men and women." *City of Cleburne v. Cleburne Living Ctr., Inc.,* 473 U.S. 432, 441, 105 S.Ct. 3249, 87 L.Ed.2d 313 (1985).

I do not believe that it is necessary to reach the question in this case, however, because in my view, the justifications asserted by the State do not satisfy even our rational-basis standard under the Common Benefits Clause, which requires that the classification be "reasonably related to the promotion of a valid public purpose." *MacCallum*, 165 Vt. at 457 n. 1, 686 A.2d at 938 n. 1 (because statute failed to pass constitutional muster under rational-basis test, no need to determine whether adopted persons are suspect class).[32] In *MacCallum*, we invalidated, under the Common Benefits Clause, a statute denying an adopted person's right of inheritance from collateral kin, stating that the statute was grounded on outdated prejudices instead of a valid public purpose. *See id.* at 460–62, 686 A.2d at 939–41. Rather than blindly accept any conceivable justification proffered by the State in that case, we carefully considered the State's rationales to determine whether the discriminatory classification rested upon a reasonable consideration of legislative policy. *See id.* at 457, 459–61, 686 A.2d at 938, 939–40; *see also Romer v. Evans*, 517 U.S. 620, 635–36, 116 S.Ct. 1620, 134 L.Ed.2d 855 (1996) (state constitutional amendment prohibiting all legislative, executive, or judicial action designed to protect homosexuals from discrimination violated Equal Protection Clause under rational-basis test because it was discriminatory and had no proper legislative end); *Cleburne*, 473 U.S. at 450, 105 S.Ct. 3249 (ordinance requiring special use permit for operation of home for mentally retarded violated Equal Protection Clause under rational-basis test because it rested on irrational prejudice rather than legitimate government purpose).

Before applying the rational-basis standard to the State's justifications, it is helpful to examine the history of the marriage laws in Vermont. There is no doubt that, historically, the marriage laws imposed sex-based roles for the partners to a marriage—male provider and female dependent—that bore no relation to their inherent abilities to contribute to society. Under the common law, husband and wife were one person. See *R. & E. Builders, Inc. v. Chandler*, 144 Vt. 302, 303–04, 476 A.2d 540, 541 (1984). The legal existence of a woman was suspended by marriage; she merged with her husband and held no separate rights to enter into a contract or execute a deed. *See id.* She could not sue without her husband's consent or be sued without joining her husband as a defendant. See id. Moreover, if a woman did not hold property for her "sole and separate use" prior to marriage, the husband received a freehold interest in all her property, entitling him to all the rents and profits from the property. *See id.*

Starting in the late nineteenth century, Vermont, like other states, began to enact statutes, such as the Rights of Married Women Act, see 15 V.S.A. §§ 61–69, to grant married women property and contractual rights independent of their husbands. See *Medical Ctr. Hosp. v. Lorrain*, 165 Vt. 12, 14, 675 A.2d 1326, 1328 (1996). The Legislature's intent in enacting the Rights of Married Women Act was to "reject [. . .] the archaic principle that husband and wife are 'one person,'" and "to set a married woman free 'from the thraldom of the common law.'" *Richard v. Richard*, 131 Vt. 98, 102, 106, 300 A.2d 637, 639, 641 (1973). Thus, we recognized that the legal existence of married women was no longer merged into that of their husbands, see *Lorrain*, 165 Vt. at 15, 675 A.2d at 1329, and that "a married woman is a 'person' under the Constitution of Vermont." *Richard*, 131 Vt. at 106, 300 A.2d at 641.

Today, the partners to a marriage are equal before the law. *See R. & E. Builders*, 144 Vt. at 304, 476 A.2d at 541 (modern statutes attempt to accord wives legal rights equal to husbands). A married woman may now enter contracts, sue and be sued without joining her husband, purchase and convey property separate from her husband, own property, and collect rents and profits from it. *See Lorrain*, 165 Vt. at 15, 675 A.2d at 1329 (women have property and contractual rights equal to men regardless of their marital status). As the Legislature enacted statutes to confer rights upon married women, this Court abolished common-law doctrines arising from the common-law theory that husband and wife were one person and that the wife had no independent legal existence. *See, e.g., Richard*, 131 Vt. at 106, 300 A.2d at 641 (abolishing interspousal immunity, which was based on "archaic principle" that husband and wife are one person, to allow passenger wife to sue husband for personal injuries arising from husband's negligence in operating automobile).

The question now is whether the sex-based classification in the marriage law is simply a vestige of the common-law unequal marriage relationship or whether there is some valid governmental purpose for the classification today. *See MacCallum*, 165 Vt. at 460–62, 686 A.2d at 939–41 (State's rationales proffered to validate statutory classification cannot rest on outdated presumptions not reasonable today when vast cultural and social changes have occurred). In support of the marriage statutes, the State advances public purposes that fall into three general categories.

In the first category, the State asserts public purposes—uniting men and women to celebrate the "complementarity" [*sic*] of the sexes and providing male and female role models for children—based on broad and vague generalizations about the roles of men and women that reflect outdated sex-role stereotyping. The State contends that (1) marriage unites the rich physical and psychological differences between the sexes; (2) sex differences strengthen and stabilize a marriage; (3) each sex contributes differently to a family unit and to society; and (4) uniting the different male and female qualities and contributions in the same institution instructs the young of the value of such a union. The State relies on social science literature, such as Carol Gilligan's *In a Different Voice: Psychological Theory and Women's Development* (1982), to support its contention that there are sex differences that justify the State requiring two people to be of opposite sex to marry.

The State attempts to analogize this case to the changes in law brought about by women's participation in the legal profession starting in the 1970s, arguing that women have brought a different voice to legal theory and practice. The State also points to *United States v. Virginia*, 518 U.S. 515, 533, 116 S.Ct. 2264, 135 L.Ed.2d 735 (1996) (hereinafter *VMI*), arguing that an institution or community made up exclusively of one sex is different from a community composed of both. The goal of diversity has been recognized to justify affirmative action programs in public broadcasting and education. *See, e.g., Metro Broadcasting, Inc. v. FCC*, 497 U.S. 547, 567–68, 110 S.Ct. 2997, 111 L.Ed.2d 445 (1990) (holding that state interest in racial diversity in broadcasting justified affirmative-action racial classification); *Regents of Univ. of Calif. v. Bakke*, 438 U.S. 265, 311–19, 98 S.Ct. 2733, 57 L.Ed.2d 750 (1978) (opinion of Powell, J.) (endorsing race classification in university admission as legitimate means of achieving diversity). Similarly, the recognition that women may contribute differently from men is a valid argument for women's full participation in all aspects of public life. The goal of community diversity has no place, however, as a requirement of marriage.

To begin with, carried to its logical conclusion, the State's rationale could require all marriages to be between people, not just of the opposite sex, but of different races, religions, national origins, and so forth, to promote diversity. Moreover, while it may be true that the female voice or point of view is sometimes different from the male, such differences are not necessarily found in comparing any given man and any given woman. The State's implicit assertion otherwise is sex stereotyping of the most retrograde sort. Nor could the State show that the undoubted differences between any given man and woman who wish to marry are more related to their sex than to other characteristics and life experiences. In short, the "diversity" argument is based on illogical conclusions from stereotypical imaginings that would be condemned by the very case cited for its support. See *VMI*, 518 U.S. at 533, 116 S.Ct. 2264 (justifications for sex-based classifications "must not rely on overbroad generalizations about the different talents, capabilities, or preferences of males and females").

In the second category, the State asserts, under several different guises, the public purpose of maintaining the sex-based classification. First, the State claims an interest in "preserving the existing marital structure." Second, the State claims an interest in "instructing the young of the value of uniting male and female qualities." This is mere tautology. The State's objective is to preserve the status quo, but that does not address the question of whether the classification can be justified. Perpetuating the classification, in and of itself, is not a valid purpose for the classification. *See id.* at 545, 116 S.Ct. 2264 (rejecting as circular governmental justification that sex-based classification is essential to governmental objective of single-sex education).

Many of the State's remaining justifications, which I place into a third category, assume highly questionable public purposes. But because none of these justifications are even remotely, much less reasonably, related to the challenged classification, I accept, for the sake of argument, the premise that each of them concerns a legitimate state interest.

The State contends, for example, that prohibiting individuals from marrying a person of the same sex promotes the public purpose of minimizing custody and visitation disputes arising from surrogacy contracts because the prohibition may deter use of technologically assisted reproduction by same-sex couples. Further, the State argues that increased use of technologically assisted reproduction "may lead men who conceive children by sexual union to perceive themselves as sperm donors, without any responsibility for their offspring." Both of these reasons suffer from the same constitutional deficiency. If the state purpose is to discourage technologically assisted reproduction, I agree with the majority that the classification is significantly underinclusive. The State does nothing to discourage technologically assisted reproduction by individuals or opposite-sex couples. Moreover, opposite-sex couples may obtain marriage licenses without regard to whether or not they will use technologically assisted reproduction.[33] The public purpose provides no rationale for the different treatment.

The State also asserts that it has an interest in furthering the link between procreation and child rearing "to ensure that couples who engage in sexual intercourse accept [. . .] responsibility for the potential children they might create." But the State cannot explain how the failure of opposite-sex couples to accept responsibility for the children they create relates at all to the exclusion of same-sex couples from the benefits of marriage. To the extent that couples, same-sex or opposite-sex, will fail to take responsibility for the children they create, the risk is greater where the couples are not married. Therefore, denying same-sex couples the benefits of marriage on this ground is not only arbitrary but completely at odds with the stated government purpose.

The State further contends that prohibiting individuals from marrying same-sex partners will deter marriages of convenience entered into solely to obtain tax benefits or government assistance. Two persons of the opposite sex are completely free to enter into a marriage of convenience, however, without the State examining their motives. Indeed, the pool of opposite-sex couples who may choose to enter into such marriages is much greater than the pool of same-sex couples. Once again, the public purpose provides no rationale for treating individuals who choose same-sex partners differently from those who choose opposite-sex partners.

Although "[a] statute need not regulate the whole of a field to pass constitutional muster," *Benning v. State,* 161 Vt. 472, 486, 641 A.2d 757, 764 (1994), there still must be some rational basis for an underinclusive classification. Here, none of the alleged governmental purposes within the third category of State justifications provides a rational basis for treating similarly situated people differently, or for applying the classification in an underinclusive manner. *See Cleburne,* 473 U.S. at 446, 105 S.Ct. 3249 (State may not impose classification where relationship to asserted goal is so attenuated as to render distinction arbitrary or irrational). The State's justifications are nothing more than post hoc rationalizations completely unrelated to any rational reason for excluding same-sex couples from obtaining the benefits of marriage.

Finally, the State claims a valid public purpose in adopting a classification to align itself with the other states. The Vermont Constitution is freestanding authority, however, and may protect rights not protected under the federal constitution or other state constitutions. *Brigham,* 166 Vt. at 257, 268, 692 A.2d at 391, 397 (recognizing right to equal education under Vermont Constitution, while acknowledging that this right is not recognized under federal constitution and is recognized under only some state constitutions). This Court does not limit the protections the Vermont Constitution confers on Vermonters solely to make Vermont law consistent with that of other states. *See id.* at 257, 692 A.2d at 391 (decisions in other states are of limited precedential value because each state's constitutional evolution is unique). Indeed, as the majority notes, Vermont's marriage laws are already distinct in several ways from the laws of other states.

In sum, the State treats similarly situated people—those who wish to marry—differently, on the basis of the sex of the person they wish to marry. The State provides no legally valid rationale for the different treatment. The justifications asserted by the State for the classification are tautological, wholly arbitrary, or based on impermissible assumptions about the roles of men and women. None of the State's justifications meets the rational-basis test under the Common Benefits Clause. Finding no legally valid justification for the sex-based classification, I conclude that the classification is a vestige of the historical unequal marriage relationship that more recent legislative enactments and our own jurisprudence have unequivocally rejected. The protections conferred on Vermonters by the Common Benefits Clause cannot be restricted by the outmoded conception that marriage requires one man and one woman, creating one person—the husband. As this Court recently stated, "equal protection of the laws cannot be limited by eighteenth-century standards." *See Brigham,* 166 Vt. at 267, 692 A.2d at 396.

III.

This case is undoubtedly one of the most controversial ever to come before this Court. Newspaper, radio, and television media have disclosed widespread public interest in its outcome, as well as the full spectrum of opinion as to what that outcome should be and what its ramifications may be for our society as a whole. One line of opinion contends that this is an issue that ought to be decided only by the most broadly democratic of our governmental institutions, the Legislature, and that the small group of men and women comprising this Court has no business deciding an issue of such enormous moment. For better or for worse, however, this is simply not so. This case came before us because citizens of the state invoked their constitutional right to seek redress through the judicial process of a perceived deprivation under state law. The Vermont Constitution does not permit the courts to decline to adjudicate a matter because its subject is controversial, or because the outcome may be deeply offensive to the strongly held beliefs of many of our citizens. We do not have, as does the Supreme Court of the United States, certiorari jurisdiction, which allows that Court, in its sole discretion, to decline to hear almost any case. To the contrary, if a case has been brought before us, and if the established procedures have been followed, as they were here, we must hear and decide it.

Moreover, we must decide the case on legal grounds. However much history, sociology, religious belief, personal experience, or other considerations may inform our individual or collective deliberations, we must decide this case, and all cases, on the basis of our understanding of the law, and the law alone. This must be the true and constant effort of every member of the judiciary. That effort, needless to say, is not a guarantee of infallibility, nor even an assurance of wisdom. It is, however, the fulfillment of our pledge of office.

Notes

CHAPTER 1

1. Sarah Kershaw, *Adversaries on Gay Rights Vow State-by-State Fight*, N.Y. TIMES, July 6, 2003. *See also* Marcia Coyle, *The Fallout Begins*, NATIONAL L.J., July 7, 2003.
2. Summer officially begins on June 21.
3. Frank Rich, *Gay Kiss: Business as Usual*, N.Y. TIMES, June 22, 2003.
4. *Id.*
5. Halpern v. Toronto, 2003 WL 34950 (Ontario Ct. App. June 11, 2003).
6. *Id.*
7. Colin Nickerson, *Ontario Court Oks Same-Sex Marriage*, BOSTON GLOBE, June 11, 2003.
8. Tom Cohen, AP, *Dozens in Canada Follow Gay Couple's Lead*, WASH. POST, June 12, 2003.
9. Colin Nickerson, *British Columbia Approves Gay, Lesbian Marriages*, BOSTON GLOBE, July 9, 2003.
10. Clifford Kraus, *Canadian Leaders Agree to Propose Gay Marriage Law*, N.Y. TIMES, June 18, 2003.
11. Hendrick Hertzberg, *Northern Light*, NEW YORKER, July 7, 2003.
12. Jeet Heer, *Canadian Rhapsody*, BOSTON GLOBE, July 13, 2003.
13. *Id.*
14. Lawrence v. Texas, ___ U.S. ___, 71 U.S.L.W. 4574 (June 26, 2003).
15. *Id.*
16. *Id.* (quoting statute).
17. *Id.*
18. Joseph Landau, *Ripple Effect*, NEW REPUBLIC, June 23, 2003.
19. *Id.*
20. *Id.*
21. Lawrence v. Texas, ___ U.S. ___, 71 U.S.L.W. 4574 (June 26, 2003).
22. *Id.* Justice O'Connor's concurring opinion made the point a bit more explicitly.
23. Howard Fineman, *A Wedge Is Born: Gay Marriage and 2004*, NEWSWEEK, July 14, 2003.
24. Evan Wolfson, *All Together Now*, in MARRIAGE AND SAME-SEX UNIONS: A DEBATE 3 (Lynn Wardle, et al, eds. 2003).
25. *See also, e.g.*, Romer v. Evans, 517 U.S. 620 (1996) (Scalia, J., dissenting); Scalia declared: "Don't believe it." *Id.*

26. *Id.*

27. *Id.*

28. *Id.*

29. *Id.*

30. *Id.*

31. *Amicus Curiae* Brief of Liberty Counsel at 5, 16, and 17 in Lawrence v. Texas, ___ U.S. ___, 71 U.S.L.W. 4574 (June 26, 2003).

32. *Amicus Curiae* Brief of Family Research Council and Focus on the Family, at 15 and 20, in Lawrence v. Texas, ___ U.S. ___, 71 U.S.L.W. 4574 (June 26, 2003).

33. *Amicus Curiae* Brief of Texas Legislators, at 17, 18, and 20, in Lawrence v. Texas, ___ U.S. ___, 71 U.S.L.W. 4574 (June 26, 2003).

34. *Id.*

35. Anna Quindlen, *Justice Rip Van Winkle*, NEWSWEEK, July 14, 2003.

36. David Broder, *Please, Mr. President, No More Scalias*, VALLEY NEWS, July 2, 2003.

37. B.J. Sigesmund, *Yee-Haw!*, NEWSWEEK on the Web, msnbc.com (June 27, 2003).

38. Safire, *The Bedroom Door*, N.Y. TIMES, June 30, 2003; Sullivan, *A Victory For Everybody's Sexual Freedom*, LA TIMES, June 28, 2003.

39. Lawrence v. Texas, ___ U.S. ___, 71 U.S.L.W. 4574 (June 26, 2003).

40. William Mann, *Frist: Ban Gay Marriage*, VALLEY NEWS, June 30, 2003.

41. Darren Allen, *Gay Marriage Deserves One Word: Congratulations*, RUTLAND HERALD, April 13, 2003.

42. Evelyn Nievens, *Passenger on Jet*, N.Y. TIMES, Jan. 16, 2003.

43. Norman Ornstein, *Planning for Disaster*, NATIONAL L.J., July 7, 2003.

44. Sheryl Stolberg, *White House Avoids Stand on Gay Marriage*, N.Y. TIMES, July 2, 2003.

45. Howard Fineman, *A Wedge Is Born: Gay Marriage and 2004*, NEWSWEEK, July 14, 2003; Evan Thomas, *The War Over Gay Marriage*, NEWSWEEK, July 7, 2003.

46. Susan Milligan, *Gay Civil Unions Find Support in Democratic Field*, BOSTON GLOBE, April 26, 2003.

47. Adam Nagourney, *Dean's Surge in Fundraising Forces Rivals to Reassess Him*, N.Y. TIMES, July 3, 2003; David Mace, *Paley Backs Rival of Dean*, RUTLAND HERALD, July 11, 2003; Will Lester, *Dean Leads Virtual Primary*, RUTLAND HERALD, June 28, 2003; *See, e.g.*, Dan Balz, Washington Post, *Dean Alters Dems' Race*, VALLEY NEWS, July 3, 2003; Adam Nagourney, *Fundraising Puts Dean in Top Tier of Contenders*, N.Y. TIMES, June 30, 2003; Ruth Marcus, Wash. Post, *They're Mad at Bush and Mad About Dean*, VALLEY NEWS, July 9, 2003; Glen Johnson, *Early-Morning Gamble by Dean Aides Made Him the Insurgent to Beat*, BOSTON GLOBE, July 10, 2003; Adam Nagourney, *Dean's Challenge*, N.Y. TIMES, July 7, 2003; Howard Fineman, *Lying in Wait for Dean*, NEWSWEEK, July 14, 2003; *Conventional Wisdom*, NEWSWEEK, July 14, 2003.

48. Tracy Schmaler, *On Road, Dean Touts Passage of Civil Unions*, RUTLAND HERALD, January 28, 2002.

49. David Gram, *Dean Won't Push Gay Marriage,* RUTLAND HERALD, July 22, 2003.

50. Thomas, *The War Over Gay Marriage, supra* note 45.

51. Goodridge v. Department of Health, ___ Mass. ___, No. SJC-08860 (Sup. Jud. Ct. Nov. 18, 2003); Kathleen Burge, *SJC Peppers Lawyers on Same-Sex Marriage,* BOSTON GLOBE, March 5, 2003

52. Editorial, *For Gay Marriage,* BOSTON GLOBE, July 8, 2003; Frank Phillips, *Support for Gay Marriage,* BOSTON GLOBE, April 8, 2003.

53. Michael Paulson, *Bishops Eye Pulpits to Fight Gay Marriage,* BOSTON GLOBE, May 29, 2003.

54. *E.g.,* Michael Paulson, *O'Mally Offers Plea,* BOSTON GLOBE, July 2, 2003. Some commentators have argued that the Catholic church's sex-abuse scandal "offers spectacular confirmation for nearly every warning ever issued by the opponents of gay marriage." *See* Stanley Kurtz, *Gay Priests and Gay Marriage: What the One Issue Has to Do with the Other,* NATIONAL REVIEW, June 3, 2002.

55. Yvonne Abraham, *Hearing Set on Measure to Ban Same-Sex Marriage,* BOSTON GLOBE, April 28, 2003.

56. Goodridge v. Department of Health, ___ Mass. ___, No. SJC-08860 (Sup. Jud. Ct. Nov. 18, 2003). *See generally, e.g.,* Kathleen Burge, *Gays Have Right to Marry, SJC Says in Historic Ruling,* BOSTON GLOBE, Nov. 19, 2003; Frank Phillips, *Lawmakers Are Divided on Response,* BOSTON GLOBE, Nov. 19, 2003; Anne Kornblut, *Some Republicans See Decision as an Issue to Run Against in '04,* BOSTON GLOBE, Nov. 19, 2003; Yvonne Abraham, *Proposals and Tears Flow in Wake of Decision,* BOSTON GLOBE, Nov. 19, 2003; Michael Paulson, *Strong, Divided Opinions Mark Clergy Reaction,* BOSTON GLOBE, Nov. 19, 2003; Editorial, *Equal Rights—and Rites,* BOSTON GLOBE, Nov. 19, 2003; Eileen McNamara, *On Marriage, Simple Justice,* BOSTON GLOBE, Nov. 19, 2003; Elizabeth Beardsley, *They Do,* BOSTON HERALD, Nov. 19, 2003; Editorial, *SJC on Marriage Not the Last Word,* BOSTON HERALD, Nov. 19, 2003; Cal Thomas, *Divorce from Decency in Mass.,* BOSTON HERALD, Nov. 19, 2003; Thomas Keane, *Gay Wedding Bells Aren't Ringing Yet,* BOSTON HERALD, Nov. 19, 2003; Howie Carr, *Layabout Legislators Left Door Open for Court Jesters,* BOSTON HERALD, Nov. 19, 2003; Joe Fitzgerald, *Inching Closer to Shameful Reality,* BOSTON HERALD, Nov. 19, 2003; Margery Egan, *Finally, Equality and Justice For All,* BOSTON HERALD, Nov. 19, 2003; Pam Belluck, *Marriage by Gays Gains Big Victory in Massachusetts,* N.Y. TIMES, Nov. 19, 2003; Adam Nagourney, *A Thorny Issue for 2004 Race,* N.Y. TIMES, Nov. 19, 2003; Frank Phillips, *Civil Union Law Sought,* BOSTON GLOBE, Nov. 20, 2003; Raphael Lewis, *Groups Muster to Fight Gay Marriage in Mass.,* BOSTON GLOBE, Nov. 20, 2003; Rick Klien, *Career on Line, Romney in Eye of Hurricane,* BOSTON GLOBE, Nov. 20, 2003; Benjamin Gedan, *Cambridge Poised to Issue Licenses Amid Controversy,* BOSTON GLOBE, Nov. 21, 2003; Pam Belluck, *Gays' Victory Leaves Massachusetts Lawmakers Hesitant,* N.Y. TIMES, Nov. 20, 2003; Katharine Steelye, *Conservatives Mobilize against Ruling on Gay Marriage,* N.Y. TIMES, Nov. 20, 2003; Editorial, *A Victory for Gay Marriage,* N.Y. TIMES, Nov. 20, 2003; Frank Phillips, *Reilly Supports Same-Sex Benefits without Marriage,* BOSTON GLOBE, Nov. 21, 2003; Editorial, *There's No Point in Rush-*

ing, Boston Herald, Nov. 21, 2003; Jay Ambrose, *Judicial Tyranny Defines Mass.,* Boston Herald, Nov. 21, 2003; Thomas Caywood, *Right Wing Revs Up for "Last Stand" in Bay State,* Boston Herald, Nov. 21, 2003; Eric Convey, *Backlash: Church Warns Pols: Gay Decision May Cost Votes,* Boston Herald, Nov. 22, 2003; Elisabeth Beardsley, *Gays Rip Pols on Union Bill,* Boston Herald, Nov. 22, 2003; Raphael Lewis, *Romney, AG Takes Heat on Marriage Issue,* Boston Globe, Nov. 22, 2003; Frank Philllips, *50% in Poll Back SJC Ruling on Gay Marriage,* Boston Globe, Nov. 23, 2003; Jeff Jacoby, *Gay Ruling Echoes Roe v. Wade,* Boston Globe, Nov. 23, 2003; David Guarino, *Same-Sex Benefits Get Voters' Blessings: Poll: Most OK Gay Marriage,* Boston Herald, Nov. 23, 2003; AP, *Expect Homily on Homosexuality,* Boston Herald, Nov. 23, 2003; David Guarino, *Constitutional Ban Will Be "Uphill Battle" in Bay State,* Boston Herald, Nov. 23, 2003; Howie Carr, *Give Reps a Ring on Gay Marriage,* Boston Herald, Nov. 23, 2003; Maggie Gallagher, *Massachusetts vs. Marriage: How to Save an Institution,* Weekly Standard, Dec. 1, 2003 (cover story); Editorial, *Mass Appeal,* New Republic, Dec. 1. 2003; Marcia Coyle, *Wedding March?,* National L.J., Nov. 24, 2004; Howard Fineman, *My Mommies Can Marry,* Newsweek, Dec. 1, 2003; Richard Lacayo, *Popping the Question,* Time, Dec. 1, 2003.

57. Goodridge v. Department of Health, ___ Mass. ___, No. SJC-08860 (Sup. Jud. Ct. Nov. 18, 2003).

58. *Id.*

59. *Id.*

60. *Id.*

61. Linda Greenhouse, *Supreme Court Paved Way for Marriage Ruling with Sodomy Law Decision,* N.Y. Times, Nov. 19, 2003.

62. *Id.*

63. Goodridge v. Department of Health, ___ Mass. ___, No. SJC-08860 (Sup. Jud. Ct. Nov. 18, 2003).

64. *Id.*

65. *Id.*

66. *Id.*

67. *Id.*

68. *Id.*

69. *Id.*

70. *Id.*

71. *Id.*

72. *Id.*

73. *Id.*

74. *Id.*

75. *Id.*

76. *Id.*

77. *Id.*

78. *Id.*

79. *Id.*

80. Frank Phillips, *Civil Union Law Sought*, BOSTON GLOBE, Nov. 20, 2003; Kathleen Burge, *Legislature Given 180 Days*, BOSTON GLOBE, Nov. 19, 2003.

81. Phillips, *Civil Union Law Sought, supra* note 80; Frank Phillips, *Reilly Supports Same-Sex Benefits without Marriage*, BOSTON GLOBE, Nov. 21, 2003.

82. *Id.* (emphasis added).

83. Goodridge v. Department of Health, ___ Mass. ___, No. SJC-08860 (Sup. Jud. Ct. Nov. 18, 2003) (emphasis added).

84. *Id.*

85. *Id.*

86. In a superb editorial, the *Rutland Herald* suggested lessons Massachusetts could learn from Vermont:

The issue of gay marriage has put the state of Massachusetts into an uproar, with fearful politicians grasping for a strategy that will protect them from angry constituents while fulfilling the constitutional mandate issuing from the state's high court.

There are lessons the people of Massachusetts could take from the experience of Vermont, which was consumed by a similar uproar four years ago.

Lesson One: There is no escaping this issue. Gay and lesbian Americans have been working for years to secure rights and protections that everyone else takes for granted. As it was for African Americans, equality in marriage for homosexuals has been the last taboo to fall. Now the Supreme Judicial Court in Massachusetts has determined that equality in marriage is required by the state constitution. No one can run away from that fact.

Lesson Two: The issue of marriage is volatile because it involves our deepest passions and our most important human connnections. But the emotion attached to the issue does not prevent political leaders from proceeding in a respectful, restrained manner, conducting a political dialogue that gives everyone his or her say and allows for constructive democratic action.

Lesson Three: A respectful dialogue requires parties on both sides of the question to recognize the humanity of the other side. Bigotry and homophobia exist. As Vermont lawmakers drew up the civil unions law in 2000, they were exposed to vicious and relentless attacks. But opposition to civil unions also arose from the legitimate beliefs of decent people who were seeking to follow the moral teaching of their churches or their consciences. Conversely, support for civil unions came from decent people, gay and straight, who were following their own moral understanding in seeking to widen the arena of tolerance and to secure equal rights for gay and lesbian Vermonters.

Lesson Four: Debate is not harmful. Vermont Chief Justice Jeffrey Amestoy wrote a ruling in 1999 that gave the Vermont Legislature the job of approving either gay marriage or a "parallel institution"—which became civil unions. He believed that involving the legislature would be healthy for the state because it would engage the people in the political process and would put a stamp of democratic legitimacy on the outcome. The debate in the legislature and around the state was often painful, bitter, and angry. But it was enormously educational. The result was that Vermonters gained an understanding of issues related to homosexuality and gay rights that few people have.

Lesson Five: Anger and extremism do not pay. Legislators on the fence were more often than not persuaded to support civil unions because of the vicious language and intolerant attitudes of the most extreme opponents. They were also impressed favorably by the strength of conviction and dignity of gay and lesbian Vermonters who were willing to stand up for themselves and to defend in straightforward language the relationships that were central to their lives. The moral force of their arguments was hard to deny.

Gay marriage is now a national issue, and Massachusetts has become the central battleground. It will be up to each participant to decide whether to exercise statesmanship or demagoguery. Statesmanship is possible. It requires a willingness to forgo cheap political points and a desire to promote a civil discourse that in the end will leave the state a better place.

Editorial, *Now Massachusetts*, RUTLAND HERALD, Nov. 21, 2003.

87. Thomas Caywood, *Right Wing Revs Up for "Last Stand" in Bay State*, BOSTON HERALD, Nov. 21, 2003.

88. Jay Ambrose, *Judicial Tyranny Defines Mass.*, BOSTON HERALD, Nov. 21, 2003.

89. Howie Carr, *Give Reps a Ring*, BOSTON HERALD, Nov. 23, 2003.

90. *Id.*

91. Cal Thomas, *Divorce from Decency in Mass.*, BOSTON HERALD, Nov. 19, 2003.

92. Joe Fitzgerald, *Inching Closer to Shameful Reality*, BOSTON HERALD, Nov. 11, 2003.

93. Eric Convey, *Backlash*, BOSTON HERALD, Nov. 22, 2003 (quoting *The Pilot*).

94. Baker v. State, 744 A.2d 864 (Vt.1999).

95. WILLIAM ESKRIDGE, EQUALITY PRACTICE: CIVIL UNIONS AND THE FUTURE OF GAY RIGHTS 148–49 (2002) [hereinafter ESKRIDGE, CIVIL UNIONS].

96. *Id.* at 149.

97. I have borrowed the "third way" phrase from Bill Clinton and Tony Blair. This phrase allowed Bill Clinton and Tony Blair to "shed the paralyzing dogmas of the old left in order to take up forceful engagement abroad along with fiscal responsibility at home." Walter Isaacson, *Fighting Words*, NEW YORKER, July 14 and 21, 2003.

98. VT. STAT. ANN., Tit. 15, Ch. 23 § 1201–1207 (Supp. 2000).

99. Greg Johnson, *Making History in Vermont*, LOQUITUR (Vermont Law School alumni magazine) (spring 2000). Johnson observed that Vermont House Judiciary Committee Thomas Little "has proudly proclaimed that the bill . . . 'would put Vermont head and shoulders ahead of any other state, [and] close to France and Canada.' Well, I'm familiar with the laws in France and Canada, and I can unequivocally state that this bill would put Vermont ahead of even those two countries. It is more akin to the Scandinavian partnership laws, except that those laws prohibit gays and lesbians from adopting, something Ver-

mont already [allowed before the domestic partnership bill]. This bill, in short, could [if passed] establish the most advanced domestic partnership plan in the world." *Id.* (quoting Vt. House Rep. Thomas Little).

100. Elizabeth Mehren, LA Times, *Vermont Senate Approves Civil Unions Bill, Sends It to House,* VALLEY NEWS, April 20, 2000.

101. Carey Goldberg, *Vermont Senate Votes for Gay Civil Unions,* N.Y. TIMES, April 20, 2000.

102. Mehren, *Vermont Senate Approves, supra* note 100.

103. Baehr v. Levin, 852 P.2d 44 (Hawaii 1993). In Baehr, "a plurality opinion by Justice Steven Levinson (speaking only for himself and Chief Justice Ronald Moon) held that the state's denial of marriage licenses to same-sex couples is sex discrimination under the equal rights amendment to Hawaii's constitution. When the court clarified its mandate in response to the state's motion for reconsideration, newly appointed Justice Paula Nakayama joined the Levinson-Moon group [*id.* at 74] (three of five justices signed the order clarifying the proceedings on remand, consistent with the Levinson opinion), assuring a majority of the court for the sex discrimination holding)." WILLIAM ESKRIDGE, THE CASE FOR SAME-SEX MARRIAGE 219 n.4 (1996) [hereinafter ESKRIDGE, THE CASE].

"For the first time in American history, a court had, even if tentatively, suggested that legally recognized marriage need not necessarily be a union between a man and a woman. The court remanded the case for a trial to determine whether the discrimination is in fact 'permissible' because it is supported by a 'compelling' state interest." *Id.* at 5.

104. Baker v. State, 744 A.2d 864 (Vt.1999).

105. Greg Johnson, *Making History in Vermont,* LOQUITUR (spring 2000). Professor Johnson was co-counsel in the Alaska case.

106. *E.g.,* Hanna Rosin, *Small Town in Vermont Mirrors Split on Gay Unions,* PITTSBURGH POST-GAZETTE, October 15, 2000; Patrick Cole, *In Vermont, Governor Feels Voters' Heat,* CHI. TRIB., October 13, 2000; Patrick Cole, *Gay Union Law Divides Vermont, Attracts Scores of Out-Of-Staters,* CHI. TRIB., October, 13, 2000; Fred Bayles, *Civil Union Law Sparks Backlash,* USA TODAY, Oct. 4, 2000; James Bandler, *Anger Over Civil-Union Law Shapes Vt. Governor Race,* WALL ST. J., Sept. 27, 2000; Daniela Altimari, *Heading to Vermont for That Coveted Piece of Paper,* HARTFORD COURANT, Sept. 18, 2000; Hubert B. Herring, *Gay Rights, Here and There,* N.Y. TIMES, Sept. 17, 2000; Steve Buttry, *State Not Ready for Gay Marriages,* OMAHA WORLD-HERALD, Sept. 17, 2000; Ben White, *Vermont Divisions Harden over Civil Unions Law,* WASH. POST, Sept. 17, 2000; Kim Cobb, *Vermont Politicians Seeing Fallout From Gay-Union Law,* Houston Chronicle, Sept. 16, 2000; *Vt. Governor Encounters Anti-Gay Backlash,* GRAND RAPIDS PRESS, Sept. 15, 2000; Richard Higgins, *Civil Union Backlash in Vt.,* BOSTON GLOBE, Sept. 14, 2000; Tom Puleo, *Civil Unions, A Political Divide in Vermont,* HARTFORD COURANT, Sept. 14, 2000; Elizabeth Mehren, *Voters Oust 5 Who Backed Vt. Civil Union Law,* LA TIMES, Sept. 14, 2000; *6 Incumbents Ousted in Vermont / Results a Backlash to "Gay-Union" Law,* NEWSDAY, Sept. 14, 2000; AP, *Gay Rights Backers Lose Seats,* CINCINNATI POST, Sept. 13, 2000; Kathleen Burge, *Vt. Legislator Gets an Earful from Voters; Campaign*

Is First Since Civil Union Bill Passed, BOSTON GLOBE, Sept. 10, 2000; Ross Sneyd, *Vermont Vote On Gays Not Over Yet; Lawmakers Facing Backlash at Polls*, CINCINNATI ENQUIRER, Sept. 7, 2000; Carey Goldberg, *Descent into a State of Anger: Civil-Unions Law Brings Out Tensions between Old-and-New-Style Vermonters*, DALLAS MORNING NEWS, Sept. 4, 2000; Carey Goldberg, *Vermont Residents Split over Civil Unions Law*, N.Y. TIMES NEW SERVICE, Sept. 3, 2000; Adam Gorlick, *State Delegates Nervous about Political Fallout from Civil Unions Law*, AP, Aug. 14, 2000; James Bandler, *Foes of Civil Unions Vow to "Take Back Vermont,"* WALL ST. J., Aug. 9, 2000; Carol Ness, *Couples Flock to Vermont Only Legal Place to Get Hitched*, S.F. EXAMINER, Aug. 7, 2000; Eleanor Yant, *Allentown Couple Celebrates Civil Unions*, ALLENTOWN MORNING CALL, Aug. 6, 2000; *Iowa Couple Takes Advantage of Vermont Civil Union Law*, Davenport, Iowa (AP), July 29, 2000; *Same-Sex Union Foe Names Surrogate*, GRAND RAPIDS PRESS, July 27, 2000; Carey Goldberg, *Gay Couples Flocking to Vermont*, PITTSBURGH POST-GAZETTE, July 25, 2000; Ross Sneyd, *Politicians Hopeful on Gay Rights*, TIMES UNION ALBANY, July 25, 2000; Kevin Kelley, *Vermont GOP Same-Sex Law Backers Face Party Backlash*, DETROIT NEWS, July 24, 2000; Raphael Lewis, *Honeymoon in Vermont. 'Flatlanders' from across US Take Advantage of State's Civil Union Law*, BOSTON GLOBE, July 14, 2000; Deb Price *Vermont Offers Welcoming Civil Unions*, DETROIT NEWS, July 10, 2000; Chuck Colbert, *"Civil Unions" Not a Religious Experience so Church Protest in Vt. Is Unfounded*, BOSTON GLOBE, July 9, 2000; *Taking Civil Action*, PALM BEACH POST, July 9, 2000; *Weekly Edition: Civil Unions Granted in Vermont May or May Not Carry Legal Weight in Other States*, (National Public Radio broadcast, July 8, 2000); *Vt. Clerks May Refuse Gay Unions*, CINCINNATI POST, July 3, 2000; *Vermont First to Legally Join Same-Sex Couples: Follows Court Ruling: Civil Union Allows Partners to Receive Rights of Marriage*, NATIONAL POST, July 3, 2000; Beth Whitehouse, *Pro-Union Stance/Precedent-Setting Vermont Law Lets Gay Couples 'Wed'*, NEWSDAY, July 3, 2000; Carey Goldberg, *Vermont Becomes First State to Hold Legal Gay Marriages*, PATRIOT LEDGER, July 3, 2000; Richard Higgins, *Vermont Licenses First Civil Unions; 2 Mass. Men Are Among Recipients*, BOSTON GLOBE, July 2, 2000; Richard Higgins, *Partners Get Rights, Responsibilities*, BOSTON GLOBE, July 2, 2000; Ross Sneyd, *Civil Unions Join Same-Sex Couples*, CHICAGO SUN-TIMES, July 2, 2000; *Gay Couples Rush to Tie Knot under New Vermont Law*, DESERET NEWS, July 2, 2000; Andy Geller and David K. Li, *Vt. Unions Make for Truly Gay Couples*, N.Y. POST, July 2, 2000; Gwen Florio, *Gays, Lesbians Legally United in Vermont*, NEWS & OBSERVER, July 2, 2000; Joshua L. Weinstein, *Just Another Couple*, PORTLAND PRESS HERALD, July 2, 2000; Carey Goldberg, *First Gay Couples Join in Civil Unions; Cheers, Boos at Vermont Ceremonies*, SAN DIEGO UNION-TRIBUNE, July 2, 2000; Pamela Ferdinand, *Gays Seal Civil Unions, Make History in Vermont. Couples Say Vows at Midnight*, SEATTLE TIMES, July 2, 2000; Linda Trischita, *New Day of Civil Unions Dawns*, TIMES UNION ALBANY, July 2, 2000; Lesley Rogers, *Civil Union Supporters Hoping Wisconsin's Next*, WISCONSIN STATE JOURNAL, July 2, 2000; *In Vermont, Judge Rejects Late Bid to Block Civil Unions*, BOSTON GLOBE, July 1, 1000; *Evening News*, (CBS News Television broadcast, July 1, 2000); *Gay Couples Ready for Vermont Civil-Union Law to Take Effect*, DALLAS MORNING NEWS, July 1, 2000;

Elizabeth Mehren, *A Historic Day in Vermont as Civil Unions Become Legal,* LA
Times, July 1, 2000; David Goodman, *A More Civil Union—Vermont's Legal
Recognition of Same-Sex Couples Has Brought the Latest Struggle for Gay Rights Out
of the Closet—and Onto the Stage of National Politics,* MOTHER JONES, July 1, 2000;
Ross Sneyd, *Vermont Judge Refuses to Block Same-Sex Unions,* TIMES UNION AL-
BANY, July 1, 2000; *Weekend Edition: Vermont Passes Civil Union Law for Gay and
Lesbian Couples,* (National Public Radio broadcast, July 1, 2000); Stephanie
Nolen, *The Dawn of Homosexual Weddings,* GLOBE AND MAIL, July 1, 2000; *All
Things Considered: Civil Unions Granted in Vermont May or May Not Carry Legal
Weight in Other States,* (National Public Radio broadcast, June 30, 2000); Jill
Young Miller, *Vermont Braces for Rush of 'Civil Unions' for Same-Sex Couples,* AT-
LANTA CONSTITUTION, June 30, 2000; Jill Young Miller, *Gay Georgians Look to Ver-
mont for Validation. DeKalb Couple Plan Trip in September to Make Their 2-Year-Old
Commitment Formal,* ATLANTA CONSTITUTION, June 30, 2000; Ross Sneyd, *Ver-
mont's Same-Sex Unions Law Stirs Unrest; Defiant Town Clerks Balk at Issuing Li-
censes to Gay and Lesbian Couples,* DETROIT NEWS, June 30, 2000; Deb Price, *Ver-
mont Gives Gay Couples First-Class Citizenship,* USA TODAY, June 29, 2000; Cheryl
Wetzstein, *Celebrations, Protests Planned for Vermont's Civil-Union Law,* WASH-
INGTON TIMES, June 29, 2000; Mike Eckel, *Civil Unions Law Spurring "Nastiness
in Vermont Race";* RECORD, North New Jersey, June 28, 2000,; Anita Manning,
Civil Unions Find Home in Vermont, USA TODAY, June 28, 2000; Eugene Sloan,
Inns, Lodges Expect a "Boom" in Bookings, USA TODAY, June 28, 2000; *Vermont
Judge Refuses to Block Civil Unions,* Orlando Sentinel, June 27, 2000; *Majority in
Poll Backs Gay Civil Unions,* the S.F. CHRON., June 20, 2000; Doug Hanchett, *N.E.
Bishops Slam Vt. for Allowing Gay "Civil Unions,"* BOSTON HERALD, June 10, 2000;
Deb Price, *Gays Prepare Vermont's Blessing,* DETROIT NEWS, June 5, 2000; *Poll
Finds Split on Gay Rights and Marriages,* LA TIMES, June 1, 2000; Kenneth Lovett,
State Dems Might Push to Legalize Gay Marriages, N.Y. POST, May 18, 2000; Lisa
Rathke, *Vermont Gay Unions May Benefit Business,* CINCINNATI ENQUIRER, May
10, 2000; Jake Halpern, *Out for a Buck,* NEW REPUBLIC, May 8, 2000; Andrew Sul-
livan, *State of the Union,* NEW REPUBLIC, May 8, 2000; Tom Mashberg, *Gays Push
Mass. Civil-Union Law; Vermont Gay Union Law Pushes Mass. Gay Issue,* BOSTON
HERALD, May 7, 2000; Tom Mashberg, *Rights Similar for Civil Unions and Mar-
riages,* BOSTON HERALD, May 7, 2000; Pamela Ferdinand, *In Vermont City, Civil
Unions Test Civility; St. Albans Residents See Anger, Resentment Lingering Long After Debate on Gay Benefits,* WASH. POST, May 5, 2000; Mark Stewart, *Panel Audience Criticize Same-Sex Marriages,* WASH. TIMES, May 2, 2000; Jill Young Miller,
Gay Couples in Georgia May Head for Vermont, ATLANTA CONSTITUTION, May 1,
2000; Deb Price, *Vermont Opens New Era for Gay Couples,* NEW ORLEANS TIMES-
PICAYUNE, May 1, 2000; Jeffery Good, *Business Owners, Residents Weigh Outcome
of Gay Law in Vermont,* BOSTON GLOBE, April 30, 2000; Carey Goldberg, *Vermont's Top Judge Moved Civil Union Debate from Court to Legislature,* PITTSBURGH
POST-GAZETTE, April 30, 2000; *Coming Out for Equal Rights,* WASH. POST, April
29, 2000; Brian MacQuarrie, *Some in Vt. Bristle at Civil Unions. Town Clerk Vows
to Deny Licenses for New Gay Right,* BOSTON GLOBE, April 28, 2000; David Boldt,

Vermont Has Got It Right on Same-Sex Unions, HOUSTON CHRONICLE, April 28, 2000; *Same-Sex Unions Now Law*, NEWSDAY, April 28, 2000; Roberto Figueroa, *Vermont Takes Lead in Equal Rights*, U-Wire, April 28, 2000, available at 2000 WL 19352958; Jeffrey Good, *Gays Ponder Breadth of a Vt. 'Civil Union'*, BOSTON GLOBE, April 27, 2000; John Roberts, Richard Schlesinger, *Vermont Couples Celebrate Civil Union Law*,(CBS News: Evening News with Day Rather, April 27, 2000); *Vermont First in Nation to OK Gay Civil Unions*, CHI. TRIB., April 27, 2000; Alexandra Marks, *Vermont Launches Revolution by Allowing Same-Sex Unions*, CHRISTIAN SCIENCE MONITOR, April 27, 2000; Deb Price, *Vermont's Courage Liberates Gays, Lesbians*, DETROIT NEWS, April 27, 2000; Sean Whaley, *Nevada Group Resists Vermont Law*, LAS VEGAS REVIEW-JOURNAL, April 27, 2000; *Vt. Governor Signs Bill on Civil Unions*, LA TIMES, April 27, 2000; *Vermont Gov Inks Gay Civil Union Law*, N.Y. DAILY NEWS, April 27, 2000; David Boldt, *A Civil Solution. Vermont's Segal "Union" For Gay Couples Is a Compromise Americans Should Accept*, PITTSBURGH POST-GAZETTE, April 27, 2000; Carolyn Lochhead, *In Gay Union Vote, Vermont Keeps Mind of Its Own / But Not All Residents Like State's Latest Way of Showing Independence*, S.F. CHRON., April 27, 2000; John Bacon, Haya El Nasser, *Vermont Governor Signs Gay Union Bill*, USA TODAY, April 27, 2000; Cheryl Wetzstein, *Vermont Governor Signs Bill Legalizing Same-Sex Unions. Foes Say Measure "Railroaded," Vow to Continue Fight*, WASH. TIMES, April 27, 2000; Marcia Scott Harrison, *Vermont's Legislature Becomes First in US to Recognize Gay "Civil Unions,"* AGENCE FRANCE-PRESSE, April 26, 2000; *Vermont Gives Gay Rights Law Final Approval*, ARIZONA REPUBLIC, April 26, 2000; Brian MacQuarrie, *Vt. House Approves Bill Allowing Same-Sex Unions*, BOSTON GLOBE, April 26, 2000; J.M. Larence, *Vt. House Approves Same-Sex Civil Union*, BOSTON HERALD, April 26, 2000; *Vermont's "Civil Unions" Option*, CHI. TRIB., April 26, 2000; *Vermont Governor Signs Nations' First Same-Sex Civil Union Law*, EFE News Service, April 26, 2000; Erin Kelly, *Vermont Decision on Gay Marriage Benefits Cheered, Denounced, as Expected*, GANNETT NEWS SERVICE, April 26, 2000; Linda Massarella, *Vt. Says "I Do" to Civil Unions For Gay Couples*, N.Y. POST, April 26, 2000; Carey Goldberg, *Vermont Gives Final Approval to Same-Sex Unions*, N.Y. TIMES, April 26, 2000; Joshua Weinstein, *Mainers Wonder if Vermont Civil Unions Will Hold Up Here*, PORTLAND PRESS HERALD, April 26, 2000; *Vermont's Civil Debate*, PROVIDENCE JOURNAL, April 26, 2000; Carolyn Lochhead, *Gay Unions Win Final Vote in Vermont / Governor to Sign Measure Extending Rights of Marriage*, S.F. CHRON., April 26, 2000; *Vermont Civil Union Law on Right Track*, SOUTH BEND TRIB., April 26, 2000; Leon M. Tucker, *Gay Marriage Move Alarms Conservatives*, TENNESSEAN, April 26, 2000; Pamela Ferdinand, *Vermont Legislature Clears Bill Allowing Civil Unions; Gay Couples Given Rights Like Those of Married People*, WASH. POST, April 26, 2000; Cheryl Wetzstein, *Vermont House OKs Gay Unions. Governor Has Said He'll Sign Legislation*, WASH. TIMES, April 26, 2000; *Vermont's Gay Marriage Bill Wins Final OK; Gov To Sign*, DOW JONES INTERNATIONAL NEWS, April 25, 2000; *All Things Considered: Gays in Vermont View Law Recognizing Gay Unions as a Step Forward for Gay Rights but Some Feel the Law Doesn't Go Far Enough*, (National Public Radio broadcast, April 25, 2000); Dan Nichols, *Vermont House Approves Civil Unions*,

CHRISTIANITY TODAY, April 24, 2000; David Crary, *Vermont's Gay Rights' Bill May Change Country*, SAN DIEGO UNION-TRIBUNE, April 23, 2000; *Vermont's Lawmakers Advance With Caution. The Unions Recognize That Rights Shouldn't Be Denied on the Basis of Sexual Orientation*, PORTLAND PRESS HERALD, April 22, 2000; Philip Delves Broughton, *Homosexuals to "Wed" In Vermont*, The Daily Telegraph, April 21, 2000; *Vermont Set to Become First US State to Allow Gay "Civil Unions,"* AGENCE FRANCE-PRESSE, April 20, 2000; *Gay Union Bill Sails through Senate*, ARIZONA REPUBLIC, April 20, 2000; J.M. Lawrence, *Vermont Senate Passes Gay Rights Bill*, BOSTON HERALD, April 20, 2000; Ross Sneyd, *Landmark Gay Unions Bill Nears Passage*, DAYTON DAILY NEWS, April 20, 2000; Elizabeth Mehren, *Vermont Senate OKs "Marriage" Rights for Gays*, LA TIMES, April 20, 2000; Carey Goldberg, *Vermont's Senate OKs Gay Unions*, NEW ORLEANS TIMES-PICAYUNE, April 20, 2000; Lisa L. Colangelo & Michael Blood, *Hil Lauds Same-Sex Marriage Bill, Rudy Mum*, NEW YORK DAILY NEWS, April 20, 2000; Steven G. Vegh, *Mainers Cheered by Legislation But Enthusiasm Is Tempered by the Imminent Law's Limitation*, PORTLAND PRESS HERALD, April 20, 2000; *All Things Considered: Vermont State Senate's Move to Approving a Bill That Would Recognize the Relationships for Gay and Lesbian Couples* (National Public Radio broadcast, April 19, 2000); *Vermont Senate Grants Preliminary Approval to Same-Sex "Civil Unions,"* CHI. TRIB., April 19, 2000; Carey Goldberg, *Vermont Senate Approves "Civil Unions" for Gay Couples*, DENVER POST, April 19, 2000; Liz Halloran, *Law on Gay Unions Nears Passage. Approval Expected Today in Vermont*, HARTFORD COURANT, April 19, 2000; Pamela Ferdinand, *Gay Civil Unions Near Legality; Following State House, Vermont Senate Votes Rights for Couples*, WASH. POST, April 19, 2000; Fred Bayles, *Vt. Gay Union Bill Leaves Questions Unanswered*, USA TODAY, April 17, 2000; David Crary, *Gay-Rights Bill Reflects Vermont's New Attitude Society: Same-Sex Couples Would Gain Legal Rights Equal to Marriage*, LA TIMES, April 16, 2000; *Same-Sex Unions Gain More Support in Committee Vote*, CHI. TRIB., April 14, 2000; *Vermont's "Civil Union" Experiment*, CHI. TRIB., April 10, 2000; Julie Deardorff, *Movement for Same-Sex Unions Picks up Steam across the U.S.*, HOUSTON CHRONICLE, April 9, 2000; *Vermont Domestic Partnership Bill Stoking Anti-Gay-Union Fire*, SALT LAKE TRIBUNE, April 8, 2000; Ross Sneyd, *Civil Union Opponents Rally in Vermont*, TIMES UNION ALBANY, April 7, 2000; *Vermont House OKs 'Civil Unions' For Gays*, CHRISTIAN CENTURY, April 5, 2000; Erin Kelly, *Socially Just or Just Crazy? Outsiders Weigh in on Vermont's Approach to Gay Unions*, GANNETT NEWS SERVICE, April 5, 2000; Julie Deardorff, *Vermont is Front Line of Gay Marriage Fight*, CHI. TRIB., April 3, 2000; Teresa Malcolm, *Vermont Bishop Decries Civil Union Bill*, NATIONAL CATHOLIC REPORTER, March 31, 2000; *Vermont Leads the Way*, HERALD ROCK HILL, March 27, 2000; Tammerlin Drummond, *A Win for Gays. Vermont Is on the Brink of Permitting "Civil Unions,"* TIME MAGAZINE, March 27, 2000; *Vermont Union*, BANGOR DAILY NEWS, March 23, 2000; *A Step Toward Equality*, BUFFALO NEWS, March 23, 2000; *Talk Nation: Civil Unions; Gay Marriages* (National Public Radio broadcast, March 22, 2000); *Vermont Closer to Gay Marriage*, CINCINNATI POST, March 21, 2000; Cheryl Wetzstein, *Gay "Civil Unions" Go to State Senate. Foes Seek Constitutional Amendment*, WASH. TIMES,

March 21, 2000; *Editorial*, PORTLAND PRESS HERALD, March 20, 2000; *Vermont: "Union" Not Gay Marriage*, ARIZONA REPUBLIC, March 19, 2000; *Vermont's Giant Step in Rights*, HARTFORD COURANT, March 19, 2000; Carey Goldberg, *Gay Couples Are Welcoming Vermont Measure on Civil Union*, N.Y. TIMES, March 18, 2000; *US State of Vermont Lower House Approves "Civil Unions" for Gays*, AGENCE FRANCE-PRESSE; Ross Sneyd, *Vt. House OKs Gay Unions. Bill Would Offer Benefits of Marriage*, CHICAGO SUN-TIMES, March 17, 2000; Liz Halloran, *Vermont House Blesses "Civil Unions,"* HARTFORD COURANT, March 17, 2000; Bill Egbert & Corky Siemaszko, *Vermont House OKs Gay, Lesbian Civil Union*, N.Y. DAILY NEWS, March 17, 2000; Damian Whitworth, *Homosexual Marriages Approved by Vermont*, TIMES (London), March 17, 2000; Steve Marshall, *Gay Marriage Nears in Vt.*, USA TODAY, March 17, 2000; March 17, 2000; Ross Sneyd, *Lawmakers Debate "Civil Unions" for Gays*, CINCINNATI ENQUIRER, March 16, 2000; *Special News Report with Brit Hume: Interview With Jonathan Turley* (Fox News broadcast, March 16, 2000); Liz Halloran, *Laid-Back Vermont as Flash Point. Legislation on Gay Unions Turning State into War Zone*, HARTFORD COURANT, March 15, 2000; Ross Sneyd, *Vermont Mulls Marriage Benefits for Gay Couples*, TIMES UNION ALBANY, March 12, 2000; *All Things Considered: Vermont Responds to the Idea of Legal Rights for Gay Couples* (National Public Radio broadcast, March 8, 2000); Carey Goldberg, *Vermont Town Meeting Turns into Same-Sex Union Forum*, N.Y. TIMES, March 8, 2000; Ann LoLordo, *Gay Rights Issue Draws a Fiery Foe to Vermont; Anti-Abortion Leader Organizes Opposition to Same-Sex Unions*, BALTIMORE SUN, March 6, 2000; Brooks Egerton, *Vermont Defying Labels in Drive for Gay Unions. Rural State Shows Support for Equality Policy*, DALLAS MORNING NEWS, March 4, 2000; *Vermont's Same-Sex Couples Move Toward Recognition*, LA TIMES, March 4, 2000; Ross Sneyd, *Vermont Panel OKs Civil Unions*, BANGOR DAILY NEWS, March 2, 2000; Lois R. Shea, *Vt. Panel OK's "Civil Unions" For Gays. Equal Marriage Rights Not Part of Measure*, BOSTON GLOBE, March 2, 2000; Stuart Taylor Jr., *A Vote For Gay Marriage—But Not by Judicial Fiat*, NATIONAL JOURNAL, February 19, 2000; Patrick Rogers & Eric Francis, *Love and . . . In a Landmark Decision, Three Gay Couples in Vermont Win the Right to Maybe—Just Maybe—Get Married*, PEOPLE MAGAZINE, February 14, 2000; Elizabeth Mehren, *New Firestorm Erupts Over Vermont's Domestic Partner Plan Law: State Appears Poised to Become First to Enact Same-Sex Benefits*, LA TIMES, February 13, 2000; *Vermont Panel Approves Gay Domestic Partners*, SAN ANTONIO EXPRESS-NEWS, February 11, 2000; Pamela Ferdinand, *Vermonters Rise to Sort Out Law on Marriage*, WASH. POST, February 6, 2000; Brooks Egerton, *Vermont Clergy Speak Out in Same-Sex Union Debate*, DALLAS MORNING NEWS, February 4, 2000; Carey Goldberg, *Forced into Action on Gay Marriage, Vermont Finds Itself Deeply Split*, N.Y. TIMES, February 3, 2000; Brian Knowlton, *Vermonters Debate Gay Marriage*, INTERNATIONAL HERALD TRIBUNE, February 3, 2000; Deb Price, *Vermont Seems Serious on Same-Sex Unions*, DETROIT NEWS, January 31, 2000; James Bandler, *Gay Marriage: Backers Plan a Softer Sell*, WALL ST. J., January 26, 2000; Ross Sneyd, *Vermont Hears Gay Marriage Opinions*, SUN-SENTINEL (Ft. Lauderdale, FL), January 26, 2000; *All Things Considered: Battle in Vermont Over Gay Marriage* (Nation Public Radio broadcast, January 20, 2000); *The Right*

Approach to Gay Marriage, PITTSBURGH POST-GAZETTE, January 16, 2000; *Calls Pour in to Vt. on Same-Sex Ruling,* BOSTON GLOBE, January 14, 2000; Jeffrey Good, *Vermonters Resist Gay Marriage Rancor,* BOSTON GLOBE, January 9, 2000; Javier Aldape, *Gay Marriage. The Benefits of Marriage (and Justice) for All,* FORT WORTH STAR-TELEGRAM, January 9, 2000; *Rights of Marriage in Extending Legal Protections to Same-Sex Couples, Vermont Takes a Bold Step,* POST-STANDARD, January 6, 2000; Rabbi Dan Judson, *Gay Unions Not Opposed by All Who Lead Religions,* PATRIOT LEDGER, January 5, 2000; Deb Price, *Vermont Ruling Alters Marriage Debate,* NEW ORLEANS TIMES-PICAYUNE, January 4, 2000; Mark A. Hofmann, *Vermont Court Ruling: Same-Sex Couples' Right to Benefits Upheld,* BUSINESS INSURANCE, January 3, 2000; State Sen. Jay Hottinger, *Marriage Bill Is Misguided, Redundant,* DAYTON DAILY NEWS, January 3, 2000; Thomas Cal, *Gay-Rights: Vermont Court Dictates Legal, Moral Policy,* DES MOINES REGISTER, January 3, 2000; E.J. Graff, *Vermont's High Court Avoids the M-Word and Makes History,* BOSTON GLOBE, January 2, 2000; Sheryl McCarthy, *Vermont Steps Ahead to the Future,* GREENSBORO NEWS & RECORD, January 2, 2000; *Bauer: Gay Rights Ruling "Terrorism,"* CINCINNATI POST, December 30, 1999; Jeff Zeleny, *Presidential Candidate Bauer Hits Landmark Court Ruling on Gays, Cites "Meltdown of Values,"* GANNETT NEWS SERVICE, December 30, 1999; M. Charles Bakst, *Same-Sex Marriage: Let's See Assembly Commit to Dignity,* PROVIDENCE JOURNAL, December 28, 1999; Deb Price, *Vermont Heralds Dawning of New Age,* DETROIT NEWS, December 27, 1999; *Enact Same-Sex Unions by Cutting Out Politics,* PALM BEACH POST, December 27, 1999; Steve Chapman, *Do Conservatives Really Believe in Marriage?,* CHI. TRIB., December 26, 1999; Carey Goldberg, *Redefining a Marriage Made New in Vermont,* N.Y. TIMES, December 26, 1999; *A Challenge in Vermont,* OMAHA WORLD-HERALD, December 26, 1999; *"Common Humanity." Once Recognized, It Seems Obvious,* STAR-TRIBUNE NEWSPAPER, December 26, 1999; Deb Price, *Light the Fireworks! Fire the Starting Pistol! Bang the Drum!,* GANNETT NEWS SERVICE, December 25, 1999; *A Step Out of Darkness,* BUFFALO NEWS, December 24, 1999; Amy Pagnozzi, *Marriage of Any Sort Ain't Easy,* HARTFORD COURANT, December 24, 1999; Cal Thomas, *Vermont Ruling Shows Raw Judicial Power,* NEW ORLEANS TIMES-PICAYUNE, December 24, 1999; *Sound Ruling in Vermont,* SALT LAKE TRIBUNE, December 24, 1999; *Mainers Divided on Impact of Vermont Ruling on Gay Couples,* BANGOR DAILY NEWS, December 23, 1999; Michael Crowley, *Gay Rights Bill Would Face Battle in Mass.,* BOSTON GLOBE, December 23, 1999; *Vermont Issues a Challenge,* CHI. TRIB., December 23, 1999; Douglas W. Kmiec, *There Cannot Be a Same-Sex Marriage,* CHI. TRIB., December 23, 1999; *Editorial,* PROVIDENCE JOURNAL, December 23, 1999; *Equality Is Inevitable,* ST. LOUIS POST-DISPATCH, December 23, 1999; Daniel Buckley, *Vt.'s Same-Sex Couples Victory Not Likely to Follow in Arizona,* TUCSON CITIZEN, December 23, 1999; *Vermont Court's Gay-Couple Rule Follows Path to Equal Treatment,* USA TODAY, December 23, 1999, at A16; *Vermont's Unelected Lawmakers,* WASH. TIMES, December 23, 1999; *A Gay Rights Breakthrough,* CAPITAL TIMES, December 23, 1999; Robert H. Bork, *Activist Judges Strike Again,* WALL ST. J., December 22, 1999; *A Vermont Court Speaks,* BOSTON GLOBE, December 22, 1999; Jeffrey Good, *Vt. Not Ready for Gay Marriages, Politicians Say. But Backers*

Say Partners Law Not Enough, BOSTON GLOBE, December 22, 1999; *Vermont Justices Rule by Arrogance,* BOSTON HERALD, December 22, 1999; Stacy A. Teicher, *Ruling Will Stir States on Same-Sex Marriages,* CHRISTIAN SCIENCE MONITOR, December 22, 1999; *Eroding Core Values. Get Ready for Same-Sex Marriages,* DAILY OKLAHOMAN, December 22, 1999; Peter Pochna, *Ruling to Stoke Maine Gay-Rights Fight,* PORTLAND PRESS HERALD, December 22, 1999; *Models of Gay Marriage. Vermont Shows Itself a Leader in the Recognition of Equal Rights for All Americans, Regardless of Race, Creed or Sexual Orientation,* S.F. EXAMINER, December 22, 1999; Brian S. McNiff, *Vermont Gay Marriage Decree to Affect Mass.,* TELEGRAM & GAZETTE, December 22, 1999; Ben Macintyre, *US Court Gives Gays Equality,* TIMES (London), December 22, 1999; *Gay Couples Win Benefits in Vermont. Court Avoids Marital Issue,* ARIZONA REPUBLIC, December 21, 1999; Jay Croft, *Gay Rights Victory in Vermont,* ATLANTA CONSTITUTION, December 21, 1999; *Vermont Court Grants Rights to Homosexual Couples,* AUGUSTA CHRONICLE, December 21, 1999; Lyle Denniston, *Gay Couples Win Vt. Ruling,* BALTIMORE SUN, December 21, 1999; Christopher Graff, *Vt. Court: Gay Couples Due Benefits,* BATON ROUGE ADVOCATE, December 21, 1999; Michael Crowley, *Vt. Court Gives Gay Couples a Victory,* BOSTON GLOBE, December 21, 1999; Matthew Taylor, *Image of Vt. Increasingly Progressive,* BOSTON GLOBE, December 21, 1999; Lois R. Shea, *Plaintiffs Rejoice in Ruling on Rights,* BOSTON GLOBE, December 21, 1999; Jack Sullivan, *Vt. Court Bolsters Rights of Gay Pairs,* BOSTON HERALD, December 21, 1999; Judy Peres, *Court OKs Gay Spousal Benefits. Legislature Ordered to Hash Out Details,* CHI. TRIB., December 21, 1999; Erin Kelly, *Same-Sex Benefits Ruling "1st Step"; Gay Couples in Line to Get Equal Rights,* CINCINNATI ENQUIRER, December 21, 1999; *Vermont to Fine-Tune Ruling on Gay Unions,* DESERET NEWS, December 21, 1999; Julian Borger, *US Court Grants Equal Rights to Gay Couples,* GUARDIAN, December 21, 1999; Lynne Tuohy, *In Vermont, Validation for Gays. Ruling by High Court Seen as Major Victory for Same-Sex Unions,* HARTFORD COURANT, December 21, 1999; *Morning Edition: Vermont Supreme Court Rules That Gay Couples Are Entitled to the Same Legal Protections and Benefits of Married Couples* (National Public Radio broadcast, December 21, 1999); David G. Savage, *Vt. Court Backs Equal Rights for Gay Couples,* LA TIMES, December 21, 1999; Carey Goldberg, *Vermont High Court Backs Rights of Same-Sex Couples,* N.Y. TIMES, December 21, 1999; Martin Wisckol, *Vermont Ruling Brings Focus to California Vote,* ORANGE COUNTY REGISTER, December 21, 1999; Elizabeth Schaefer, *Vermont Ruling May Open Door in R.I.,* PROVIDENCE JOURNAL, December 21, 1999; Elaine Herscher, *Vermont Supreme Court Rules in Favor of Gay Couples' Rights,* S.F. CHRON., December 21, 1999; Gregory Lewis, *Vermont Ruling Cheered by Gay Couples. California Initiative Would Erect the Same Barriers Court Banned,* S.F. EXAMINER, December 21, 1999; *Talk Nation: Vermont Supreme Court's Landmark Decision on Same-Sex Unions and Its Likely Impact* (National Public Radio broadcast, December 21, 1999); Fred Bayles, *Vt. Court Upholds Gay Couples' Rights,* USA TODAY, December 21, 1999; Hanna Rosin, *Same-Sex Couples Win Rights in Vermont; Gay Activists Say Ruling Is a Legal Breakthrough,* WASH. POST, December 21, 1999; Cheryl Wetzstein, *Ver-*

mont Supreme Court OKs Same-Sex "Protections." Legislature "Exhorted" to Enact Laws Guaranteeing Benefits, WASH. TIMES, December 21, 1999.

107. Carey Goldberg, *Vermont's High Court Extends Full Rights to Same-Sex Couples,* N.Y. TIMES, Dec. 21, 1999; Michael Crowley, *Vt Court Gives Gay Couples a Victory,* BOSTON GLOBE, Dec. 21, 1999.

108. Editorial, *Vermont's Momentous Ruling,* N.Y. TIMES, Dec. 22, 1999.

109. Editorial, *A Vermont Court Speaks,* BOSTON GLOBE, Dec. 22, 1999.

110. For an excellent discussion of the legal status of same-sex marriage in other nations, *see* Greg Johnson, *Vermont Civil Unions,* 25 VT. L. REV. 15 (2000). *See also,* Hana Rosin, *Civil Dis-Union in America's "Gay State,"* TORONTO STAR, October 22, 2000; Carey Goldberg, *In Anti-Gay Backlash, Traditional Vermonters Go on Offensive,* INTERNATIONAL HERALD TRIBUNE, September 4, 2000; Carey Goldberg, *Vermont's New Civil Union Law Luring Out-of-State Gay Couples,* INTERNATIONAL HERALD TRIBUNE, July 24, 2000; Carey Goldberg, *Gay Couples Visiting Vermont,* INTERNATIONAL HERALD TRIBUNE, July 24, 2000; *Same Sex Couples "Wed,"* TORONTO STAR, July 2, 2000; *Vermont Becomes First US State to Recognize Gay Unions,* AGENCE FRANCE PRESS, July 1, 2000; *Vermont Becomes First US State to Give Legal Rights to Gay Couples,* AGENCE FRANCE PRESSE, April 27, 2000; Toby Harnden, *Homosexuals Given Right to "Marry,"* DAILY TELEGRAPH (London), April 27, 2000; Marcia Scott Harrison, *Vermont's Legislature Becomes First in US to Recognize Gay "Civil Unions,"* AGENCE FRANCE PRESSE, April 26, 2000; *Vermont to Allow Gay Marriages,* INDEPENDENT (London), April 26, 2000; *Vermont Same-Sex Bill a First,* TORONTO STAR, April 26, 2000; Philip Delves Broughton, *Homosexuals to "Wed" in Vermont,* DAILY TELEGRAPH (London), April 21, 2000; *Vermont Set to Become First US State to Allow Gay "Civil Unions,"* AGENCE FRANCE PRESSE, April 20, 2000; *US State Backs Gay Rights Bill,* GUARDIAN (London), April 20, 2000; *State Senate Approves Gay "Civil Unions" Bill,* JOURNAL (Newcastle, UK), April 20, 2000; *Same Sex Bill Nears Approval,* TORONTO STAR, April 20, 2000; *Matrimony Not an Exclusive Club for Heterosexuals,* TORONTO STAR, April 1, 2000; *Vermont Should Be Proud,* INTERNATIONAL HERALD TRIBUNE (Neuilly-sur-Seine, France), March 20, 2000; Hanna Rosin & Pamela Ferdinand, *Vermont Bill Approves Gay Civil Unions,* INTERNATIONAL HERALD TRIBUNE (Neuilly-sur-Seine, France), March 18, 2000; *US State of Vermont Lower House Approves "Civil Unions" for Gays,* AGENCE FRANCE PRESSE, March 17, 2000; *Vermont Bill Gives Gay Couples Rights,* HERALD (Glasgow), March 17, 2000; Damian Whitworth, *Homosexual Marriages Approved by Vermont,* TIMES (London), March 17, 2000; *Vermont Approved Legislation Yesterday Allowing Gays to Form "Civil Unions,"* TORONTO STAR, March 17, 2000; Eamonn O'Neill, *State of the Union,* SUNDAY HERALD (Scotland), March 5, 2000; William Frankel, *Battle for Gay Marriages,* STATESMAN (India), February 22, 2000; *Gay Marriage Loses a Test in Vermont,* INTERNATIONAL HERALD TRIBUNE (Neuilly-sur-Seine, France), February 11, 2000; Mary Dejevsky, *Vermont Gives Equal Rights to All Gay Couples,* INDEPENDENT (London), December 22, 1999; Ben Macintire, *US Court Gives Gays Equality,* TIMES (London), December 22, 1999; *Vermont Court Rules in Favor of Gay Partner Benefits,* AGENCE FRANCE PRESSE, December 21, 1999; *Homosexual Couples Gain Legal Pro-*

tection, DEUTSCHE PRESSE-AGENTUR, December 21, 1999; Christopher Graff, *Vermont Court Backs Same Sex Couples*, TORONTO STAR, December 21, 1999.

111. Shannon Duffy, *Pushing the States on Gay Unions*, NAT'L L.J., Dec. 4, 2000.

112. Recent Legislation, 114 HARV. L. REV. 1421, 1423 n. 39 (2001).

113. Shannon Duffy, *Pushing the States on Gay Unions, supra* note 111.

114. AP, *Texas Bans Recognition of Same-Sex Unions*, RUTLAND HERALD, May 29, 2003.

115. Jack Hoffman, *Panel Tackles Marriage Issue*, RUTLAND HERALD, Jan. 12, 2000.

116. Defense of Marriage Act of 1996, 28 U.S.C. § 1738 (2000).

117. *Id.*

118. *Id.*

119. *Id.*

120. ESKRIDGE, CIVIL UNIONS *supra* note 95 at 39.

121. ESKRIDGE, THE CASE, *supra* note 103.

122. ESKRIDGE, CIVIL UNIONS, *supra* note 95.

123. Darren Allen, Chief, Vermont Press Bureau, *Gay Marriage*, RUTLAND HERALD, July 13, 2003 (citing Rich McCoy).

124. Debra Rosenberg, *Breaking Up is Hard to Do*, NEWSWEEK, July 7, 2003 (noting that 85% of Vermont's 5,000 civil unions went to out-of-state couples); Patricia Wen, *A Civil Tradition*, BOSTON GLOBE, June 29, 2003 (nearly 5,700 civil unions had been performed in Vermont as of June 2003).

125. AP, *Georgia Woman Tests Vermont's Civil Union Law*, VALLEY NEWS, April 27, 2001.

126. AP, *Georgia Appeals Court: Vermont Civil Unions Don't Equal Marriage*, VALLEY NEWS, Jan. 28, 2002.

127. Kathryn Masterson, AP, *Connecticut Can't Dissolve Vermont Civil Union*, VALLEY NEWS, July 25, 2002.

128. Debra Rosenberg, *Breaking Up Is Hard to Do, supra* note 124.

129. *Id.*

130. *Id.*

131. *Id.*

132. Anne Allen, AP, *Lesbian Couple Prevail in Ruling About Adoption*, RUTLAND HERALD, March 20, 2003.

133. Trudy Tynan, *Gay Activists Sue Over Right to Marry in Massachusetts*, RUTLAND HERALD, April 12, 2001.

134. Mark Strasser, *The Privileges of National Citizenship*, 52 RUTGERS L. REV. 553 (2000).

135. The landmark U.S. Supreme Court decision invalidating Virginia's ban on interracial marriage, Loving v. Virginia, 388 U.S. 1010 (1967), was, in a way, a "full faith and credit" portability case. The Lovings were married in D.C. and settled in Virginia. They were prosecuted under Virginia's statutory ban on interracial marriage. Because the Supreme Court invalidated the statutes as unconstitutional, the Court had no need to reach the issue of "full faith and credit."

The *Romer* case in 1996 is especially instructive in *Romer v. Evans*, 517 U.S. 620 (1996). The Supreme Court held unconstitutional, under the Equal Protection Clause of the Fourteenth Amendment, a provision of the Colorado Constitution that repealed local ordinances to the extent they prohibited discrimination on the basis of sexual orientation. The *Romer* Court's majority opinion began by quoting the First Justice Harlan's dissent in *Plessy v. Ferguson*: "One century ago, the First Justice Harlan admonished this court that the Constitution 'neither knows nor tolerates classes among citizens.' Unheeded then, those words now are understood to state a commitment to the law's neutrality where the rights of persons are at stake. The Equal Protection Clause enforces this principle and today requires us to hold invalid a provision of Colorado's Constitution." *Plessy*, 163 U.S. at 559.

136. Barbara Cox, *Applying the Usual Marriage-Validation Rules to Marriages of Same-Sex Couples*, in DEBATE, *supra* at 313 (arguing that choice-of-law doctrine, rather than full faith and credit clause, would control issue).

137. Even before *Lawrence*, the DOMAs were of questionable constitutionality. E.g., Mark Strasser, *Mission Impossible*, 9 WM. & MARY BILL OF RT'S J. 1 (2000); Mark Strasser, *Loving the Romer Out of Baehr*, 58 U. PITT. L. REV. 279 (1997); Melissa Provost, *Disregarding the Constitution in the Name of Defending Marriage*, 8 SETON HALL CONST. L.J. 157 (1997); Andrew Koppelman, *Dumb and DOMA*, 83 IOWA L. REV. 1 (1997); Jon-Peter Kelly, *Act of Infidelity*, 7 Cornell J.L. & Pub. Policy 203 (1997); Kevin Lewis, *Equal Protection After* Romer v. Evans, 49 HASTINGS L.J. 175 (1997).

138. Greg Johnson, *Vermont Civil Unions*, 25 VT. L. REV. 15, 54 (2000).

139. Shannon Duffy, *Pushing the States on Gay Unions*, *supra* note 111.

140. Sarah Kershaw, *supra* note 1.

141. *Id.*

142. *Id.*

143. *Id.*

144. William Raspberry, *Civil Unions Don't Threaten Marriage*, BURLINGTON FREE PRESS, May 2, 2000 (quoting Gary Bauer).

145. *Id.*

146. Diane Derby, *Vermont Gets Loud Cheers During March at the Capital*, RUTLAND HERALD, May 1, 2000.

147. *Id.*

148. Ross Sneyd, AP, *Vermonters Get Hero's Welcome at Gay March*, VALLEY NEWS, May 1, 2000 (quoting U.S. Rep. Jerrold Nadler).

149. *Who Lost Vermont?*, WEEKLY STANDARD, June 26, 2000.

150. Geoffrey Norman, *The New Vermont: Give It To Canada*, WEEKLY STANDARD, June 26, 2000.

151. *Id.*

152. David Coolidge, *The Civil Truth About "Civil Unions,"* WEEKLY STANDARD, June 26, 2000.

153. David Goodman, *A More Civil Union*, MOTHER JONES, July/Aug. 2000.

154. *Id.*

155. *E.g.*, Debbie Zielinski, *Domestic Partnership Benefits*, 13 J.L. & HEALTH 281 (1999); Craig Christianson, *If Not Marriage?*, 66 FORDHAM L. REV. 1699 (1998); David Coolidge and William Duncan, *Definition or Discrimination?*, 32 CREIGHTON L. REV. 3 (1998); Barbara Cox, *"The Little Project"*, 15 WISC. WOMEN'S L.J. 77 (2000); Richard Posner, Book Review, *Sex, Law and Equality*, 95 MICH. L. REV. 1578 (1997); David Coolidge, *Playing the Loving Card*, 12 BYU J. PUB. L. 201 (1998); Lynn Wardle, *Legal Claims for Same-Sex Marriage*, 39 S. TEX. L. REV. 735 (1998); Sandra Cavazos, *Harmful to None*, 9 UCLA WOMEN'S L.J. 133 (1998); Linda Eckols, *The Marriage Mirage*, 5 MICH. J. GENDER & L. 353 (1999); Evan Wolfson, *Crossing the Threshold*, 31 NYU REV. L. & SOC. CHANGE 567 (1993-94); Nancy Polikoff, *We Will Get What We Ask For*, 79 VA. L. REV. 1535 (1993); Barbara Cox, *The Lesbian Wife*, 33 CAL. W. L. REV. 155 (1997); Barbara Cox, *Same-Sex Marriage and Choice of Law*, 1994 WISC. L. REV. 1033; William Eskridge, *A History of Same-Sex Marriage*, 79 VA. L. REV. 1419 (1993); Lynn Wardle, *A Critical Analysis of Claims for Same-Sex Marriage*, 1996 BYU L. REV. 1; Gerard Bradley, *Same-Sex Marriage*, 14 IND. J. L. ETHICS & PUB. POLICY 729 (2000); David Chambers, *What If?*, 95 MICH. L. REV. 447 (1996); Richard Myers, *Same-Sex Marriage and the Public Policy Doctrine*, 32 CREIGHTON L. REV. 45 (1998); Richard Duncan, *From Loving to Romer*, 12 BYU J. PUB. L. 239 (1998); Mark Strasser, *The Privileges of National Citizenship*, 52 RUTGERS L. REV. 553 (2000); Greg Johnson, *Vermont Civil Unions*, 25 VT. L. REV. 15 (2000); Barbara Cox, *But Why Not Marriage*, 25 VT. L. REV. 113; David Collidge and William Duncan, *Beyond Baker*, 35 VT. L. REV. 61.

156. *See e.g.*, ESKRIDGE, CIVIL UNIONS *supra* note 95; MARRIAGE AND SAME-SEX UNIONS: A DEBATE (Lynn Wardle, et al eds. 2003); MARK STRASSEN, ON SAME-SEX MARRIAGE, CIVIL UNIONS, AND THE RULE OF LAW (2002).

157. KAI FRIESE, ROSA PARKS 52 (1993).

158. *Vermont Gay Rights Milestones*, BURLINGTON FREE PRESS, April 26, 2000.

159. *Id.*

160. *Id.*

161. For an excellent treatment of the arguments in favor of legal recognition of same-sex marriage, *see* ESKRIDGE, THE CASE, *supra* note 103.

162. Special Report, John Leland, *Shades of Gay*, NEWSWEEK, March 20, 2000.

163. Steven Lee Myers, *Survey of Troops Finds Antigay Bias Common in Service*, N.Y. TIMES, March 25, 2000.

164. *Id.*

165. *Id.*

166. *Id.*

167. *Id.* (quoting Columbia researcher Alan Yang).

168. *Id.*

169. *See generally, e.g.*, Reuters, *Senator, under Fire, Defends His Remarks on Gays*, BOSTON GLOBE, April 23, 2003; Carl Hulse, *Republican Lawmakers Back Senator in Gay Dispute*, N.Y. TIMES, April 30, 2003; Sheryl Stolberg, *Persistent Conflicts for Gays and GOP*, N.Y. TIMES, April 23, 2003; Hendrick Hertzberg, *Dog Bites Man*, NEW YORKER, May 5, 2003; Editorial, *"An Inclusive Man,"* NEW REPUBLIC, May 12, 2003; Dan Savage, *GOP Hypocrisy*, N.Y. TIMES, April 25, 2003;

Cathy Young, *Santorum's Odious Comparisons*, Boston Globe, April 26, 2003; Editorial, *Santorum's Passions*, Boston Globe, May 2, 2003; Editorial, *In the Mud*, Rutland Herald, April 25, 2003; Steve Nelson, *Dean Challenging One of GOP's Fundamentalist Crusaders*, Valley News, April 27, 2003.

170. Christopher Graff, Commentary, *Vermont: What America Wants to Be*, Valley News, April 16, 2000.

171. *Id.*

172. *Id.*

173. *Id.*

174. *Id.*

175. *Id.*

176. Katherine Seelye and Adam Clymer, *Senate Republicans Step Out and Democrats Jump In*, N.Y. Times, May 25, 2001; Glen Johnson, *Upheaval in Halls of Power*, Boston Globe, May 25, 2001; Jack Hoffman, *Independent!*, Rutland Herald, May 25, 2001.

177. *Mr. Jeffords Blows Up Washington*, Newsweek, May 4, 2001 (cover); *Bushwhacked!: The Senate's Flip Makes It a Whole New Ball Game*, Time, June 4, 2001; *Bringing Down the Senate*, Nation, June 18, 2001 (cover); *Don't Blow It*, New Republic, June 11, 2001 (cover).

178. *Mr. Jeffords Blows Up Washington*, Newsweek, *supra* note 177.

179. Karen Tumulty, *A One-Man Earthquake*, Time, June 4, 2001.

180. *Bringing Down the Senate*, Nation, *supra* note 177.

181. *A Struggle for Our Leaders to Deal with Me and for Me to Deal with Them*, Transcript of Jeffords' Announcement, N.Y. Times, May 25, 2001.

182. Jon Karl, *Jeffords Reports Death Threats in Wake of Defection*, CNN Comm, May 31, 2001.

183. *Id.*

184. Editorial, *Bringing Down the Senate*, Nation, June 18, 2001.

185. Micah Sifry, *Independent's Day*, Nation, June 18, 2001.

186. However, as Professor Greg Johnson has noted, "Although slavery was abolished in Vermont in 1777, nevertheless, persons purporting to be slaves were present in Vermont. The first census in the United States in 1790 noted sixteen slaves in Vermont." Greg Johnson, *Vermont Civil Unions*, 25 Vt. L. Rev. 15, 25 n. 47 (quoting William C. Hill, The Vermont State Constitution: A Reference Guide 28 (1992)).

187. Christopher Graff, Commentary, *Lawmakers Will Give Gay Marriage Issue Intelligent Treatment*, Rutland Herald, Jan. 25, 2000.

188. *Id.*

189. *Id.*

190. *Id.*

191. Eskridge, Civil Unions, *supra* note 95.

192. The phrase *badge of inferiority* is a constitutional term of art; that is, it was a term coined by the courts. The phrase was employed in *Plessy v. Ferguson* in reference to the separate-but-equal status imposed on African Americans.

193. Brown v. Board of Education, 347 U.S. 483 (1954).

194. *E.g.,* Barbara Cox, *But Why Not Marriage: An Essay on Vermont's Civil Unions Law, Same-Sex Marriage, and Separate-but-(Un)Equal,* 25 Vt. L. Rev. 113 (2000); Evan Wolfson, *All Together Now,* in Debate, *supra* note 24 at 5–6.

195. Eskridge, Civil Unions, *supra* note 95 at 133–39 and at 140.

196. Greg Johnson, *Vermont Civil Unions: A Success Story* in Marriage and Same-Sex Unions: A Debate 283 and 292 (Lynn Wardle, et al., eds. 2003).

197. I owe a debt of gratitude to the newspaper reporters and commentators on whose work I draw in this book, including Christopher Graff, Jack Hoffman, Ross Sneyd, Adam Lisberg, Nancy Remsen, Frederick Bever, Diane Derby, Jim Kenyon, Steve Nelson, Heather Stephenson, and Carey Goldberg.

198. *E.g.,* Michael Mello, Dead Wrong (2002); Michael Mello, The Wrong Man (2001); Michael Mello, Dead Wrong (1997); Michael Mello, Against The Death Penalty (1996).

199. Michael Mello, Dead Wrong 116–117 (1997).

200. *Id.* at 117 (quoting Deborah Cameron & Elizabeth Frazer, The Lust to Kill: A Feminist Investigation Into Sexual Murder [1987]).

Chapter 2

1. Quoted in Jack Bass, Unlikely Heroes (1981).

2. Baker v. State, 744 A.2d 864 (Vt.1999).

3. Baker v. State, 744 A.2d 864 (Vt.1999). Hawaii was instructive because the Hawaii Supreme Court's decision was overturned by an amendment to the state constitution. *Id.* (citing and quoting Hawaii Const., art. I, § 23).

4. Diane Derby, *Same-Sex Rights Affirmed,* Rutland Herald, Dec. 21, 1999.

5. Tom Weiner, *Gay Rights Leader Sees Shift Toward Public Acceptance,* N.Y. Times, April 24, 2000 (quoting Elizabeth Birch, a lesbian mother and director of the Human Rights Campaign).

6. James Q. Wilson, The Marriage Problem: How Our Culture Has Weakened Families (2003).

7. Many same-sex couples don't. *See* Don Aucion, *For Gays, No Unanimity on Marriage,* Boston Globe, July 10, 2003.

8. Linda Greenhouse, *Considering Gay-Scout Case, Justices Explore Implications,* N.Y. Times, April 27, 2000. The U.S. Supreme Court heard oral arguments in the Scout case on April 26, a week after Vermont's *Baker* statute became law.

9. Mello, *"In the Years When Murder Wore the Mask of Law,"* 24 Vt. L. Rev. 583 (2000).

10. William Eskridge, Gaylaw (1999) [hereinafter Eskridge, Gaylaw].

11. Carey Goldberg, *Gay Couples Welcoming Idea of Civil Union,* N.Y. Times, March 18, 2000.

12. Eskridge, Gaylaw, supra note 10 at 53.

13. Goldberg, *Gay Couples Welcoming, supra* note 11.

14. William Eskridge, The Case For Same-Sex Marriage 219 n.4 (1996) [hereinafter Eskridge, The Case] at 58 [footnotes omitted].

15. *Id.* at 48.

16. *Id.* The "Nelson" in *Baker v. Nelson* was Gerald Nelson, the clerk of the Hennepin County District Court who had denied Baker and McConnell a marriage license; "Baker and McConnell sued Nelson on the ground that denying them a marriage license is unconstitutional." *Id.*

17. Eskridge, Gaylaw *supra* note 10 at 223 (quoting *Baker v. Nelson,* 191 N.W. 2d 185, 186 [Minn. 1971], *appeal dismissed,* 409 U.S. 810 [1972]).

18. Eskridge, The Case, *supra* note 14 at 48–9.

19. *See also* Greg Johnson, *Vermont Civil Unions,* 25 Vt. L. Rev. 15, 27–36 (2000).

20. Memo from Pamela Gatos & Brook Hopkins to Michael Mello, June 21, 2000.

21. Diane Derby, *Couples Anticipate Becoming "CU'ed,"* Rutland Herald, April 26, 2000 [hereinafter Derby, *Couples Anticipate*].

22. Carey Goldberg, *Vermont Supreme Court Takes Up Gay Marriage,* N.Y. Times, Nov. 19, 1998.

23. *Id.*

24. *Id.*

25. Nancy Remsen, *Plaintiffs in Lawsuit Watch Historic Vote,* Burlington Free Press, April 26, 2000 [hereinafter Remsen, *Plaintiffs*]. Derby, *Couples Anticipate, supra* note 21.

26. Remsen, *Plaintiffs, supra* note 25.

27. Derby, *Couples Anticipate, supra* note 21.

28. *Id.* (quoting Stan Baker).

29. Baker v. State, 744 A.2d 864 (Vt.1999).

30. *Id.* (quoting the trial court).

31. Ross Sneyd, *Who Gets to Marry?,* Valley News, Nov. 19, 1998. *Accord* Audio Tape, Oral Argument in Baker v. State (Nov. 18, 1998).

32. Jim Kenyon, *A Chance to Sit In on History,* Valley News, Nov. 19, 1998. *Accord* Audio Tape, Oral Argument in Baker v. State (Nov. 18, 1998).

33. *Id. Accord* Audio Tape, Oral Argument in Baker v. State (Nov. 18, 1998).

34. For an excellent discussion of the miscegenation analogy to same-sex marriage, *see* Eskridge, The Case, *supra* note 14.

35. Ross Sneyd, *From Vermont Justices, Many Questions,* Valley News, Nov. 19, 1998. *Accord* Audio Tape, Oral Argument in Baker v. State (Nov. 18, 1998).

36. Ross Sneyd, *Who Gets to Marry?, supra* note 31.

37. *Id. Accord* Audio Tape, Oral Argument in Baker v. State (Nov. 18, 1998).

38. Kenyan, *supra* note 32. *Accord* Audio Tape, Oral Argument in Baker v. State (Nov. 18, 1998).

39. Buck v. Bell, 274 U.S. 200 (1927); *see generally* Stephen Jay Gould, *Carrie Buck's Daughter,* 2 Constitutional Commentary 331 (1985) (cited in Eskridge, The Case, *supra* note 14.

40. Baker v. State, 744 A.2d 864 (Vt.1999) (citing and quoting Webster's New International Dictionary and Black's Law Dictionary).

41. Baker v. State, 744 A.2d 864 (Vt.1999).

42. *Id.*
43. *Id.*
44. *Id.*
45. *Id.*
46. *Id.*
47. *Id.*
48. *Id.*
49. *Id.*

50. On the one hand, the court rejected the state's argument that recognizing same-sex couples could not be reconciled with "the long history of official intolerance of intimate same-sex relationships," Baker v. State, 744 A.2d 864 (Vt.1999). The court reasoned that "to the extent that state action has historically been motivated by an animus against a class, that history cannot provide a legitimate basis for continued unequal application of the law," *id.* The court also rejected as speculative the government's argument that recognition of same-sex unions "might foster marriages of convenience" or otherwise destabilize the existing institution of marriage. On the other hand, in the portion of the opinion dealing with remedy, the court said that "while the state's prediction of 'destabilization' cannot be a ground for denying relief, it is not altogether irrelevant," *id.* Any "sudden" change in marriage "may have disruptive and unforseen consequences." Thus, the court held that the existing marriage would remain in effect to allow the legislature to respond to the constitutional right recognized in *Baker.*

51. Baker v. State, 744 A.2d 864 (Vt.1999).
52. Baker v. State, 744 A.2d 864 (Vt.1999).
53. Baker v. State, 744 A.2d 864 (Vt.1999).
54. Editorial, *Johnson in Dissent,* Rutland Herald, Dec. 29, 1999.
55. Baker v. State, 744 A.2d 864 (Vt.1999) (quoting Cass Sunstein, *Forward,* 100 Harv. L. Rev. 6, 101 (1996).
56. Christopher Graff, Associated Press, Commentary *Court's Gradualism May Work Out Best,* Dec. 26, 1999.
57. Baker v. State, 744 A.2d 864 (Vt.1999).
58. *Id.*
59. *Id.*
60. Baker v. State, 744 A.2d 864 (Vt.1999).
61. *Id.*
62. *Id.*
63. *Id.*
64. Watson v. City of Memphis, 373 U.S. 526, 533 (1963); Baker v. State, 744 A.2d 864 (Vt.1999).
65. Baker v. State, 744 A.2d 864 (Vt.1999).
66. *Id.*
67. Id. This may have been true at the time *Baker* was decided. However, the post-*Baker* homophobic reaction, discussed in a later chapter, suggests it may not be true today. As discussed below, the reason the House Judiciary Com-

mittee opted for domestic partnerships, rather than marriage, was "political reality." That "political reality" was the wave of homophobia that swept across Vermont in the wake of *Baker*.

68. E.J. Graff, *Vermont's High Court Avoids the M-Word and Makes History*, BOSTON GLOBE, Jan. 2, 2000.

69. *Id.*

70. *Id.*

71. President Jackson's alleged remark referred to Worchester v. Georgia, 31 U.S. (6 Pet.) 515 (1822). "Though the historians seem to agree that Jackson held such views, the statement itself may be apocryphal. The only first-hand report of such a statement is by Horace Greeley," DAVID GETCHES, ET AL., FEDERAL INDIAN LAW: CASES AND MATERIALS (3rd ed. 1993) (citing HORACE GREELEY, AMERICAN CONFLICT 106 [1864]).

72. Jack Hoffman, *Gay Marriage Opponents State Case*, RUTLAND HERALD, Jan. 13, 2000 [hereinafter Hoffman, *Gay Marriage Opponents*].

73. *Id.*

74. VT. CONST., Ch. I, art. 7.

75. Editorial, *Our Common Humanity*, VALLEY NEWS, Dec. 26, 1999.

76. Baker v. State, 744 A.2d 864 (Vt.1999).

77. *Id.*

78. Hoffman, *Gay Marriage Opponents, supra* note 72.

79. Actually, as the amicus brief in *Baker* makes clear, the brief's real quarrel is with what he calls "poststructuralism," a school of literary and linguistic theory that, as far as I can tell, has no relevance at all to the issue before the court in *Baker* or before the legislature now. *See* Brief of Amicus Curiae, Take It to the People, Baker v. State, No. 98-032 (filed April 29th, 1998).

I must confess to having tried—and failed—to understand what the poststructuralism debate is all about. I own a dozen or so books on the subject, and a few summers ago I plowed through a few of them. Unfortunately, I began with Derrida's *Of Grammatology*, and I don't have a clue about what Derrida was trying to say in that book. To me, it all seemed like a lot of word games and punmanship.

Although I certainly make no claim of understanding either poststructuralism, or the movement's critics, I do think that the amicus committed the very fallacy of which it accuses the poststructuralists. At page 9, the brief seems to argue against a plain reading of the Common Benefits Clause. This refusal to give words their plain meaning seemed to be the very sin of which the brief accuses the poststructuralists. In other words, Goldman himself used poststructural devices in attacking poststructuralism.

Finally, the brief's critique of poststructuralism had no relevance to the constitutional methodology used by the *Baker* court to decide the case. The methodology of following and applying the plain language and meaning of the constitutional text at issue predated structuralism, poststructuralism, post-poststructuralism and all the rest of the schools of literary theory with which the brief takes such issue.

80. *Id.*

81. Baker v. State, 744 A.2d 864 (Vt.1999) (emphasis added).
82. *Id.* (emphasis added).
83. *Id.*
84. Baker v. State, 744 A.2d 864 (Vt.1999).
85. Baker v. State, 744 A.2d 864 (Vt.1999).
86. ESKRIDGE, THE CASE, *supra* note 14.
87. On the whole, the civil rights of gays and lesbians have fared well in the Vermont legislature. Associated Press writer Christopher Graff noted that Vermont was one of the first states to enact statewide legislation prohibiting discrimination in employment, housing, and other areas based on sexual orientation. Vermont has laws protecting gays from hate crimes and, most significantly, the legislature has recently sanctioned adoptions by same-sex partners, a step taken by just a few states.

I don't know what to make of the apparent dissonance between this legislative record and the recent outpouring of vitriol against same sex couples. Perhaps these statutes did not really register on the radar screens of average Vermonters. Or perhaps Vermont's homophobes find that the marriage/partnership issue hits too close to home. Regardless of the reason, *Baker* has exposed an ugly aspect of Vermont's tradition of tolerance and equality.

We do know a couple of things. First, the Vermont legislature has found it necessary to enact legislation to combat discrimination against gays and lesbians in Vermont. Second, the recent outpouring of antihomosexual feeling—strong enough to compel the *Rutland Herald* to editorialize, *e.g.* Editorial, *The Political Dimension*, Rutland Herald, Feb. 4, 2000, that the supporters of same-sex marriage ought to back off for fear of sparking an even more significant backlash against civil rights for gays and lesbians—shows the need for protection of the civil rights of this particular discrete and insular minority.

88. RICHARD KLUGER, SIMPLE JUSTICE 645 (1975).
89. Loving v. Virginia, 388 U.S. 1 (1967).

CHAPTER 3

1. Loving v. Virginia, 388 U.S. 1 (1967) (quoting trial court's statements during sentencing). This order was affirmed by the Virginia Supreme Court, which upheld Virginia's ban on interracial marriage "to preserve the racial integrity of its citizens" and to prevent "the corruption of blood" and the obliteration of racial pride." *Id.* It was reversed by the U.S. Supreme Court in *Loving v. Virginia,* 388 U.S. 1 (1967).

2. *E.g.*, State of Vermont, House of Representatives, Summary: Work of the House Judiciary Committee for the Week January 17–21, 2000 (on file with the author) [hereinafter, House Summary].

3. Jack Hoffman, *Gay Marriage Opponents State Case at Hearing,* RUTLAND HERALD, Jan. 13, 2000.

4. *Id.*

5. *Id.*

6. *Id.*(quoting Hal Goldman).

7. *Id.*

8. House Summary, *supra* note 2.

9. Christopher Graff, AP, *Gay Marriage Law Is in Deep Trouble,* Jan. 30, 2000.

10. Jack Hoffman, *Marriage Hearing Draws Overflow Crowd,* Rutland Herald, Jan. 26, 2000.

11. Ross Sneyd, *Same-Sex Marriage Opinions Split in Second Vt. Hearing,* Valley News, Feb. 2, 2000.

12. Heather Stephenson, *Big Crowd Rallies Against Gay Marriage,* Rutland Herald, Feb. 2, 2000.

13. *Id.*

14. Christopher Graff, Commentary, *Opponents of Same-Sex Marriage Make Mistake in Attacking Court,* Valley News, Feb. 6, 2000.

15. Carey Goldberg, State House Journal, *A Kaleidoscopic Look at Attitudes on Gay Marriage,* N.Y. Times, Feb. 6, 2000; *accord* Carey Goldberg, *Forced to Act on Gay Marriage, Vermont Finds Itself Deeply Split,* N.Y. Times, Feb. 3, 2000.

16. Jack Hoffman, *Second Round of Hearings Held,* Rutland Herald, Feb. 3, 2000.

17. Christopher Graff, *Gay Marriage Law Is in Deep Trouble,* Rutland Herald, Jan. 30, 2000.

18. AP, *Catholic Legislators Take Case to Bishop,* Burlington Free Press, March 23, 2000.

19. *Id.*

20. Photo and Caption, Rutland Herald, Feb. 18, 2000. The photo accompanied a story, Jack Hoffman, *Proposal Bars Gay-Couple Rights,* Rutland Herald, Feb. 18, 2000.

21. *Id.*

22. Ross Sneyd, AP, *Clergy Members Testify on Gay Marriage Issue,* Rutland Herald, Feb. 3, 2000.

23. As discussed earlier, Senator Rick Sartorum paid no political price for comparing gay love with bestiality.

24. Carey Goldberg, *Vermont Moves Step Closer to Same-Sex Civil Unions,* N.Y. Times, April 19, 2000.

25. Letter to the Editor, Burlington Free Press, April 18, 2000.

26. Letter to the Editor, Burlington Free Press, April 18, 2000.

27. Letter to the Editor, Burlington Free Press, April 18, 2000.

28. Letter to the Editor, Burlington Free Press, April 18, 2000.

29. Letter to the Editor, Rutland Herald, March 9, 2000.

30. Letter to the Editor, Times Argus [Barre and Montpelier, Vt.], Feb. 22, 2000.

31. Letter to the Editor, Times Argus [Barre and Montpelier, Vt.], Feb. 22, 2000 (quoting an earlier letter to the editor).

32. Letter to the Editor, Valley News, Feb. 6, 2000.

33. Letter to the Editor, Rutland Herald, Feb. 27, 2000.

34. Letter to the Editor, Valley News, Feb. 27, 2000.

35. *Id.*

36. Letter to the Editor, Rutland Herald, Feb. 26, 2000.

37. *Id.*

38. *Id.*

39. Letter to the Editor, Times Argus [Barre and Montpelier, Vt.], Feb. 29, 2000.

40. Letter to the Editor, Times Argus, Feb. 29, 2000.

41. Letter to the Editor, Times Argus, Feb. 29, 2000.

42. Letter to the Editor, Times Argus, Feb. 29, 2000.

43. Letter to the Editor, Burlington Free Press, April 11, 2000.

44. Letter to the Editor, Rutland Herald, March 5, 2000.

45. *Id.*

46. Letter to the Editor, Burlington Free Press, March 5, 2000.

47. Letter to the Editor, Burlington Free Press, March 5, 2000.

48. Letter to the Editor, Burlington Free Press, March 5, 2000.

49. Letter to the Editor, Burlington Free Press, March 5, 2000.

50. Letter to the Editor, Burlington Free Press, April 17, 2000 (ellipses in original).

51. Letter to the Editor, Burlington Free Press, April 16, 2000 (quoting Leviticus, ch. 20, verse 13).

52. Letter to the Editor, Burlington Free Press, April 16, 2000.

53. *Id.*

54. *Id.*

55. Letters to the Editor, Burlington Free Press, April 16, 2000.

56. Letter to the Editor, Rutland Herald, April 16, 2000.

57. Letter to the Editor, Rutland Herald, April 16, 2000.

58. Letter to the Editor, Rutland Herald, March 5, 2000.

59. Letter to the Editor, Rutland Herald, March 7, 2000.

60. Letter to the Editor, Rutland Herald, Jan. 16, 2000.

61. Letter to the Editor, Rutland Herald, March 10, 2000.

62. Letter to the Editor, Burlington Free Press, March 11, 2000.

63. *Id.*

64. *Id.*

65. Letter to the Editor, Valley News, April 12, 2000.

66. Letter to the Editor, Valley News, April 12, 2000.

67. Letter to the Editor, Rutland Herald, April 12, 2000.

68. Letter to the Editor, Rutland Herald, April 12, 2000.

69. Letter to the Editor, Rutland Herald, April 13, 2000.

70. Letter to the Editor, Rutland Herald, April 13, 2000.

71. *Id.*

72. Letter to the Editor, Rutland Herald, Feb. 12, 2000.

73. Letter to the Editor, Rutland Herald, Feb. 19, 2000.

74. Letter to the Editor, Rutland Herald, Feb. 20, 2000.

75. Letter to the Editor, Rutland Herald, Feb. 17, 2000.

76. Letter to the Editor, Valley News, Feb. 22, 2000.
77. Letter to the Editor, Burlington Free Press, March 23, 2000.
78. Letter to the Editor, Burlington Free Press, March 23, 2000.
79. Letter to the Editor, Burlington Free Press, March 23, 2000.
80. Letter to the Editor, Rutland Herald, March 23, 2000. This letter's reference to the boy's bigotry—and the adult letter-writer's endorsement of that bigotry—reminded me of the song from the film *South Pacific, You've Got to Be Taught to Hate.*
81. Letter to the Editor, Rutland Herald, April 27, 2000.
82. Letter to the Editor, Burlington Free Press, May 2, 2000.
83. *Id.*
84. Letter to the Editor, Rutland Herald, April 30, 2000.
85. Letter to the Editor, Rutland Herald, April 30, 2000
86. Letter to the Editor, Rutland Herald, April 30, 2000.
87. *Id.*
88. Letter to the Editor, Burlington Free Press, April 30, 2000.
89. *Id.*
90. *Id.*
91. Letter to the Editor, Burlington Free Press, April 30, 2000.
92. Letter to the Editor, Burlington Free Press, March 26, 2000.
93. Letter to the Editor, Burlington Free Press, March 26, 2000.
94. Letter to the Editor, Burlington Free Press, March 26, 2000.
95. Letter to the Editor, Burlington Free Press, March 26, 2000.
96. Letter to the Editor, Burlington Free Press, March 26, 2000.
97. Letter to the Editor, Rutland Herald, March 29, 2000.
98. Letter to the Editor, Rutland Herald, March 29, 2000.
99. Letter to the Editor, Rutland Herald, March 29, 2000.
100. Letter to the Editor, Rutland Herald, April 4, 2000.
101. Letter to the Editor, Rutland Herald, April 20, 2000.
102. Letter to the Editor, Burlington Free Press, April 19, 2000.
103. Letter to the Editor, Rutland Herald, Jan. 12, 2000.
104. *Id.*
105. *Id.*
106. *Id.*
107. Letter to the Editor, Burlington Free Press, April 2, 2000.
108. Letter to the Editor, Burlington Free Press, April 2, 2000.
109. Letter to the Editor, Burlington Free Press, April 2, 2000
110. Letter to the Editor, Burlington Free Press, April 2, 2000
111. Letter to the Editor, Valley News, April 5, 2000
112. Letter to the Editor, Burlington Free Press, April 4, 2000.
113. Letter to the Editor, Burlington Free Press, April 4, 2000.
114. Letter to the Editor, Herald of Randolph, April 20, 2000.
115. Letter to the Editor, Rutland Herald, April 21, 2000.
116. Letter to the Editor, Rutland Herald, April 21, 2000.
117. Letter to the Editor, Valley News, May 3, 2000.

118. *Id.*

119. *Id.*

120. Letter to the Editor, Rutland Herald, March 14, 2000 (emphasis added).

121. Letter to the Editor, Burlington Free Press, March 19, 2000.

122. Letter to the Editor, Burlington Free Press, March 19, 2000.

123. Letter to the Editor, Burlington Free Press, March 19, 2000.

124. Letter to the Editor, Burlington Free Press, March 19, 2000.

125. Letter to the Editor, Burlington Free Press, March 19, 2000.

126. Letter to the Editor, Burlington Free Press, March 19, 2000.

127. Letter to the Editor, Rutland Herald, March 30, 2000.

128. *Id.*

129. Letter to the Editor, Rutland Herald, March 30, 2000.

130. Letter to the Editor, Rutland Herald, March 30, 2000.

131. Letter to the Editor, Rutland Herald, March 30, 2000.

132. *Id.*

133. Letter to the Editor, Rutland Herald, March 17, 2000.

134. Letter to the Editor, Rutland Herald, March 17, 2000.

135. Letter to the Editor, Rutland Herald, April 25, 2000.

136. *Id.*

137. Letter to the Editor, Rutland Herald, April 25, 2000.

138. Letter to the Editor, Rutland Herald, April 26, 2000.

139. Letter to the Editor, Rutland Herald, April 26, 2000.

140. Letter to the Editor, Burlington Free Press, April 26, 2000.

141. Letter to the Editor, Burlington Free Press, May 5, 2000.

142. *Id.*

143. Letter to the Editor, Burlington Free Press, May 5, 2000.

144. Letter to the Editor, Burlington Free Press, May 5, 2000 (ellipses in original).

145. *Id.* (ellipses in original).

146. Letter to the Editor, Burlington Free Press, May 5, 2000.

147. Letter to the Editor, Burlington Free Press, May 5, 2000.

148. *Id.*

149. *Id.*

150. Letter to the Editor, Burlington Free Press, May 4, 2000.

151. Letter to the Editor, Burlington Free Press, May 6, 2000.

152. *Id.*

153. *Id.*

154. Letter to the Editor, Burlington Free Press, May 6, 2000.

155. Letter to the Editor, Rutland Herald, March 18, 2000.

156. *Id.*

157. Letter to the Editor, Rutland Herald, March 18, 2000.

158. Letter to the Editor, Herald of Randolph, March 23, 2000.

159. Letter to the Editor, Rutland Herald, March 25, 2000.

160. Jack Hoffman, *Gay Marriage Lawyer Makes Emotional Plea*, Rutland Herald, Feb. 5, 2000.

161. *Id.*

162. Sharon Underwood, *Ignorant Cruelty Robbed Me of the Joys of Motherhood,* VALLEY NEWS, April 25, 2000.

163. Editorial, *Our Common Humanity,* VALLEY NEWS, Dec. 26, 1999.

164. *Id.*

165. *Id.*

166. Editorial, *Delay in Montpelier,* VALLEY NEWS, Feb. 29, 2000.

167. *Id.*

168. The Rev. William Sloane Coffin, *Let Us Be Impatient with Prejudice,* RUTLAND HERALD, Jan. 20, 2000.

169. Eugene Rayner, *Valentine's Day Gift Wish for Loving Couples,* RUTLAND HERALD, Feb. 13, 2000.

170. Rama Schneider, *How I Would Have Testified on Same-Sex Marriage,* RUTLAND HERALD, Jan. 30, 2000.

171. Victor Nuovo, *Law, Morality, and Same-Sex Marriage,* RUTLAND HERALD, Aug. 26, 1999.

172. Adam Lisberg, *Unions Divide Religions,* BURLINGTON FREE PRESS, March 30, 2000.

173. Gustav Niebuhr, *Reform Rabbis Back Blessings of Gay Unions,* N.Y. TIMES, March 30, 2000.

174. Jack Hoffman, *Poll: Majority Say No to Same-Sex Benefits,* RUTLAND HERALD, Jan. 25, 2000.

175. Nancy Remeson, *Vermonters to Have Their Say on Gay Marriage,* BURLINGTON FREE PRESS, March 3, 2000.

176. *Id.*

177. Jack Hoffman, *Panel Affirms Marriage Tradition,* RUTLAND HERALD, March 1, 2000 [hereinafter Hoffman, *Panel Affirms*].

178. Ross Sneyd, AP, *Gay Rights Bill Expanded, Revised,* VALLEY NEWS, March 1, 2000 [hereinafter Sneyd, *Gay Rights Bill*]; Hoffman, *Panel Affirms, supra* note 177.

179. Sneyd, *Gay Rights Bill, supra.*

180. Patrick Garahan, State Chairman, Republican Party, Letter to the Editor, RUTLAND HERALD, March 1, 2000.

181. Sneyd, *Gay Rights Bill, supra* note 178.

182. Ross Sneyd, AP, *Civil Unions Are Endorsed in Close Vote,* RUTLAND HERALD, March 4, 2000.

183. *Id.*

184. Alex Hanson, *Local Group Emerges to Fight Same-Sex Rights,* VALLEY NEWS, March 10, 2000.

185. Jack Hoffman, *Will Gay Marriage Ruling by Court Be Next-to-Last-Step?,* RUTLAND HERALD, Dec. 26, 1999 [hereinafter Hoffman, *Next-to-Last Step*].

186. Vermont State Senator William Doyle "has been asking Vermonters questions each town meeting for 32 years." Nancy Remsen, *Vermonters to Have Their Say on Gay Marriage,* BURLINGTON FREE PRESS, March 3, 2000 [hereinafter Remsen, *Vermonters to Have Their Say*].

187. Hoffman, *Next-to-Last Step, supra* note 185.

188. THE BOB MITCHELL YEARS 110 (1993).

189. Christopher Graff, AP, Commentary, *If the Debate Over Civil Unions Sounds Familiar, Here's Why,* VALLEY NEWS, March 26, 2000.

190. *Id.*

191. *Id.*

192. *Id.*

193. Jack Hoffman, *Same-Sex Marriage Is Opposed,* RUTLAND HERALD, March 8, 2000.

194. Remsen, *Vermonters to Have Their Say, supra* note 175.

195. Jack Hoffman, *Same-Sex Marriage Is Opposed,* RUTLAND HERALD, March 8, 2000.

196. Nancy Remsen, *Gay Marriage Loses at Ballot Box,* BURLINGTON FREE PRESS, March 8, 2000 [hereinafter Remsen, *Gay Marriage Loses*].

197. *Id.*

198. Jack Hoffman, *Same-Sex Marriage Is Opposed,* RUTLAND HERALD, March 8, 2000.

199. *Id.*

200. *Id.*

201. *Id.*

202. Editorial, *Public Resistance,* RUTLAND HERALD, March 8, 2000.

203. Jack Hoffman, *Reactions Vary to Town Votes on Civil Unions,* RUTLAND HERALD, March 9, 2000 [hereinafter Hoffman, *Reactions Vary*].

204. Editorial, *Public Reactions, supra.*

205. Chris Graff, AP, Commentary, *How Will History Judge Lawmakers?*, RUTLAND HERALD, March 12, 2000.

206. *Id.*

207. *Id.*

208. *Id.*

209. *Id.*

210. *Id.*

211. Carey Goldberg, *Vermont Town Meeting Turns into Same-Sex Union Forum,* N.Y. TIMES, March 8, 2000.

212. *Id.*

213. Representative Deen was as good as his word: He voted in favor of the comprehensive civil unions bill both times the bill came to a vote in the House. He also was one of two co-sponsors of an amendment to the bill that would have extended the right of marriage to same-sex couples. *See* Jack Hoffman, *House Backs Civil Union Bill,* March 16, 2000; *see also Roll Call Is 79-68 for Civil Unions,* RUTLAND HERALD, March 16, 2000 (noting that Rep. Deen voted for the bill on the preliminary vote); *House Passes Civil Unions Bill with 76-69 Roll Call,* RUTLAND HERALD, March 17, 2000 (noting that Rep. Deen voted for the bill on the final vote).

214. *Id.*

215. *Id.*

216. Hoffman, *Reactions Vary, supra* note 203.

217. Wilson Ring, AP, *Marriage Question Unclear, Dean Says,* BURLINGTON FREE PRESS, March 9, 2000.

218. Hoffman, *Reactions Vary, supra* note 203. Governor Howard Dean's criticism of the news media was wrong here, I believe. This aspect of the bill received extensive coverage in the *Rutland Herald* and *Valley News,* for example.

219. Editorial, *Yes to Civil Unions,* RUTLAND HERALD, March 12, 2000. The newspaper also argued that the questions before the voters were different from the question before the legislature. The *Herald* framed the latter: "Do you favor civil unions in light of the fact that the supreme court has said that civil unions or marriages are necessary to redress injustice and in light of the fact that if you don't approve civil unions the court will probably impose same-sex marriage." *Id.*

220. Remsen, *Gay Marriage Loses, supra* note 196.

221. *Id.*

222. *Id.*

223. Remsen, *Gay Marriage Loses, supra* note 196.

CHAPTER 4

1. Part Five, *From the Earth to the Moon* (HBO), 1995.

2. Baker v. State, 744 A.2d 864 (Vt.1999).

3. WILLIAM SHAKESPEARE, MACBETH, act IV, scene I. I am grateful to Deanna Mello for remembering that this scene is from *Macbeth* and for tracking down the precise passage.

4. Leslie Staudinger, *VLS Community Participates in Same-Sex Marriage Debate,* LOQUITUR (spring 2000) (quoting Professor Greg Johnson).

5. Frederick Bever, *Senate Leaders Are Confident,* RUTLAND HERALD, March 17, 2000.

6. *Id.*

7. Jack Hoffman, *Panel Backs Domestic Partnership,* RUTLAND HERALD, Feb. 10, 2000 (quoting Gov. Howard Dean) [hereinafter Hoffman, *Panel Backs*].

8. Jack Hoffman, *Panel Tackles Marriage Issue,* RUTLAND HERALD, Jan. 12, 2000.

9. *Id.* (quoting Susan Murray).

10. *Id.* (quoting Susan Murray).

11. *Id.* (quoting Susan Murray).

12. *Id.* (quoting Beth Robinson) (parenthetical in original).

13. *Id.*

14. *Id.* (quoting Beth Robinson).

15. *Id.*

16. *Id.* (quoting Peter Teachout).

17. Christopher Graff, *Gay Marriage Law Is in Deep Trouble,* RUTLAND HERALD, Jan. 30, 2000.

18. Ross Sneyd, AP, *Domestic Partnership Supported*, VALLEY NEWS, Feb. 10, 2000.

19. Hoffman, *Panel Backs, supra* note 7 (quoting Gov. Dean).

20. Ross Sneyd, AP, *12 Lawmakers: Impeach Court for Same-Sex Ruling*, VALLEY NEWS, Feb. 11, 2000.

21. *See generally* Jack Hoffman, *House Panel Approves Bill on Civil Unions*, RUTLAND HERALD, March 2, 2000 [hereinafter Hoffman, *House Panel Approves Bill*]; Ross Sneyd, AP, *Gay Rights Bill Clears Big Hurdle*, VALLEY NEWS, March 2, 2000 [hereinafter Sneyd, *Gay Rights Bill Clears*].

22. Jeffrey Good, *Gays Ponder Breadth of a Vermont "Civil Union,"* BOSTON GLOBE, April 27, 2000.

23. *Id.*

24. Jack Hoffman, *Panel Affirms Marriage Tradition*, RUTLAND HERALD, March 1, 2000 (quoting the bill).

25. The day before the vote in the full House, "Dean was hard at work on the issue, buttonholing lawmakers in the State House corridors and inviting those who had not made up their minds into his office for personal encounters." Ross Sneyd, *Fate of Civil Unions May Hinge on Who's Out Ill*, VALLEY NEWS, March 15, 2000; *see also* Nancy Remsen and Adam Lisberg, *"Civil Union" Debate Hits Apex*, BURLINGTON FREE PRESS, March 15, 2000 [hereinafter Remsen and Lisberg, *"Civil Union" Debate*].

26. Ross Sneyd, *Dean to Lawmakers: Let Your Conscience Guide*, VALLEY NEWS, March 16, 2000.

27. *Id.*

28. Sneyd, *Gay Rights Bill Clears, supra* note 21.

29. *Id.*

30. Hoffman, *House Panel Approves Bill, supra*; Sneyd, *Gay Rights Bill Clears, supra* note 21.

31. *Id.*

32. *Id.*

33. Adam Lisberg, *Panel OKs Marriage Substitute*, BURLINGTON FREE PRESS, March 2, 2000.

34. *Id.*

35. Remsen and Lisberg, *"Civil Union" Debate, supra* note 25.

36. *Id.*

37. Hoffman, *House Panel Approves Bill, supra* note 21.

38. Ross Sneyd, AP, *Civil Unions Are Endorsed in Close Vote*, RUTLAND HERALD, March 4, 2000.

39. Editorial, *Through the Minefield*, RUTLAND HERALD, March 7, 2000.

40. *Id.*

41. This language had been added to the bill by the Judiciary Committee. *See* Ross Sneyd, AP, *Panel Affirms Marriage Tradition*, March 1, 2000.

42. Hoffman, *House Panel Approves Bill, supra* note 21.

43. Sneyd, *Gay Rights Bill Clears, supra* note 21.

44. HBO, *From the Earth to the Moon*.

45. *E.g.* Editorial, *Yes to Civil Unions*, RUTLAND HERALD, March 12, 2000; Christopher Graff, Commentary, *Historical Perspective on Gay Rights Debate*, VALLEY NEWS, March 12, 2000.

46. Editorial, *Yes to Civil Unions*, RUTLAND HERALD, March 12, 2000.

47. Ross Sneyd, AP, *2000 Legislature: Key Bills*, BURLINGTON FREE PRESS, March 13, 2000.

48. Ross Sneyd, *Obuchowski Predicts Votes for Unions*, RUTLAND HERALD, March 14, 2000.

49. *Id.*

50. *Id.*

51. *Id.*

52. Adam Lisberg, *Senators Rule Out Gay Right to Marry*, BURLINGTON FREE PRESS, March 18, 2000.

53. Remsen and Lisberg, *"Civil Union" Debate, supra* note 25.

54. *Id.*

55. *Id.*

56. Sandy Cooch, *Legislators Explain Their Votes*, HERALD OF RANDOLPH, March 23, 2000 (citing Rep. Ann Seibert).

57. Sam Hemmingway, *Hard to Tell Which Way Marriage Mood Is Swinging*, BURLINGTON FREE PRESS, March 15, 2000.

58. *Id.*

59. Jack Hoffman, *Foes See Votes to Block Civil Unions*, RUTLAND HERALD, March 15, 2000.

60. Remsen and Lisberg, *"Civil Union" Debate, supra* note 25.

61. Diane Derby, *Well-Oiled Machine Was Decisive Factor*, RUTLAND HERALD, March 17, 2000.

62. Carey Goldberg, *Vermont's House Backs Wide Rights for Gay Couples*, N.Y. TIMES, March 17, 2000.

63. *Id.*

64. Adam Lisberg, *House Agonized over Civil Unions*, BURLINGTON FREE PRESS, March 19, 2000 (referring to Rep. Robert Starr) [hereinafter Lisberg, *House Agonized*].

65. Ross Sneyd, *Fate of Civil Unions May Hinge on Who's Out Ill*, VALLEY NEWS, March 15, 2000 (quoting Rep. Peg Flory).

66. *Id.*

67. Jack Hoffman, *House Backs Civil Unions Bill*, RUTLAND HERALD, March 16, 2000 [hereinafter Hoffman, *House Backs*].

68. Ross Sneyd, AP, *Civil Unions Bill Clears House*, March 17, 2000.

69. Hoffman, *House Backs, supra* note 67.

70. *Id.*

71. *Id.*

72. *Id.*

73. Hoffman, *House Backs, supra* note 67 (emphasis added).

74. Barbara Dozetos, *House Approves Civil Rights Bill*, Out in the Mountains: Vermont's Forum For Lesbian, Gay, Bisexual, and Transgender Issues, April 2000 [hereinafter Dozetos, *House Approves*].

75. *Id.*

76. *Id.*

77. *Id.* (quoting Rep. Michael Vinton).

78. I have to admit that I found these statements—made in support of a separate but equal system of matrimony—a bit odd. Voting for a "civil rights" bill that enshrines into law the second-class matrimonial status of same-sex couples seems to me an odd principle on which to sacrifice a political career. If I were a legislator determined to vote my conscience in favor of full marital equality for same-sex couples, I'd vote for marriage and only for marriage—as Rep. William Mackinnon initially did, much to the very public outrage of the supporters of the civil unions bill on which they insisted on voting their "conscience." For Mackinnon's many detractors, "voting your conscience" seems really to mean "voting the way I think your conscience should dictate—not voting *your* conscience, but rather voting *my* conscience."

79. Hoffman, *House Backs*, *supra* note 67 (quoting Rep. George Allard).

80. *Id.* (quoting Rep. Nancy Sheltra).

81. *Id.* (quoting Rep. Mary Mazzariello).

82. Nancy Remsen and Adam Lisberg, *House Backs Civil Unions*, Burlington Free Press, March 16, 2000 (quoting Rep. Francis Brooks) [hereinafter Remsen and Lisberg, *House Backs*].

83. Ross Sneyd, AP, *Lippert Gives Impassioned Plea for Justice*, Valley News, March 16, 2000.

84. Lisberg, *House Agonized*, *supra* note 64.

85. Adam Lisberg, *Lawmaker Listens, Then Decides*, Burlington Free Press, March 16, 2000.

86. Remsen and Lisberg, *House Backs*, *supra* note 82.

87. Lisberg, *House Agonized*, *supra* note 64.

88. Jack Hoffman, *For Little, Civil Union Debate Is Immediate, Not Yet Historic*, Rutland Herald, March 19, 2000 (quoting Rep. Thomas Little).

89. Lisberg, *House Agonized*, *supra* note 64.

90. Jack Hoffman, *Final Approval for Landmark Law*, Rutland Herald, March 17, 2000.

91. *Id.*

92. *Id.* (quoting Rep. Nancy Sheltra).

93. *Id.*

94. Dozetos, *House Approves*, *supra* note 74.

95. Ross Sneyd, AP, *Civil Unions Bill Clears House*, March 17, 2000.

96. Adam Lisberg and Nancy Remsen, *Bill Wins Final Approval*, Burlington Free Press, March 17, 2000.

97. *Id.*

98. *Id.*

99. Carey Goldberg, *Vermont's House Backs Wide Rights for Gay Couples*, N.Y. Times, March 17, 2000; Carey Goldberg, *Gay Couples Welcoming Idea of Civil Union*, N.Y. Times, March 18, 2000.

100. Editorial, *Legal Unions for Gays in Vermont*, N.Y. Times, March 18, 2000.

101. Senator Sears made this comment, spoken with some exasperation, near the end of the final public hearing on the civil unions bill. The quote comes from my contemporaneous notes on the hearing, which was broadcast live by Vermont Public Radio on April 3, 2000.

102. Ross Sneyd, *Civil Union Bill Clears House*, Valley News, March 17, 2000; Frederick Bever, *Senate Leaders Are Confident*, Rutland Herald, March 27, 2000; Nancy Remsen and Adam Lisberg, *Legislation's Passage Predicted in Senate*, Burlington Free Press, March 17, 2000 [hereinafter Remsen and Lisberg, *Legislation's Passage Predicted*].

103. Ross Sneyd, AP, *Debate on Civil Unions Begins in Vermont Senate Committee*, Valley News, March 22, 2000.

104. Adam Lisberg, *Two Senators on Panel Seek Gay-Marriage Ban*, Burlington Free Press, March 22, 2000.

105. *Id.*

106. *Id.* (quoting Sen. Vincent Illuzzi).

107. Jack Hoffman, *Now It's Sears' Turn*, Rutland Herald, March 26, 2000 (quoting Sen. Richard Sears).

108. *Id.*

109. Supporters of these amendments to the state constitution might have been wise to recall that in *Romer v. Evans*, the U.S. Supreme Court held that a state constitutional amendment violated the *federal* constitution because the amendment was based on antigay animus. The Colorado amendment invalidated in *Romer* was far more comprehensive in its denial of civil rights than might be the case with the proposed amendments to the Vermont Constitution. Still, the discriminatory animus behind the proposed Vermont amendments would render them vulnerable to attack under the federal Constitution. Even under an easygoing rational basis test, the classification must serve *some* legitimate legislative goal—and animus against gays is not a legitimate legislative goal. *See also* Lawrence v. Texas, ___ U.S. ___, 71 U.S.L.W. 4574 (June 26, 2003).

110. Ross Sneyd, *Debate on Civil Unions Begins in Vermont Senate Committee*, Valley News, March 22, 2000.

111. *Id.*

112. AP, *House Speaker Angry over "Gay Marriage" Advertisements*, Valley News, March 22, 2000.

113. The ad was page 18 of the *Rutland Herald*, March 21, 2000. The ad appeared as an unnumbered page in the *Burlington Free Press*, March 21, 2000.

114. *Id.*

115. *Id.*

116. *Id.* (phone and fax numbers omitted).

117. *Id.*

118. These ads ran in the *Valley News* on March 23, 2000, and in the *Burlington Free Press* and *Rutland Herald* on March 22, 2000.

119. *Id.* (emphasis in original).

120. *Id.* (emphasis in original).

121. *Id.*

122. *Id.*

123. Frederick Bever, *Postcards, Ads Target Officials*, RUTLAND HERALD, March 24, 2000 (quoting Gov. Howard Dean) [hereinafter Bever, *Postcards*].

124. Ross Sneyd, AP, *Dean: Ads Condemning Civil Unions Are "Asinine,"* VALLEY NEWS, March 24, 2000.

125. *Id.* (quoting advertisement by a group called Who Would Have Thought, Inc.)

126. *Id.*

127. Nancy Remsen, *Dean Says Civil-Union Foes Cross Line*, BURLINGTON FREE PRESS, March 24, 2000.

128. Advertisement, RUTLAND HERALD, March 30, 2000.

129. Advertisement, RUTLAND HERALD, April 5, 2000.

130. *Id.* (capitalization original).

131. *Id.* (emphasis and exclamation points in original).

132. Advertisement, BURLINGTON FREE PRESS, April 2, 2000.

133. *Id.*

134. *Id.* (quoting the bill) (emphasis in original ad).

135. Bever, *Postcards, supra* note 123.

136. *Id.*

137. Adam Lisberg, *Anti–Civil Union Mail Blitzes Vt*, BURLINGTON FREE PRESS, April 5, 2000.

138. Letter From Rev. D.A. Stertzbach to Michael Mello, March 30, 2000 (emphasis in original).

139. Letter to the Editor, VALLEY NEWS, April 5, 2000.

140. Letter to the Editor, VALLEY NEWS, April 5, 2000.

141. Adam Lisberg, *Lobbying on Gay Marriage Cost $100,000*, BURLINGTON FREE PRESS, March 25, 2000.

142. *Id.*

143. *Id.*

144. *Id.*

145. *Id.*

146. Vermont Press Bureau, *Legislators Angry About Ads by Terry*, RUTLAND HERALD, April 6, 2000.

147. *Id.* (quoting Randall Terry).

148. Remsen and Lisberg, *Legislation's Passage Predicted, supra* note 102.

149. Ross Sneyd, AP, *Vt. Weighs Impact of Civil Union Bill*, VALLEY NEWS, March 18, 2000; *see also* Adam Lisberg, *Senators Rule Out Gay Right to Marry*, BURLINGTON FREE PRESS, March 18, 2000 [hereinafter Lisberg, *Senators Rule Out*].

150. *Id.*

151. Frederick Bever, *Senate Leaders Are Confident*, RUTLAND HERALD, March 17, 2000 (quoting Senate President Pro Tem Peter Shumlin).

152. *Id.*

153. Lisberg, *Senators Rule Out, supra* note 149 (quoting Sen. Richard Sears).

154. Ross Sneyd, AP, *Gay Rights Plaintiff Addresses Vt. Panel*, VALLEY NEWS, March 23, 2000 [hereinafter Sneyd, *Gay Rights Plaintiff*].

155. *Id.*

156. *Id.* (quoting House Rep. Thomas Little).

With all due respect, I think Representative Little missed the point. A same-sex marriage law is not about changing the "perceptions" of homophobes. It is about *the law* institutionalizing a separate parallel system of matrimonial equality—when the only reason for the inequality is public hostility to homosexuality.

Representative Little was absolutely right that "symbols matter" and "words matter." *Id.* It is unfortunate that *the law*, bending to the "political reality" of homophobia, refuses to allow same-sex couples access to the word and symbol that is marriage. The unmistakable message of any civil unions bill enacted in the 2000 climate of hatred of homosexuals was that they were second-class matrimonial citizens. Symbols do matter, and *that* is a terrible symbol.

157. For a defense of the proposed constitutional amendment, see David Coolidge and William Duncan, *Beyond Baker*, 25 VT. L. REV. 61 (2000).

158. Sneyd, *Gay Rights Plaintiff, supra* note 154 (quoting Sen. Julius Canns).

159. Bev Marker, *Professor Kujovich Speaks to the Vermont Judiciary Committee*, FORUM [the student newspaper of Vermont Law School]), April 7, 2000.

160. *Id.* (quoting Sen. Vincent Illuzzi and Prof. Gil Kujovich).

161. *Id.*

162. *Id.* As I suggested earlier, I do not believe that the argument that same-sex marriage undermines heterosexual marriage holds up under even minimal scrutiny. Same-sex marriage undermines heterosexual marriage only if the former is so inherently immoral or evil that its very existence destabilizes the latter.

This rationale is nothing more than a thinly veiled criticism of homosexuality itself and homosexuals themselves. The homophobia at the heart of this argument means that it ought not pass constitutional muster, even under the most easygoing of rational basis tests.

163. Adam Lisberg, *Unions Divide Religions*, BURLINGTON FREE PRESS, March 30, 2000.

164. Ross Sneyd, AP, *Clergy Members Air Views on Civil Unions for Senate*, RUTLAND HERALD, March 30, 2000 (quoting Vermont Bishop Kenneth Angell).

165. Adam Lisberg and Nancy Remsen, *Same-Sex Opponents Rally*, BURLINGTON FREE PRESS, April 7, 2000.

166. Ross Sneyd, AP, *March Against Civil Unions*, VALLEY NEWS, April 7, 2000 (quoting Rev. Fred Barker).

167. *Id.* (quoting Rev. Fred Barker).

168. Tracy Schmaler, *Civil Union Foes Hold Capital Rally*, Rutland Herald, April 7, 2000 [hereinafter Schmaler, *Civil Union Foes Hold*].

169. *Id.* (quoting Alan Keyes).

170. Sneyd, *March Against, supra* note 166 (quoting Alan Keyes).

171. *Id.*

172. Jack Hoffman, *Keyes' Visit Could Define GOP Stance on Civil Unions,* RUT-LAND HERALD, April 9, 2000.

173. *Id.*

174. Letter to the Editor, HERALD OF RANDOLPH, April 13, 2000.

175. Schmaler, *Civil Union Foes Hold, supra* note 168 (quoting Randall Terry).

176. Photograph accompanying Lisberg and Remsen, *Same-Sex Opponents Rally, supra* note 165.

177. Lisberg and Remsen, *Same-Sex Opponents Rally, supra* note 165.

178. *Id.*

179. Photo Accompanying Schmaler, *Civil Union Foes, supra* note 168.

180. Photo and Caption, BURLINGTON FREE PRESS, April 9, 2000.

181. *Id.*

182. Jim Kenyon, *Legislators Apparently Sticking with Votes,* VALLEY NEWS, April 23, 2000 (quoting the anonymous, handwritten note).

183. AP, *Legislators Forgo License Plates, Citing Insults over Civil Union Bill,* BURLINGTON FREE PRESS, April 16, 2000 [hereinafter AP, *Legislators Forgo*].

184. *Id.*

185. *Id.* (quoting Rep. Michael Flaherty).

186. *Id.*

187. Carey Goldberg, *Vermont Senate Votes for Gay Civil Unions,* N.Y. TIMES, April 20, 2000.

188. *Id.* (quoting House Sergeant-at-Arms Kermit Spaulding).

189. *Id.*; AP, *Legislators Forgo, supra* note 183.

190. *Id.*

191. *Id.* (quoting Rep. Hank Gretowski).

192. Kenyon, *Legislators Apparently Sticking with Votes, supra* note 182.

193. *Id.* (quoting a note threatening Rep. Marilyn Rivero).

194. Editorial, *Separate but Equal?,* NEW REPUBLIC, Jan. 10, 2000.

195. Ross Sneyd, *Senate Panel Is Close to House on Civil Unions,* VALLEY NEWS, April 11, 2000.

196. *Id.*

197. Nancy Remsen, *Residency Union Rule Considered,* BURLINGTON FREE PRESS, April 11, 2000 [hereinafter Remsen, *Residency Union Rule*].

198. Jack Hoffman, *Senate Follows House Approach,* RUTLAND HERALD, April 11, 2000 [hereinafter Hoffman, *Senate Follows*].

199. Remsen, *Residency Union Rule, supra* note 197 (quoting Beth Robinson).

200. Hoffman, *Senate Follows, supra* note 198.

201. *Id.*

202. *Id.* (quoting Beth Robinson).

203. Remsen, *Residency Union Rule, supra* note 197 (quoting Jerry Smiley).

204. Jack Hoffman, *Senate Panel Sends Constitutional Amendment to Floor,* RUTLAND HERALD, April 12, 2000 [hereinafter Hoffman, *Senate Panel Sends*].

205. *Id.*
206. *Id.* (quoting the Illuzzi amendment).
207. Ross Sneyd, AP, *Amendment Would Nullify Same-Sex Ruling,* VALLEY NEWS, April 12, 2000.
208. *Id.* (quoting Sen. John Bloomer).
209. Adam Lisberg, *Senate Will Get Chance to Debate Gay-Marriage Ban,* BURLINGTON FREE PRESS, April 12, 2000 (quoting Senate President Pro Tem Peter Shumlin).
210. Hoffman, *Senate Panel Sends, supra* note 204.
211. *Id.*
212. Helen Simon, *Civil Union Issue Brings Out 500 People in Franklin County,* BURLINGTON FREE PRESS, April 12, 2000.
213. *Id.*
214. *Id.*
215. *Id.* (quoting Town Clerk Gerry Longway).
216. *Id.*
217. *Id.*
218. *Id.* (quoting Rep. William Lippert).
219. *Id.*
220. *Id.*
221. Jack Hoffman, *Panel Advances Civil Unions Bill,* RUTLAND HERALD, April 14, 2000 [hereinafter Hoffman, *Panel Advances*].
222. Adam Lisberg, *Panel Clears Way for Civil Unions,* BURLINGTON FREE PRESS, April 14, 2000.
223. Ross Sneyd, AP, *Two Senate Committees Back Civil Unions Bill,* VALLEY NEWS, April 14, 2000.
224. *Id.* (quoting Sen. John Bloomer).
225. *Id.*
226. Hoffman, *Panel Advances, supra* note 221 (quoting William Shouldice).
227. Ross Sneyd, AP, *Senate Girds for Civil Unions Vote,* VALLEY NEWS, April 17, 2000.
228. *Id.*
229. *Id.*
230. Adam Lisberg, *OK Near on Civil Unions,* BURLINGTON FREE PRESS, April 15, 2000 [hereinafter Lisberg, *OK Near*].
231. Tracy Schmaler, *Tuesday Debate Looms,* RUTLAND HERALD, April 15, 2000 (quoting Sen. President Pro Tem Peter Shumlin) [hereinafter Schmaler, *Tuesday Debate*].
232. The calendar-thrower was Senator Gerald Morrissey.
233. *Id.*
234. *Id.* (quoting Sen. John Bloomer).
235. *Id.*
236. *Id.*
237. Lisberg, *OK Near, supra* note 230.
238. *Id.*

239. *Id.*

240. *How Senators Will Vote,* BURLINGTON FREE PRESS, April 15, 2000.

241. *Id.*

242. Lisberg, *OK Near, supra* note 230. Recall that the final House vote on the bill was 76-69.

243. *Id.* (quoting Rep. George Schiavone). These comments were made at a Friday press conference. *See* Schmaler, *Tuesday Debate, supra* note 231.

244. Schmaler, *Tuesday Debate, supra* note 231.

245. *Id.* (quoting Senate President Pro Tem Peter Shumlin).

246. Ross Sneyd, AP, *Senators Prepare for Battle,* BURLINGTON FREE PRESS, April 17, 2000.

247. Ross Sneyd, *Senate Girds for Civil Union Vote,* VALLEY NEWS, April 17, 2000.

248. *Id.*

249. *Id.*

250. *Id.*

251. *Id.*

252. *Id.* (quoting Rep. Robert Starr).

253. *Id.*

254. *Id.* (quoting Sen Richard Sears).

255. *Id.* (quoting Rep. Robert Starr).

256. Ross Sneyd, AP, *Senate Expected to Pass Civil Unions,* RUTLAND HERALD, April 18, 2000.

257. *Id.* (quoting Sen. Peter Shumlin).

258. *Id.*

259. Tracy Schmaler, *Dwyer, Meub Air Views,* RUTLAND HERALD, April 18, 2000.

260. *Id.*

261. *Id.* (quoting William Meub).

262. I'm not sure if, in Vermont, "to demagogue" is properly used as a verb. Where I come from, it is—as in, "politician X sure is demagoging the race issue."

263. Advertisement, RUTLAND HERALD, April 17, 2000.

264. Advertisement, BURLINGTON FREE PRESS, April 11, 2000.

265. *Id.*

266. *Id.*

267. *Id.*

268. Nancy Remsen and Adam Lisberg, *Lawmakers Preserve Constitution,* BURLINGTON FREE PRESS, April 19, 2000 (quoting Sen. Julius Cannes) [hereinafter Remsen and Lisberg, *Lawmakers Preserve*].

269. Ross Sneyd, *Vermont Civil Unions Bill Passes First Senate Vote,* VALLEY NEWS, April 19, 2000 (quoting Sen. Julius Cannes) [hereinafter Sneyd, *Vermont Civil Unions Bill Passes*].

270. Remsen and Lisberg, *Lawmakers Preserve, supra* note 268 (quoting Sen. Julius Cannes).

271. *Id.*

272. *Id.* (quoting Sen. Vincent Illuzzi).

273. *Id.* (quoting Sen. Richard McCormack).

274. *Id.*

275. Jack Hoffman, *Senate Backs Civil Unions,* Rutland Herald, April 19, 2000 [hereinafter Hoffman, *Senate Backs*].

276. *Statehouse Quotes,* Burlington Free Press, April 19, 2000 (quoting Sen. John Crowley).

277. *Id.*

278. David Gram, AP, *Senate Unions Debate Brings Out a Crowd,* Valley News, April 19, 2000.

279. Elizabeth Mehren, LA Times, *Vermont Senate Approves Civil Unions Bill, Sends It to House,* Valley News, April 20, 2000 [hereinafter Mehren, *Vermont Senate*].

280. Sneyd, *Vermont Civil Unions Bill Passes, supra* note 269.

281. Hoffman, *Senate Backs, supra* note 275 (quoting Sen. John Bloomer).

282. Christopher Graff, AP, Commentary, *Senators Agonized over Civil Unions,* Valley News, April 23, 2000.

283. *Id.*

284. Jim Kenyon, *Senator Tempts Fate, Votes Conscience,* Valley News, April 19, 2000.

285. *Id.*

286. *Id.*

287. *Id.*

288. *Id.*

289. *Id.*

290. *Id.*

291. *Id.*

292. *Id.*

293. *Id.*

294. *Id.* (quoting Sen. Richard Sears).

295. Letter from Sen. Elizabeth Ready to Pamela Gatos and Pete Peiffer, April 19, 2000 (copy on file with author). I am grateful to Pamela Gatos for sharing this letter with me.

296. Jack Hoffman, *Senate Backs, supra* note 275 (quoting a statement of Bishop Kenneth Angell).

297. *Id.* (quoting statement of Bishop Kenneth Angell).

298. Adam Lisberg, *Civil Union Bill in Stretch-Run,* Burlington Free Press, April 20, 2000.

299. *Id.*

300. *Id.* (quoting Sen. Julius Canns).

301. *Id.* (quoting Sen. Richard Sears).

302. *Id.* (quoting Sen. Richard Sears).

303. Carey Goldberg, *Vermont Senate Votes for Gay Civil Unions,* N.Y. Times, April 20, 2000 (quoting Sen. Peter Shumlin) [hereinafter Goldberg, *Vermont Senate Votes*].

304. *Id.* (quoting Peter Shumlin).

305. Mehren, *Vermont Senate, supra* note 279.

306. Goldberg, *Vermont Senate Votes, supra* note 303.

307. Adam Lisberg, *Randall Terry Packs Up to Leave State*, BURLINGTON FREE PRESS, April 20, 2000 [hereinafter Lisberg, *Randall Terry Packs Up*].

308. Lisberg, *Civil Union Bill in Stretch Run, supra* note 298.

309. Tracy Schmaler, *Amendment Defeated, Eyes Turn Back to House*, RUTLAND HERALD, April 19, 2000.

310. *Id.* (quoting Rep. George Schiavone).

311. *Id.*

312. *Id.*

313. Nancy Remsen, *Civil Union Divisions Remain*, BURLINGTON FREE PRESS, April 21, 2000.

314. *Id.* (quoting Leigh Pfenning).

315. *Id.* (quoting Susan Senger).

316. *Id.* (quoting William Lippert).

317. *Id.* (quoting Helena Blair).

318. Postcard, received by the author on April 22, 2000 (postcard on file with author).

319. Letter to the Editor, RUTLAND HERALD, April 22, 2000.

320. *Id.*

321. *Id.*

322. *Id.*

323. *Id.*

324. *Id.*

325. Letter to the Editor, BURLINGTON FREE PRESS, April 23, 2000.

326. Letter to the Editor, RUTLAND HERALD, April 23, 2000.

327. *Id.*

328. *Id.*

329. *Id.*

330. *Id.*

331. Kenyon, *Legislators Apparently Sticking with Votes, supra* note 182.

332. *Id.*

333. *Id.* (quoting TIP e-mail) (parenthetical in original news story).

334. *Id.*

335. *Id.* (quoting Rep. Bill MacKinnon).

336. Ross Sneyd, AP, *Civil Unions Head Toward House Vote*, BURLINGTON FREE PRESS, April 24, 2000.

337. *Id.*

338. *E.g.*, Advertisement, RUTLAND HERALD, April 24, 2000.

339. *Id.*

340. Adam Lisberg, *Civil Unions Bill Goes to Dean*, BURLINGTON FREE PRESS, April 26, 2000 (quoting Rep. Henry Gray).

341. Adam Lisberg, *House Expected to Make History Today*, BURLINGTON FREE PRESS, April 25, 2000 (quoting David Rice).

342. *Id.*

343. *Id.* (quoting House Speaker Michael Obuchowski).

344. Advertisement, Burlington Free Press, April 25, 2000.

345. Jim Kenyon, *It's Still Sinking In*, Valley News, April 26, 2000.

346. Lisberg, *Civil Union Bill Goes to Dean, supra* note 340.

347. Jack Hoffman, *Civil Unions Approved*, Rutland Herald, April 26, 2000 (quoting Rep. George Allard).

348. Lisberg, *Civil Union Bill Goes to Dean, supra* note 340 (quoting Rep. Nancy Sheltra).

349. Carey Goldberg, *Vermont Gives Final Approval to Same-Sex Unions*, N.Y. Times, April 26, 2000 [hereinafter Goldberg, *Vermont Gives*].

350. Kenyon, *It's Still Sinking In, supra* note 345 (quoting Rep. Neil Randall).

351. Brian McQuarrie, *Vermont House Approves Bill Allowing Same-Sex Unions*, Boston Globe, April 26, 2000 (quoting Rep. Neil Randall).

352. Goldberg, *Vermont Gives, supra* note 349 (quoting Rep. George Schiavone).

353. *Id.* (quoting Rep. George Schiavone).

354. *Id.* (quoting Rep. Henry Gray).

355. *Id.* (quoting bumper stickers).

356. Hoffman, *Civil Unions Approved, supra* note 347.

357. Goldberg, *Vermont Gives, supra* note 349 (quoting Rep. Bill Lippert).

358. *Id.* (quoting Rep. Bill Lippert).

359. Ross Sneyd, AP, *Vermont in the Forefront*, Valley News, April 26, 200 (quoting Rep. Bill Lippert).

360. Fax dated April 5, 2000 (copy on file with author).

361. Lisberg, *Civil Union Bill Goes to Dean, supra* note 340.

362. Hoffman, *Civil Unions Approved, supra* 347.

363. *Id.*

364. Carey Goldberg, *Vermont Gives Final Approval to Same Sex Unions*, N.Y. Times, April 26, 2000 (quoting Stacy Jolles, speaking to Nina Beck).

365. Adam Lisberg, *Dean Signs Civil Unions into Law*, Burlington Free Press, April 27, 2000.

366. *Id.*

367. *Id.*

368. Ross Sneyd, AP, *Privately, Governor Signs Civil Unions Legislation*, Valley News, April 27, 2000.

369. *Id.*

370. *Id.* (quoting Governor Howard Dean).

371. *Id.*

372. Sandi Switzer, *Civil Union Vote Spurs Challenge*, Rutland Herald, March 22, 2000.

373. *Id.*

374. *Id.* (quoting Ronald Boucher).

375. *Id.* (quoting Ronald Boucher).

376. Lisberg, *Randall Terry Packs Up, supra* note 307.

377. Memorandum From Pamela Gatos and Brook Hopkins to Michael Mello, May 21, 2000 (original on file with author).

378. Frederick Bever, *Foes of Civil Unions Contact Town Clerks*, RUTLAND HERALD, May 27, 2000.

379. *Id.*

380. *Id.*

381. *Id.* (quoting Nancy Sheltra letter)

382. *Id.*

383. Editorial, *Sheltra's Bludgeon*, RUTLAND HERALD, May 28, 2000.

384. Alex Leary, *Tunbridge Town Clerk Quitting over Civil Unions Law*, VALLEY NEWS, June 15, 2000.

385. *Id.*

386. Heather Stephenson, Topsham Clerk Against Civil Unions, RUTLAND HERALD, June 25, 2000 (quoting town clerk).

387. *Id.*

388. *Id.*

389. David Gram, AP, *Civil Unions Foes Sue over Bet Pool*, VALLEY NEWS, June 2, 2000.

390. *Id.*

391. *Id.* (quoting the lawsuit)

392. David Gram, AP, *Judge Asked to Block Unions*, VALLEY NEWS, June 24, 2000.

393. Editorial, *Uncivil Action*, VALLEY NEWS, June 7, 2000.

394. *Id.* (quoting Rep. Ann Seibert.

395. David Gram, *Judge Asked to Block Unions*, RUTLAND HERALD, June 24, 2000.

396. Ross Sneyd, AP, *Judge Rejects Bid to Block Civil Unions*, RUTLAND HERALD, June 27, 2000.

397. *Id.* (quoting trial court's order denying injunction relief).

398. Ross Sneyd, AP, *Civil Union Opponents Renew Legal Maneuvers*, RUTLAND HERALD, June 28, 2000.

399. *Id.* (quoting counsel for plaintiffs).

400. Ross Sneyd, *Judge Refuses to Block Start of Civil Unions*, VALLEY NEWS, July 1, 2000.

401. Susan Smallheer, *First Couple Joined in Civil Union*, RUTLAND HERALD, July 1, 2000.

402. *Id.*

403. Memorandum from Ted Sweet to Michael Mello, July 14, 2000 (copy on file with author).

404. *Id.*

405. *Id.*

406. *Id.*

407. *Id.*

408. *Id.*

409. Carey Goldberg, *Vermonters Are Caught Up in a Civil War over Civil Unions*, N.Y. TIMES, Nov. 2, 2000.

410. Carey Goldberg, *Gay and Lesbian Couples Head for Vermont to Make It Legal, but How Legal Is It?*, N.Y. Times, July 23, 2000.

411. Ralph Lewis, *Honeymoon in Vermont*, Boston Globe, July 14, 2000.

412. E.g., Editorial, *A Slogan's Fallacy*, Rutland Herald, Aug. 2, 2000; David Smith, *Signs of These Times Defaced*, Rutland Herald, July 29, 2000; Editorial, *Take Back Vermont*, Valley News, Aug. 8, 2000.

413. Steve Nelson, *No One Has Taken Vermont and No One Needs to Take It Back*, Valley News, July 30, 2000.

414. *Id.* (capitalization in original).

415. AP, *Take Back Vermont—or Syrup*, Valley News, Oct. 6, 2000.

416. Frederick Bever, *Tourists in Vermont on the "Take,"* Rutland Herald, Oct. 5, 2000.

417. Ross Sneyd, AP, *Heated Campaign Sparks Uncivil Behavior*, Valley News, Oct. 29, 2000.

418. *Id.*

419. *Id.*

420. *Id.*

421. I obtained this information from my confidential sources. It remains in my files.

422. *Id.*

423. I obtained this information from my confidential sources. It remains in my files.

424. *Id.*

425. *Id.*

426. *Id.*

427. Alexis Jetter, *Students Feel the Nasty Edge of Take Back Vermont Movement*, Valley News, Oct. 17, 2000.

428. Jack Hoffman, *Dwyer: Lawmakers Moving Too Fast on Same-Sex Legislation*, Times Argus (Barre and Montpelier, VT), March 14, 2000.

429. *Id.* (quoting Ruth Dwyer).

430. M.D. Drysdale, *GOP Reps Thrashed for Their "Yes" Votes*, Herald of Randolph, March 23, 2000 (quoting Rep. Richard Mallary).

431. Tracy Schmaler, *Dwyer, Meub Attack Administration*, Rutland Herald, March 28, 2000.

432. *Id.*

433. *Id.*

434. *Id.* (quoting Ruth Dwyer).

435. *Id.*

436. *Id.*

437. *Id.* (quoting William Meub).

438. *Id.*

439. Frederick Bever, *Civil Union Tack Irks Some in GOP*, Rutland Herald, May 4, 2000.

440. *Id.* (quoting fundraising letter of GOP Chairman Patrick Garahan) (exclamation point and capitalization in original).

441. *Id.* (quoting Patrick Garahan).

442. AP, *Dwyer: NEA Promotes Homosexual Agenda,* VALLEY NEWS, August 18, 2000 (quoting Ruth Dwyer).

443. *Id.; Id.* (quoting Ruth Dwyer).

444. Editorial, *Dwyer's Agenda,* VALLEY NEWS, Aug. 22, 2000; Editorial, *Exploiting Hate,* RUTLAND HERALD, Aug. 22, 2000.

445. Tracy Schmaler, *Valsangiacomo Leads Defectors to Dwyer,* RUTLAND HERALD, Oct. 12, 2000.

446. *Id.* (quoting Rep. Oreste Valsangiacomo).

447. *E.g.,* Ross Sneyd, AP, *Vermont Gubernatorial Debate Is Dominated by Civil Unions Issue,* VALLEY NEWS, Sept. 25, 2000.

448. VALLEY NEWS, Sept. 23, 2000.

449. VALLEY NEWS, Aug. 25, 2000.

450. VALLEY NEWS, Aug. 30, 2000.

451. VALLEY NEWS, Sept. 10, 2000.

452. VALLEY NEWS, Oct. 2, 2000.

453. RUTLAND HERALD, Oct. 6, 2000.

454. VALLEY NEWS, Oct. 8, 2000.

455. RUTLAND HERALD, Oct. 20, 2000.

456. VALLEY NEWS, Oct. 20, 2000.

457. VALLEY NEWS, Nov. 1, 2000.

458. *Vermont Law on Gay Rights Proves a Factor in Primaries,* N.Y. TIMES, Sept. 14, 2000.

459. *Id.*

460. Christopher Graff, *Election All about Civil Unions,* RUTLAND HERALD, Sept. 17, 2000; Ross Sneyd, *Civil Unions Resonating in Primary,* RUTLAND HERALD, Sept. 7, 2000.

461. Editorial, *A Call for Civility,* RUTLAND HERALD, Sept. 17, 2000; Cary Goldberg, *Vermont Residents Split over Civil Unions Law,* N.Y. TIMES, Sept. 3, 2000.

462. Editorial, *A Call for Civility,* RUTLAND HERALD, Sept. 17, 2000.

463. Tracy Schmaler, *Valsangiacomo Leads Defectors to Dwyer,* RUTLAND HERALD, Oct. 12, 2000; Editorial, *Conspiracy Theories,* VALLEY NEWS, Oct. 15, 2000; Christopher Graff, Commentary, *Bizarre Theory an Insult to Dean and Amestoy,* RUTLAND HERALD, Oct. 15, 2000.

464. David Gram, AP, *Buchanan Assails Civil Unions,* VALLEY NEWS, Oct. 13, 2000.

465. David Ross and Heather Rider, *A Note from the Editors,* 25 VT. L. REV. 1, 2 (2000) [hereinafter Ross and Rider, *A Note*].

466. Jim Kenyon, *VT GOP Grabs Control of House,* VALLEY NEWS, Nov. 9, 2000.

467. Ross and Rider, *A Note, supra* note 465.

468. *Id.* at 2.

469. Frederick Bever, *GOP Controls VT House; Democrats Hold Senate,* RUTLAND HERALD, Nov. 9, 2000.

470. Tracy Schmaler, *State's Voter Turnout Close to 75%*, Rutland Herald, Nov. 15, 2000.

471. Ross Sneyd, AP, *Judge Thwarts Anti–Civil Unions Suit by Citizens, Lawmakers, and Clerks*, Valley News, Nov. 11, 2000.

472. *Id.*

473. Ross Sneyd, AP, *Vt. Justices Uphold Civil Unions*, Valley News, Jan. 4, 2002; Ross Sneyd, AP, *Court Hears Challenge to Civil Unions Law*, Rutland Herald, Nov. 30, 2001.

474. Ross Sneyd, AP, *Republicans in House Take Aim at Civil Unions*, Valley News, May 23, 2001.

475. Ross Sneyd, AP, *VT House Votes Civil Unions Repeal*, Valley News, May 24, 2001; Tracy Schmaler, *House Backs Repeal of Civil Unions*, Rutland Herald, May 24, 2001; Ross Sneyd, AP, *House Passes Reciprocal Partnerships Measure*, Valley News, May 25, 2001; Tracy Schmaler, *GOP-Controlled House Passes Reciprocal Partnerships Bill*, Rutland Herald, May 25, 2001; Editorial, *Making Arrangements*, Valley News, May 26, 2001; Editorials, *GOP and Civil Unions*, Rutland Herald, May 20, 2001.

476. Tracy Schmaler, *Dean Decries Bid to Repeal Civil Unions*, Rutland Herald, May 17, 2001.

477. Christopher Graff, AP, *2001 Legislature Defined the Issue*, Rutland Herald, June 17, 2001.

478. *Id.*

479. Alex Hanson, *Civil Unions Stay; Foes' Last Hurrah?*, Valley News, May 29, 2001 (quoting Rep. Michael Kainen).

480. *Id.*

481. Wilson Ring, AP, *Practical, Emotional Changes in Vermont*, Rutland Herald, Dec. 23, 2001.

482. For my conflicting thoughts on the legal issues raised by September 11, *see, e.g.*, Michael Mello, Keynote Address, *Are We All "Undocumented Aliens" Now?: Collateral Damage of the National Security State*, Symposium, *Homeland Security and the Constitution*, Middlebury College, Middlebury, Vermont, April 3–6, 2003; Michael Mello, *Friendly Fire: Privacy vs. Security After September 11*, 38 Crim. L. Bull. 367 (2002); Michael Mello, *The Law at War*, Jonathon B. Chase Student Center, Vermont Law School, Sept. 11, 2002; Michael Mello, Statement to Vermont Legislature on Senate Bill 298, a State Anti-terrorism Bill (March 2002) (copy available from Vermont ACLU); Michael Mello, *Dr. Martin Luther King, Jr. Was Right: Anti-Zionism Is (Perhaps Unconscious and Unintentional) Anti-Semitism*, Chase Student Center, Vermont Law School, Jan. 30, 2003; *but see* Michael Mello, Statement and Testimony on Joint House Resolution 9: A Bill Urging the Federal Government to Scale Back the USA PATRIOT ACT, Government Affairs Committee, House of Representatives, Vermont General Assembly, The Capitol, Montpelier, Vermont (April 22, 2003); Michael Mello, *The Ultimate Role-Play: John Ashcroft Chats with the ACLU about the USA PATRIOT ACT, PATRIOT ACT II, Military Commissions, Monitoring Certain Attorney/Client Communications*,

and Nearly Everything Else, Windjammer Conference Center, South Burlington, Vermont, June 19, 2003.

483. *See generally, e.g.,* Evelyn Nievens, *Passenger on Jet: Gay Hero or Hero Who Was Gay?,* N.Y. Times, Jan. 16, 2002; Margarie Mason, *Passenger Who Battled Terrorists Hailed as Gay Hero,* Rutland Herald, Oct. 23, 2001.

484. Norman Ornstein, *Planning for Disaster,* National L.J. July 7, 2003.

485. *Id.*

486. *Id.*

487. *Id.*

488. *Id.*

489. Elisabeth Bumiller, *The Most Unlikely Story behind a Gay Rights Victory,* N.Y. Times, June 22, 2003.

490. *Id.*

491. *Perspectives,* Newsweek, Sept. 29, 2001 (quoting Rev. Jerry Falwell).

492. Lawrence v. Texas, ___ U.S. ___, 71 U.S.L.W. 4574 (June 26, 2003).

493. *E.g.,* AP, *Democrats Question Bush Credibility,* Rutland Herald, July 11, 2003; Anne Kornblut, *Democrats Rip Bush,* Boston Globe, July 11, 2003.

494. David Mace, *Civil Unions Are Low-Key Issue for This Election,* Valley News, Oct. 8, 2002.

495. *E.g.,* Christopher Graff, *Vt. Governor's Race: Calm after the Storm,* Valley News, Oct. 20, 2002; Alex Hanson, *Calm Rules Vermont Races,* Valley News, Nov. 2, 2002.

496. Ross Sneyd, *Election Assures Survival of Civil Union Law,* Valley News, Nov. 24, 2002.

497. *Id.*

498. David Gram, AP, *Douglas Urges Supreme Court Restraint,* Valley News, July 4, 2003.

499. *E.g.,* David Mace, *Comments on Court Have Welch Concerned,* Rutland Herald, July 9, 2003; Editorial, *Courage to Change,* Rutland Herald, July 8, 2003.

500. *E.g.,* Tracy Schmaler, *Curriculum Issue Pushed by Sheltra,* Rutland Herald, Jan. 19, 2002.

501. Editorial, *Affirmative in Vermont,* Rutland Herald, March 14, 2003.

502. Christopher Graff, *A Quiet Anniversary,* Rutland Herald, April 27, 2003.

503. *See* William Eskridge, Equality Practice: Civil Unions and the Future of Gay Rights 148–49 (2002).

Chapter 5

1. J.W. Peltason, 58 Lonely Men 104 (1961).

2. William Eskridge, Equality Practice: Civil Unions and the Future of Gay Rights 148–49 (2002) [hereinafter Eskridge, Civil Unions] at 133–39.

3. *Id.* at 139–140.

4. Greg Johnson, *Vermont Civil Unions: A Success Story*, in MARRIAGE AND SAME-SEX UNIONS: A DEBATE 291–92 (Lynn Wardle, et al, eds. 2003).

5. Michael Mello, *Dead Reckoning: The Duty of Scholarship*, 35 CRIM. L. BULL. 478 (Sept./Oct. 1999).

6. *E.g.*, WILLIAM ESKRIDGE, THE CASE FOR SAME-SEX MARRIAGE 219 n.4 (1996) [hereinafter ESKRIDGE, THE CASE].

7. OLIVER WENDELL HOLMES, THE COMMON LAW 1 (1881).

8. Editorial, *Polling the Public*, RUTLAND HERALD, March 5, 2000 (emphasis added).

9. *E.g.*, Michelle Cummings, President, Take It To The People, *Opposing Same-Sex Marriage Not Bigotry*, RUTLAND HERALD, March 26, 2000.

10. Sandy Cooch, *Legislators Explain Their Votes*, HERALD OF RANDOLPH, March 23, 2000 (quoting Rep. Phillip Winters).

11. Jack Hoffman, *Senate Backs Civil Unions*, RUTLAND HERALD, April 19, 2000.

12. "Until the early 1970s, the [American Psychiatric Association] regarded homosexuality as a pathology. After heavy lobbying from gay rights activists, including a psychiatrist who was a member of the APA and who spoke at the 1972 annual meeting, his face concealed by a mask to preserve his anonymity, the board of trustees voted to remove homosexuality from the [Diagnostic and Statistical Manual IV]. The membership followed suit in 1974. (One bemused observed labeled it 'the single greatest cure in the history of psychiatry.')" Emily Eakin, *Bigotry as Mental Illness, or Just Another Norm*, N.Y. TIMES, Jan. 15, 2000.

As recently as 1968, the APA's DSM II labeled homosexuality (and oral sex, it appears) as a mental illness called "Sexual Deviation." The DSM II defined "Sexual Deviation" in this way: "This category is for individuals whose sexual interests are directed primarily towards objects other than people of the opposite sex, toward sexual acts not usually associated with coitus. . . ." *See* Word for Word, *Mental Disorders Defining the Line between Behavior That's Vexing and Certifiable*, N.Y. TIMES, Dec. 19, 1999.

13. For a thoughtful examination of this issue, see Heather Stephenson, *Why Gay? Science Can Offer Only Clues*, RUTLAND HERALD, March 12, 2000.

14. *Id.*

15. Alex Hanson, *Issue Won't Go on Windsor Ballot*, VALLEY NEWS, Feb. 2, 2000 (quoting Michael Quinn).

16. *Id.*

17. For example, the president of Take It To The People explained: "When homosexuals are told they cannot marry someone of the same gender, they are not being discriminated against. The marriage law applies equally to them and to heterosexuals who must abide by the same (and other reasonable) restrictions." Michelle Cummings, President of Take It To The People, *Opposing Same-Sex Marriage Not Bigotry*, RUTLAND HERALD, March 26, 2000.

Similarly, Republican gubernatorial candidate Ruth Dwyer reasoned: " 'I don't consider it a civil rights issue,' Dwyer said. 'Civil rights, as far as I'm concerned, have already been granted to just about every group out there. So civil rights have been addressed. Marriage is an institution, a union between a man and a woman, has been for thousands of years. *Every man and woman in this state has equal rights to marry"* a member of the opposite sex. *See* Jack Hoffman, *Dwyer: Lawmakers Moving Too Fast on Same-Sex Legislation,* Times Argus (Barre and Montpelier, VT), March 14, 2000 (quoting Ruth Dwyer) (emphasis added).

18. Editorial, *Dwyer's World,* Valley News, March 17, 2000.

19. The Supreme Court came close to recognizing this reality in *Lawrence v. Texas,* ___ U.S. ___, 71 U.S.L.W. 4574 (June 26, 2003).

20. Martin Luther King, Jr. *Letter From Birmingham City Jail* (1963) in A Testament of Hope: The Essential Writings of martin Luther King, Jr. (James Washington ed. 1986) at 294.

21. Mark Miller, *To Be Gay—And Mormon,* Newsweek, May 8, 2000 at 38–39.

22. *Id.*

23. *Id.*

24. *Id.*

25. *Id.*

26. *Id.*

27. *Id.*

28. *Id.*

29. *Id.*

30. *Id.*

31. Jack Hoffman, *Gay Marriage Lawyer Makes Emotional Plea,* Rutland Herald, Feb. 5, 2000 [hereinafter Hoffman, *Gay Marriage Lawyer*].

32. *Id.*

33. Interview with Vermont Law School Professor James May, Shari's Headquarters, South Royalton, Vermont, May 2003.

34. William Safire, *The Bedroom Door,* N.Y. Times, June 30, 2003.

35. For an outstanding analysis argument that civil unions are analogous to the separate-but-equal laws in the race context, see Barbara Cox, *But Why Not Marriage?,* 25 Vt. L. Rev. 113, 123–146 (2000).

36. Editorial, *A Vermont Court Speaks,* Boston Globe, Dec. 21, 1999.

37. *Id.*

38. Jeff Jacoby, *The Threat from Gay Marriage,* Boston Globe, July 3, 2003.

39. Steve Swayne, *Separate State-Sanctioned Unions from Religious Marriages,* Valley News, June 21, 2003.

40. Diane Derby, *Randall Terry Is Told to "Go Home,"* Rutland Herald, Feb. 4, 2000.

41. *Id.*

42. In my youth, I committed an abomination or two myself. I lived with a woman who I wasn't married to when I was in college—"living in sin" was what it was called then—and we made love. Both the cohabitation and the unmarried lovemaking were illegal under Virginia law at the time (they may well still be illegal, for all I know), and unmarried cohabitation remains illegal in some states today, New Mexico and Arizona, for instance. *See* Jim Yardley, *Unmarried and Living Together, Till the Sheriff Do Us Part,* N.Y. Times, March 25, 2000.

43. In one of life's delicious little ironies, while Vermont's debate over "traditional [read heterosexual] marriage" was raging—and while the three Republican Presidential candidates were condemning same-sex marriage—the Fox television network aired a wildly popular TV show called *Who Wants to Marry a Millionaire?* On the show, a millionaire bachelor selected (based on her appearance and choice of wedding gown) a woman he had never previously met and immediately married her on national TV. The whole thing was a ratings bonanza (23 million viewers):

> In a live broadcast from Las Vegas, a real estate developer selected an instant bride from among 50 contestants, who vied for his lifetime commitment via swimsuit displays and perfunctory interviews. No pretense of a "talent" competition was thought necessary.
>
> When appalled viewers wondered why this wasn't prostitution, Nevada Deputy District Attorney J. Charles Thompson explained, "It's often the case that people have sex and then get married, but you can do it the other way. We don't mind." His office had higher enforcement priorities. And it should.
>
> Fox's blushing bride emerged from her self-confessed "error of judgment" with a quick annulment and prizes worth more than $100,000.
>
> Deborah Rhode, *Fox Ignored Real Sex Trade,* NAT'L L.J., March 13, 2000.

The fierce critics of same-sex marriage were relatively silent, presumably because this counted as "traditional marriage," because it was heterosexual.

44. Letter to the Editor, BURLINGTON FREE PRESS, April 16, 2000.

45. *Id.*

46. *Id.*

47. Anna Quindlen, *The Right to Be Ordinary,* NEWSWEEK, Sept. 11, 2000.

48. *Id.*

49. *Id.*

50. Leslie Staudinger, *VLS Community Participates in Same-Sex Marriage Debate,* LOQUITUR (spring 2000) (emphasis added). Senator Ptashnick made this statement at a panel discussion at Vermont Law School on February 8, 2000.

51. Jack Hoffman, *Panel Tackles Marriage Issue,* RUTLAND HERALD, Jan. 12, 2000.

52. Baker v. State, 744 A.2d 864 (Vt.1999).

53. Ross Sneyd, AP, *Domestic Partnership Supported,* VALLEY NEWS, Feb. 10, 2000.

54. Jack Hoffman, *Panel Backs Domestic Partnership,* RUTLAND HERALD, Feb. 10, 2000 (quoting Gov. Howard Dean).

55. Tammerlin Drummond, *A Win for Gays,* TIME, March 27, 2000.

56. *Id.*

57. Jack Hoffman, *Caution Urged on Amendment,* RUTLAND HERALD, March 24, 2000.

58. *Id.*

59. Adam Lisberg, *Two Senators on Panel Seek Gay-Marriage Ban*, BURLINGTON FREE PRESS, March 22, 2000 (quoting Sen. Vincent Illuzzi).

60. Sandy Cooch, *Legislators Explain Their Votes*, The Herald of Randolph, March 23, 2000 (quoting Rep. Marion Milne).

61. *Id.* (quoting Rep. Carolyn Kehler).

62. Ross Sneyd, *Vermont House Votes in Favor of Civil Unions*, VALLEY NEWS, March 16, 2000.

63. Nancy Remsen and Adam Lisberg, *Senate Backs Civil Unions*, BURLINGTON FREE PRESS, April 19, 2000 (quoting Sen. Julius Canns and citing Sen. Judiciary Committee Chairman Richard Sears).

64. *Id.*

65. Ross Sneyd, AP, *Ad Campaign Sparks Criticism by Speaker*, RUTLAND HERALD, March 22, 2000.

66. AP, *House Speaker Angry over "Gay Marriage" Advertisements*, VALLEY NEWS, March 22, 2000.

67. *Id.*

68. *Id.* (quoting House Speaker Michael Obuchowski).

69. Editorial, *Misinformation Campaign*, RUTLAND HERALD, March 26, 2000.

70. *Id.*

71. *Id.*

72. Vermont Press Bureau, *Legislators Angry About Ad by Terry*, RUTLAND HERALD, April 6, 2000.

73. Advertisement, RUTLAND HERALD (citing Rep. Cathy Voyer).

74. Vermont Press Bureau, *supra* note 72.

75. Governor Howard Dean, *Rise above Rancor When Debating Equal Rights for Gays*, BURLINGTON FREE PRESS, March 29, 2000.

76. *Id.*

77. Sandy Cooch, *Legislators Explain Their Votes*, HERALD OF RANDOLPH, March 23, 2000 (quoting Rep. Philip Angell) [hereinafter Cooch, *Legislators Explain*].

78. *Id.* (citing Rep. Henry Holmes).

79. Cooch, *Legislators Explain*, *supra* note 77 (quoting Rep. William Mackinnon).

80. Jim Kenyon, *Civil Union Debate: The Winners and Losers*, VALLEY NEWS, March 19, 2000.

81. *Id.*

82. *Id.*

83. *Id.*

84. Steve Nelson, *Mackinnon Shouldn't Be Bashed for Sticking to Principle*, VALLEY NEWS, March 26, 2000.

85. *E.g.*, Letter to the Editor, VALLEY NEWS, March 26, 2000.

86. Brown v. Board of Education, 347 U.S. 483 (1954).

87. Plessy v Ferguson, 163 U.S. at 559.

88. *Id.*

89. Anthony Lewis, *"Imposing on Them a Badge of Inferiority,"* N.Y. TIMES, Jan. 22, 2000.

90. Brown v. Board of Education, 347 U.S. 483 (1954).

91. Plessy v Ferguson, 163 U.S. at 559.

92. Brown v. Board of Education, 347 U.S. 483 (1954).

93. Editorial, *Separate-but-Equal*, New Republic, January 2000.

94. *See generally*, Taylor Branch, Parting the Waters (1988). Rosa Parks was arrested on December 1, 1955. *Id.* at 128. Although the precise moment "marking the origins of the Montgomery bus boycott would become hotly contested ground to future generations of civil rights historians," *id.* at 132 n.*, the first moves to organize the boycott began shortly after Ms. Parks's arrest.

95. Jack Bass, Taming the Storm 111 (1993).

96. *Id.*

97. *Id.*

98. Richard Kluger, Simple Justice 750 (1975).

99. *Id.*

100. *Id.*

101. *Id.*

102. *Id.* at 750–51.

103. *Id.* at 750.

104. *Id.*

105. *Brown* of course doesn't preclude things like separate-but-equal bathrooms for men and women—having separate washrooms does not imply inferiority. But separate marriage substitutes would indeed stamp same-sex couples with a badge of inferiority—in fact, that is the only reason for "civil unions."

106. Brent Staples wrote an eloquent op-ed piece in the *New York Times* on September 8, 1999, making the connection between the same-sex marriage issue of today and the civil rights struggles of yesterday:

> The civil rights movement had made spectacular gains in the courts—including *Brown v. Board of Education*—before Rosa Parks galvanized public opinion in a way that lawsuits had not. Ms. Parks became an emblematic figure when she was arrested in Montgomery, Ala., for refusing to sit in the "colored only" section of a bus. The sight of this dignified woman being denied the simplest courtesy because she was black crystallized the dehumanizing nature of segregation and rallied people against it.

> Racism began to wane as white Americans were introduced to members of the black minority whom they could identify as "just like us." A similar introduction is underway for gay Americans, but the realization that they are "just like us" has yet to sink in. When it finally does, the important transitional figures will include State Representative Steve May, a 27-year-old Republican from Arizona.

> Mr. May is a solid conservative who supports issues like vouchers and charter schools. He was raised a Mormon and recalls himself as the kid who "had to go out and bring in the wayward souls." He is also a former

active-duty soldier and an Army reservist, whose record shows that he could have moved up swiftly and been given a command.

But Mr. May is about to be hounded out of the Reserve for publicly admitting that he loves and shares his life with another man. This acknowledgment came last winter during a heated exchange in the Arizona Legislature over a bill that would have barred counties from offering domestic-partner benefits, stripping them from gay couples who currently enjoy them.

Mr. May could have sat quietly, protecting his career. Instead he exposed the provision as bigoted and told the Arizona House: "It is an attack on my family, an attack on my freedom. . . . My gay tax dollars are the same as your straight tax dollars. . . . I'm not asking for the right to marry, but I'd like to ask this Legislature to leave my family alone."

When Rosa Parks declined to yield her seat on that bus, she was telling Alabama that she was not just a *colored* person, but a human being who deserved the respect and protection of the law. Mr. May's words in the Arizona House were similarly clarifying. Fearful of a backlash, gay politicians rarely mention their mates in public—and shy away from speaking of them in terms that might disturb even constituents who know that they are gay. But by framing his argument in the context of "the family," Mr. May disarmed his bigoted colleagues and took the debate on same-sex unions exactly where it needed to go.

When Mr. May's comments became public, the Army Reserve began an investigation that legal experts say will certainly end in discharge. Lieutenant May will then become a casualty of "don't ask, don't tell," which ended more than 1,100 military careers in 1998, on the grounds that homosexuals who reveal the fact are nor longer fit to serve.

This is a staggering loss at a time when the armed services are canvassing strip malls and lowering entrance requirements to find personnel. By the time this policy is abandoned, thousands of talented Americans will have been lost to a purge that will come to be recognized as contrary to the public good and morally wrong.

Republicans began the 1990s refusing campaign contributions from gay organizations and demonizing homosexuals for political gain. But in the race for 2000, the most prominent candidates are accepting the money and say that they would hire gay workers as long as they refrained from pressing "a gay agenda"—a code phrase for keeping quiet about issues of same-sex intimacy, up to and including marriage. The trouble with this approach is that legitimacy for same-sex unions is the heart of the matter. By denying that legitimacy, we declare gay love less valid than heterosexual love and gay people less human. We cut them off from the rituals of family and marriage that bind us together as a culture.

The legislator who wished to revoke benefits from same-sex partners in Arizona viewed those partnerships as culturally alien and morally illegitimate. The military establishment may force Mr. May out of the service—despite an exemplary record—because his family consists of two men who are indistinguishable from their neighbors, except that they sleep together.

This persecution finds a parallel in statutes that made it illegal for blacks and whites to get married up until 1967, when the Supreme Court declared the laws unconstitutional. The laws were based on the primitive belief that blacks and whites were set apart on the tree of life by God Himself. Interracial couples were initially seen as a threat to the social order and to the institution of marriage. Over time, the culture began to discard the filter of race, viewing the couples as "just like the rest of us." The same process will probably work out for same-sex couples—but only after an extended battle. When the matter is settled, historians will look back at people like Steve May, who declined to go quietly to the back of the American bus.

Brent Staples, *Why Same-Sex Marriage Is the Crucial Issue*, N.Y. Times, Sept. 8, 1999.

107. Jack Hoffman, *Panel Affirms Marriage Tradition*, Rutland Herald, March 1, 2000.

108. Adam Lisberg, *Panel OKs Marriage Substitute*, Burlington Free Press, March 2, 2000.

109. Diane Derby, *Dean Says Issue Is One of Conscience*, Rutland Herald, March 16, 2000.

110. *Id.* (quoting Governor Howard Dean).

111. Ross Sneyd, AP, *Dean to Lawmakers: Let Your Conscience Guide*, Valley News, March 15, 2000.

112. Jack Hoffman, *Panel Backs Domestic Partnership*, Rutland Herald, Feb. 10, 2000.

113. Eskridge, Civil Unions, *supra* note 2 at 136–37.

114. *Id.* at 137–38.

115. Jack Hoffman, *Partnership and Marriage Won't Ever Be Equal*, Rutland Herald, Jan. 16, 2000.

116. Editorial, *Our Common Humanity*, Valley News, Jan. 26, 1999.

The issues of "portability," full faith, and credit are worth a footnote. The possible lack of portability of Vermont same-sex marriages is not a reason not to recognize such marriages here. We are talking about the law of *Vermont*. I don't think we should resurrect *Plessy* in the twenty-first century because other states might be bigoted against gays.

And Vermont hasn't in the past. When much of the south outlawed interracial marriages, did Vermont law forbid interracial marriage in Vermont because such marriages might not be "portable"? Did Vermont enact a racist marriage law because of fears that racist states might not give full faith and credit—as the

Constitution requires them to give—to our nonracist marriage laws? Vermont did not, because Vermont says it's different. Now is the time to prove it.

117. The *Valley News* editorialized that "if the legislature believes that it is worth its time to make [an] extraordinary effort to create a parallel institution, would it not thereby concede that it is creating an inferior institution, not just a separate one?" *See* Editorial, *Our Common Humanity*, VALLEY NEWS, Dec. 26, 1999.

118. Eileen McNamara, *Marriage Lite Won't Cut It*, RUTLAND HERALD, Dec. 23, 1999.

119. *Id.*

120. Letter to the Editor, RUTLAND HERALD, March 9, 2000.

121. Lawrence v. Texas, ___ U.S. ___, 71 U.S.L.W. 4574 (June 26, 2003).

122. Loving v. Virginia, 388 U.S. 1 (1967).

123. *Id.*

124. *Id.*

125. *Id.* (quoting trial court).

126. *Id.*

127. MAY IT PLEASE THE COURT 282–83 (Peter Irons and Stephanie Guitton eds 1993) (quoting oral arguments in *Loving v. Virginia*).

128. *Id.* at 285.

129. *Id.*

130. Hoffman, *Gay Marriage Lawyer, supra* note 31.

131. Dennis O'Brien argued in a newspaper op-ed piece that the separate-but-equal principle of *Brown* is not apposite to the present debate because domestic partnerships are "not truly comparable to being made by law to attend a segregated school." Dennis O'Brien, *Let's Cool Rhetoric about Gay Marriage*, RUTLAND HERALD, Dec. 30, 1999. But, as the post-*Brown* cases make clear, *Brown's* rejection of separate-but-equal applied to the entire Jim Crow south, a south that segregated everything from water fountains to lunch counters; *Brown* did not only apply to schools.

Further, O'Brien suggests that because domestic partnerships would be a minor form of "segregation" (same-sex couples would not be segregated from housing, schools, jobs, legal benefits, etc.), the only damage to homosexuals may be "to some measure of self-esteem or social acceptance." This reasoning echoes the *Plessy v. Ferguson* Court's argument that any sense of inferiority African Americans may feel from being segregated on railroad cars was their own hypersensitivity.

But that was exactly the argument rejected in *Brown*: Legally *sanctioned* segregation is unlawful when it imposes badges of inferiority. That will be the unmistakable message of Vermont's rejection of same-sex marriage in favor of domestic partnerships.

O'Brien is incorrect that gays who feel that domestic partnerships are inferior simply have a self-esteem problem. The recent outpouring of homophobic sentiment suggests that gays are not paranoid—they do have real enemies in Vermont. More importantly, gays will feel inferior under a marriage substitute because *the law* will be telling them they *are* inferior: They can ride the marriage bus, but only if they sit in the back.

132. Ross Sneyd, *Who Gets to Marry?*, VALLEY NEWS, Nov. 19, 1998.

133. Ross Sneyd, AP, *From Vermont Justices, Many Questions*, VALLEY NEWS, Nov. 19, 1998.

134. Martin Luther King, Jr. *Letter From Birmingham City Jail* (1963) in A TESTAMENT OF HOPE: THE ESSENTIAL WRITINGS OF MARTIN LUTHER KING, JR. (James Washington ed. 1986) at 293.

135. Jack Hoffman, *Poll: Majority Say No to Same-Sex Benefits*, RUTLAND HERALD, Jan. 25, 2000.

136. JACK BASS, UNLIKELY HEROES 117 (1981).

137. *Id.*

138. *Id.* (emphasis in original).

139. *Id.*

140. *Id.* at 118.

141. Quoted in BASS, UNLIKELY HEROES, *supra* note 136 at 11.

142. Editorial, *Gay Rights Ping Pong?*, RUTLAND HERALD, Dec. 26, 1999 (quoting Vermont Governor Howard Dean.) "Later, Dean was chagrined to say that his lawyer had advised him that 'different but equal' was not a good way to describe the goals of a domestic partnership bill." *Id.*

143. KLUGER, *supra* note 98.

144. 23 USLW 2356–60 (April 19, 1955).

145. *Id.* at 3257.

146. ARGUMENT (Chelsea House Publishers 1969) 439.

147. *Id.* at 393.

148. *Id.* at 3526 and 3260.

149. ARGUMENT, *supra* note 146 at 394.

150. Gil Kujovich, *An Essay on the Passive Virtue of Baker v. State*, 25 VT. L. REV. 93 (2000).

151. CAROL POLSGROVE, DIVIDED MINDS (2001).

152. King, *Letter, supra* note 134 at 293 (emphasis added).

153. *Id.* at 296.

154. *Id.* at 296.

155. *Id.* at 296. Beth Robinson, one of the lawyers for the plaintiffs *in Baker*, read to the House Judiciary Committee this passage from Dr. King's letter. *See* Hoffman, *Gay Marriage Lawyer, supra* note 31. She also quoted another passage from King's letter:

I have almost reached the regrettable conclusion that the Negro's great stumbling block on the stride toward freedom is not the White Citizen's Counciler or the Ku Klux Klanner, but the white moderate who is more devoted to 'order' than to justice; who prefers a negative peace which is the absence of tension to a positive peace which is the presence of justice; who constantly says, "I agree with you in the goal you seek, but I can't agree with your methods of direct action," who paternalistically feels that he can set the timetable for another man's freedom; who lives by the myth of time and who constantly advises the Negro to wait until a "more convenient season."

156. Letter to the Editor, VALLEY NEWS, April 5, 2000.

157. Heather Stephenson, *Couples Cheer Decision: "There's No Stopping Us,"* RUTLAND HERALD, Dec. 21, 1999.

158. *Id.*

159. Brigham v. State, 166 Vt. 246 (1997).

160. *See generally* BASS, UNLIKELY HEROES, *supra* note 136.

161. *E.g.,* Editorial, *The Political Dimension,* RUTLAND HERALD, Feb. 4, 2000.

162. King, *Letter, supra* note 134 at 302.

163. The *Rutland Herald's* longtime publisher, Robert Mitchell, put it well in 1964: "Here in Vermont we have a certain sense of superiority because there is so little evident among us the racial prejudice that has brought bloodshed to other parts of the country. . . . The absence of overt race friction in Vermont is, of course, not due to any special virtue on our part, but rather to the fact that in most of our communities there are few if any Negro residents." THE BOB MITCHELL YEARS 109–110 (1993). Notwithstanding Vermont's whiteness, Mitchell and his newspaper were fighters against prejudice and bigotry. *Id.* at 106–131.

164. David Gram, *Report Cites Racism in Vermont Schools,* VALLEY NEWS, Feb. 6, 1999. Actually, Vermont is tied with Maine as the "whitest" state in the union. Diane Derby, *"Widespread" Racism Is Found in Vermont Schools,* RUTLAND HERALD, Feb. 6, 1999 [hereinafter Derby, *Widespread*].

165. Derby, *Widespread, supra.*

166. *See generally, e.g.,* Michael Mello, *Dr. Martin Luther King, Jr. Was Right: Anti-Zionism Is (Perhaps Unconscious and Unintentional) Anti-Semitism,* Chase Student Center, Vermont Law School, Jan. 30, 2003.

167. David Mace, *Group Seeking to End Police Bias Remaining Mum,* RUTLAND HERALD, July 9, 2003.

168. *Id.*

169. Derby, *Widespread, supra* note 164.

170. David Gram, AP, *Report Cites Racism in Vermont Schools,* VALLEY NEWS, Feb. 6, 1999 (quoting report) (emphasis added).

171. Derby, *Widespread, supra* note 164 (emphasis added).

172. Gram, *Report, supra* note 170.

173. *Id.*

174. Derby, *Widespread, supra* note 164.

175. *Id.*

176. *Id.*

177. *Id.*

178. *Id.*

179. *Id.*

180. Gram, *Report, supra* note 170.

181. Derby, *Widespread, supra* note 164.

182. Christopher Graff, Commentary, *Racism in Vermont Is a Subtle Matter,* RUTLAND HERALD, Jan. 17, 1999.

183. *Id.*

184. *Id.*

185. Letter to the Editor, RUTLAND HERALD, March 9, 2000. The specific threat to which the letter referred occurred years previously, when the writer was in college.

186. Yes, yes, I know that Pickett's charge was neither a charge nor done by Pickett's division alone, But the Pickett-Pettigrew-Trimble-advance-with-a-brief-charge-at-the-end doesn't have the same charm. Besides, I'm a Virginian, as was Pickett and every man serving under him at Gettysburg. And Pickett's troops—led by Armistead—were the only Confederates to pierce the Union's line that day, except as captives or as corpses.

187. New York Trust v. Eisner, 265 U.S. 345, 349 (1921) (quoted in John Witte, *The Tradition of Traditional Marriage,* in DEBATE, *supra* note 4 at 47).

188. Baker v. State, 744 A.2d 864 (Vt.1999).

189. Ross Sneyd, AP, *Gay Rights Suit Ended,* RUTLAND HERALD, May 10, 2000.

190. *Id.* (quoting Beth Robinson).

191. As a strategic matter, I was not at all sure that the gay community ought to have partied in the legislative process or supported *any* domestic partnership or civil unions bill. Under *Baker,* a comprehensive domestic partnership approach was the *minimum* that *might* pass constitutional muster. Thus, I wonder whether the gay community ought to have endorsed anything short of same-sex marriage. I saw no real downside here.

I did see a downside in the gay community's supporting legislation that is anything short of marriage. The downside was that it provided legislators, Governor Dean, and perhaps even a supreme court justice or two political cover in compromising for civil unions: These folks could point proudly to the second-class citizenship conferred by civil unions, and say, "See, even the gay leadership thinks domestic partnership is enough." With gay support behind a civil unions statute, the supreme court would have a tougher time voiding that statute in favor of requiring same-sex marriage.

How's this for a strategy: The gay community conscientiously abstains from participation in the legislative process and cedes the field to the haters. The legislature passes a second-rate domestic partnership bill (which it was likely to do regardless of whether or not the gay community participated in the legislative process), which Governor Dean happily signs into law (as opposed to a marriage bill, which Dean might well have vetoed, in the unlikely event that the legislature would ever pass such a bill). Then the law comes before the Vermont Supreme Court, which must pass on its constitutionality. If the new law is a shoddy enough example of separate but obviously unequal—and the haters and the governor all but guarantee that it would be—then the supreme court would have little difficulty striking it down, and, by then, there might be three votes on the court for same-sex *marriage.*

The foregoing was the Machiavellian game plan I articulated in the original February 8, 2000, version of this book. Beth Robinson, a lawyer for the same-sex couples in *Baker,* took a different approach—she worked hard and in good faith with the House Judiciary Committee to produce the best, most comprehensive system of domestic partnerships possible—and I don't blame her.

In her testimony before the Senate Judiciary Committee, Ms. Robinson reportedly said the lawyers "remain convinced that the only way to provide same-sex couples with true equality would be to allow them to marry. . . . [However, the] 'freedom to marry community supports this [comprehensive domestic partnership] bill as a step to equity,' Robinson said." *See* Ross Sneyd, AP, *Gay Rights Plaintiff Addresses Vt Panel*, VALLEY NEWS, March 23, 2000. Nina Beck, the only one of the *Baker* plaintiffs to speak to the legislature, also argued in favor of marriage. *Id.*

Had I been in Ms. Robinson's position, I'm honestly not sure what I would have done. The *Baker* court's punt to the legislature presented Ms. Robinson, and the other lawyers for the same-sex couples, with a heart-wrenching moral, tactical, and strategic dilemma. On the one hand, ought they to work with the legislature to fashion the best possible version of a civil unions bill, which would greatly improve the day-to-day lives of same-sex couples in Vermont, but knowing (1) that such a bill would be most likely to pass constitutional muster when the new statute comes before the court for review in *Baker*, and (2) that the *Baker* lawyers' participation in the legislative process would compromise their subsequent ability to argue, in the Vermont Supreme Court, that the bill on which they had worked was in fact unconstitutional? Or, on the other hand, ought they to boycott the legislative process, knowing that, without their input, the resulting bill would probably be inadequate and thus vulnerable to attack in the Vermont Supreme Court? The second option would be a high-stakes gamble, because the court might well uphold the watered-down version of domestic partnership.

Had the legislature rejected the comprehensive civil unions bill in favor of some sort of marriage *lite*, the *Baker* lawyers would be in a strong position to argue in the Supreme Court: "Look we participated in good faith in the legislative process and endorsed the only marriage substitute that passes muster under *Baker*: a truly comprehensive system of domestic partnership. The watered-down version enacted by the full legislature fails under *Baker*, and this court should so hold." The problem is that, in that case, the *Baker* counsel would have a hard time arguing that *Baker* requires marriage or anything other than a comprehensive partnership system, since that was what the lawyers supported in the legislature.

It is important to keep in mind that the *Baker* "majority" was such only by the margin of a single vote. Justice Johnson would require marriage, and Justice Dooley's concurrence might well require marriage as well. That left chief Justice Amestoy's opinion for the three-justice majority. We know where the Chief Justice was on the issue—domestic partnerships are sufficient—but the other two justices remained silent in *Baker*. We don't know what either or both of them might do when confronted with an actual system of domestic partnerships—particularly with a statute that was not marriage solely due to the homophobic reaction to *Baker*. The ultimate holding could still be that same-sex couples must be allowed the right of civil marriage.

Stay tuned.

192. Greg Johnson, *Vermont Civil Unions*, 25 VT. L. REV. 15, 50 (2000).

193. Bass, Unlikely Heroes, *supra* note 136.

194. Baker v. State, 744 A.2d 864 (Vt.1999).

195. Rep. Derek Levin, *Civil Union Issue Winds through Legislative Maze*, Vermont Standard (Woodstock), March 30, 2000.

196. Lawrence v. Texas, ___ U.S. ___, 71 U.S.L.W. 4575 (June 26, 2003).

197. *Id.*

198. *Id.* at 4576 (quoting Bowers v. Hardwick, 478 U.S. 186, 190 (1986)).

199. *Id.*

200. *Id.*

201. *Id.* at 4579.

202. Johnson, *Vermont Civil Unions, supra* note 4 at 283.

203. Eskridge, Civil Unions, *supra* note 2 at 140.

204. Johnson, *Vermont Civil Unions, supra* note 4 at 283.

205. *Id.* at 392.

206. Halpern v. Toronto, 2003 WL34950 (Ontario Ct. App. June 11, 2003).

207. Tom Cohen, AP, *Dozens in Canada Follow Gay Couple's Lead*, Wash. Post, June 11, 2003.

208. Hendrick Hertzberg, *Northern Lights*, New Yorker, July 7, 2003.

209. Patricia Wen, *A Civil Tradition*, Boston Globe, June 29, 2003.

210. Editorial, *Canada's Celebration of Marriage*, N.Y. Times, June 19, 2003.

211. Tim O'Brien, If I Die in a Combat Zone (1969).

212. *Id.*

213. *Id.*

214. *Id.* (quoting Plato).

215. *Id.* (quoting Plato).

216. *Id.*

217. *Id.*

218. Steve Nelson, *Mackinnon Shouldn't Be Bashed for Sticking to Principle*, Valley News, March 26, 2000.

219. *Id.*

Chapter 6

1. Martin Luther King, Jr., *Letter from Birmingham City Jail* (April 16, 1963), in A Testament of Hope: The Essential Writings of Martin Luther King, Jr. 296 (James Washington ed. 1986).

2. Darren Allen, *Gay Marriage*, Rutland Herald, July 13, 2003.

3. Debra Rosenberg, *Breaking Up Is Hard to Do*, Newsweek, July 7, 2003.

4. Exodus, ch. 7, verse 20.

5. Exodus 8:6; Exodus 8:24; Exodus 9:9; Exodus 11:14.

6. Exodus, ch. 9, verse 3.

7. Tammerlin Drummond, *The Marrying Kind*, Time, May 14, 2001.

8. Trudy Tynan, *Gay Activists Sue over Right to Marry in Massachusetts*, Rutland Herald, Apr. 12, 2001.

9. Sarah Kershaw, *Adversaries on Gay Rights Vow State-by-State Fight*, N.Y. TIMES, July 6, 2003.

10. *E.g.*, Laurie Goodstein, *New Hampshire Episcopalians Choose Gay Bishop, and Conflict*, N.Y. TIMES, June 8, 2003.

11. Sarah Kershaw, *Wal-Mart Sets a New Policy That Protects Gay Workers*, N.Y. TIMES, July 2, 2003.

12. *Gay Old Times*, NEW YORKER, Sept. 2, 2002.

APPENDIX A

1. In their motions, each of the parties presented the trial court with extensive extra-pleading facts and materials, including legislative history, scientific data, and sociological and psychological studies. *See* V.R.C.P. 12(b) & (c) (motion treated as one for summary judgment where "matters outside the pleadings are presented to and not excluded by the court"); *Fitzgerald v. Congleton*, 155 Vt. 283, 293–94, 583 A.2d 595, 601 (1990) (court effectively converted motion to dismiss into motion for summary judgment where it considered matters outside pleadings and parties had reasonable opportunity to submit extra-pleading materials). The parties have continued to rely on these materials on appeal. In addition, the Court has received numerous amicus curiae briefs, representing a broad array of interests, supportive of each of the parties.

2. Although plaintiffs raise a number of additional arguments based on both the United States and the Vermont Constitutions, our resolution of the Common Benefits claim obviates the necessity to address them.

3. Conventional equal protection analysis under the Fourteenth Amendment employs three "tiers" of judicial review based upon the nature of the right or the class affected. *See generally City of Cleburne v. Cleburne Living Center, Inc.*, 473 U.S. 432, 440–41, 105 S.Ct. 3249, 87 L.Ed.2d 313 (1985); 3 R. Rotunda & J. Nowak, *Treatise on Constitutional Law* § 18.3, at 216–20 (3d ed.1999). The first step in that analysis is to categorize the class affected as more or less similar to race based upon certain judicially-developed criteria. *See Personnel Administrator of Mass. v. Feeney*, 442 U.S. 256, 272, 99 S.Ct. 2282, 60 L.Ed.2d 870 (1979); *see generally* J. Baer, *Equality under the Constitution: Reclaiming the Fourteenth Amendment* 253–64 (1983); C. Sunstein, *The Anticaste Principle*, 92 Mich. L.Rev. 2410, 2441–44 (1994). If a legislative classification implicates a "suspect" class, generally defined in terms of historical discrimination, political powerlessness, or immutable characteristics, the law is subject to strict scrutiny, and the state must demonstrate that it furthers a compelling governmental interest that could not be accomplished by less restrictive means. In addition to race (the original suspect class), alienage and national origin have also been recognized as suspect. *See Cleburne*, 473 U.S. at 440, 105 S.Ct. 3249. The United States Supreme Court has created a "middle-tier" level of review for legislative classifications based on gender or illegitimacy; laws affecting these groups must be substantially related to a sufficiently important governmental interest to withstand constitu-

tional scrutiny. *See id.* The balance of legislative enactments, including nearly all economic and commercial legislation, are presumptively constitutional and will be upheld if rationally related to any conceivable, legitimate governmental interest. *See Minnesota v. Clover Leaf Creamery Co.,* 449 U.S. 456, 466, 101 S.Ct. 715, 66 L.Ed.2d 659 (1981); *see also Cleburne,* 473 U.S. at 440, 105 S.Ct. 3249. Thus, as one commentator has explained, rationality review may be "used to uphold laws justified even by hypothesized or ad hoc state interests." J. Wexler, *Defending the Middle Way: Intermediate Scrutiny as Judicial Minimalism,* 66 Geo. Wash. L.Rev. 298, 300 (1998).

4. In this respect, *Ludlow* was consistent with an older line of Vermont decisions which, albeit in the Fourteenth Amendment context, routinely subjected laws involving economic classifications to a relatively straightforward reasonableness evaluation, explicitly balancing the rights of the affected class against the State's proffered rationale. *See, e.g., State v. Hoyt,* 71 Vt. 59, 64, 42 A. 973, 975 (1899) (peddler-licensing classifications must be "based on some reasonable ground, some difference that bears a just and proper relation to the attempted classification, and is not a mere arbitrary selection"); *State v. Cadigan,* 73 Vt. 245, 252, 50 A. 1079, 1081 (1901) (State must establish "reasonable basis" to support law distinguishing between business partnerships organized in Vermont and those formed in other states); *State v. Haskell,* 84 Vt. 429, 437, 79 A. 852, 856 (1911) (mill regulation must be "based upon some difference having a reasonable and just relation to the object sought"). These opinions are notable for their detailed examination of the context and purposes of the challenged legislation, the impact on the affected class, and the logical fit between the statutory classification and the public ends to be achieved.

5. Cass Sunstein, among others, has documented the United States Supreme Court's unacknowledged departures from the deferential rational-basis standard without defining a new kind of scrutiny. *See* C. Sunstein, *Foreword: Leaving Things Undecided,* 110 Harv. L.Rev. 4, 59–61 (1996). These cases include *Romer v. Evans,* 517 U.S. 620, 635, 116 S.Ct. 1620, 134 L.Ed.2d 855 (1996) (holding Colorado statute that banned state or local laws forbidding sexual-orientation discrimination was not rationally related to legitimate governmental objective), *Cleburne,* 473 U.S. at 450, 105 S.Ct. 3249 (applying rational basis review, Court invalidated zoning discrimination against mentally retarded as based on "irrational prejudice"), and *United States Dep't of Agriculture v. Moreno,* 413 U.S. 528, 534, 93 S.Ct. 2821, 37 L.Ed.2d 782 (1973) (invalidating regulation that excluded nonfamily members of household from food stamp program). In each of these decisions, the Court employed a highly contextual, fact-based analysis balancing private rights and public interests even while ostensibly applying minimal rational-basis review. Conversely, in *Adarand Constructors, Inc. v. Pena,* 515 U.S. 200, 237, 115 S.Ct. 2097, 132 L.Ed.2d 158 (1995), the high court itself questioned the notion that strict scrutiny was inevitably "fatal in fact." *See* G. Gunther, *The Supreme Court 1971 Term—Foreword: In Search of Evolving Doctrine on a Changing Court: A Model for a Newer Equal Protection,* 86 Harv. L.Rev. 1, 8 (1972) (observing that strict scrutiny is generally " 'strict' in theory and fatal in fact"). Viewed

together, these cases have prompted one commentator to suggest that "[t]he hard edges of the tripartite division have thus softened," and that the Court has moved "toward general balancing of relevant interests." Sunstein, *supra*, at 77.

6. The current version differs from the original only in that the gender-neutral terms "person" and "persons" have been substituted for "man" and "men." *See* Vt. Const., ch. II, § 76. This revision was not intended to "alter the sense, meaning, or effect of the" provision. *Id.*

7. There is little doubt as to the obligatory nature of the Common Benefits Clause, which provides that "government is, or ought to be, instituted for the common benefit, protection, and security." Indeed the State does not argue that it is merely hortatory or aspirational in effect, an argument that would not be persuasive in any event. *See Brigham*, 166 Vt. at 261–62, 692 A.2d at 393–94 (framers "drew no distinction between 'ought' and 'shall' in defining rights and duties").

8. The use of the word "family" in the Pennsylvania Common Benefits Clause reflects Pennsylvania's history, where elite "proprietors" including the Penns and other established families, had long dominated colonial politics, religion, and economic interests. The revolt against Great Britain presented an opportunity for western Pennsylvania farmers, urban gentry, and dissenting Presbyterians nursing "deep seated and long-felt grievances" to end Eastern domination of the colony, and establish a more democratic form of government. *See* J. Selsam, *The Pennsylvania Constitution of 1776: A Study in Revolutionary Democracy* (1936), 255–56.

9. This Court has noted that interpretations of similar constitutional provisions from other states may be instructive in understanding our own. *See Benning*, 161 Vt. at 476, 641 A.2d at 759. "Common Benefits" decisions from other states, however, are scarce. Pennsylvania eliminated the Common Benefits Clause when it replaced its constitution in 1790, and Virginia courts have not explored in any depth the meaning of its clause. The New Hampshire Constitution of 1783 also included a Common Benefits section substantially similar to Vermont's. *See* N.H. Const., Pt. 1, art. 10. Although New Hampshire courts have not developed an independent Common Benefits jurisprudence, several early New Hampshire decisions noted the provision's significance. *See State v. Pennoyer*, 65 N.H. 113, 18 A. 878, 881 (1889) (relying on Common Benefits Clause to strike down physician-licensing statute that exempted physicians who had resided in one place for four years); *Rosenblum v. Griffin*, 89 N.H. 314, 197 A. 701, 706 (1938) (noting that under Common Benefits Clause, "[e]quality of benefit is no less required than equality of burden. Otherwise equal protection is denied. . . ."). Massachusetts included a variation on Vermont's Common Benefits Clause in its Constitution of 1780, as well as a separate "emoluments" provision. *See* Mass. Const., Pt. 1, arts. VI & VII (adopted 1780). Massachusetts has not relied on the Common Benefits provision as a separate source of equal protections rights. *See Town of Brookline v. Secretary of Com.*, 417 Mass. 406, 631 N.E.2d 968, 978 n. 19 (1994). In the nineteenth century, a number of additional states adopted variations on the Common Benefits Clause. *See, e.g.,* Conn. Const. of 1818, art. 1, § 2 ("[A]ll political power is inherent in the people, and all free gov-

ernments are founded on their authority, and instituted for their benefit."); Ohio Const. of 1851, art. I, § 2 ("All political power is inherent in the people. Government is instituted for their equal protection and benefit."); W. Va. Const., art. III, § 3 (adopted 1872) ("Government is instituted for the common benefit, protection and security of the people, nation or community."). Even assuming that provisions enacted in the nineteenth century have some bearing on the meaning of a Revolutionary-era document, these sister-state constitutions provide little guidance. Ohio has held that the state clause is the "functional equivalent" of the Equal Protection Clause with similar standards. See American Ass'n of Univ. Professors v. Central State Univ., 83 Ohio St.3d 229, 699 N.E.2d 463, 467 (1998). The West Virginia Supreme Court, in contrast, has relied on the Common Benefits Clause to hold that the state constitution provides greater individual protection than the United States Constitution. See United Mine Workers of America, Intl. Union v. Parsons, 172 W.Va. 386, 305 S.E.2d 343, 353–54 (1983). Apart from noting the absence of an equivalent provision in the federal constitution, however, the West Virginia court has not engaged in any extensive textual or historical analysis.

A number of states during the Revolutionary and early National periods also adopted separate provisions, apparently modeled on the Pennsylvania and Virginia clauses, declaring that no men, or set of men, are entitled to exclusive or separate emoluments or privileges from the community, but in consideration of public services. See, e.g., N.C. Const. of 1776, Decl. of Rights, § 3; Mass. Const., Pt. 1, art. VI; Conn. Const. of 1818, art. I, § 1; Miss. Const. of 1832, art. I, § 1; Ky. Const. of 1792, art. XII, § 1. These "emoluments and privileges" clauses have been extensively cited and applied, often in the context of taxpayer suits challenging public expenditures as unconstitutional "gifts" of public funds without consideration of public service, or suits challenging legislative acts granting special credits, payments, or exemptions to a specific class. See, e.g., Commissioner of Pub. Works v. City of Middletown, 53 Conn.App. 438, 731 A.2d 749, 757 (1999) (challenge to tax exemption); Driscoll v. City of New Haven, 75 Conn. 92, 52 A. 618, 622 (1902) (taxpayer suit to enjoin municipal grant of land to private company); Kentucky Union R.R. v. Bourbon County, 85 Ky. 98, 2 S.W. 687, 690 (1887) (taxpayer suit to enjoin subscription of bonds for railroad purposes); Brumley v. Baxter, 225 N.C. 691, 36 S.E.2d 281, 286 (1945) (taxpayer suit to enjoin municipal grant of real property for use by military veterans); see also Gross v. Gates, 109 Vt. 156, 159, 194 A. 465, 467 (1937) (Article 7 challenge to payment to sheriff's widow as "emolument" without consideration of public service). These cases generally turned on whether the challenged action promoted a public purpose or was made without some consideration of public service. They represent, in effect, the reverse of the Common Benefits Clause, prohibiting the grant of special privileges to a select class of persons over and above those granted to the general community, as the Common Benefits Clause requires the equal enjoyment of general benefits and protections by the whole community.

10. The concurring opinion would tie its analysis to the presumably "objective" test of suspect class. But suspect class analysis has never provided a stable

mooring for constitutional application of Vermont's Common Benefits Clause. Although the concurrence identifies precedents of this Court holding that a more searching scrutiny is required when a statutory scheme involves suspect classes, we have never established the criteria for determining what constitutes a suspect class under the Vermont Constitution nor have we ever identified a suspect class under Article 7. Moreover, the concurrence applies strict scrutiny predicated on a finding that lesbians and gay men are a suspect class, although the overwhelming majority of decisions have rejected such claims. *See Ben-Shalom v. Marsh,* 881 F.2d 454, 464–66 (7th Cir.1989), cert. denied, 494 U.S. 1004, 110 S.Ct. 1296, 108 L.Ed.2d 473 (1990); *Equality Found. of Greater Cincinnati, Inc. v. City of Cincinnati,* 128 F.3d 289, 292–93 (6th Cir.1997); *Thomasson v. Perry,* 80 F.3d 915, 927 (4th Cir.), cert. denied, 519 U.S. 948, 117 S.Ct. 358, 136 L.Ed.2d 250 (1996); *Richenberg v. Perry,* 97 F.3d 256, 260–61 (8th Cir.1996), cert. denied, 522 U.S. 807, 118 S.Ct. 45, 139 L.Ed.2d 12 (1997); *High Tech Gays v. Defense Indus. Sec. Clearance Office,* 895 F.2d 563, 571–72 (9th Cir.1990); *Woodward v. United States,* 871 F.2d 1068, 1076 (Fed.Cir.1989), cert. denied, 494 U.S. 1003, 110 S.Ct. 1295, 108 L.Ed.2d 473 (1990); *Padula v. Webster,* 822 F.2d 97, 103 (D.C.Cir.1987); *Baker v. Wade,* 769 F.2d 289, 292 (5th Cir.1985) (en banc), cert. denied, 478 U.S. 1035, 107 S.Ct. 23, 92 L.Ed.2d 774 (1986); *National Gay Task Force v. Board of Educ.,* 729 F.2d 1270, 1273 (10th Cir.1984), *aff'd,* 470 U.S. 903, 105 S.Ct. 1858, 84 L.Ed.2d 776 (1985); Opinion of the Justices, 129 N.H. 290, 530 A.2d 21, 24 (1987). The Court—no less than the concurrence—seeks a rationale faithful to our Constitution and careful in the exercise of this Court's limited powers. The concurrence suggests that the Oregon Supreme Court's decision in *Hewitt v. State Accident Insurance Fund Corp.,* 294 Or. 33, 653 P.2d 970, 977–78 (1982), should be relied upon to supply the missing Vermont jurisprudence of suspect class criteria. Yet, the Oregon Court of Appeals found it necessary to abandon the immutable personal-characteristic criterion of *Hewitt* in order to find that homosexuals were a suspect class entitled to heightened scrutiny. *See Tanner v. Oregon Health Sciences Univ.,* 157 Or.App. 502, 971 P.2d 435, 446 (1998). The "adverse stereotyping" analysis used in its place, *see id.,* may provide one intermediate appellate court's answer to the question of whether homosexuals are a suspect class, but it is far from an "exacting standard" by which to measure the prudence of a court's exercise of its powers. It is difficult to imagine a legal framework that could provide less predictability in the outcome of future cases than one which gives a court free reign to decide which groups have been the subject of "adverse social or political stereotyping." *Id.* The artificiality of suspect-class labeling should be avoided where, as here, the plaintiffs are afforded the common benefits and protections of Article 7, not because they are part of a "suspect class," but because they are part of the Vermont community.

11. The concurring and concurring and dissenting opinions are mistaken in suggesting that this standard places identical burdens upon the State regardless of the nature of the rights affected. As explained above, the significance of the benefits and protections at issue may well affect the justifications required of the State to support a statutory classification. This is plainly demonstrated in the

discussion of marriage benefits and protections which follows. Nor is there any merit to the assertion that this standard invites a more "activist" review of economic and social welfare legislation. See 744 A.2d at 896 (Dooley, J., concurring). Characterizing a case as affecting "economic" interests, "civil rights," "fundamental" rights, or "suspect classes"—as our colleagues apparently prefer—is no less an exercise in judgment. Indeed, it may disguise the court's value judgments with a label, rather than explain its reasoning in terms that the public and the litigants are entitled to understand. "It is a comparison of the relative strengths of opposing claims that informs the judicial task, not a deduction from some first premise." *Glucksberg*, 521 U.S. at 764, 117 S.Ct. 2258 (Souter, J., concurring). That is a task we trust will continue to be undertaken in a legal climate that recognizes that "constitutional review, not judicial lawmaking, is a court's business here." *Id.* at 768, 117 S.Ct. 2258.

12. Justice Harlan has described the process of constitutional interpretation as follows:

> If the supplying of content to this Constitutional concept has of necessity been a rational process, it certainly has not been one where judges have felt free to roam where unguided speculation might take them. The balance of which I speak is the balance struck by this country, having regard to what history teaches are the traditions from which it developed as well as the traditions from which it broke. That tradition is a living thing. A decision of this Court which radically departs from it could not long survive, while a decision which builds on what has survived is likely to be sound. No formula could serve as a substitute, in this area, for judgment and restraint.
>
> *Poe*, 367 U.S. at 542, 81 S.Ct. 1752 (Harlan, J. dissenting).

13. Relying largely on federal precedents, our colleague in her concurring and dissenting opinion suggests that the statutory exclusion of same-sex couples from the benefits and protections of marriage should be subject to heightened scrutiny as a "suspect" or "quasi-suspect" classification based on sex. All of the seminal sex-discrimination decisions, however, have invalidated statutes that single out men or women as a discrete class for unequal treatment. *See, e.g., United States v. Virginia*, 518 U.S. 515, 555–56, 116 S.Ct. 2264, 135 L.Ed.2d 735 (1996) (repudiating statute that precluded women from attending Virginia Military Institute); *Mississippi Univ. for Women v. Hogan*, 458 U.S. 718, 731, 102 S.Ct. 3331, 73 L.Ed.2d 1090 (1982) (invalidating admission policy that excluded males from attending state-supported nursing school); *Craig v. Boren*, 429 U.S. 190, 204, 97 S.Ct. 451, 50 L.Ed.2d 397 (1976) (invalidating statute that allowed women to purchase nonintoxicating beer at younger age than men); *Frontiero v. Richardson*, 411 U.S. 677, 690, 93 S.Ct. 1764, 36 L.Ed.2d 583 (1973) (striking statute that imposed more onerous requirements upon female members of armed services to claim spouses as dependents).

Although this Court has not addressed the issue, *see State v. George*, 157 Vt. 580, 588, 602 A.2d 953, 957 (1991), we do not doubt that a statute that discriminated on the basis of sex would bear a heavy burden under the Article 7 analysis set forth above. The difficulty here is that the marriage laws are facially neutral; they do not single out men or women as a class for disparate treatment, but rather prohibit men and women equally from marrying a person of the same sex. As we observed in *George*, 157 Vt. at 585, 602 A.2d at 956, "[i]n order to trigger equal protection analysis at all . . . a defendant must show that he was treated differently as a member of one class from treatment of members of another class similarly situated." Here, there is no discrete class subject to differential treatment solely on the basis of sex; each sex is equally prohibited from precisely the same conduct.

Indeed, most appellate courts that have addressed the issue have rejected the claim that defining marriage as the union of one man and one woman discriminates on the basis of sex. *See, e.g., Baker v. Nelson*, 291 Minn. 310, 191 N.W.2d 185, 186–87 (1971); *Singer v. Hara*, 11 Wash.App. 247, 522 P.2d 1187, 1191–92 (1974); *see also Phillips v. Wisconsin Personnel Comm'n*, 167 Wis.2d 205, 482 N.W.2d 121, 129 (Ct.App.1992) (holding that health insurance regulation limiting state employee's dependent coverage to spouse did not constitute sex discrimination because coverage was "unavailable to unmarried companions of both male and female employees"); *State v. Walsh*, 713 S.W.2d 508, 510 (Mo.1986) (rejecting claim that sodomy statute imposed sex-based classification because it "applie[d] equally to men and women [in] prohibit[ing] both classes from engaging in sexual activity with members of their own sex"). *But see Baehr v. Lewin*, 74 Haw. 530, 852 P.2d 44, 64 (1993) (plurality opinion holding that state's marriage laws discriminated on basis of sex).

Although the concurring and dissenting opinion invokes the United States Supreme Court decision in *Loving v. Virginia*, 388 U.S. 1, 87 S.Ct. 1817, 18 L.Ed.2d 1010 (1967), the reliance is misplaced. There, the high court had little difficulty in looking behind the superficial neutrality of Virginia's antimiscegenation statute to hold that its real purpose was to maintain the pernicious doctrine of white supremacy. *Id.* at 11, 87 S.Ct. 1817. Our colleague argues, by analogy, that the effect, if not the purpose, of the exclusion of same-sex partners from the marriage laws is to maintain certain male and female stereotypes to the detriment of both. To support the claim, she cites a number of antiquated statutes that denied married women a variety of freedoms, including the right to enter into contracts and hold property.

The test to evaluate whether a facially gender-neutral statute discriminates on the basis of sex is whether the law "can be traced to a discriminatory purpose." *Feeney*, 442 U.S. at 272, 99 S.Ct. 2282. The evidence does not demonstrate such a purpose. It is one thing to show that long-repealed marriage statutes subordinated women to men within the marital relation. It is quite another to demonstrate that the authors of the marriage laws excluded same-sex couples because of incorrect and discriminatory assumptions about gender roles or anxiety about gender-role confusion. That evidence is not before us. Accordingly, we are not persuaded that sex discrimination offers a useful analytic framework for determining plaintiffs' rights under the Common Benefits Clause.

14. It would, for example, serve no useful purpose to remand this matter for hearings on whether marriages of convenience (i.e., unions for the purpose of obtaining certain statutory benefits) would result from providing same-sex couples with the statutory benefits and protections accorded opposite-sex couples under marriage laws. For the reasons we have stated in this opinion, it is not a failure of proof that is fatal to the State's arguments, it is a failure of logic.

15. Contrary to the characterization in the concurring and dissenting opinion, we do not "decline [. . .] to provide plaintiffs with a marriage license" because of uncertainty and confusion that change may bring. 744 A.2d at 902. Rather, it is to avoid the uncertainty that might result during the period when the Legislature is considering potential constitutional remedies that we consider it prudent to suspend the Court's judgment for a reasonable period.

16. J. Boswell, *Life of Johnson* (1791) (reprinted in *Bartlett's Familiar Quotations* 54 (15th ed.1980)).

17. The majority's characterization of *Brigham* is neither fair nor accurate. The majority states that *Brigham* "acknowledged the federal standard," but "eschewed the federal categories of analysis." 744 A.2d at 873. Far beyond "acknowledging" the federal standards, *Brigham* held explicitly that they applied under Article 7—a holding now implicitly overruled by the majority decision. Rather than eschewing the federal standards, we held that the educational financing system advanced no "legitimate governmental purpose" under any standard. *See Brigham*, 166 Vt. at 265, 692 A.2d at 396.

18. The majority's statement that suspect class analysis is "often effectively ignored in our more recent decisions" is inaccurate, unless our statements that we need not reach the issue in a case somehow "ignores" suspect-class analysis. 744 A.2d at 873. *See, e.g., MacCallum*, 165 Vt. at 457 n. 1, 686 A.2d at 938 n. 1 (in view of our disposition, we need not reach plaintiff's claim that adopted persons are suspect class).

19. My concern about the effect of this decision as a precedent is heightened by the majority's treatment of the *Ludlow* decision. It is fair to say that for some purposes, there have been two versions of the *Ludlow* decision. First, there is the one we have described in dicta, usually as a historical event. *See State v. Brunelle*, 148 Vt. 347, 351, 534 A.2d 198, 201–02 (1987); Hodgeman, 157 Vt. at 464, 599 A.2d at 1373. This one holds that Article 7 is "more stringent than the federal constitutional standard, which requires only a rational justification." *Brunelle*, 148 Vt. at 351, 534 A.2d at 201–02. Second, there is the *Ludlow* decision that we have actually used in deciding cases. *See, e.g., Choquette*, 153 Vt. at 52, 569 A.2d at 459; *In re Property of One Church Street*, 152 Vt. 260, 263–65, 565 A.2d 1349, 1350–51 (1989). This version of *Ludlow* holds that the Article 7 standard is the reasonable-relationship test applicable under the Fourteenth Amendment to the United States Constitution. *See Choquette*, 153 Vt. at 52, 569 A.2d at 459; *see also Lorrain*, 160 Vt. at 212, 628 A.2d at 550 (test under Article 7 is same as that under federal Equal Protection Clause). Obviously, these versions of *Ludlow* are irreconcilable, and only one can be accurate. In case after case, advocates pursuing Article 7 challenges have tried, and failed, to get us to adopt the first version of *Ludlow*

as the basis for a favorable decision. The first version has appeared only in dicta in two isolated cases. Today, seventeen years after the *Ludlow* decision, the advocates have finally succeeded, with a begrudging acknowledgment from the majority that our decisions "have consistently recited" the federal test and are now wholesale overruled.

In view of this history of treatment of *Ludlow*, I find incredible the majority's statement that "Vermont case law has consistently demanded in practice that statutory exclusions from publicly conferred benefits and protections must be 'premised on an appropriate and overriding public interest,'" 744 A.2d at 873, quoting *Ludlow* as if all of our decisions after *Ludlow* disingenuously mouthed one deferential constitutional standard but silently employed a more activist standard. If one general statement could be made, it would be that we have never actually employed the standard quoted by the majority in any case, until this one.

My fear is that once we get beyond this controversial decision, we will end up with two versions of it. Will we go back to minimalist review when we get a claim of discrimination, for example, between large stores and small ones, or will the more activist review promised by this decision prevail? Our history in applying *Ludlow* says that we will do the former, which I find to be the more desirable, but a serious blow will have been dealt to our ability to develop neutral constitutional doctrine.

20. In the 1999 legislative session, while the instant case was pending before this Court, fifty-seven representatives signed H. 479, which sought to amend the marriage statutes by providing that a man shall not marry another man, and a woman shall not marry another woman.

21. Although the State's licensing procedures do not signal official approval or recognition of any particular lifestyles or relationships, commentators have noted that denying same-sex couples a marriage license is viewed by many as indicating that same-sex relationships are not entitled to the same status as opposite-sex relationships. *See, e.g.,* C. Christensen, *If Not Marriage? On Securing Gay and Lesbian Family Values by a "Similacrum of Marriage"*, 66 Fordham L.Rev. 1699, 1783–84 (1998) (most far-reaching consequence of legalizing same-sex marriage would be symbolic shedding of sexual outlaw image and civil recognition of shared humanity); D. Chambers, *What If? The Legal Consequences of Marriage and the Legal Needs of Lesbian and Gay Male Couples*, 95 Mich. L.Rev. 447, 450 (1996) (allowing same-sex couples to marry would signify acknowledgement of same-sex couples as equal citizens). This Court has recognized that singling out a particular group for special treatment may have a stigmatizing effect more significant than any economic consequences. *See MacCallum v. Seymour's Administrator*, 165 Vt. 452, 460, 686 A.2d 935, 939 (1996) (noting that symbolic and psychological damage resulting from unconstitutional classification depriving adopted children of right to inherit from collateral kin may be more significant than any concern over material values). The United States Supreme Court has also recognized this phenomenon. *See Romer v. Evans*, 517 U.S. 620, 634, 116 S.Ct. 1620, 134 L.Ed.2d 855 (1996) (laws singling out gays and

lesbians for special treatment "raise the inevitable inference that the disadvantage imposed is born of animosity toward the class of persons affected"); *Heckler v. Mathews,* 465 U.S. 728, 739–40, 104 S.Ct. 1387, 79 L.Ed.2d 646 (1984) (stigmatizing members of disfavored group as less worthy participants in community "can cause serious noneconomic injuries . . . solely because of their membership in a disfavored group"). Because enjoining defendants from denying plaintiffs a marriage license is the most effective and complete way to remedy the constitutional violation we have found, it is not necessary to reach the issue of whether depriving plaintiffs of the "status" of being able to obtain the same state-conferred marriage license provided to opposite-sex couples violates their civil rights.

22. Unlike the Vermont Constitution, *see* Vt. Const. ch. II, § 5 ("The Legislative, Executive, and Judiciary departments, shall be separate and distinct, so that neither exercise the powers properly belonging to the others."), the United States Constitution does not contain an explicit separation-of-powers provision; however, the United States Supreme Court has derived a separation-of-powers requirement from the federal constitution's statement of the powers of each of the branches of government. *See, e.g., Bowsher v. Synar,* 478 U.S. 714, 721–22, 106 S.Ct. 3181, 92 L.Ed.2d 583 (1986). Because we have relied upon federal separation-of-powers jurisprudence in interpreting Chapter II, § 5, *see Trybulski v. Bellows Falls Hydro-Elec. Corp.,* 112 Vt. 1, 7, 20 A.2d 117, 120 (1941), I draw upon federal case law for analysis and support in discussing separation-of-powers principles. *See In re D.L.,* 164 Vt. 223, 228 n. 3, 669 A.2d 1172, 1176 n. 3 (1995); *see also In re Constitutionality of House Bill 88,* 115 Vt. 524, 529, 64 A.2d 169, 172 (1949) (noting that judicial power of Vermont Supreme Court and United States Supreme Court is same).

23. I do not misinterpret the majority's holding. See 744 A.2d at 887. I am aware that the Legislature is not obligated to give plaintiffs a marriage license, or any other remedy for that matter. It is this Court, not the Legislature, that has the duty to remedy the constitutional violation we have found. We are left to speculate why the majority is not enjoining defendants from denying plaintiffs the regulatory license that they seek and that would entitle them to the same benefits and protections to which they are entitled under the majority's holding.

24. The majority states that my analogy to the circumstances in *Watson* is "flawed" because (1) we are not confronting the evil of institutionalized racism; and (2) our ruling today is "decidedly new doctrine." 744 A.2d at 888. The majority's first point implies that our duty to remedy unconstitutional discrimination is somehow limited when that discrimination is based on sex or sexual orientation rather than race. I would not prioritize among types of civil rights violations; our duty to remedy them is the same, once a constitutional violation is found.

25. This rule requires the exclusion of evidence obtained as the result of unconstitutional searches and seizures.

26. Judicial authority is not, however, the ultimate source of constitutional authority. Within our constitutional framework, the people are the final arbiters

of what law governs us; they retain the power to amend our fundamental law. If the people of Vermont wish to overturn a constitutionally based decision, as happened in Alaska and Hawaii, they may do so. The possibility that they may do so, however, should not, in my view, deprive these plaintiffs of the remedy to which they are entitled.

27. The majority misconstrues my opinion. *See* 744 A.2d at 880 n. 13. I do not reach the issue of whether heightened scrutiny is appropriate for sex-based classifications under the Common Benefits Clause. *See Ashwander v. Tennessee Valley Auth.,* 297 U.S. 288, 347, 56 S.Ct. 466, 80 L.Ed. 688 (1936) (Brandeis, J., concurring) (courts should not formulate rules of constitutional law broader than is required by precise facts to which they are to be applied). I mention federal law and that of other states merely to acknowledge the approach of other jurisdictions on an issue that we have not yet decided. I analyze the sex-based classification under our current test for rational-basis review.

28. In its brief, the State notes that if the Court declares that heightened scrutiny is applicable, it might offer additional arguments and justifications to demonstrate a compelling State interest in the marriage statutes. Obviously, in its extensive filings both in the trial court and here, which included a one-hundred-page appellate brief, the State made every conceivable argument in support of the marriage laws, including what it perceived to be its best arguments. For the reasons stated by the majority, *see* 744 A.2d at 868 n. 1, 885 n. 14, I agree that it would be pointless to remand this matter for further proceedings in the trial court.

29. Under the State's analysis, a statute that required courts to give custody of male children to fathers and female children to mothers would not be sex discrimination. Although such a law would not treat men and women differently, I believe it would discriminate on the basis of sex. Apparently, the Legislature agrees. By prohibiting consideration of the sex of the child or parent in custody decisions, *see* 15 V.S.A. § 665(c), the Legislature undoubtedly intended to prohibit sex discrimination, even if the rules applied equally to men and women. *See Harris v. Harris,* 162 Vt. 174, 182, 647 A.2d 309, 314 (1994) (stating the family court's custody decision would have to be reversed if it had been based on preference that child remain with his father because of his gender).

30. I do not contend, as the majority suggests, that the real purpose of the exclusion of same-sex partners from the marriage laws was to maintain certain male and female stereotypes. *See* 744 A.2d at 880 n. 13. As noted above, I agree that the original purpose was very likely not intentionally discriminatory toward same-sex couples. The question is whether the State may maintain a classification today only by giving credence to generally discredited sex-role stereotyping. I believe our decision in *MacCallum* says no. *See* Sunstein, *supra* note 5 at 23, 27 (exclusion of same-sex couples from marriage is, in reality, impermissible sex-role stereotyping, and therefore, is discrimination on basis of sex); J. Culhane, *Uprooting the Arguments Against Same-Sex Marriage,* 20 Cardozo L.Rev. 1119, 1171–75 (1999) (accord).

31. *See, e.g., United States v. Virginia,* 518 U.S. 515, 533, 116 S.Ct. 2264, 135

L.Ed.2d 735 (1996) (concluding that sex-based classifications are subject to heightened standard of review less rigorous than that imposed for race or national origin classifications); *Frontiero*, 411 U.S. at 684, 686, 93 S.Ct. 1764 (plurality opinion) (concluding that sex is suspect classification under two-part test inquiring whether class is defined by immutable characteristic and whether there is history of invidious discrimination against class); *Sail'er Inn. Inc. v. Kirby*, 5 Cal.3d 1, 95 Cal.Rptr. 329, 485 P.2d 529, 540 (1971) (applying federal two-part test and concluding that sex is immutable trait and women have historically labored under severe legal and social disabilities); *Hewitt v. State Accident Ins. Fund Corp.*, 294 Or. 33, 653 P.2d 970, 977 (1982) (applying federal two-part test and concluding that sex is immutable personal characteristic and purposeful unequal treatment of women is well-known).

32. The question remains why I feel it is necessary to identify the class of persons being discriminated against in this case if the majority and I reach the same conclusion. It is important because I have concerns about the test that the majority devises to review equal-protection challenges under the Common Benefits Clause. The majority rejects the notion that the Court should accord some measure of heightened scrutiny for classifications denying benefits to historically disadvantaged groups. It argues that the history of the Common Benefits Clause supports the Court's adoption of a uniform standard that is reflective of the broad inclusionary principle at its core. Therefore, rather than accord any particular group heightened scrutiny, it will balance all the factors in the case and reach a just result. While this notion is superficially attractive in its attempt to achieve fundamental fairness for all Vermonters, it is flawed with respect to an equal-protection analysis. The guarantee of equal protection is about fundamental fairness in a large sense, but its most important purpose is to secure the rights of historically disadvantaged groups whose exclusion from full participation in all facets of society has resulted from hatred and prejudice.

I share Justice Dooley's concern that the new standard enunciated by the majority may not give sufficient deference to the Legislature's judgment in economic and commercial legislation. See 744 A.2d at 896–97 (Dooley, J., concurring). It is the Legislature's prerogative to decide whether, for example, to give "optometrists" more protection than "opticians." See *Cleburne*, 473 U.S. at 471, 105 S.Ct. 3249 (Marshall, J., concurring in part and dissenting in part). Such classifications ought not to become a matter of serious constitutional review, even though optometrists and opticians comprise "a part of the community" and may have vital economic interests in the manner in which they are regulated. I am certain the majority would agree with that proposition and argue that its balancing of all the relevant factors in that kind of a case would not result in striking down a classification that treated those two groups differently. But therein lies my concern with the majority's approach. Although we might agree on the optometrists/opticians classification, a balancing of all relevant factors in all equal-protection cases puts the rule of law at "excessive risk." C. Sunstein, *Foreword: Leaving Things Undecided*, 110 Harv. L.Rev. 4, 78 (1996). As Professor Sunstein explains:

The use of "tiers" has two important goals. The first is to ensure that courts are most skeptical in cases in which it is highly predictable that illegitimate motives are at work. . . . The second goal of a tiered system is to discipline judicial discretion while promoting planning and predictability for future cases. Without tiers, it would be difficult to predict judicial judgments under the Equal Protection Clause, and judges would make decisions based on ad hoc assessments of the equities. The Chancellor's foot[*] is not a promising basis for antidiscrimination law.

Id. The majority argues that subjective judgment is required to make choices about classes who are entitled to heightened review and, therefore, that a tiered approach is not more precise than the balancing-of-factors approach. *See* 744 A.2d at 878 n. 10. But, in choosing the suspect class, it would be incumbent upon the Court to articulate its rationale, thereby providing predictive value in future cases of discrimination rather than depending on the perspicacity of judges to see it. *Cleburne*, 473 U.S. at 466, 105 S.Ct. 3249 (Marshall, J., concurring in part and dissenting in part).

[* The reference to the Chancellor's foot in the Sunstein quote is from John Seldon's (1584–1654) critique of equity, which is relevant here:]

Equity is a roguish thing. For Law we have a measure, know what to trust to; Equity is according to the conscience of him that is Chancellor, and as that is larger or narrower, so is Equity. 'Tis all one as if they should make the standard for the measure we call a "foot" a Chancellor's foot; what an uncertain measure would this be! One Chancellor has a long foot, another a short foot, a third an indifferent foot. 'Tis the same thing in the Chancellor's conscience.

J. Bartlett, Familiar Quotations, 263 (15th ed.1980).

33. The State does not address the apparent conflict between the public purposes it asserts and the legislative policy of this State. Vermont does not prohibit the donation of sperm or the use of technologically assisted methods of reproduction. Thus, same-sex partners and single individuals may use technologically assisted reproduction, all without the benefit of marriage. It is impossible to accept that the classification in the marriage statutes serves as a reasonable deterrent to such methods.

Index

advertisements: attacking Howard Dean, 89–90; mailed letters opposing same-sex marriage, 91–93; regarding same-sex marriage in Vermont, 88–95; by supporters of H 847, 119; in support of same-sex marriage, 90–91; "Take Back Vermont" signs, 131–32; by Take It To The People, 88–90, 110, 120

AIDS: fear of increase in Vermont, 56–58; ideological influence on gay couples, 29–30.

Alaska: ruling on gay marriage in, 12

Amestoy, C.J., 32, 179; concluding thoughts on *Baker v. State*, 224–25; majority opinion written for *Baker v. State* by, 35–40, 197–224

Angell, Bishop Kenneth, 98–99

Article 7: analysis of Common Benefits Clause under, 210–12; application of Common Benefits Clause under, 212–20; Chapter I of, 229–30; compared with Oregon's § 20 jurisprudence, 229–32; Vermont Supreme Court's ruling based on, 220–24, 232–37

Baker, Stan, 34

Baker v. Nelson, 30

Baker v. State: arguments opposed to decision in, 46–48; as civil rights case, 187–88, 226; criticism of Court's decision in, 41–42; criticism of Court's rationale for decision in, 232–37; disagreement with decision to limit same-sex couples to civil unions, 252–55; disagreement with implementation of decision in, 238–47; gay couples involved in, 33–34, 198; influence of popular opinion on decision in, 157; in-state reaction to, 27;

interpretation of Article 7 in decision of, 210–24, 232–37; legislative hearings on, 45–48; letters-to-the-editors in response to, 48–68; main reason for decision in, 178–79; oral arguments in, 34–35; plaintiffs in, 33–34, 198; praise for Vermont court justices in, 179; public hearings following decision of, 46–48; responses of religious figures to, 47–48; role of Common Benefits Clause in, 201–24; Senate Judiciary Committee's vote to overrule decision in, 103–4; starting points for, 30–33; *Valley News'* response to, 67–68; Vermont Catholic Church's response to, 47; Vermont legislature's options in response to, 74–75; Vermont Supreme Court's decision for, 35–40, 197–256; Vermont Supreme Court's remedy concerning benefits denied to same-sex couples, 220–24; vote on amendment to overrule decision in, 111

Bauer, Gary, 16

Beck, Nina, 33–34; before Senate Judiciary Committee, 96–97

Bible: used to oppose past civil rights decisions, 180

Bingham, Mark, 6, 139

Blair, Helena, 116

Bloomer, John, 105

Bonuato, Mary L., 32–33

Boston Globe: on Vermont's civil union legislation, 12–13

Bowers v. Hardwick, 189–90, 227–28

Boynton v. Virginia, 164

Browder v. Gayle, 164

Brown v. Board of Education, 162, 163–65; Supreme Court's follow-up to decision in, 175–76

331